The
Emotionally Disturbed Child
in the Classroom

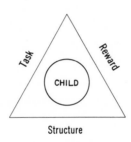

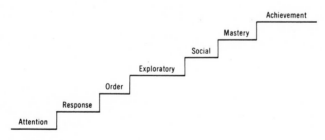

The Emotionally Disturbed Child in the Classroom

A DEVELOPMENTAL STRATEGY FOR EDUCATING CHILDREN WITH MALADAPTIVE BEHAVIOR

FRANK M. HEWETT

Associate Professor of Education and Psychiatry
University of California, Los Angeles

Allyn and Bacon, Inc.
Boston

LIBRARY OF CONGRESS CATALOG CARD NUMBER: 68-19922

Printed in the United States of America

Fifth printing . . . July, 1970

Preface

This book is about educational deeds. It presents the emotionally disturbed child as a learning problem which teachers can do something about and attempts to dispel some of the formidable multidisciplinary mystique which often surrounds such a child and suggests he is far too fragile and complex for his difficulties to be substantially remedied by the teacher and the school.

In the chapters which follow, the author shares a set of hypotheses formulated over a period of 15 years in special, hospital, and public school settings with emotionally disturbed children. The intent of these hypotheses is to link description, diagnosis, and practice within a distinctly educational context and provide guidelines for the development of school programs for the disturbed which are more efficient and which take better advantage of the teaching expertise of the teacher, particularly in the public school. Section 1 (Chapters I–IV) reviews three major strategies used in the education of emotionally disturbed children and introduces the goals, methodology, and assessment of a developmental strategy. Section 2 (Chapters V–IX) relates the developmental strategy to specific classroom practices, and Section 3 (Chapters X–XII) delineates and evaluates a total classroom design which implements the developmental strategy in the public school.

In writing a text in a field already clouded and confused by bias, conjecture, and opinion, the author would like to be able to claim that all of his statements were supported by objective research evidence. Unfortunately, this book must be presented largely as a working paper, still in the process of being written as it is published. Much of what is included is based on the author's observation and experience and awaits further refinement and development. The major contribution of the book is its attempt to bring a measure of order into a somewhat chaotic field of special education through delineation of a continuous and consistent strategy for educating children called "emotionally disturbed" which is focused on observable behavior.

The ideas, suggestions, and experiences of numerous teachers and other professionals with whom the author has had the privilege of working are represented in much of the content of this book. In this respect, admiration and appreciation are due the staff of the UCLA Neuropsychiatric Institute School—Frank H. Langdon, Juanita J. Ferjo, Donald L. Mayhew, Ethel Rabb, and Howard M. Richer as well as James Q. Simmons, III, M.D., Chief, Children's Inpatient Service, UCLA Neuropsychiatric Institute.

The staff of the Santa Monica Unified School District, particularly Dr. Alfred A. Artuso, Superintendent, Dr. Frank D. Taylor, Director of Special Services, and Mr. Thomas J. Taglianetti, Coordinator, the Santa Monica Project, which is discussed in detail in Chapters XI and XII, have greatly contributed to the translation of the educational strategy presented in this text to the public school. Mrs. Blanche Warson and Mr. Lou Rienzi of the Tulare County Schools in California and Miss Sylvian You of the Waipahu School District in Hawaii have also provided valuable assistance in this translation. Regardless of the success of a particular approach in private, residential, and hospital school programs with the disturbed, its ultimate worth will be determined by whether it is applicable—not just to the select few in these settings—but to the tens of thousands of disturbed children in the community who are enrolled in public schools.

Dr. James C. Coleman, Department of Psychology, and Dr. Frances Berres, Assistant Director of the Fernald School, University of California, Los Angeles, deserve special acknowledgment for the guidance and support they provided the author during his early work with children with learning problems.

The author is also grateful to several colleagues who reviewed drafts of the manuscript for this book: Justin Call, M.D., Department of Psychiatry, University of California, Los Angeles; George A. Fargo, Ph.D., Department of Education, University of Washington; Barbara Keogh, Ph.D., Area of Special Education, University of California, Los Angeles; Nadine Lambert, Ed.D., Department of Education, University of California, Berkeley; Francis E. Lord, Ph.D., Department of Special Education, California State College, Los Angeles; Robert Schwitzgebel, Ed.D., Ph.D., Department of Psychology, University of California, Los Angeles; and Janet Switzer, Ph.D., Area of Special Education, University of California, Los Angeles. Peggy Groves also deserves special mention for the helpful editorial and secretarial assistance she provided.

Finally to my wife, Ruth, son, Michael, and daughter, Julie Anne, I am most indebted for the "absentee" husband and father status which they so patiently granted during the preparation of this book.

F.M.H.

Contents

Appendices

Bibliography

Index

1 *Goals, Methodology, Assessment*

I EDUCATIONAL STRATEGIES WITH EMOTIONALLY DISTURBED CHILDREN

The emotionally disturbed child is a socialization failure. Underlying all of the specialized terms and complex diagnostic labels used to describe him is the implication that his behavior, for whatever reason, is maladaptive according to the expectations of the society in which he lives. The term *socialization* is used in this text to refer to the process by which these expectations are learned and met by members of a society during the course of their development from infancy to adulthood. At each age level, certain behaviors, capabilities, knowledge, beliefs, and customs must be acquired if successful adaptation to the environment is to occur. As an individual's behavior deviates from what is expected for his age, sex, and status it is *maladaptive* and he may experience serious difficulties in getting along.

The term *emotional disturbance* has very little pragmatic value in the classroom. To some it implies the child is psychiatrically ill and a victim of deep-seated emotional conflicts which necessitate psychotherapy for resolution. To others it implies he has a hidden minimal organic defect which accounts for the hyperactivity, poor concentration, and oversensitivity to stimuli seen in some emotionally disturbed children, and as a result medication of one kind or another is required before successful learning in school can take place. Such approaches search for underlying causal factors and view the child first in a psychiatric or medical context and only secondly as an educational problem.

While this book retains the term "emotionally disturbed" in the title because of its widespread acceptance and usage in describing children who are inattentive, withdrawn, aggressive, nonconforming, disorganized, immature, and unable to get along with others, it is the subtitle's

3

reference to "maladaptive behavior" which more accurately reflects the author's orientation. For an increasing number of special educators have come to focus on children labeled "emotionally disturbed" as children with "maladaptive behavior" which teachers can modify rather than as "sick" or "defective" "patients" who require psychiatric or medical treatment before the school can effectively teach them (Hobbs, 1966; Haring and Phillips, 1962; Quay, 1966; Whelan, 1966). This is not to say that disturbed children do not profit from such treatment but rather to emphasize that maladaptive behavior interferes with learning and that such behavior can be modified in the classroom using resources unique to the school and training unique to the teacher. From this point on in the text, the terms "emotionally disturbed child" and "child with maladaptive behavior" will be used interchangeably.

Estimates of the actual incidence of children with emotional problems in the United States vary considerably, for the pinning of the label "emotionally disturbed" on a given child will depend on the nature of his maladaptive behavior, its severity, and frequency of occurrence as perceived by the psychiatrist, psychologist, teacher, peer group, and parents, individually or in combination. Pate (1963) suggests that a figure of 0.5 percent of the school age population reflects the number of emotionally disturbed children who need intensive special education while Abrahamson (1955) and Bower (1961) estimate that 10 percent need some help for emotional problems. Morse (1967) has found that teachers judge 8 percent of junior high pupils studied as severely maladjusted. White and Harris (1961) surveyed studies done to determine the incidence of emotional maladjustment in the school population from 1928 to 1958. They concluded that the incidence of serious maladjustment is somewhere between four and seven percent but that the incidence of mild maladjustment is too difficult to estimate due to problems of definition and variability in sampling techniques and methods of assessment.

It is the author's contention that the incidence of emotional disturbance or maladaptive behavior which the teacher must be concerned with would far exceed the 10 percent figure if a broader definition of the problem were employed. In actuality there are at least four types of children who qualify for the label "emotionally disturbed" in school.

First, there is the child like nine-year-old Clyde who became depressed and apathetic following his father's death. This behavior was in marked contrast to Clyde's usual outgoing and enthusiastic classroom participation and precluded his learning anything for a time. The situational stress brought about by his father's unexpected passing had precipitated a transient disturbance which disappeared over a two-week period but which required special attention from the teacher.

Second, there is Bobby who clung to his mother's skirts in terror as she attempted to leave him the first day of kindergarten. During the next two years, Bobby came to school with great reluctance, screamed and ran from other children when they approached him, and frequently claimed he was ill in the morning in what seemed an attempt to avoid going to school. Bobby's maladaptive behavior had become a way of life and seriously interfered with his learning in school. Other children like Gordon, a third grader, have chronic emotional problems of a less severe nature. Gordon was passive and pleasant in the classroom but became so anxious when a reading assignment was presented that he looked through, over, under, and around the printed symbols but never directly at them and hence had a serious reading problem.

Blair is a third example of an emotionally disturbed child. He was a ten-year-old mentally retarded boy with an IQ of 75 and was capable of acquiring certain basic academic skills in school. But his impulsivity and unwillingness to follow directions were constant limiting factors in his learning. While most of the other children functioning at the same intellectual level in his class could participate in a number-counting lesson using disc counters, Blair quickly and carelessly sorted out his discs with little attention to teacher directions and as a result often made errors. Blair's primary problem in school was one of mental retardation, but it was further complicated by a secondary problem of emotional disturbance.

Jeffrey had gradually lost his hearing and became totally deaf at the age of ten. He acquired lipreading skills and had mastered many basic arithmetic and printed language skills. But Jeffrey could not remain in a group of other children for more than a few minutes before his extreme suspiciousness caused him to strike out at one or more of them. He became violent at the slightest glance or minor provocation from others, apparently convinced that they intended to hurt him. His great mistrust and hostility also extended to the teacher and he had to be withdrawn from school. Here an emotional disturbance constituted Jeffrey's primary problem in learning and his deafness a problem of secondary importance.

Long, Morse, and Newman (1965) have compiled an interesting collection of excerpts from fictional works which describes the maladaptive behavior of many types of emotionally disturbed children. They also present a cross-section of the available literature covering techniques and approaches for identifying, teaching, and managing disturbed children as well as methods of evaluating school programs for them.

The present text is written to help teachers understand and more effectively teach all types of disturbed children. It is concerned with adaptive behaviors necessary for learning and maladaptive behaviors which interfere with learning. This chapter first reviews three major educational strategies which have been used with children called "emotionally disturbed." Finally it introduces a developmental educational strategy which underlies the remainder of the text. In an effort to assess and compare these strategies, it is important to first establish the significance of both *goals* and *methodology* in the education of emotionally disturbed children. Teachers must not only know where they are going with such children but also how they are going to get there.

Miss Brown, a third-grade teacher, is standing in front of the classroom waiting to get her children's attention. She is about to start a reading lesson when she notices Billy is still turned around in his seat. He is trying to distract several other class members, including Susan, whose right shin is still covered with a bandage over the spot where he kicked her the day before. Through Miss Brown's mind flash a host of crayon-throwing, paint-spilling, classroom-upsetting, and teacher-defying episodes involving Billy over the past several weeks. He cannot read, and when presented with a book he becomes noticeably anxious and blocks on even the simplest words. He seldom concentrates, has done no work, has refused to conform, and has been a constant source of harassment. He is at this time just about to provide "the last straw" which will provoke Miss Brown to have him excluded from school.

Billy qualifies, as do some one or two other of his classmates in the room, for the label "emotionally disturbed." His acting out behavior, however, puts him at the top of the class problem-list, considerably ahead of shy, fingernail-biting Mary, who cries at the slightest upset, and immature, distractible Kenneth, who sits quietly and daydreams.

As Miss Brown surveys this familiar scene, she wonders what in the world can be done with Billy. All of her third-grade goals with him have failed. He is totally unable to behave and learn as are the typical eight-year-olds with whom she is familiar. It is obvious he needs to learn to pay attention, follow directions, and respect the rights of others, but Miss Brown has difficulty viewing such goals as appropriate in themselves when the other children can do so much more. In addition, she is puzzled regarding how she might go about accomplishing any goals with a student who is so unresponsive to her teaching efforts.

Billy has a problem. Miss Brown has a problem. Special education has a problem. What are the goals of an effective educational program with emotionally disturbed children, and what methodology can be utilized to achieve them?

Rabinow (1955) has approached the problem of selecting educational goals for emotionally disturbed children as follows:

1. The school is not one school, but many schools; in the final analysis it is for each child a different school.
2. What may be taught is only what the child is ready to learn and despite apparent uneducability, all children are ready to learn *something*.
3. Normal children on entering school already have had a childhood which has prepared them for the culture of the school; for most of our (emotionally disturbed) boys and girls this is not so. The teacher and other staff become the primary persons, the people on whom the youngsters may build new concepts of worthwhile life; they incorporate our goals and purposes for them and through us, somewhat late, get *ready* for school while attending school.
4. It is possible to do a tremendous amount of individualization if the adult really believes in it; the youngsters catch on to the greater justice of different *right* things for everybody rather than the same things for all.[1]

Rabinow's statement furnishes the teacher of emotionally disturbed children with the guidelines needed for the selection of goals: *All such children are ready to learn something and despite their deviate behavior, the major educational goal is to get them ready for school while they are actually in school.*

The methodology which will assist the child in learning the "somethings" he needs to learn, and which will aid in getting him ready to be in school while he is actually there, is another matter. If Miss Brown accepts Rabinow's statement about goals, she will have to give serious thought to just how she might teach Billy "something," indeed *anything*. Perhaps concentrating on building a more positive relationship through accepting and trying to understand the meaning of Billy's behavior will win him over and decrease his hostility and nonconformity; perhaps introducing him to a preacademic, perceptual-motor training program will help him become a more successful learner; or perhaps selecting the most deviant behavior he displays (e.g., assaulting other children) and attempting to modify this by rewarding him for more appropriate interactions with his peers will accomplish more in the long run.

Miss Brown, like all teachers who are confronted with emotionally disturbed children in their classrooms, is faced with the problem of

[1] B.B. Rabinow, "The Role of the School in Residential Treatment," *The American Journal of Orthopsychiatry*, 1955, 25, p. 691. Copyright, The American Orthopsychiatric Association, Inc. Reproduced by permission.

selecting an educational strategy which holds promise for working with Billy. The term "strategy" implies both the selection of goals and the procedures or methodology for attaining those goals.

The selection of an educational strategy for use with the emotionally disturbed will depend in large measure on how such children are viewed. In this respect the teacher may be likened to a visitor to an art gallery where a unique piece of sculpture is on display. For some, the question of greatest concern is the origin of the work, the intent of the artist, and the message he is attempting to convey. For others, the physical structure of the sculpture and the nature of the materials used to fashion it may be of primary interest. Still others may be concerned with function. How does the work fit into the surroundings, and how appropriate and useful is it?

The three major strategies which have been utilized by teachers of emotionally disturbed children each reflect one of these points of view. One, focusing on the meaning and origin of the child's behavior, will be called the *psychodynamic-interpersonal strategy*. Another concerned with possible underlying organic causal factors related to behavior will be referred to as the *sensory-neurological strategy*. The final approach which views the child's behavior in terms of its adaptive function we will call the *behavior modification strategy*.

Neat categorization of diverse points of view is seldom possible, and the following attempt is no exception. In some cases, the headings are overly restrictive since the work of individuals grouped under them is relevant to more than one strategy. In others, the headings themselves lack explicit reference to a particular approach or individual. Nevertheless, an effort has been made to subsume the major distinguishing characteristics associated with current practices in classrooms for emotionally disturbed children under these headings.

Bateman (1967) has attempted a similar organization of approaches to the education of children with learning disabilities. Her *etiological approach* shares in common with the psychodynamic-interpersonal strategy a concern for causative factors. Bateman's *diagnostic-remedial approach* is related to the sensory-neurological strategy in that it focuses on diagnosis of specific sensory and perceptual-motor deficits. Finally, her *task analysis approach* views the child behavioristically and concentrates on defining specific educational tasks the child needs to learn in much the same manner as the behavior modification strategy. Bateman introduces her discussion with a statement that the three approaches are "neither mutually exclusive nor irreconcilable" and that all three might be used. The author concurs with this position with respect to the three strategies to be discussed in the next sections and will expand on this notion during the introduction to a *developmental strategy* at the close of the chapter.

In the section which follows, each of the strategies will be discussed in terms of its historical background, representative advocates, goals, methodology, teacher's role, and how it might be applied in the case of Billy.

THE PSYCHODYNAMIC-INTERPERSONAL STRATEGY

The psychodynamic-interpersonal educational strategy is concerned with the psychic origin and meaning of maladaptive behavior, as well as the child's interpersonal relationships with others, particularly the teacher. This orientation, shared by most psychotherapists, is consistent with the high priority given by them to understanding psychological causal factors and the development of a positive, trusting relationship between adult and child in formal educational training.

For purposes of discussion this strategy will be divided into two sub-strategies—one related to psychoanalysis and the other to a psycho-educational approach.

Psychoanalysis has had a marked influence on educational practices with emotionally disturbed children in residential and special schools and to some extent in the public school. In this section we will review psychoanalytic theory and its implication for special education with the disturbed.

The term psychoanalysis has three meanings. It is a body of data on human behavior. It is a method of treatment for individuals with mal-adaptive behavior. Psychoanalytic theory also describes stages of personality development, starting with infancy and proceeding through childhood, adolescence, and adulthood. The maladaptive behavior exhibited by emotionally disturbed children is viewed in part as resulting from arrested intellectual and psychological functions occurring during these critical periods of personality development.

Psychoanalysis has undergone, and continues to undergo, continuous revision since Freud's first psychoanalytic papers in the 1890's. In this discussion, a brief sketch of Freudian psychoanalytic theory will be presented (Freud, 1937, 1949).* Psychoanalytic theory is concerned with mental activity. Thus, it is psychodynamic and focused on the "workings" of the mind. Psychoanalytic theory postulates three mental structures: the *id, ego,* and *superego,* which underlie all mental activity. The *id* contains the mental representatives of instinctual life. Two basic

---

* The author is indebted to Justin Call, M.D., Department of Psychiatry, University of California, Los Angeles, for collaboration in the writing of this section.

instinctual drives are recognized, libido and aggression. Libido may be defined as a fixed quantity of sexual energy available to the individual from birth onward. Because of its close connection with instinctual drives, the id contains powerful forces and energies and is devoted to obtaining satisfaction of these drives which the child possesses at birth. The mental representatives of the instinctual life of a child are in the form of unconscious wishes, urges, and feeling states. Such unconscious activity is made known in fantasy life, dream life, symptoms, inhibitions, slips of the tongue, mistakes, and impulses.

The *ego* acts as an arbitrator between the child's inner needs and wishes found in the id and the external demands of the environment. Freud (1937) postulated primary congenital variations in the ego and suggested that id and ego were originally one and that even before the ego exists as such its subsequent lines of development, tendencies, and reactions were already determined. The ego is the seat of adaptation and learning. The ego judges situations according to circumstances. It gathers and weighs data. All of these functions require energy which comes from instinctual energy neutralized for these functions, and also from primary sources in the ego. Early psychoanalytic theory emphasized the strength of the id, and later Freudian theory (1926 and 1937) emphasized the strength of the ego. This changing emphasis has resulted in the broadening of psychoanalytic theory to become a general psychology of human behavior, rather than a theory of psychopathology alone.

The *superego* is a specialized part of the ego containing the conscience and the ego ideal, the agency by which one measures oneself. The conscience is the policy-maker of the mind which formulates permissible action from a moral viewpoint. Most of the directives issued from the conscience are verbal, utilizing the moral imperative in the subjective mood, i.e., "Thou shalt" and "Thou shalt not." The superego continues to grow and change throughout life. The superego is most closely related to the expectations of the environment, which are then internalized and exert a private influence from within. The early superego is mother-centered. The superego of the latency-aged child is parent- and family-centered, and the superego of adolescence is socially oriented. The school as a social institution transmits the values of the society to the child just as the parents do. These values become internalized as conscience and ego-ideal. The school acts as an external reinforcer for the superego. Like the id, most of the functions of the superego occur out of conscious awareness. The superego serves as a guide for achieving socially acceptable solutions to problems which confront the child.

These three structures make up a psychodynamic system which Freud called "the psychic apparatus."

Much of the child's behavior at any moment is viewed as unconsciously determined by the interaction of these structures and historically related to his psychological experiences during preceding stages of psychosexual development. The first of these stages is conceived as an *oral* stage, when the child is brought into contact with his environment through the feeding process, when early interpersonal relationships are initiated, and when basic attitudes, such as trust vs. mistrust, are established. Next the child moves to an *anal* stage, where confrontation with demands for control and adherence to routine occur, crystalizing around elimination processes. The child may emerge from the anal phase with feelings of autonomy or with feelings of shame and doubt. The next phase, the *phallic* phase, begins as the child becomes increasingly interested in the feelings of pleasure associated with the genital region of his body, and with fantasies about his parents. Taking his lead from the classic Greek tragedy, Oedipus Rex, Freud postulated an Oedipal conflict for the child at this stage. The child, awakened to the sexual pleasures of the genital area, seeks to establish an affectionate relationship with the opposite-sexed parent and *unconsciously* wishes to have exclusive possession of the opposite-sexed parent. He also fears retaliation from the parent of the same sex. The resolution of this conflict is usually accomplished through the child's identification with the like-sexed parent. This accomplishes several important things. It gives the child vicarious gratification, confirms the child's own identity and is a major point around which the child's superego crystalizes, since the child takes in through the process of identification the values of the parents and applies them to himself as his own, sometimes in a very strict fashion. If the child emerges from the Oedipal conflict relatively unscathed, he is ready to pursue the next phase of development with initiative rather than feelings of guilt.

The next phase of development, called *latency,* usually persists during the time the child is in elementary school. During this period of time the Oedipal wishes are repressed, and the child's energies are channeled into learning. His interests are directed to the peer group, and he tends to use teachers as substitutes for parents.

As the child moves into adolescence and further shifts his interest away from the family, and begins the process of selecting an appropriate partner for life, much of his earlier development is recapitulated before it becomes solidly established into what is called the *genital* stage of psychosexual development. It is during this time that all previous identities become consolidated and instinctual pressures from the id become greater, but are usually met with expanding ego and superego capacities as well.

Psychoanalytic theory is far more complex than implied by the brief summary above. Its specific relevance to the education of the emotionally disturbed child has been and still is being debated by special educators, who identify themselves with the psychodynamic-interpersonal strategy. For some educators, Freudian psychoanalytic theory is considered "ancient history" and of only passing interest to special education of the disturbed today. Despite the changing times, the author is impressed with how often he encounters the use of hypotheses and concepts derived from psychoanalytic theory by teachers, psychologists, and psychiatric consultants as they seek to describe and understand problem behaviors exhibited by emotionally disturbed children in the classroom. Such problem behaviors are often seen as symptoms of psychic conflict. If the child is to function and to learn in school, these symptoms must be thoroughly understood and every effort made to establish a positive, trusting relationship between teacher and child. The causes of maladaptive behavior or "learning blocks" in the classroom may be traced to problems during psychosexual stages of development. For example, a child who experienced psychological trauma during the oral stage may refuse to "take in" information. A child with problems during the anal stage may "withhold" what he is capable of doing and refuse to "give out." A child with difficulties during the phallic stage may greatly fear loss of anything and resist learning the subtraction process in arithmetic or have problems with fractions.

Call (1968), a psychoanalyst interested in developmental psychology, summarizes the relationship between psychoanalytic theory and education at present as follows:

Psychoanalysts, most notably Anna Freud (1965) have had a continuing interest in the relationship between the data derived from psychoanalytic treatment and the developmental aspects of psychoanalytic theory to education. Despite all the talk on both sides, the two fields have not really begun to grapple with the realities of the educational process as it is practiced with groups of children in the classroom with one teacher. The explanatory aspects of psychoanalytic theory may reduce or increase the anxiety and guilt in a teacher, but they have little to say at the practical level of how the teacher, as a teacher, should approach the child with an emotional disturbance. Psychoanalytic theory has in fact been better at defining the nature of problems than it has been in offering solutions. This does not mean that psychoanalysis and education cannot constructively meet in the classroom.[2]

---

[2] J. Call, Personal Communication, 1968.

Call (1963) has also discussed this problem elsewhere. In a discussion of the relationship between psychoanalysis and pedagogy, Anna Freud (1954) suggests that psychoanalysis has done three things for education. First, it has offered criticism of existing educational methods; second, it has extended the teacher's knowledge of human beings; and third, as a method of treatment it has attempted to "repair the injuries which are inflicted upon the child during the process of education."

The work of August Aichhorn with severely socially and emotionally maladjusted youth described in the original 1925 edition of his famous book *Wayward Youth* (Viking Press, 1965) represents an early attempt to apply psychoanalytic principles to education. Aichhorn set up a unique residential training school program for aggressive delinquent boys in marked contrast to the punitive, rigidly authoritarian approach of the day to such children. In an effort to establish a trusting and positive relationship with his charges, Aichhorn's motto was "as far as possible, let the boys alone." He was convinced that almost total acceptance of their behavior and continual expression of friendliness and warmth would eventually compensate for the lack of love these boys had experienced in earlier life and would make possible the gradual introduction of demands for conformity and learning. Such complete permissiveness resulted in many assaultive and destructive acts, but these reportedly diminished over time. When such behaviors had run their course, Aichhorn found that the boys were more amenable to staff contact and the formation of more appropriate relationships.

Aichhorn is credited with "warm sympathy and intuitive understanding" by Freud himself who wrote the introduction to Aichhorn's text. Freud also recommended psychoanalytic training for the educator and admitted that the contribution of psychoanalysis to education was still largely to be determined. Aichhorn's sympathetic and intuitive giftedness has also been recognized by Rabinow (1960) who concludes "the artistry of the teacher is more significant than the trainable competencies."

This early, totally permissive approach to the education and treatment of the emotionally disturbed has been modified over the years and programs utilizing the psychodynamic-interpersonal strategy in which children are completely "let alone" are certainly the exception rather than the rule. However, establishing a positive and trusting relationship between the teacher and child and relating behavior to causal factors before exerting demands for conformity and learning are still cardinal principles of the strategy.

Bettelheim (1950), Director of the University of Chicago's Orthogenic School, a residential treatment center for severely disturbed children,

comments regarding the important role the teacher plays in the therapeutic program as an object for relationship and identification.

> The satisfaction of a child's wants must become the means which will
> induce him to form a positive relation to the adults who provide for his
> well being. Then to the satisfaction of the child's needs is added the
> unique gratifying experience that only a genuine human relationship can
> offer. The relation to this person eventually challenges the child to change
> his personality at least in part in the image of the person or persons who
> are now so important to him. He identifies with them, as we say, and
> this identification is often the starting point for the organization of his
> personality. Those aspects of the adult's personality with which the child
> identifies then form the nucleus around which he organizes his talents,
> his desires and his temperament, all of which have until now been chaotic
> and undeveloped.[3]

Berkowitz and Rothman (1960) define the teacher's role in the classroom for disturbed children as follows:

> The role of teacher-academician concerned with skill and discipline has
> given way to a new concept of teaching concerned with education of the
> emotions. In order to accomplish this goal the teacher has to accept
> the behavior of the child from his first moment in class, no matter how
> unacceptable that behavior may be. The disturbed child who is aggressive
> is permitted to express his aggression without harming himself or others,
> while the withdrawn child is not pressured into socializing but is treated
> with intelligent neglect. Every child is made to feel that the teacher
> accepts him as an individual and that his behavior will be met with
> understanding.[4]

Pearson (1949, 1954) and Devereaux (1956) have also contributed
to the translation of psychoanalytic principles to the education of emotionally disturbed children.

During the course of its development the relationship of psychoanalytic theory as a general psychology to child development rather
than rigid adherence to earlier doctrines of psychic energy and activity
and psychosexual milestones has been emphasized. This emphasis relates the concepts of ego development and socialization more closely.
The child is viewed as an ever-adapting organism in an ever-changing

---

[3] B. Bettelheim, *Love Is Not Enough* (Glencoe: The Free Press, 1950), p. 28. Reproduced by permission of The Free Press and of George Allen & Unwin Ltd.,
London.
[4] P. Berkowitz and E. Rothman, *The Disturbed Child* (New York: New York
University Press, 1960), pp. 119–120.

environment, and the environmental events associated with his personality development assume added significance.

Redl and Wineman (1952) present a contrasting position to the one taken earlier by Aichhorn with respect to residential treatment with emotionally disturbed children. While still concerned with the communication of acceptance to the child, environmental realities are not ignored.

> A treatment home is interested not in avoiding and squashing the problem behavior resulting from the disturbances of the children but in giving it a chance to come out in the open so that it can be manipulated and used for treatment purposes. This means that we must convey to the children from the very onset the awareness that the difficulties which are part of their natural problem can be expressed and lived out without too severe consequences or rejection from the adult. On the other hand it is equally important to avoid the impression of "total permissiveness" in the children's mind. For, if they thought we not only tolerated but really enjoyed or did not mind their disturbed behavior what motivation in terms of gradual treatment changes would there be left? In a nutshell the treatment home must convey to the youngsters from the very start a climate which could be summarized in the following words: We like you, we take you the way you are, but of course in the long range we'd like you to change.[5]

Newman (1959) has focused on the public school setting and the problems facing teachers of hyperaggressive children with learning disturbances. Gradual introduction and increase of behavioral limits has been considered important in her work.

> Differences between acceptable and tolerated activities and behavior in the classroom had to be clearly communicated and a great deal of time and effort had to be spent on transmitting the message that what is tolerated at one period would not be tolerated at a later date. For example, the reading of comics was tolerated in school originally in order to communicate the message that the child was wanted in school and could stay there as long as he was not too disturbing to others. Later comics were tabooed in school since this time the message to be communicated was that there were some things appropriate to school and others inappropriate for the best use of school time.[6]

[5] F. Redl and D. Wineman, *Controls from Within* (Glencoe: The Free Press, 1952), p. 59.
[6] R. G. Newman, "The Assessment of Progress in the Treatment of Hyperaggressive Children with Learning Disturbances within a School Setting," *The American Journal of Orthopsychiatry*, 1959, 29, pp. 641–642. Copyright, The American Orthopsychiatric Association, Inc. Reproduced by permission.

Recently, there has been a growing interest in a psychoeducational approach to the education of disturbed children and the establishment of an effective mental health program in the public schools (Morse, 1966). Morse advocates organization of a psychoeducational team in a local region of the school system consisting of special education teachers, a psychometrist, social worker, and other specialists such as guidance workers, speech personnel, and psychiatric and psychological consultants. Thus, the orientations and skills of several disciplines would be mobilized to assist the disturbed child in the schools. Morse conceives of such a team as being focused on the child's behavior and his interpersonal relationships as well as his entire educational experience.

Following identification and referral of a particular child for assistance, the team would select a member to go into the classroom and observe the problem firsthand. As a result of this observation, a possible solution to the problem such as modification of the classroom, referral to another teacher, or placement in a special class or resource center would be considered. When the team has settled on a way to help the child, the regular teacher who will work with him would avail herself of consultation services from the special education teachers and other consultants on the team and be closely involved in all follow-up planning. Team responsibility would also include regular checking of the teacher and provision for additional assistance as needed.

Morse (1965) has also described the use of a "crisis teacher" in the school to assist regular teachers when a given child's behavior can no longer be tolerated in the classroom. The crisis teacher might work individually with the child until such time as he could be returned to his regular room. Such a teacher must be skilled in remedial teaching techniques and management of difficult behavior problems.

One of the management techniques suggested by Morse (1963) and others (Redl, 1959; Morse and Small, 1959) is life-space interviewing. The life-space interview is a form of instant therapeutic first aid in which the child is helped with problems in the immediate context in which they have occurred (e.g., playground) by individuals normally associated with such events (e.g., teacher). It is designed to deal with "now" events rather than past events in the child's life related to the problem such as might be brought up by a professional psychotherapist, and it relies on the direction of individuals such as teachers and group leaders who are not trained therapists. Newman, Bloomberg, Emerson, Keith, Kitchner, and Redl (1964) have investigated the effectiveness of providing "technical assistance," a form of psychoanalytically oriented consultation offered by professionals in the mental health field to the school. Stark and Bentzen (1958) have also reported on the use of psychiatric team and special teacher assistance as a means of aiding disturbed children in the public school.

The work of Aichhorn, Bettelheim, Berkowitz, and Rothman, Redl and Wineman, and Newman and Morse has been presented as illustration of the application and development of a psychodynamic-interpersonal educational strategy. Their approaches, while covering a wide range of specific emphases, share in common a concern for understanding the antecedent psychological problems associated with the child's behavior and reliance on building a positive, trusting relationship between teacher and child as prelude to training and academic learning.

Project Re-ED (Hobbs, 1966; Lewis, 1967) is an educational program for emotionally disturbed children which provides brief residential treatment and which primarily uses educational procedures and personnel. It has been developed over a several-year period at George Peabody College in Tennessee. Project Re-ED does not utilize a single educational strategy but focuses on the child's adaptation to his total environment.

The Project Re-ED model is ecological and is concerned with the child's relationship with his family, regular school, and community. This project is discussed here because of its reliance on the unique contribution of a teacher-counselor who, while not a psychotherapist, is thoroughly trained in the characteristics of disturbed children and the nature of community mental health resources and who is expected to work with consultants from other disciplines as well as be an expert in special teaching techniques and recreational skills. Each Project Re-ED school has an enrollment of 40, and students are placed in classes of eight under the supervision of two teacher-counselors. Every effort is made to preserve a link with the child's parents, regular school, and the community and to prepare the child for return to his natural environment as quickly as possible (usually after six or seven months). The teacher-counselors not only conduct classroom programs for the children but analyze clinical records and direct social living experiences in the total school program for the child. They actively participate and work with parents and other individuals who are a part of the child's ecological unit.

Despite differences in emphasis, proponents of a psychodynamic-interpersonal strategy tend to perceive goals and methodology in the education of the emotionally disturbed as follows:

Goals

A primary goal is to understand why the child is behaving as he is in school. This goal may be achieved by some through interpretation of behavior in a psychodynamic context, using psychoanalytic concepts.

Others may view the child more in relationship to his total environment and be concerned with understanding why he lacks adaptive capacities for dealing with the stresses and demands associated with learning and adjustment in school. For the teacher, a major goal is the communication of acceptance to the child and the establishment of a secure and meaningful relationship. Formal educational goals are of secondary importance.

Methodology

In the process of working toward the goals of the psychodynamic-interpersonal strategy, the teacher must possess expertise normally associated with disciplines other than education. In addition to sound training in special education, the teacher may be expected to be knowledgeable regarding personality dynamics and the interpertation of clinical data from psychological testing and psychiatric interviews and to be able to relate effectively to consultants from social work, clinical psychology, and psychiatry. While these are valuable attributes for any teacher, they are probably relied on to a greater extent in educational programs for the disturbed following a psychodynamic-interpersonal strategy than in any other type of educational program for exceptional children.

The teacher may also need to be able to offer some type of counseling or therapeutic assistance in classroom and related activities. Although most of the individuals advocating the use of this strategy would not classify the teacher as a "psychotherapist" in such a role, the line between the supportive help they recommend and more typical therapeutic approaches used by professionals in social work, clinical psychology, and psychiatry may be ill-defined, particularly from the teachers' point of view.

In the actual educational program, the child is accepted without censure since his psychopathology may be considered "grist for the mill." An accepting nondemanding climate is also considered essential for establishment of a positive relationship between teacher and child. Complete permissiveness, however, is not likely to exist. The child will be given academic and learning tasks it is felt he is ready for, and attempts will be made to guarantee him success in all that he does in school.

The teacher pursuing the psychodynamic-interpersonal strategy may assume the role of *educational therapist*. In this role, artistry and intuition may be of greater import than teaching competence, and the teacher may identify more closely with the psychotherapist than the special educator.

As an educational therapist, Miss Brown might set the goals of classroom conformity and reading instruction aside for Billy, her problem third grader, and concentrate on building a more positive and accepting relationship with him. She might work with him individually before or after class in an effort to communicate her interest and genuine concern for helping him succeed in school. While her responsibility to other children will not permit abandoning all demands for conformity in the classroom, Miss Brown would make every attempt to let Billy know that it was his behavior she was rejecting and not his value as a person. When she cannot handle the situation, perhaps the help of a crisis teacher will restore his composure and control and permit early return to the classroom.

On some occasions, when Billy is upset and angry with the other children, Miss Brown might reflect his feelings and, in effect, communicate to him, "I know you are angry with Sally. You cannot hit her but you can come and tell me about it and I will understand." Or she may take Billy aside and engage in life-space interviewing, allowing him to drain off frustration and anger and supporting him but attempting to get him to view the reality of the situation and the rules and rights of others. Billy's relationships at home with his siblings and parents will be important to Miss Brown as she seeks to relate Billy's behavior in school to its antecedents outside the classroom. With regard to Billy's anxiety in the reading situation, Miss Brown may hypothesize that it is related to a traumatic psychological experience of earlier childhood. Since reading involves "looking at" something, perhaps Billy saw something as a young child which deeply troubled him, such as sexual activity between his mother and father, and as a result "looking at" anything has become psychologically conflictual for him. She most likely would not attempt to verify this possibility or interpret it to Billy, but what transpires in the classroom might markedly be influenced by such an attempt to understand the "why" of Billy's reading problem. In addition, serious consideration might be given to referring Billy and his parents to a clinical psychologist or psychiatrist for personality testing and/or psychotherapy.

The psychodynamic-interpersonal strategy has probably exerted more influence on educational practices with emotionally disturbed children than any other approach. Just as psychoanalytic theory has had an impact on child rearing practices and has constituted the basis for much child psychotherapy, so it has strongly influenced special education with the disturbed. While no one can argue with its goal of a thorough understanding of the child's problems, the emphasis on psychosexual stages, feeling states, and a quasi-therapist role for the teacher has not produced a truly translatable strategy for the typical classroom. Its greatest success seems to have been in special school settings where control exists over the child on a 24-hour basis and where teachers work intimately and intensively with psychotherapists.

More recent attempts at development of a psychoeducational approach are aimed at helping the public school teacher who works with a disturbed child from four to six hours a day. The emphasis here is on creating a mentally healthy learning climate through mobilization of various disciplines associated with child care and treatment. In general, however, more attention seems to have been paid to establishment of this climate rather than to development of specific teaching techniques and curriculum materials for helping the child learn and the teacher to fulfill a primary role of educator.

THE SENSORY-NEUROLOGICAL STRATEGY

In the introduction to this chapter, it was pointed out that maladaptive behavior or emotional disturbance could be found in combination with the full range of exceptionalities. For that reason it is not as containable in a single category as other classifications such as the mentally retarded, deaf, and visually handicapped. In fact, if you are going to discuss emotional disturbance and special education what you say must have relevance to all possible combinations of disturbed exceptional children.

One type of exceptional child who often manifests maladaptive behavior or emotional disturbance is the child with suspected neurological impairment. His difficulties have been referred to as the brain damage behavior syndrome, hyperkinetic-impulse disorder, Strauss syndrome, and postencephalitic behavior syndrome (Clements and Peters, 1962). He may also be described as a victim of minimal cerebral dysfunction or a learning disability. Among the maladaptive behaviors often seen in these children are specific learning deficits, perceptual-motor deficits, general coordination deficits, hyperactivity, impulsivity, emotional lability, and short attention span and/or distractibility. Since all of these may also be seen in children called emotionally disturbed, a question often asked in special education at the present time is whether such behaviors are organic or functional in origin. How much of what the teacher sees is the result of an actual organic insult to the brain, how much is due to intellectual deficits, how much to psychological conflict and faulty learning, and how much to cultural and educational deprivation?

Whether the answer to this question really has a bearing on the best educational approach for helping the child is debatable, and the author will expand on this in subsequent chapters in the text. For purposes of the present discussion we shall review the work of individuals who have approached the education of children with maladaptive behavior from a sensory or neurological point of view.

The sensory-neurological strategy predates the psychodynamic-interpersonal strategy. One of its most significant landmarks occurred at the beginning of the nineteenth century with the work of Itard. Itard (1962) undertook a lavish five-year program of individual training with Victor, "the wild boy of Aveyron," who had been found at about age 11 living in a forest near the Province of Aveyron in France. Although Victor was considered an incurable idiot by some, Itard, inspired by the philosophy of sensationalism, the French post-revolutionary belief that man had unlimited possibilities and that environment was the chief determining factor in development, set out to demonstrate that with proper training of the senses Victor could be made "human."

Through special exercises designed to teach Victor to discriminate extremes of temperature, differences in taste, touch, vision, and sound, Itard achieved some success; but in his attempts to teach human wants and desires and appropriate social behavior, very little progress was made. Auditory training and speech instruction were particularly difficult and Victor remained nonverbal.

In his training program Itard not only established methods of sensory training used today with exceptional children and gave support to the premise that all children regardless of their apparent degree of noneducability are ready to learn something, but he also demonstrated aspects of the behavior modification and operant conditioning methodology to be discussed in the next section.

During the nineteenth century Seguin (Talbot, 1964), a student of Itard, continued exploration of sensory-motor training with handicapped children. His work strongly influenced Montessori (1912), whose "scientific approach to pedagogy" included development of unique sensorial materials for visual, auditory, tactile, and olfactory training.

The exceptional children with whom Itard, Seguin, and Montessori worked included those with physical and sensory impairments as well as mental retardation, and few might be solely classifiable as emotionally disturbed today. Nevertheless, the sensory-motor training approach which they introduced has been applied to the education of children labeled emotionally disturbed because of continuing interest in explaining maladaptive behavior on an organic basis.

In the 1930's implications of the principle of cerebral dominance for education of children with learning problems was explored by Orton (1937). Word reversals in reading (e.g., the child's reading "was" as "saw") were considered indications of "incomplete" or "mixed" cerebral dominance. Unless the child demonstrated a clearcut preference for use of a hand and eye on the same side of the body, it was assumed that dominance had not been established and that this was central to his learning problem. Orton coined the impressive term "strephosymbolia" (twisted symbol) to describe the problem of word reversal.

Various other medical-neurological terms have been utilized to describe children's learning problems, such as "specific dyslexia" (partial inability to read due to cerebral dysfunction), and "alexia" (total inability to learn to read due to cerebral dysfunction). A complete discussion of dyslexia may be found in texts by Money (1962, 1966) and Critchley (1964). Mykelbust (1957) has intensively studied language development in children with cerebral dysfunction.

Others who have contributed to the sensory-neurological strategy are Fernald, Strauss, Kephart, Cruickshank, and Frostig.

The Fernald (1943) method of kinesthetic word tracing is a multisensory approach to learning that has proven useful teaching reading and spelling to children with learning and behavior problems. The child traces with his finger over words written in large form in crayola on a slip of paper. He looks at the word and says it aloud as he engages in the kinesthetic tracing procedure. Fernald's approach to remedial education is still practiced in the Fernald School (formerly the Clinic School) of the University of California, Los Angeles, and includes a highly individualized educational program for each child, in which continued success experience is emphasized and competition is eliminated.

Strauss's (Strauss and Lehtinen, 1947) work has been with children termed "brain-injured," but who often manifest problems of emotional disturbance as well. With Werner (1941) he contributed to a broader understanding of the relationship between neurological impairment and psychological adjustment among exceptional children. In collaboration with Lehtinen, Strauss, like Itard, Seguin, and Montessori earlier, conceived of training procedures that have relevance for many types of exceptional children. Control of stimulation in the classroom, separation of children to lessen distraction, and heightening the stimulus value of teaching materials are environmental planning considerations recommended by Strauss to counteract organic disturbances of behavior and attention.

Cruickshank (1961) has recognized the considerable degree of overlap which exists between brain-injured and emotionally disturbed children and has devloped a sensory-neurological strategy with implications for both. As a result of an experimental study with these children he concluded that the following conditions for teaching were desirable:

1. reduced environmental stimuli
2. reduced space
3. a structured school program and life plan
4. an increase in the stimulus value of the teaching materials which are constructed to cope with the specific characteristics of the psychopathology under consideration.[7]

Cruikshank states the objectives of the teacher as follows:

The teacher works with children in terms of enlisting the support of the ego, in acquiring mastery of the learning skills. The existence and resolution of psychopathological aspects of the personality is secondary to the instructional goal and the success of the teaching situation is gauged in relation to the degree to which children achieve academic progress.[8]

Kephart's (1960) approach emphasizes establishing perceptual-motor skills before undertaking formal academic training.

The teacher already spends a great deal of time with the slow learning child. Much of this time could be more profitably spent by concentrating on pre-academic skills, rather than by continued drilling on the academic activities, from which the child has already demonstrated that he is not ready to profit. If readiness can be achieved by giving him such special training early, many slow learners will fall in with the rest of their fellows and continue learning through the customary activities of the group.[9]

Kephart has formulated a developmental framework stressing the importance of perceptual-motor functioning underlying complex learning and behavior. He emphasizes establishment of efficient and consistent motor patterns as a basis for a generalized, stable perceptual orientation in space and time. The Achievement Center for Children at Purdue University under Kephart's direction offers diagnosis and training for children with perceptual-motor deficits.

Frostig (Frostig, Lefever, and Whittlesey, 1961) has developed an assessment device for measuring the level of visual-perceptual functioning in children and has produced specific materials for remediating diffi-

---

[7] W. Cruikshank, F. Bentzen, F. Ratzeburg, and M. Tannhauser, *A Teaching Method for Brain-Injured and Hyperactive Children* (Syracuse: Syracuse University Press, 1961), p. 14.
[8] Ibid., p. 424.
[9] N. Kephart, *The Slow Learner in the Classroom* (Columbus: Charles E. Merrill Books, Inc., 1960), p. viii.

culties in hand-eye motor coordination, figure-ground perception, recognition of constancy of shape, determination of position in space, and spatial relationships. Haeussermann (1958) has developed psycho-educational procedures for use with preschool brain-injured children.

Kirk and McCarthy (1961) have devised a quantitative test of psycholinguistic abilities for children between the ages of two-and-one-half and nine. Their Illinois Test of Psycholinguistic Abilities (ITPA) consists of a battery of nine sub-tests designed to assess the linguistic assets and deficits of children, based on a model of the communication process postulated by Osgood (1953). Utilizing the ITPA, the teacher can identify the relative abilities and disabilities of children with learning problems and develop remedial instructional procedures accordingly.

A thorough reading of the major references associated with each of these authors will clarify their similarities and differences in points of view and training procedures. For purposes of this text an attempt will be made to summarize the sensory-neurological strategy which they represent in terms of goals and methodology.

Goals

The primary goal of the sensory-neurological strategy is to discover the child's sensory and neurologically based deficits often through extensive observation and diagnostic testing. Once these deficits are uncovered the child is viewed as a learner who must be trained to accurately perceive and comprehend stimuli and to demonstrate motor efficiency before he is given complex learning tasks.

Methodology

The sensory-neurological strategy places great emphasis on order and routine. Development of pre-academic perceptual motor skills has to be accomplished through clearcut goal setting, constant repetition, and mastery of one level before proceeding to the next. There is a specificity in the methodology which directs the teacher in each step of the program. This specificity may extend to the exact type of classroom environment including neutral wall color to reduce distraction, and the type of curriculum assignments and activities given to the child. Special materials such as walking boards and sequential work sheets are suggested. Criteria for evaluating the child's improvement and readiness for more advanced training are also offered the teacher.

The sensory-neurological strategy provides the role of *diagnostician* for the teacher of the emotionally disturbed. This role establishes a liaison between education, medicine, and neurology which, like the liaison between education, psychology, and psychiatry inherent in the psychodynamic-interpersonal strategy, is often particularly attractive to teachers of disturbed children. In general, there is little concern with inferred psychological meaning of the child's behavior although the authors cited admittedly vary in this regard.

Billy's distractibility and hyperactivity in the classroom might lead Miss Brown to refer him to the school physician or a medical specialist in order to ascertain whether his problems are related to some type of cerebral dysfunction. The physician may prescribe medication in an attempt to reduce Billy's maladaptive behavior. A thorough neurological examination including an electroencephalogram (EEG) might also be undertaken.

Although such an approach to Billy's school problem may be highly desirable regardless of the particular strategy used in the classroom, it probably is more readily taken and the results obtained given greater credence by teachers oriented toward the importance of sensory-neurological factors in learning. In addition, Miss Brown might concern herself with observing Billy and having him further assessed to determine among other things his visual acuity, auditory discrimination, the presence or absence of established hand-eye dominance, degree of laterality, spatial orientation, and gross and fine motor coordination. Where difficulties were found Billy may then be placed in a program of training designed to bring him up to a level deemed necessary for formal reading instruction.

As appealing as the specificity of diagnosis, labeling, and training associated with the sensory-neurological strategy may be to the educator, when it results in educational narrowness and rigidity it may have serious drawbacks. In addition terms such as "brain damage," "cerebral dysfunction," and "neurological impairment" often sidetrack the teacher. Being told by a physician or neurologist that a given child is "dyslexic" or has "strephosymbolia" may cause the teacher to decide that such an ominous problem really precludes the child's being helped in the classroom.

Gallagher (1966) has stressed the potential danger of dependence on labels in special education.

The tranquilizing effect on a profession of the application of some distinguished label and accompanying description such as schizophrenia, infantile autism, or minimal brain injury is too well known to require extended comment. These terms describe extraordinary, vague entities, explain nothing, and lead to no clear description as to what should be done. They provide only a false sense of order and knowledge. The relief that is obvious at a case conference once one of these labels is convincingly pinned on the child gives evidence that all tend to seek certainty and security, sometimes at the expense of broadening professional wisdom.[10]

With regard to the wisdom and efficacy of labeling children as "brain-injured" Reger (1965) has offered strong advice to school psychologists.

1. The only time that a diagnosis of brain injury can be made with certainty is at autopsy.
2. There are no psychological tests that can actually diagnose injury to the brain except in the more obvious cases; for the so-called "Strauss-type" brain injury, psychological or medical tests are of unknown validity.
3. Most of what is assumed to be known about the "brain-injured child" today is folklore.
4. The flippant way the label of brain injury is tagged on to children by persons who "frankly," do not know what they are talking about is hardly likely to further the causes of the profession.
5. School psychologists should study this area carefully. The available evidence is against the current direction of program developments for so-called brain injured children. School psychologists may be diagnostic impresarios by promoting the brain-injured child "myth," but it is *scientific evidence* and not popularity that eventually will hold the field.[11]

The mounting of scientific evidence to support the hypothesis that maladaptive behavior and emotional disturbance may indeed be the result of injury to the child's brain is a complex proposition.

Clements and Peters (1962) have spoken out strongly for consideration of possible organic factors in cases of emotional disturbance and learning problems and not undue preoccupation with environmental influence. They state that "most" childhood psychoses are based on brain deviations and that traumatic experiences, methods of teaching, or emotional blocking are not major causes of reading disability. They cite the following as evidence that minimal brain dysfunction conditions do exist and determine behavior: the similarities of perceptual deficit and symptoms of children with questionable histories and adults with known brain damage, the clustering of these symptoms into recognizable entities, the positive correlation between complications of pregnancy and later behavior and learning problems, studies which link

---

[10] J. Gallagher, "Children with Developmental Imbalances: A Psychoeducational Definition," in W. Cruikshank, ed., *The Teacher of Brain-Injured Children* (Syracuse: Syracuse University Press), 1966, p. 27.
[11] From R. Reger, *School Psychology*, 1965, pp. 190–191. Courtesy of Charles C. Thomas, publisher, Springfield, Mass.

heredity and dyslexia, the good response of children with suspected brain damage to drugs and training without psychotherapy, and differences between siblings reared in similar environments.

Clements (1966) has described hyperactivity as the most prominent symptom of the minimal brain dysfunction syndrome. Werry (1967) has challenged this and states that the belief that the majority of hyperactive children have cerebral dysfunction is at present no more than an "unsubstantiated hypothesis" and that treatment should be "multifaceted."

That definitive linking between brain functioning and behavior is extremely difficult to establish has been pointed out by Isom (1967), a neurologist. He cites the case of three infants with hydrocephaly (virtual absence of a cerebral cortex). All three had characteristically abnormal EEG's and abnormal transillumination. Two of the infants were clearly retarded, but the third case was normal by any clinical examination. Mabry (1959) has also reported a case of prolonged neonatal anoxia (lack of oxygen) without apparent subsequent developmental or behavioral abnormalities. Additional evidence which advises caution regarding making assumptions that "such and such" behaviors are clearly representative of "such and such" brain deviations has been presented by Lorber (1965) and Williams (1966).

In the author's experience many highly respected neurologists have cautioned educators with regard to uncritically assuming that word-reversals, hyperactivity and perceptual-motor problems are organic in origin. They honestly admit their limited ability to relate problems of learning and behavior to specific functions of the brain. However, such conservatism and humility is not always found in the field of special education. The author has heard numerous educators declare with an air of strong conviction and authority that a given child's learning or behavior problems were "obviously organic," based on the flimsiest of observational data. Such attempts at pseudoneurological expertise are indicative of the educator's strong need to bring a degree of order out of the educational chaos created by children with unexplained learning and emotional problems.

Certainly not all emotionally disturbed children demonstrate sensory or neurological problems in school, but as long as maladaptive behavior such as inattention, distractibility, hyperactivity, poor coordination, and perceptual-motor deficits are commonly found among them, an attempt to establish a link between the child's behavior and possible organic contributing factors will undoubtedly continue. As definitive evidence is obtained it may greatly aid the physician and neurologist in treating such children but perhaps assist the teacher confronted with the problem of teaching them to a far lesser extent.

THE BEHAVIOR MODIFICATION STRATEGY

Instead of asking "why" an emotionally disturbed child behaves as he does or attempting to relate his problems to "how" the central nervous system is functioning, the teacher may ask simply "what" behavior does the child exhibit which interferes with learning. The behavior modification strategy to which we now turn is primarily concerned with asking "what" rather than "why" or "how."

The interfering behaviors which the emotionally disturbed child exhibits in the classroom are considered learned in the context of this strategy. By assisting the child in modifying his behavior and hence increasing the probability of his success in and acceptance by the environment, underlying core or causal factors are largely ignored. The teacher using this strategy is also more concerned with the disadvantages and negative consequences inherent in allowing the child to maintain maladaptive behavior rather than the long-standing controversy over whether symptom removal constitutes a cure or mere masking of the real problem.

Teachers of emotionally disturbed children are well acquainted with examples of the two types of behavior with which this strategy is concerned. One type is involuntary and not under the control of the individual. It includes the fear and avoidance reactions seen in children who are confronted with assignments, rules, competition, and other classroom demands which they cannot handle. It is unlikely that Todd, a nonreader, will objectively evaluate the situation when he is given an oral reading assignment by the teacher the first day he is in a new class. There is a good chance he will become fearful, "freeze" in front of the class, and wish more than anything else at that moment that he could escape. These reactions on Todd's part are the result of learning or conditioning.

The fact that such negative reactions are learned was recognized by John Locke in the year 1700. In the fourth edition of the *Essay* he wrote:

> Many children imputing the pain they incurred in school to their books . . . so join these ideas together that a book becomes their aversion . . . and thus reading becomes a torment to them, which otherwise possibly they might have made the greatest pleasure of their lives.

Todd's behavior has been learned through respondent or classical conditioning. It is the result of previously neutral stimuli (books and reading before Todd entered school) acquiring properties for automatically eliciting a response (fear and avoidance on Todd's part) due to repeated pairings with unpleasant and painful events (ridicule of other children, criticism of teacher and parents because of failure to learn to read).

Keller (1954) provides a striking example of the classical conditioning of reflexive behavior.

> Suppose that, in a warm room, your right hand is immersed in a pitcher of ice water. Immediately the temperature of the hand will be lowered, due to a shrinkage or constriction of its blood vessels. This is an instance of respondent behavior. It will be accompanied by a similar, and more easily measured, change in the temperature of the left hand, where blood-vessel constriction will also be induced. Now, suppose that your right hand is dipped into the ice water a number of times, say at intervals of three or four minutes; and suppose further that an electric buzzer is heard briefly just before each dip. By the 20th pairing of the buzzer sound with the cold water, the temperature change can be elicited by the sound alone—that is, without the moistening of either hand.[12]

Eysenck (1960) and Wolpe, Salter, and Renya (1965) have written regarding the application of classical conditioning procedures to the treatment of individuals with emotional problems.

The second type of behavior with which the behavior modification strategy is concerned is voluntary and under the control of the individual. It is behavior learned in accord with Thorndike's (1913) Law of Effect which simply states, "An act may be altered in its strength by its consequences."

The "act" in question is considered a "response" on the part of the individual to a particular "stimulus" presented him, and the "consequences" are positive or negative reinforcements provided on the basis of a specific set of expectations or a contingency.

The teacher holds up a card with the word "milk" on it (the stimulus) and points to Lee. Lee is expected to read it (the contingency). Lee looks at the card and says "milk" (the response); the teacher smiles and says "Good boy!" (the positive reinforcement). Lee is being conditioned to give this response in the presence of the printed stimulus. If, however, Lee has read the word "milk" as "house" he would not have given the correct response according to the expectation or contingency set by the teacher. Such an incorrect response might elicit a frown from

[12] F. Keller, *Learning: Reinforcement Theory* (New York: Random House, 1954), pp. 3–4.

the teacher or giggles from his classmates (negative reinforcement), and Lee might work harder than ever to avoid having this happen again in the future. In addition if Lee's incorrect response had not produced any reaction on the part of the teacher, he might also have been negatively reinforced through the withholding of positive reinforcement. In these examples Lee is learning through operant conditioning which has been described by Skinner (1963).

Teachers hearing "operant conditioning" and "reinforcement" often conjure up images of experimental studies with animals and birds (e.g., rats running mazes, pigeons pecking at buttons) and dismiss these terms as nonapplicable to education with children. The author is reminded of one such teacher who, after hearing operant conditioning discussed in detail, exclaimed with surprise, "Why you aren't talking about animal conditioning at all. You're just describing *good teaching!*"

Application of behavior modification principles to education *does* constitute good teaching, but unfortunately the valuable contribution which such principles can make to the education of the disturbed child is often overlooked because of the discomfort some educators experience in relating a theoretical framework which has largely emerged from the animal laboratory to the human classroom. Whelan (1966) has written a knowledgeable and comprehensive account of the relevance of the behavior modification strategy to the education of emotionally disturbed children.

Some educators view positive and negative consequences as so obviously related to changing and controlling behavior that they exclaim, "So what else is new?" What is *new* is that teachers often do not recognize the potency of positive and negative consequences in the classroom or understand how to effectively and appropriately utilize them with children who have learning and behavior problems.

Martin and Stendler (1959) provide us with an example of a powerful purveyor of positive and negative consequences in action.

Consider Miss A., a third-grade teacher. Miss A.'s class is writing letters to Tony who is ill at home. Miss A. walks up and down the aisles, supervising the children's work. She stops at Pete's desk and picks up his paper.

"Boys and girls," she says to get the attention of the group, "may I have your attention? That means you too, Matilda."

"This is Pete's paper. I want you to notice how carefully Pete has followed my directions. See, he has left margins at both sides and has written the heading exactly right. See how neat and clean his paper is too?"

Miss A. returns Pete's paper with a beam of approval and goes on. She stops at Raymond's desk. Raymond does not fare so well.

"Boys and girls!" Again the heads go up. "Look at Raymond's paper. Raymond needs some help. See the smudges and spots on his paper? What can we tell Raymond to help him improve?"

"He should wash his hands before he starts and not erase," say the children.

The teacher returns the paper to Raymond with a look of disapproval.

"It will have to be done over, Raymond, and that's wasting paper you know."

Some of the children finish their letters and must wait for the others to finish. Several sit and do nothing. Miss A. comments to the class.

"I like the way some people are finding jobs to do when they finish. I see two children studying spelling and one boy doing his workbook. That's using time wisely, isn't it, boys and girls? You'll have five more minutes to finish and I expect all of you to be done if you haven't been dawdling."

Miss A. did not distribute gold stars as rewards or spankings as punishments. Yet she made certain ways of behaving pleasurable to the children and other ways painful by her approval and disapproval of their actions. In the space of five minutes she indicated her liking for children who obeyed her requests for attention, followed her directions, did neat clean work, kept obviously busy, did not waste supplies and finished work on time. The children in Miss A.'s class did not learn obedience, respect for authority and neatness and cleanliness, avoidance of waste and the importance of time in this one lesson but when day after day, school year after school year, teacher after teacher, the same kinds of actions are rewarded and punished, these responses become reinforced in the child.[13]

In the preceding example, Pete's responses (e.g., leaving margins on his paper, writing neatly) were completely in line with Miss A.'s expectations and were rewarded by her "beam of approval." Miss A. was utilizing operant conditioning to strengthen Pete's appropriate work habits.

Raymond, on the other hand, responded inappropriately, according to the teacher's expectations. The smudges on his paper resulted in negative consequences. For many emotionally disturbed children, school and learning are associated with such experiences. Because they are not able to meet teacher expectations and obtain desired rewards, the school becomes an unpleasant environment, and like Todd in the earlier example they acquire, through classical conditioning, negative associations to learning.

While Pete undoubtedly reacted positively to Miss A.'s criticism whenever it was directed at him and worked harder than ever to avoid future disapproval, children like Raymond often "give up" as a result of repeated failure. If they are not helped to achieve success by having

---

[13] W. Martin and C. Stendler, *Child Behavior and Development* (New York: Harcourt, Brace & World, 1959), pp. 349–350.

expectations reduced to a realistic level and opportunities provided for obtaining positive consequences for their efforts, school and learning become part of a vicious circle. The more you are in school and given assignments, the more you fail. The more you fail, the less you try, and your chances of failure increase.

Application of the behavior modification strategy in the field of education is seen in the development of teaching machines and programed instruction and the work of Birnbrauer, Bijou, Kidder, and Wolf, Hewett, Haring, and Phillips, Whelan, Quay, Patterson, and Ebner, and Zimmerman and Zimmerman.

Teaching machines are behavior modification devices in a pure form, and programs presented on them adhere closely to basic learning theory principles: clearly defined stimuli and expectations, active responses required of the learner, immediate reinforcement through knowledge of results, use of prompts when necessary to guarantee success, and gradual increase in complexity of the material.

Programed instruction presented on a teaching machine appears to hold promise for enlisting the active participation of some seriously emotionally disturbed children who demonstrate inability to function in a social learning situation. The machine-child relationship, however, is a highly impersonal one which does not assist the child in improving his functioning in a social setting.

Operant conditioning techniques have been applied in a classroom program with exceptional children by Birnbrauer, Bijou, Kidder, and Wolf (1965) at the Ranier School in Buckley, Washington. Although the children in the experimental classroom established in the project were mentally retarded, some severely, they manifested the hyperactivity and distractibility often seen in children with emotional problems. Small teacher-pupil ratios, careful programing of reading, written language and number concepts, systematic use of token and extrinsic rewards, and a high degree of structure have made academic training possible with children often considered noneducable. The hypothesis that exceptional children do not always fail in learning but that the teacher may often fail in teaching is suggested by the preliminary results of this research.

An operant conditioning educational program teaching word-picture association, alphabet recognition, and handwriting instruction was successfully undertaken (Hewett, 1964) with a twelve-year-old nonverbal autistic boy who had never responded to intellectual skill training before. Proceeding from color and form discrimination training to word-picture matching and alphabet recognition and writing, this boy was taught to communicate his basic wants through writing on a pad of paper which he carried with him. A later training program with a nonverbal autistic boy of four-and-a-half established beginning speech skills through application of operant conditioning procedures (Hewett, 1965). Both of these programs will be discussed in detail in later chapters.

Haring and Phillips (1962) found the use of a structured classroom with clearcut expectations and rewarding consequences for academic accomplishments resulted in a sizable achievement gain for emotionally disturbed children, in contrast to that obtained for similar children in a more traditional educational setting.

Whelan and Haring (1966) later reported the usefulness of a negative reinforcement—removal of the child from the classroom for inappropriate behavior for a specified period in a "time out" room, which had far fewer rewarding properties than the actual classroom.

Quay (1966) has utilized behavior modification techniques within a classroom program with "conduct disorder" children who manifested unsocialized and aggressive behavior in school. In an illustration of building preacademic before academic skills, Quay rewarded his students by periodically flashing a light on their desks if they were paying attention to the teacher during a group listening period. The light flash later was rewarded with a piece of candy, and attending behavior of the students increased dramatically during the time of the study.

Patterson and Ebner (1965) also have used a similar signaling device with hyperactive children during individual training sessions. When a child was paying attention to an assigned task, a light on his desk flashed and a piece of candy was placed before him. The authors found that children rewarded in this way for appropriate behavior improved their functioning in the regular classroom and on the playground.

Whelan (1966) reported on the use of the Premack (1959) principle in the education of emotionally disturbed children. This principle states that behavior normally occurring at a low rate may increase in frequency when it is followed by activities which are highly desirable to the child. The teacher who promises her students a class movie or field trip if they satisfactorily accomplish a unit on social studies is in effect utilizing this principle.

In Whelan's program, at the Children's Rehabilitation Unit in the University of Kansas Medical Center, emotionally disturbed children can earn points for appropriate behavior and task completion. At any time during the day these points may be traded for free time to spend on the playground, doing arts and crafts work, or various other activities. During this free time the child carries a small timer with him which reminds him (by the ringing of a bell) when he has spent his number of earned minutes.

Zimmerman and Zimmerman (1962) demonstrated that the spelling disability of a student who continually misspelled every word and received constant teacher attention as a result improved markedly when the teacher withheld attention until the correct spelling of the word was produced.

Application of the behavior modification strategy has been made in public school classrooms with emotionally disturbed children (Hewett, 1966, 1967). A more detailed discussion of this application will be presented in Chapters X through XII.

All the studies in this section involved a variety of children functioning in several types of settings. Their common implications for education of the emotionally disturbed child can be summarized through reference to goals and methodology.

Goals

The basic goal for the behavior modifier is the identification of maladaptive behaviors which interfere with learning and assisting the child in developing more adaptive behavior. Every child is considered a candidate for learning something regardless of his degree of psychopathology or other problems. This "something" may only represent a starting point (e.g., chair sitting) and be but a small part of the eventual "something" the teacher hopes to accomplish (e.g., reading), but care will be taken to insure its mastery before more complex goals are introduced. The child's behavior is viewed in the broadest possible context without rigid adherence to a priority ranking of behavioral goals on the basis of inferences regarding emotional conflicts or brain dysfunction.

Methodology

In the process of assisting the child in the development of adaptive behaviors for learning, the teacher will present the child with tasks he needs to do, is ready to do, and can be successful doing. Once a starting point is established the complexity of tasks assigned will gradually be increased with the teacher ever ready to reduce expectations if it becomes apparent the child is unable to comply. Care is taken to provide positive consequences which are meaningful to the child following successful accomplishment of a task. These consequences may cover a broad range from tangible rewards such as food and candy to praise or letter grades. Negative consequences may be used when the child fails to respond appropriately, but in general such consequences in the extreme (punishment) are avoided because of their undesirable and disruptive side effects on complex school learning. However, once the teacher has set a demand for the child which in light of all that is known about him is appropriate and reasonable to expect, he will be held for the meeting of that demand before being rewarded.

Rewarding children if what they do is correct, nonrewarding them if it is incorrect, is hardly new to education. In fact, many teachers, after reading this section, may exclaim, "Why I've been doing the same thing for years!" No doubt they have, but it is not the mere presence of aspects of this methodology in the classroom that is essential to the behavior modification strategy but rather, their *systematic* application. The child finds himself in a highly predictable learning environment. What is expected is clearly presented, and the rewards the child receives are contingent upon his meeting the expectations operating in the classroom. When he responds, something happens, for knowledge of the results is an important part of the behavior modification strategy. Consequences in the classroom are not subject to haphazard distribution or interminable delays. They occur in close temporal relationship to the behavior in question so that at all times the child knows where he stands in the classroom and what the consequences are for his actions.

The role of the teacher utilizing the behavior modification strategy is that of a *learning specialist*. It is not, as some may assume from the emphasis on structure and routine, mere emulation of a teaching machine. Selection of the appropriate "something" to assign the child as a beginning task, the elaboration of this task until the child reaches the desired standard of functioning in the classroom, and selection of the type of meaningful positive consequences for appropriate behavior and the type of negative consequences for inappropriate behavior in order to insure learning requires a considerable knowledge of child developmental processes, a degree of clinical judgment, and familiarity with sound educational practices.

Billy, our nonreading behavior problem introduced earlier, would be primarily viewed as a candidate for learning by Miss Brown in terms of the behavior modification strategy, rather than a victim of psychic conflicts or perceptual-motor dysfunction.

This approach does not by any means preclude consideration of Billy's interpersonal, emotional, sensory, and neurological problems in the selection of appropriate tasks to assign him. Those situations producing withdrawal or anxiety initially will be avoided. Tasks which demand visual, auditory, or motor skills which Billy does not possess will not be given him. Previous school records, case study information, and diagnostic test information will all be utilized in the development of a suitable program for Billy in the classroom.

Miss Brown will select a task, no matter how simple, to undertake with Billy (e.g., getting him to sit behind his desk for longer periods each day) which will guarantee a measure of success in the class and start him developing standards of behavior necessary for learning. While the goal of reading instruction will be ever present, Miss Brown will reduce expectations toward achieving that goal to zero, if necessary. Step by step, Billy will be given increasingly complex assignments which will be *systematically* increased in difficulty and *systematically* rewarded. If Miss Brown is successful in modifying Billy's behavior and getting him to learn through adherence to the goals and methodology of this strategy, the goals of the interpersonal-psychodynamic and sensory-neurological strategies (e.g., building a positive relationship between teacher and child, helping the child achieve a more adequate self concept, developing trust, improving visual, auditory, and motor skills) may also be largely accomplished.

As has been pointed out in this section, the strength of the behavior modification strategy is its focus on observable behavior, rather than inferred psychological or neurological factors, its simplicity and lack of reliance on labeling, and its close relationship to principles of good teaching utilized by teachers in all classrooms.

However, Porter (1962) warns against accepting the behavioral modification strategy as a "panacea" in education. He also suggests that educators question advice given them by proponents of this strategy in the following ways:

First of all, is the advice real? Does it refer to actual operations you can carry out or is it just a collection of general, vague, psychological jargon? If you are to take action on the advice received, it has to have reference to the world of deeds, not words. Too often, psychological advice is of the latter sort.

Does the advice give suggestions about how to modify behavior or does it consist of explanations? The relation between an educator and a learning theorist parallels that of an engineer and a scientist. Both the engineer and the educator have practical jobs to do while the scientist usually tries to explain, but not control, phenomena. For example, the knowledge that "motivation" makes a person act does not tell you how to modify behavior any more than the knowledge that "gravity" makes an object fall tells you how to modify its rate of descent. As teaching engineers you need practical advice from applied psychologists, not theories.

With what kind of rationale does the psychologist support his advice? If he cannot provide it in terms you can understand, you should beware— he may not understand it himself.

If the evaluation of empirical evidence is a tricky business for researchers, how can an educator—even a very sophisticated one—hope to make sound decisions from the facts and figures presented in support of a point of view? Perhaps the best way is through direct questioning.

The plainest forms of questions are this: How did you get these facts? What exactly did you do? What does that mean? If such questions are embarrassing to your psychological advisor, he is either a charlatan or incompetent.

Finally, beware of panaceas. Human behavior is so complex and teaching so subtle that dealing with them successfully *must* involve complicated techniques.[14]

Three strategies for educating emotional disturbed children have been reviewed in this chapter. The psychodynamic-interpersonal strategy asks "why" the child behaves as he does and focuses on the underlying psychological causal factors related to problems presented in the classroom. The sensory-neurological strategy is most concerned with "how" the child's behavior might be linked to organic deficits. The behavior modification strategy focuses on "what" the child presents in the classroom and attempts to shape deviant behavior so that it falls in line with standards required for learning.

All three strategies have produced positive results for some emotionally disturbed children. Each also has certain limitations. The author recalls three severely disturbed children each of whom was enrolled in an educational program operating under one of these strategies.

The first boy, David, was 12 years of age with apparently normal intelligence. He had been in a special residential school since age four where he had received intensive individual psychotherapy. Training of self-care and intellectual skills was deemphasized and delayed because the program stressed resolution of David's psychological conflicts first. He could not talk, but speech was considered a skill which would emerge when David was secure in relation to his environment. He could not read, write, or do number work but such skills were considered unimportant until David formed a relationship with his therapist in a permissive therapy setting. The school waited patiently for eight years for David to "get ready" but he made little noticeable progress. The parents out of desperation finally withdrew the boy because his advancing age and almost nonexistent capacity to care for himself or communicate alarmed them. Subsequent training in another school oriented differently proved slow and most difficult, and one wonders how much better David's chances of acquiring speech and other skills might have been had they been systematically introduced during his younger years. The interpersonal focus during the first long period of schooling was not necessarily bad, but its extremely narrow view of David's problem and

---

[14] D. Porter, "What Does Learning Theory Contribute to the Classroom?," *Audiovisual Instruction*, 1962, 7, pp. 14–15.

refusal to include some specific socialization training in the program raises questions of theoretical rigidity and poor judgment.

Robert was 11 when the author first encountered him. He was a classical, nonverbal autistic boy who had been diagnosed by several competent child psychiatrists. During the course of the parents' search for a suitable educational program, when Robert was eight, they met an individual with a strong, sensory-neurological bias. Robert was evaluated and found to be very deficient in motor coordination and spatial orientation. He was recommended for a special school which stressed resolution of such problems through repetitive daily training procedures. For three years Robert was drilled in exercises designed to promote balance, coordination, and laterality. At the end of this period Robert emerged as a somewhat better coordinated autistic boy who had not progressed at all in areas of social behavior, self-care, or intellectual skill development. While Robert may have been a candidate for some type of perceptual-motor training, the exclusion of these other areas from his educational program provides a further illustration of the detrimental effects of an overly strong bias.

Virgil was a six-year-old, severely disturbed boy who participated in an experimental program involving application of operant conditioning to the teaching of attention, direction following, and social imitation. He was seen individually over a period of one year and conditioned to perform specific responses in the presence of discrete stimuli such as light flashes or the experimenter's command. These responses were followed by scheduled rewards of candy. Virgil readily acquired a repertoire of responses including eye contact, participation in simple hand games, and a capacity to pick up and give the experimenter objects on demand. At the end of the year Virgil was placed in a special nursery-kindergarten setting with other emotionally disturbed children. The experimenter who had worked with him was disappointed when Virgil's behavior completely regressed to the level seen before the operant conditioning began. Without a one-to-one training situation, carefully controlled stimuli, and maintenance of a reinforcement schedule the effects of training were eliminated. The fallacy of expecting experimentally acquired behaviors to readily generalize and be sustained in a noncontrolled environment is illustrated here. Before Virgil's experimental repertoire would have any significance careful provision for transfer to many individuals and different types of situations would have to be made.

Strong theoretical bias, when it results in complete exclusion of considerations of other points of view, has limited value in education because of the vast differences which exist among children with problems in the classroom and the great variability found among teachers with respect to background, experience, and personality. Teachers who review the three strategies presented in this chapter will undoubtedly think of certain children for whom a particular approach would be ideal and other children for whom it would not seem appropriate. In addition, some teachers will react positively to a particular approach because it "strikes home" and is consistent with their beliefs, values, experience, and previous successes in the classroom, while they will reject another approach because it is inconsistent.

After 15 years of teaching emotionally disturbed children and training teachers to work with them, the author has come to the conclusion that not one of these strategies discussed earlier can be implemented in pure form in the public school classroom and achieve widespread success. This opinion is based on the differences existing among these strategies with respect to provision for educational goals and methodology for the teacher.

The psychodynamic-interpersonal strategy has contributed significant goals to the field of education of emotionally disturbed children. Communicating acceptance, building positive relationships, allowing self-expression, attempting to understand the meaning of the child's behavior, and remedying ego defects are goals directed toward helping the child get ready for learning. However, they are so global and difficult to define operationally that teachers of the disturbed may not clearly understand them.

But the most serious limitation of the strategy is in terms of its implications for methodology in the classroom. What the teacher *does* to implement the goals of the strategy appears largely dependent on how sensitive, intuitive, and psychologically sophisticated she *is*, rather than on her knowledge of child development, the learning process, and educational practices. If teacher giftedness and artistry are the prime requisites for success in teaching emotionally disturbed children, serious problems are going to arise in locating enough gifted teachers to work with the increasing number of such children being identified in public schools throughout this country.

The psychodynamic-interpersonal strategy is probably most often successful in the residential and special school where a close working relationship exists between teacher and psychotherapist. Indeed, since the methodology inherent in this strategy is in many ways closer to psychotherapy than pedagogy, teachers successfully using it may have to work intimately with the therapist or have a considerable knowledge and understanding of psychotherapeutic techniques.

The psychodynamic-interpersonal strategy, then, is viewed as being primarily relevant to education in terms of goals, even though they are difficult to define operationally, but seriously limited in terms of the methodology it offers average teachers in the public schools.

In contrast, the sensory-neurological strategy is strong in both goals and methodology. The educational goals of this strategy can be defined as observable acts (e.g., hand-eye coordination), rather than inferred psychological states (e.g., ego-functioning), and as such are more readily communicated to the teacher.

In addition, there are specific methodologies available to the teacher for accomplishing these goals and measurement techniques for assessing progress. The child who has not established a left-right orientation can be identified fairly quickly, assigned a goal of laterality training, and provided with a series of exercises and work sheets to assist him. His daily performance will give a ready indication of the progress he is making.

Despite such specificity of both goals and methodology the sensory neurological strategy is limited because of the narrowness of its focus. Rigid sensory-motor training procedures may minimize or overlook broader socialization goals for emotionally disturbed children.

The behavior modification strategy offers a powerful methodology but essentially no specific educational goals. Ullman and Krasner (1965) describe the goals of the behavior modifier as 1) defining maladaptive behavior, 2) determining the environmental events which support the behavior, and 3) manipulating the environment in order to alter maladaptive behavior. While these are general guidelines for the teacher they are totally lacking in developmental or educational implications. Defining "maladaptive behavior" is left up to the teacher. In the author's experience many teachers working with emotionally disturbed cannot "see the trees for the forest," and the task of accurately assessing the components of the child's behavior which are interfering with successful adaptation in school is a difficult one. This emphasis on methodology without clearly defined goals is in direct contrast to the emphasis on goals with only limited implications for educational methodology inherent in the psychodynamic-interpersonal strategy.

It is the author's opinion that both goals and methodology must receive strong emphasis if the field of education of emotionally disturbed children is to develop and provide adequate programs in the public schools. Despite the 19 or 20 hours emotionally disturbed children must spend outside the school each day, often in deplorable surroundings and malignant family relationships, the author is convinced four to six positive hours in the classroom can make a significant difference in their lives.

This text is written primarily about these classroom hours. It does not include emphasis on community mental health programs, parent counseling, or the roles of the school psychologist, social worker, physician, or psychiatrist in the education of emotionally disturbed children. Such omissions do not consititute a dismissal of the important contributions made by these programs and individuals, but it is the intent of this text to deal practically and directly with the classroom phase of education of the emotionally disturbed child. Toward this end a developmental educational strategy is the subject of the remaining chapters in this book.

A DEVELOPMENTAL STRATEGY

As has been stated, an effective educational strategy for the child who is emotionally disturbed must also be effective with all other exceptional children. Far from a discrete diagnostic category, "emotional disturbance" frequently appears in combination with other types of exceptionality. Children with physical, sensory, intellectual, and neurological handicaps are often subjected to considerable stress as they seek to adapt and succeed in a society oriented toward self-reliance, conformity, and success. As a result, maladaptive behavior patterns may develop which are sources of additional handicaps either on a primary or secondary basis.

Attempts to devise educational programs for exceptional children have followed both the specialist and generalist approach. Teacher training programs, credentialing procedures, and legislative requirements have tended to separate the various exceptionalities. The teacher of the deaf who has pursued a specialized course of training in college and who holds a specialized credential for teaching such children may consider a deaf child who is obviously mentally retarded unacceptable in her class. The number of additional such examples which might be offered is almost limitless. An effort to deal with the problem of overlapping conditions is currently seen in the growing interest in a category for exceptional children called the "multiple-handicapped." The emergence of this category may shift the focus of the field from specialization to generalization.

In the author's opinion, such a shift in focus is highly desirable. Indeed, if problems of learned maladaptive behavior are considered as belonging to a separate category, then perhaps a majority of all exceptional children are multiple-handicapped.

The developmental strategy which represents the author's point of view and about which the remainder of the text is written was originally devised as an approach to the education of children with emotional disturbances or maladaptive behavior. During the course of its development, it became increasingly apparent that what was emerging was a generalist approach which had direct relevance to the problem of all exceptional children. As was stated in the opening sentence of this section this was a logical and necessary state of affairs.

For purposes of this text, continuous reference to all exceptional children when discussing the developmental strategy will not be made. It is the child called "emotionally disturbed" who will receive our major attention. However, it is hoped that the relevance to all children —exceptional, including gifted and culturally disadvantaged—and normal—will be readily apparent.

The developmental strategy was formulated by the staff of the Neuropsychiatric Institute (NPI) School of the Neuropsychiatric Institute in the Center for Health Sciences of the University of California, Los Angeles (UCLA). The NPI is a State of California, Department of Mental Hygiene facility located on the UCLA campus to provide resources for research and training in the field of mental illness. Forty-two children and adolescents with severe emotional disturbances are hospitalized on the NPI Children's Service and attend classes in the NPI School. Central to the strategy is a developmental framework describing the essential behaviors and competencies all children must possess if they are to successfully learn in school. This has been called a *developmental sequence of educational goals* and has undergone continuous revision (Hewett, 1964, 1967). It hypothesizes that in order for successful learning to occur, the child must pay attention, respond, follow directions, freely and accurately explore the environment, and function appropriately in relation to others. It further hypothesizes that the learning of these behaviors occurs during the normal course of development from infancy to school age, and failure to learn any or all of them may preclude the child's being ready for school. For such a child they constitute the "somethings" he must learn in the process of getting ready for school while he is actually there.

The developmental sequence which is illustrated in Figure I-1 also includes mastery of self-care and intellectual skills and achievement of self-motivation in learning as the highest level goals. While presented in hierarchal form, the behaviors described by the developmental sequence are not seen as discrete or as developing separately. They are rather a part of a continuous sequence of development related to the learning process.

The behaviors described on the developmental sequence are educational and learning behaviors. They attempt to establish a firsthand educational framework for viewing children with maladaptive behavior

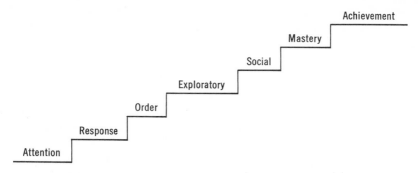

FIGURE I-1. A developmental sequence of educational goals.

and to replace the secondhand framework borrowed from disciplines of medicine, psychiatry, clinical psychology, and neurology which essentially have no educational significance. The most notorious example of a secondhand descriptive term with simply no educational relevance is "emotionally disturbed." Teachers are not trained to deal with "disturbed emotions" in the classroom. They are specialists who can assist children in acquiring essential knowledge about the world in which they live and in developing skills which are indispensable for successful adaptation.

The critical question for the teacher is: "What are the somethings emotionally disturbed children need to learn, which can be learned in the environment over which I have complete control and which I can teach as an educator?" The critical question is most certainly not: "How can I become a junior psychiatrist or a pseudo neurologist?"

Whether teachers are better therapists or diagnosticians in the long run than psychiatrists and neurologists is of little consequence. But what is crucial is that a teacher can teach, and without a full commitment to that role the important contribution which only the school can make to the treatment of the emotionally disturbed child may be minimized.

The developmental sequence is a statement of the goals of the developmental strategy. It is also a statement of many of the goals of the psychodynamic-interpersonal and sensory-neurological strategies expressed in a continuous, interrelated educational context. The relationship between the goals of the developmental strategy and those of the other strategies will be discussed in the next chapter. The methodology of the developmental strategy is derived pragmatically—not rigidly—from the behavior modification strategy. The next three chapters are devoted to discussing the goals and methodology of the developmental strategy in detail.

II A DEVELOPMENTAL SEQUENCE OF EDUCATIONAL GOALS

A developmental sequence implies an orderly progression of stages, each occurring in relation to the other.

From longitudinal studies of large numbers of children we have learned that physical and motor development follow such an orderly progression. In the case of motor development, the typical child raises his chin at about one month of age. At two months he lifts his chest; he sits with support at four months, stands with help at eight months, and walks alone early in the first year of life (Shirley, 1933). Such normative data enable us to determine if a particular infant's motor behavior at a particular age is retarded, advanced, or within the normal range.

As we move from infancy and from areas such as physical and motor development which permit direct observation and measurement, verification of the existence and nature of developmental sequences becomes less certain and precise. In fact as we enter the realm of perceptual, social, cognitive, and personality development in children we are largely dependent on the hypotheses of child development specialists rather than established bodies of knowledge. While such hypotheses are not always accepted by all and many await further research and study for validation, they have nonetheless proven useful in the evaluation of children with emotional and learning problems, assessment of the extent of their difficulties according to expectations for children of like age and sex, and the formulation of special education programs for them.

The developmental sequence of educational goals which is used in this text as the basis for assessment and education of emotionally disturbed children reflects stages of development described in the work of

Kephart, Doll, Havighurst, Piaget, Sigmund Freud, Anna Freud, Erikson, Maslow, and Sears. It attempts translation of these stages into operations associated with learning in the classroom. As an introduction to a discussion of the goals on the developmental sequence in relation to both the normal course of child development and classroom learning, a brief summary of the work of each of the authors cited above will be presented.

Kephart (1964) has concerned himself with perceptual-motor development. The first key learnings in Kephart's developmental sequence are motor, with balance and maintenance of posture, locomotion, contact through manipulation, receipt, and propulsion emphasized. From this point spatial and directional relationships are developed and the child learns laterality, or left-right orientation. Temporal dimensions of synchrony (the origin of a point in time), rhythm, (the development of a scale for estimating temporal intervals), and sequence (the ordering of events in time) are later developed and associated with the child's efficient learning in school.

The Vineland Social Maturity Scale developed by Doll (1946) describes children according to social competencies generally found at various chronological age levels. It consists of a series of rating scales arranged in a developmental series. These scales are organized with respect to the ages at which certain social behaviors appear in most children. According to the Vineland, a child before his sixth birthday "goes to school unattended" and functions "on his own outside his neighborhood." Before his eighth birthday he takes part in group play, boys preferring games of limited skill such as follow-the-leader and girls preferring games related to the home and social affairs. Between his twelfth and fifteenth birthdays, the child takes part in games requiring skill, such as cards, basketball, and pool and understands the scoring systems used. He also attends social affairs with children his own age.

Havighurst (1952) has described a series of developmental tasks which confronts all children during the course of growing up and which must be mastered for successful adjustment. These tasks parallel periods of critical societal demands on the child (e.g., early childhood: learning a sense of right and wrong; middle childhood: learning to get along with age mates; adolescence: achieving emotional independence from parents and other adults), and accomplishment of each task is considered requisite for future success.

Piaget (1950) has contributed a large amount of fascinating writing on cognitive development in children. His highly individualized style of research and vast experience observing, interacting with, and questioning children has provided much information regarding the stages children pass through in the process of perceiving, thinking, and developing concepts about the world around them. The cognitive scheme of Piaget is divided into phases—the *sensori motor, preconceptual,* and *cognitive,* the latter divided into stages of intuitive thought, concrete operations, and formal operations. An elaboration of Piaget's system is beyond the scope of this text, but for present purposes we are concerned only with establishing his work as a source of developmental guidelines for the understanding of the development of children's thinking processes.

Sigmund Freud's (1949) psychoanalytic theory and resultant hypotheses regarding the relation of the child's early psychological experience to later adjustment were introduced in the previous chapter.

Anna Freud (1965) has related the stages of classical Freudian psychosexual development to the socialization process with her concept of developmental lines. These lines trace such growth as dependency toward self-reliance, irresponsibility toward responsibility in body management, and egocentricity toward companionship.

The work of Erikson (1950) also reflects a basic adherence to Freudian psychology but presents a further elaboration and expansion of the processes of socialization. Erikson's scheme parallels Freud's and focuses on the psychosocial tasks of the various psychosexual stages outlined by Freud. Trust vs. mistrust (oral), autonomy vs. shame (anal), initiative vs. guilt (phallic), industry vs. inferiority (latency), identity vs. diffusion (adolescence), intimacy vs. solidarity, generativity vs. self-absorption, and integrity vs. despair (genital) are contrasting traits dealt with during each developmental stage.

Maslow (1954) has organized all human motivation on a hierarchy which emphasizes, from one level to the next, *satisfying bodily drives* such as hunger, *assuring self-preservation, gaining status and acceptance* from others, *attaining adequacy and esteem,* and *finally fulfilling one's ultimate potential.*

Sears (1951) is a child development specialist operating from a contrasting theoretical position to that of Freud and Erikson. He has devoted more attention to the relation of environmental events in the shaping of personality and considers the child's behavior at any point in time to be basically the result of systematic learning or conditioning.

According to Sears, the child's earliest learnings occur on the basis of primary need satisfaction (e.g., hunger). From these early feeding transactions between mother and child, the child generalizes the reward value of the food itself to the mother's presence and all its attendant cues (e.g., voice, touch, smell). This generalization becomes the basis for a secondary or acquired motivational system which enables the child to learn in the family and in later social situations. A related learning theory approach has been taken by Bijou and Baer (1961). Their work somewhat more specifically relates the theories of behavioral scientists such as Pavlov (1927), Watson (1925), Thorndike (1913), Hull (1943), and Skinner (1953) to child development.

The individuals already briefly discussed have described child development from perceptual-motor, social, cognitive, motivational, and emotional points of view. Each approach is relevant to the education of emotionally disturbed children although the descriptive terms and concepts which are utilized defy easy translation to classroom practice.

The staff of the NPI School regularly attends case conference meetings held to discuss children and adolescents on the Children's Service. These meetings give the disciplines of psychiatry, clinical psychology, social work, nursing, and occupational therapy as well as education an opportunity to participate in discussions directed toward describing the child's problem and formulating an interdisciplinary treatment program for him.

At one time or other the viewpoints of each of these authors, particularly Freud and Erikson, have been presented by members of the various disciplines in an attempt to explain a given child's behavior and to suggest possible treatment approaches. Over the course of several years, the teachers working with the children and participating in the discussions found they:

1. Did not have the sophistication to thoroughly understand child behavior and development from these varied points of view.
2. Could not clearly formulate classroom goals even when they familiarized themselves with the terms and concepts involved.
3. Lacked a true educational frame of reference within which to set goals for the children and describe their work in the classroom to other disciplines.

These three problems undoubtedly are encountered by most teachers working in institutional, special, and public school settings with disturbed children and led the NPI School staff to develop a *practical* approach for describing emotionally disturbed children *educationally*, which was consistent with many of the perceptual-motor, social, cognitive, motivational, and emotional developmental schemes of the authors discussed earlier. The result was the developmental sequence of educational goals.*

---

* The author is indebted to the staff of the NPI School and to James Q. Simmons III, M.D., Chief, Children's In-patient Service, Neuropsychiatric Institute for their valuable assistance in the formulation of the developmental sequence.

The sequence is *practical* in that it describes behaviors which the teachers know something about and can do something about in the classroom. It is *educational* because *each* level in the sequence relates to getting the child ready to learn and finally teaching him in school.

Exactly at which chronological age the behaviors associated with each level develop and whether they develop independently of each other in the order described are not considered key issues. The sequence is a statement of the necessary behaviors for successful learning in school and implies that normal children have acquired the majority of them before they enter school. It is the emotionally disturbed child's failure to master the basic levels that constitutes the most serious problem for the teacher.

The developmental sequence of educational goals will be introduced with a discussion of each level in relation to normal child development.

ATTENTION

Before learning can begin, the child must notice something. Since human organisms seldom exist in a total sensory vacuum, there is no shortage of "somethings" for him to notice. Shortly following birth, when the sense organs are not fully developed, the stimuli which impinge on the infant are more of internal than external origin. The distress of hunger pangs may therefore be the signal most frequently eliciting the infant's "attention." But in a short time, external stimulation is felt, heard, seen, smelled, and tasted. As the infant attends to this stimulation, he begins to associate it with events which are pleasant, neutral, or unpleasant, and his knowledge of the environment around him rapidly accumulates.

The number of stimuli which bombard him greatly increases during early childhood, and with entrance into school the child begins a program of many years' duration designed to get him to attend to specific cues in the environment as a basis for his formal education.

Suppose Jack is to learn to ride a bicycle. Before this process may begin, Jack must notice that the bike is there. He must exclude for the moment paying attention to his blocks or his toy soldiers. He must remain in the vicinity of the bicycle and notice that it has a seat, handlebars, pedals, and wheels. Finally he must first notice a demonstration of bike riding by his brother or someone else and remember what he has seen.

Before Mary learns how to play house, there will be a period of time devoted to her paying attention to her mother's household routine.

Mary must attend to the differences between a broom and a dish, the sink and the refrigerator. Finally, she must watch her mother handle and use these objects.

Bill is taking part in a beginning reading lesson in school. In order to profit from the teacher's instruction, he will have to look at the letter symbols being displayed rather than out the window. He will have to listen to the teacher as she points out differences between the letters and remember what she has said.

We can assume with some certainty that Jack, Mary, and Bill will not learn if they do not pay attention. The ability to focus on relevant cues in the environment is fundamental in all learning.

RESPONSE

While noticing something starts the learning process, the child next must do something, that is, make a response, in order to learn. Children, even from earliest infancy, are seldom unresponsive. Hunger pangs lead to flailing of the limbs and loud crying; a new rubber toy may lead to poking, squeezing, biting, sucking, smelling, or throwing; the sound of daddy's voice may cause the child to run for the door with his arms outstretched. In fact, as any parent will attest, children are notorious responders and once they become talkers and walkers, their repertoire increases at a tremendous rate. Many of the responses children make gain them the attention of others, and this social contact becomes an important source of motivation.

When the child enters school, active participation in learning is a must. Every teacher has favorite techniques for getting children to respond. Curriculum guides are filled with directions for eliciting the child's attention and getting him to do something related to the skill or subject under study.

Jack can notice his bicycle all day long, but until he actually gets on it he will not learn to ride. He must sit on the seat, put his feet on the pedals, and grasp the handlebars. The pedals must be pushed in order for the bike to move. Jack must make a variety of responses in order to learn bicycle riding. As he responds, Jack will be concerned about the attention he draws from his father, big brother, or neighborhood friend.

Mary's careful attention to her mother's behavior will inevitably lead to Mary's trying some of the things she has seen her mother do. This responding on Mary's part is essential if she is to learn to play house. In her own playhouse Mary may put toy dishes on the table in the same way her mother puts them on the dining room table. Other responses may include putting on an apron, sweeping the floor, cleaning or dusting furniture, all of which may elicit considerable attention from Mary's mother.

Bill will undoubtedly be asked by his teacher to make a response during the reading lesson. He may be asked to discriminate between a big and little box, given the name of a letter, or actually try to read a word. Bill cannot sit back passively while the reading lesson is going on. In order for him to learn to read, he must first attend to the teacher and the learning cues being provided and then become actively involved through responding. Such responses on Bill's part will readily gain him the attention of teacher and classmates.

Once Jack, Mary, and Bill have noticed something which in turn has led them to do something, they have begun the learning process.

ORDER

Noticing and doing, however, do not guarantee that systematic learning will take place. The child must also follow directions and develop order in his attending and responding. In early life it is not long before definite routines are imposed on the child. Sleeping and eating become routinized. The weaning process introduces a new and specific method of feeding. When toilet training is initiated, the child is dramatically confronted with the demand that his behavior conform to established rules of order. From this point on, direction following becomes more and more important. Toys have particular uses, clothes are put on in a specific sequence, and shoes are tied as a result of a step-by-step process. Entrance into school brings with it numerous order requirements and during the course of all the child's future learning, he will be involved in ordered sequences of behavior.

Jack, on his bicycle, must follow a prescribed routine if he is to learn to ride. He must sit facing the handlebars, not backwards on the seat; the pedals must be pushed one after another and he must coordinate his leg movements accordingly. Jack must learn not to ride in front of oncoming cars or drive his bike into the path of pedestrians. He must not leave it behind his father's car in the driveway, and he will be expected by his parents to return it to a specific place in the yard when he is through riding.

Mary's playing house will continuously involve her in following routines. The dishes go on her play table in a specific way; the broom is pushed back and forth if the floor is to be swept; the furniture must be gone over carefully if all the dust is to be removed. Should Mary want to borrow her mother's kitchen utensils or supplies, these must be cared for properly and returned to their place.

Bill will soon discover that learning to read is no haphazard matter. Words are read from left to right and once you finish a line, you start the next one just below it on the left-hand side of the page. In a reading group you wait your turn and don't interrupt the teacher or another child. When a reading exercise is given, it is supposed to be completed, the first part done before the end. Bill will also learn that stories he reads have a beginning, middle, and end and that the complete story must be read if he wants to obtain all the information in it.

Once the child is attending and responding in an ordered manner, his learning efficiency increases considerably. Jack, Mary, and Bill are on their way toward developing important and useful skills.

EXPLORATORY

The more things the child notices, the more he does; and the more systematic he is in attending and responding, the more he learns about his environment. The world is a fascinating place and the child finds out through exploration that some things are hot, some cold, some smooth, some sticky, some heavy, some light, some sweet, some bitter, some loud, and some soft. Children are often described as "into everything" and while a mixed blessing for parents, it constitutes a necessary stage in the learning process. Multisensory exploration provides the child with the raw material, the basic facts which he needs in learning. In school, teachers augment cognitive learning with actual exploratory experiences and children learn not only by looking and listening but by touching, smelling, and tasting. Art, music, and recreation are exploratory activities engaged in by the child periodically during his school career.

Jack will become an explorer on his bicycle. He will feel the muscles in his legs expand and contract. He will experience motion and sense the difference between going slow and going fast. Jack's newly acquired mobility will also increase his exploratory potential. There will be bumps on the sidewalk, sharp turns around corners, differences in riding on cement and grass, and a large assortment of new sights to see, sounds to hear, and smells to smell as he rides around the neighborhood.

Mary will also be engaged in exploratory behavior while playing house. Dishes break if they are dropped, cookies burn if the oven is too hot, and the floor gets muddy if you walk on it with dirty shoes while it is wet. Mary cannot learn all there is to know about housework by just watching her mother and doing exactly what she does; she must innovate and explore some on her own.

Reading will be a source of discovery and exploration for Bill. Although colored pictures first enhance the printed content, soon the words themselves will convey interesting new ideas and information to him. This type of symbolic exploration, while in contrast to the more concrete exploration being pursued by Jack and Mary, becomes the primary means by which the child amasses the tremendous amount of information which must be covered during the school years.

SOCIAL

The first four task levels focus largely on the child as an individual getting ready to learn. At this point the fact that the child often is not learning in isolation but as a member of a reacting social group must be taken into account. It is impossible to restrict the significance of the child's relations with others to this fifth level, for at the attention, response, order, and exploratory levels, his experiences were influenced by what he was given, shown, and told by parents, peers, and other individuals. While gaining social *attention* was a by-product of the response level, at the social level it is the child's gaining social *approval* that is the major concern.

The desire to please others and avoid their displeasure stems from the early period of infancy when maternal care is indispensable for the child's survival. As an agent who satisfies primary needs of hunger, thirst, temperature regulation, and who removes pain, the mother as a prototype of all humans who will later interact with the child becomes a highly valued person. Child rearing is accomplished largely because of this strong influence parents exert over their children. Once outside the home, the child encounters a multitude of social standards not directly set by his parents. Play has rules but these are subject to change, depending on who is the leader of the play group. In order to be included, the child must maintain the approval of those with whom he wishes to play.

Social relationships in the school are extremely important for the child. Working and playing successfully with other children and relating appropriately to the teacher are essential for effective learning to take place.

Sooner or later Jack's bike riding will engage him with others. Gaining big brother's approval in light of progress made riding a bicycle, improving status with neighborhood peer leaders by letting them have a turn on the bike, or racing with friends to see who can ride the fastest are social experiences Jack will encounter. He will be motivated by a desire to gain the approval of others, avoid their disapproval, and establish a position of some social esteem with his peers.

Mary will undoubtedly invite a friend or two to play house with her. They may take turns being "mother," the "baby" of the house, or the "neighbor" who drops by for coffee. Sometimes Mary will get her way; other times she will have to acquiesce to the wishes of her friends.

Bill will find that his success or lack of it in learning to read will have definite social ramifications. His teacher may express criticism or exasperation if he loses his place in the book or is unable to recognize a word which has just been gone over in class. His classmates may giggle aloud at his failure, or when he is the only one able to provide the answer to the teacher's question, nod their approval.

Social tasks are inextricably woven into the learning process, and all children test and expand their knowledge and skills in a world of people.

MASTERY

The mastery task level all but completes the learning process in school for the child. This level is concerned with the mastering of basic intellectual and adaptive skills and acquisition of a fund of information about the environment which will enable the child to function independently and successfully within the limits of his abilities. Fundamental mastery skills such as speech and concept formation begin to develop in early childhood and are continually refined and expanded during the process of growing up. Children also learn to function independently of their parents and master such skills as eating, toileting, dressing, and bathing on their own. In addition, they learn to tell time, stay out of the streets, and to obey rules of safety away from home. They become increasingly proficient at solving problems and mastering the requirements of rules and games.

But the primary center in the child's life for undertaking mastery goals is school. In the classroom he will become competent at reading, written language, and arithmetic. He will learn to read street signs, write his name, and make change. He will become more and more concerned with accuracy and competition with peers for grades. He will study science and social studies. During the course of the child's education he will be required to master these basic areas at increasingly complex levels.

Jack's bicycle riding constitutes a mastery task when the quality of his performance as a rider is considered. As he decreases his number of spills, increases his control over the bicycle, approaches a level of competence commensurate with his chronological age, and functions more and more independently of adult supervision, he is a mastery learner.

Hopefully Mary will be able to put her house play experiences to use on the mastery level. Her increased reliability as a dishwasher and competency as a floor sweeper and cook may win her actual responsibilities in her mother's kitchen. An allowance may be given Mary for her efforts and she may come to take her duties very seriously and continually try to improve.

Bill was launched on a mastery task the day he took part in the first reading lesson. As he became more skilled on the readiness levels which normally emphasize building of attention, response, order, exploratory and social skills, in that order of importance, he found he could actually read, understand, and recall what he read, do follow-up assignments, and later receive a good grade in reading on his report card.

While mastery goals are the major focus of the upper elementary grades, the significance of the readiness goals which precede them cannot be overlooked when dealing with children with learning problems.

ACHIEVEMENT

The achievement level occupies the highest level on the developmental sequence. This is the enrichment level where self-motivation in learning is developed and where pursuit of intellectual and adaptive skills in depth is important. In early life children often do more than just master the basic essentials of a learning task. Struggling on the swing until your legs pump in better and better coordination, practicing with a jump rope until you can consistently keep from being tripped up when it is rapidly being swung, attempting to catch a ball over and over until it is caught with precision, and pounding nail after nail until one finally goes in straight are a few examples.

Children take pride in accomplishment, and as they improve in swinging, jumping, catching, and pounding, they experience increased self-satisfaction and a desire for greater improvement.

Once in school, achievement goals are given great importance. Blockbuilding and painting and later, handwriting and reading, are skills consistently refined and improved. What is accomplished at one grade level is merely the raw material for elaboration and further development at the next. Children who operate on the achievement level are the joy of all teachers. In the upper elementary grades, teaching the child who not only does his basic assignment but who asks questions, volunteers for extra work, and researches out additional facts provides a genuine sense of teaching accomplishment.

Jack may not be content just to make his bicycle move and to ride it with minimum efficiency. He may attempt to ride without holding on and to perform various feats of daring and skill on it. He may enter a "bicycle rodeo" at school, practice long hours maneuvering his bicycle with precision, and compete with other boys to see who is the best bike rider in his grade.

Mary's housekeeping play may lead her into developing cooking as her own special hobby. Concern over cookies that are "just so brown" and cakes with "just the right" consistency may result in her reading recipes with ever-increasing care and measuring out ingredients more accurately. She may develop her own special techniques for assuring success and become increasingly critical of the results of her efforts.

Reading, Billy may discover, can open up a world of untold adventures about people, places, and events. One book about deep sea diving may be so exciting and stimulating to him that he combs the library shelves for additional material on this subject.

At this point, Jack, Mary, and Bill are highly efficient learners. They have learned to attend, respond, follow directions, explore, operate successfully with other children, master basic skills, and extend their learning in breadth and depth. The goal of all education is to promote children's eventual involvement with learning on such a self-directed basis.

The developmental sequence does not represent the first attempt to describe learning in the classroom by means of a sequence or hierarchy of behaviors. Krathwohl, Bloom, and Masia (1956) have developed a taxonomy of educational objectives. In *Handbook II: Affective Domain* they postulate a five step hierarchy of objectives. Starting with *Receiving* (*attending*) at the lowest level the hierarchy moves through *Responding, Valuing, Organization,* and *Characterization by a value or value complex.* While the first two objectives of their hierarchy are practically identical with the initial levels of the developmental sequence of educational goals, the final levels move toward consideration of values, attitudes, and beliefs in learning in contrast to the operational orientation of the developmental sequence introduced in this chapter.

Gagné (1965) has distinguished eight types of learning: *signal learning, stimulus-response learning, chaining, verbal-associate learning, multiple discrimination, concept learning, principle learning,* and *problem solving.* He has also described the conditions within the learner and conditions in the learning situation which must exist in order for each type of learning to take place. Although not presented from a developmental point of view, Gagné's work aims at providing the educator with a better understanding of the application of learning principles to instructional programs.

Valett (1967) has proposed a classification of basic developmental tasks for use in individualized training programs with children with learning problems. He arranges these tasks sequentially under the headings: *Motor Integration and Physical Development, Tactile Discrimination, Auditory Discrimination, Language Development and Verbal Fluency, Visual-Motor Coordination,* and *Conceptual Development.* An assessment instrument—The Valett Developmental Survey of Basic Learning Abilities—has been devised to measure the child's competencies in each of the areas.

Bereiter and Engelmann (1966) have organized a core preschool curriculum to prepare children for demands presented in the primary grades. Some 15 specific tasks have been defined along with highly specific teaching techniques for aiding the child in learning them. Bereiter and Engelmann's approach is similar to the one taken in this text and focuses on building basic competencies in learning before the child is confronted with the traditional school curriculum.

In his book, *Prescriptive Teaching,* Peter (1965) presents a model for translating medical, psychological, and social work diagnoses of children with emotional and learning problems into educational terms. His model is more comprehensive than the developmental sequence of educational goals and not only considers variables associated with the child's problem but those concerned with the total educational situation as well.

The levels on the developmental sequence of educational goals were not selected on the basis of a definitive longitudinal assessment of children which established them as describing behaviors developing in a specified order or during specific chronological age periods. Rather, they were chosen on the basis of the following:

1. Their relevance to the stages of perceptual-motor, social, cognitive, motivational, and personality development described by the writers cited earlier in this chapter.
2. The author's observations of the necessary competencies, in order of importance, which must be acquired by emotionally disturbed children if they are to learn efficiently in school and the relevance of such competencies to educational diagnosis.
3. Their relevance to actual teaching operations which the teacher can understand and do something about in the classroom.

The relationship of the developmental sequence of educational goals to the first point presented above will be illustrated by a brief comparison of the levels on the sequence with the stages of development found in the writings of Kephart, Piaget, Freud, Erikson, and Sears. The relationship of the developmental sequence to the second point will be discussed in Chapter IV. The remainder of the text is devoted to elaboration of the third point.

The *attention* and *response* levels are primarily concerned with establishing contact with the child, orienting him toward learning, and helping him begin to participate in the learning process. For Kephart the motor and spatial aspects of the child's behavior are fundamental in initiating early learning. For Piaget the child's *sensori-motor* experiences introduce him to the environment. Freud and Erikson are more concerned with the interpersonal aspects of the child's earliest learnings. For Freud, the early mother-child dependency which is initiated during the *oral* stage is a crucial determiner of later development. Erikson sees this relationship as generating the *trust* necessary for the child to reach out and learn. Sears also views the mother-child interaction as a basis for later learning because of the primary reward properties the early feeding experiences have for the child.

At the *order* level the goal for the child is learning to adapt to routines and structure. The concept of order is central to Kephart's perceptual-motor approach. Balance, maintenance of posture, and later laterality and temporal discrimination all involve ordered behavior. Piaget's *preconceptual* stage involves the child ordering the concepts of space and spatial relationships according to subjective experience. The *anal* stage of Freud, which follows the oral period, is conceived of as a time when bringing elimination processes under control according to an expected societal routine is a critical task for the child. Erikson postulates that the young child engages in the struggle for *autonomy* and constantly tests regulations imposed on him by others. Toilet training is a task to be learned according to Sears. The positive reward value of the mother's presence and praise and the negative value of her disapproval are determiners of the child's learning to "order" his behavior.

The *exploratory* level goal for the child is to increase his multisensory involvement with the environment. Kephart emphasizes the child's orientation to the physical environment; as the child's perceptual-motor efficiency increases he can interact more and more completely and accurately with the physical universe through all of his sense modalities. Piaget's *preconceptual* and *intuitive thought* phases overlap with reference to the child's increasing ability to react realistically to his environment through exploration, with the child given to greater self-expression and attempts at achieving a sex role. Erikson labels this stage *initiative* and views the child as expanding his interests and increasing his communication with the environment. In Sears' framework, touching, smelling, looking, listening, and tasting provide rewards of their own which move the child toward greater exploration of the world around him.

The *social* level confronts the child with the necessity of learning standards of social appropriateness. Kephart's concern with the child's social environment is primarily from the point of view that mastery of the physical environment is a requisite for adapting to the complex demands of the social world. Piaget's phase of *concrete operations* includes the child's development of the capacity to view himself objectively as a member of a peer group. The *Oedipal conflict* in Freudian theory, encountered during the *phallic* period, results in the child identifying with the like-sexed parent and increasing his concern with the social role expected. Erikson's phases of *industry* and *identity* overlap the social task level; the child experiences a need to find a place among those of his own age and to establish an identity for making mature decisions. Social rewards exert an increasingly powerful influence over the child's behavior in early life. Gaining approval and avoiding disapproval and punishment are viewed by Sears as a part of a secondary motivational system which enables the child to take his place in a larger social environment outside the home.

The *mastery* and *achievement* goal levels complete the developmental sequence. Here the child acquires adaptive and intellectual skills and develops a self-motivation for learning. Kephart's perceptual-motor component of adaptive and intellectual tasks is generally applicable at this level although its primary application is at the attention, response, order, and exploratory level. Piaget's last phase of intellectual development is *formal operations* when the individual systematically approaches problem solving, ponders ideas, and establishes hypotheses about his environment. During the *latency* period Freud postulates that the child's energies are freed from the incestuous striving of the *Oedipal conflict*, thereby becoming more readily available for formal learning in the school. Erikson's last three stages—*intimacy, generativity,* and *integrity*—describe a postchildhood and youth period when participation in the community, readiness for marriage, and development of a philosophy of life occur. These represent a mastery and achievement phase in a larger context than provided by the developmental sequence of educational goals, but both are concerned with the culmination of a developmental process. Sears views the school as a major socializing agency which will assist the child in developing adaptive and intellectual skills by means of secondary motivational systems which originate in the family setting.

This discussion of the compatibility of a developmental sequence of educational goals with the work of Kephart, Piaget, Freud, Erikson, and Sears does no justice in depth to the authors cited. Hopefully, it has sufficed to introduce the concept of the developmental sequence and its relationship to social, cognitive, maturational, and personality development as viewed by these authors.

Since several of the authors considered in this chapter were also mentioned in connection with the three strategies discussed in the previous chapter the relationship of the goals of the developmental sequence to the goals of these strategies should be apparent. The psycho-dynamic-interpersonal strategy is concerned with making contact with the child, getting him involved with his environment, and relating to others in it. The attention, response, exploratory, and social levels are of major importance with the order and mastery levels receiving less emphasis, particularly at first. The sensory-neurological strategy is focused on getting the child to pay attention and respond in an accurate and orderly manner before social and mastery tasks are demanded. The attention, response, order, and exploratory levels are therefore of primary concern initially. The behavior modification strategy, as was stated earlier, is not committed to any specific educational goals and hence might approach the developmental sequence without special emphasis on any level.

This chapter has established the developmental sequence as the source for the educational goals of the developmental strategy. The next chapter introduces the methodology for accomplishing these goals.

III THE LEARNING TRIANGLE

The developmental sequence of educational goals introduced in the previous chapter organizes the "somethings" all children need to learn in order to be ready for school and to function efficiently in the classroom. During the period of preschool socialization most children at least partially achieve the first five goals of the developmental sequence and arrive in school ready to learn on the mastery and achievement levels and to increase their proficiency at the lower levels.

Emotionally disturbed children, however, often arrive never having achieved such goals as paying attention, responding in learning, ordering their behavior, readily and accurately exploring their environment, and getting along with their teachers and classmates. And as they are exposed to stresses with which they cannot deal and encounter failure and frustration in school, their lack of readiness for learning may seriously increase. The problems of some so-called "drop-outs" in secondary school may well be the result of a slow but steady process of being "pushed out" because the necessary opportunities for getting ready to learn were never provided from the time they entered school. These children can be considered as never having "dropped in" to school in the first place.

The child with emotional and learning problems is often viewed as a child failure by the teacher who throws up her hands in disgust and exclaims, "I've done all I can. He could learn if he wanted to, but he won't!" The practice of so easily dismissing such problems is highly questionable. It is the author's contention that many of the children labeled "impossible" in the classroom are the result of teacher failure, not child failure, although educators may not readily recognize or admit it. Coaladarci (1967) has studied comments made by teachers

60

next to failing or near-failing grades on report cards of several thousand elementary age children in regular classes. The majority of such comments tended to explain the poor grades on the basis of child failure and a much smaller percentage referred to possible teacher-failure factors. To succeed in teaching any child, the teacher must be highly oriented toward success and firmly believe that despite a lack of readiness to be in school, every child is ready to learn "something" and if he learns "nothing" the fault lies in the teaching program.

Having established the developmental sequence of educational goals as the basis for defining the "somethings" needed by emotionally disturbed children for success in school, we now turn to methodology and the problem of getting the child ready to be in school while he is actually there. It is postulated that if the teacher can appropriately provide three ingredients in a learning program for each child, there is no emotionally disturbed, or, for that matter, no exceptional child who cannot be taught "something." These three ingredients may be conceived of as the sides of a triangle, the central position of which is occupied by the emotionally disturbed learner. This learning triangle is illustrated in Figure III-1.

If the teacher can select the task the child is ready to undertake and which is consistent with the educational goals most relevant to his problem, provide him with a truly meaningful reward for his efforts, and maintain the degree of structure or control necessary to insure efficient learning, the learning process is under way.

In addition to significance for the child the learning triangle is equally important to consider from the teacher's point of view. Teachers can only effectively teach when they understand what tasks are suitable for them to undertake with a given child, receive some personal rewards for their teaching efforts, and operate within an understandable theoretical structure. Thus, the teacher, like the child, occupies a central position in the learning triangle as shown in Figure III-2.

THE TASK

A learning task is defined in this text as any activity, lesson, or assignment given the child which is directed toward assisting him in achieving one or more goals on the developmental sequence.

The educational goals organized on the developmental sequence can seldom be accomplished directly with one type of assignment or series of activities. Instead, the teacher usually must break the goal down into a sequence of tasks which progressively moves the child toward the end goal in steps which assure his continued success. This sequencing of

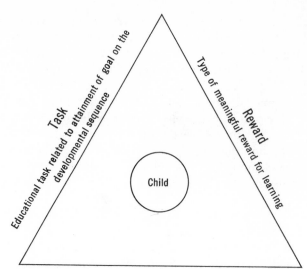

Teacher expectations associated with task assigned child which determine conditions under which reward will be provided

Structure

FIGURE III-1. The learning triangle (child).

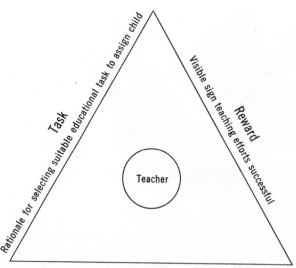

A practical and understandable educational strategy

Structure

FIGURE III-2. The learning triangle (teacher).

tasks also requires the teacher to be prepared to reduce the level of complexity of a given task at any moment rather than arbitrarily pursuing a program of instruction according to a preplanned design.

Suppose Miss Brown, introduced in Chapter I, were concerned with the behavior of Billy, her problem third grader, and wanted to work toward helping him attain the goal of order on the developmental sequence. Rather than demand that he immediately obey all class rules and limits she might pick one order task and start working with him on it while deemphasizing the many other tasks which were relevant. Perhaps getting Billy to sit in his seat and not turn around might be an appropriate first level task to help him on his way toward achieving the goal of order.

In focusing on "seat sitting" initially rather than "good citizenship" Miss Brown would be settling for a "thimbleful" accomplishment related to the eventual goal. Educators are often not comfortable producing mere "thimbleful" changes in children. Many prefer to pursue the "bucket" approach and effect major teaching accomplishments. It is, however, a "thimbleful" orientation that is required in helping children who are not ready to be in school get ready while they are actually there. More emphasis should be placed on such discrete tasks as "seat sitting," "turn waiting," and "mouth closing" rather than on the global goal of "citizenship." The "thimbleful" of learning orientation is well illustrated in the case of Louis which follows.

Louis was an eleven-year-old, hospitalized, catatonic schizophrenic child, carried, in an immobilized state, into the elementary classroom of the NPI School. Since the basic philosophy of the school is "something for everyone," Louis was not to be an exception. But Louis' severe psychological difficulties had resulted in his almost total withdrawal from the environment. He did not speak, eat, walk, or move any part of his body and had lapsed into a serious state of psychological, social, and physical deterioration. What could you do with Louis in school? He appeared no more ready for learning than a desk or a chair.

After studying Louis' case, the teacher decided on a task that would be suitable for him. A large box with a lever in the middle was placed on his lap. The lever activated a small slide projector. The projector was focused on a frosted glass screen set up on a table directly in front of Louis. A slight push of the lever to the right turned the projector on, a slight push to the left turned it off. Since Louis was known to like pictures of prehistoric life, particularly dinosaurs, some colored slides of these creatures were procured. They were placed in the projector, and Louis was shown how he could turn them on and off. After a long period of time Louis finally responded and interacted with the environment for the first time in months by pushing the lever to the right in order to see the picture and then to the left to turn it off so the teacher could put on the next slide. The initial stage in Louis' educational program is illustrated in Figure III-3 showing the arrangement of the projector and lever box.

The NPI School teacher was very pleased, but a visiting teacher who observed Louis in the classroom had reservations.

"This is all very interesting," she remarked, "but one thing bothers me. Louis is eleven years old and should be in the sixth grade. I don't know of any science curriculum in the sixth grade which includes the study of dinosaurs."

Obviously, her selection of a suitable educational task for Louis would have differed markedly from the one selected by the NPI School teacher and would no doubt have been aimed toward a "bucketful" accomplishment.

Louis had been an outstanding student prior to his hospitalization, but at this point in time academic tasks were not appropriate or practical to assign him. Here was a boy who had regressed so completely that the teacher had to reduce expectations almost to zero in order to make contact with him. The simple task of moving a lever back and forth was chosen because it required so little of Louis and the probability of success was great. He was not asked to speak, to move his body, to write, or to do anything but pay attention and make a simple motor response. Since the attention and response levels are considered the most basic on the developmental sequence, this task was suitable for initiating an educational program for this seriously emotionally disturbed boy.

It was because the teacher viewed Louis as a candidate for doing "something" in school, no matter how far removed from what is ordinarily expected of a sixth-grade student, and then went to work designing a "thimbleful" task which practically guaranteed his success and moved him slightly toward the goals of attention and response that the NPI School program played a large part in helping Louis regain his former level of functioning.

From this significant beginning step, the teacher went on to present Louis with more and more complex tasks, until, in three months, he was sitting at a desk and working efficiently at the sixth-grade level. One of the intermediate tasks employed included having him move his hand slowly across the table and stop at the correct answers to simple arithmetic problems, as shown in Figure III-4.

A pencil was later placed in his hand, and Louis drew lines under multiple choice answers in much the same way. Louis' case illustrates one of the basic tenets of this text: that a suitable beginning task

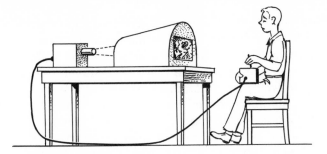

Figure III-3. Arrangement of projector, screen, and lever box in program for Louis.

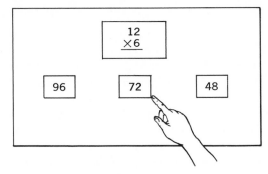

Figure III-4. Multiple choice arithmetic task in program for Louis.

leading to an essential educational goal exists for every child, regardless of the severity of his emotional problems.

While the degree of disturbance seen in this boy is seldom encountered by teachers of emotionally disturbed children, particularly in a public school, the principle of a teacher's reducing expectations in accord with the child's readiness for learning is equally applicable to all disturbed children.

REWARD

Reward in this text refers to a positive consequence which tends to maintain or increase the strength or frequency of behavior associated with accomplishing tasks related to the achievement of educational goals on the developmental sequence.

It can be simply stated that learning is facilitated by the learner receiving a reward for his efforts. In classrooms for normal children these rewards for learning are readily apparent. Teachers nod approval, smile, and verbally praise students who give evidence of learning. They write comments such as "Good work" or stamp a cartoon picture of a smiling face on papers which meet or exceed expectations. A major reward for learning in school is the grade given on the student's report card which may have far-reaching effects with the child's peers and parents. Children are also rewarded by the stimulation provided by looking and listening in the classroom. The world is an exciting place to learn about, and impressing others with newly acquired knowledge and demonstrations of such skills as reading and arithmetic provide a source of reward. In addition normal children are rewarded by avoiding disapproval and failure in school. This accounts for much of their motivation to learn.

Emotionally disturbed children often have a difficult time finding anything rewarding in school. Teacher's frowns, looks of exasperation, and angry comments following the child's misbehavior hardly constitute a meaningful reward, although in the light of some emotionally disturbed children's problems with adult authority, "getting the teacher's goat" may provide some form of gratification. Just being noticed by others and gaining social attention may also be rewarding even though it occurs in a negative context.

In the main, however, school may be viewed as essentially negative. Books and assignments come to represent failure, reactions from classmates predominantly consist of rejection or ridicule, and grades and report cards become sources of parental criticism and disgust.

Before emotionally disturbed children can learn in school, the teacher must guarantee that some form of reward is present in the classroom for each child. Social rewards such as approving glances and remarks may be meaningful with some, but in many cases the child's previous unsatisfactory relationships with adults makes these rewards of limited value. Task completion and success and multisensory experiences may also vary in effectiveness. Indeed, each child may have to be rewarded in different ways, utilizing a continuum ranging from tangible rewards to intrinsic satisfaction from acquiring knowledge and skill. The range of rewards available in the classroom will be related to the developmental sequence of educational goals in the next chapter and discussed in detail in Chapters V–IX.

In planning the program for Louis, the teacher gave serious consideration to providing something rewarding for him. In the case of this extremely disturbed boy, who had withdrawn from all interaction with the environment, this was an initially difficult ingredient to locate. In the report from Louis' previous school, however, it had been mentioned that he was highly motivated by subject matter pertaining to prehistoric life. Since Louis' eyes were open and he had been observed looking for brief moments at objects around him, the teacher selected the colored slides described earlier as a source of reward. Getting Louis to move the lever was thus largely accomplished by the rewarding consequences it provided for him.

Teachers in normal classrooms find that their students' social awareness, desire to please, motivation to achieve, and responsiveness to curriculum content provide a constant source of satisfying feedback. It is rewarding to teach a receptive and appreciative learner.

Perhaps no one factor contributes so greatly to the discouragement and defeat of teachers of the emotionally disturbed as the dearth of immediate teaching rewards. Emotionally disturbed children often go out of their way to reject, ridicule, and ignore conscientious teachers' most valiant efforts. Such reactions are not only defeating, but self-devaluating for the teacher. Obviously, what is expressed by the emotionally disturbed child is not always a measure of his true feelings or the amount of real learning which has occurred. But the fact remains that teachers are human, and humans in our society place great value on the approval of others and demonstrated success.

As a result, the teacher of the emotionally disturbed child should make every effort to select tasks which are appropriate and rewarding for the student in order to promote mutual success. In addition the teacher must develop a personal detachment and objectivity which makes the immediate rewards of teaching success less important and increases his tolerance for "failing gracefully." One of the givens in special education is that occasional failure with students is inevitable. The teacher who objectively asks why a particular approach has failed and then objectively goes about revising it is in a far better position to assist disturbed children than one who views it largely as a personal defeat.

STRUCTURE

Structure refers to the limits or "strings" the teacher or the school attaches to particular tasks assigned the child which determine whether or not he will be rewarded. In essence, it is the degree of teacher control present in the learning situation. Wayne must arrive at school by 9:00 A.M. (not 9:05) in order to keep from being counted tardy. The structure or string attached to the task of arriving at school is thus based on time (when) and the reward of an "on time" notation in the class record book is contingent on this behavior. Wayne must go to his own seat and not sit at someone else's desk if he is to receive a rewarding smile of approval from the teacher. Structure here involves location or space (where). When reading begins, Wayne is expected to take out his reader and follow the teacher's directions. The strings attached to this task are concerned with the type of activity or assignment (what) and the teacher may comment favorably when Wayne, or the members of the reading group to which he is assigned, sit quietly and indicate they are ready to work. When it comes time for Wayne to read in his book he must hold the book right side up and read, not sing a song if he is to avoid a disapproving glance or comment from the teacher. The structure here dictates the way (how) the task is performed. As he reads, the number of words he misses will be recorded by the teacher who will attach the string of correctness (how well) to Wayne's reading task before giving him an approving glance or an eventual "A" in reading on his report card.

The socialization process largely involves assigning children tasks with limits or strings attached to them. When, where, what, how, and how well are considerations made by parents and teachers alike as they attempt to assist the child in adapting to his environment.

This definition of structure is by no means the only one to be found in special educational literature. The differences of opinion and confusion regarding the term are illustrated in the following excerpts which relate to the concept of structure and its supposed opposite extreme permissiveness.

Haring and Phillips (1962) in their text have defined structure in educational programs for emotionally disturbed children in terms of fixed environmental expectations and state their rationale as follows:

> Broadly speaking, structure refers to the clarification of the relationship between behavior and its consequences. More specifically, the term refers to the following procedures: setting up a definite and dependable classroom routine; giving at first very specific and limited tasks, which can later be extended and embellished as the child increases in emotional self-control and educational application; having the teacher remain consistent and giving and following through on requirements to the child until they are reasonably fulfilled; forwarding the impression that the children are at school for work, with recreational activities coming after acceptable work has been completed; having the child repeat or redo careless or incomplete work; fostering a persistent pattern of returning to work at hand after an emotional blowup or after other distractions; fostering in the child a strong and healthy respect for the requirements set by the teacher; and fostering in the teacher an equally strong respect for the child's efforts and achievements.
>
> The main hypothesis advanced in this study was that children suffer from emotional disturbance because they lack order or structure or definiteness in their daily living at home and at school, and that within the confines of the school program it would be desirable and constructive to rectify past excesses in habits, attitudes and achievement.[1]

---

[1] N. Haring and E. Phillips, *Educating Emotionally Disturbed Children* (New York: McGraw-Hill Book Company, 1962), pp. 9–10.

A comparison was made by these authors between the "structured" approach of the program cited in their text and the "permissive" approach attributed to such educators as Bettelheim, Director of the University of Chicago's Orthogenic School.

This comparison was not long in provoking Bettelheim (1963) to write a review of the text which included the following:

> Basically, all the authors have done in this book is to grind an axe called "the firmly structured classroom situation" and to slay with it a straw man of their own creation which they call "permissive education." In this permissive education "the social emotional changes were sought in their own right, without reference to educational progress of the child." So anxious are they to believe this, that they cannot see how the very authorities they quote contradict their assertions.
>
> Still speaking of the Orthogenic School the authors say that "very little structure is set" (p. 19) but on the next page we read that "no educational plan was too elaborate to follow if it was consistent with the interpretation of the child's needs" (p. 20). How elaborate planning can be carried out in a classroom without elaborate structuring is hard to see but having spent most of my professional life on structuring a very special environment that would further the education and rehabilitation of emotionally disturbed children I may be over-sensitive to hear I have wasted my efforts since there is no structure to speak of in the Orthogenic School.[2]

Obviously structure *does* exist in the Orthogenic School as it must in all educational and therapeutic situations. Child psychiatrists do not permit young patients to physically assault them, burn up their furniture, or jump out of office windows. Permissiveness is not synonomous with open license.

But the type of structure in the Orthogenic School probably is determined differently than the type of structure discussed by Haring and Phillips. It may well relate to the goals and methodology of the psychodynamic-interpersonal strategy and center on the child, his psychic conflicts, and psychological needs of the moment, rather than on a set of fixed environmental limits. Haring and Phillips, on the other hand, in pursuing the behavior modification strategy are more concerned with directly influencing the child's behavior and bringing it into line with standards required for learning in the classroom.

Both are structured programs but derive their basis for structuring from somewhat different sources. These sources—the child, his psycho-

---

[2] B. Bettelheim, "A Noncontribution to Educational Research," *Harvard Educational Review*, 1963, 33, p. 329.

logical problems, and changing needs, as compared to the environment and its requirements for learning—tend to separate the two strategies.

Despite Haring and Phillips' emphasis on fixed environmental expectations their position is not synonomous with rigid, irrational authority. These authors were "permissive" in the sense that they readily accepted the child's academic limitations and modified assignments when these tended to be conflictual.

The approach to structure taken in this text is similar to that advocated by Haring and Phillips, and it readily concedes to the child's limitations whenever his success and, hence, opportunity to obtain rewards in the classroom is threatened. Attainment of the first two goals of the developmental sequence, attention and response, may have to be fostered by reducing the number of limits or strings attached to tasks assigned the child and modifying environmental expectations. On the order, exploratory, social, and mastery levels, environmental expectations increase but diminish at the achievement level where the child's self-motivation and direction take over.

When speaking of structure and degree of teacher control it is difficult to avoid consideration of the role of punishment in education. Miss A's critical comments toward the quality of Raymond's work in the example in Chapter I may be mild compared to what some children with learning and behavior problems are exposed to in school. Although the use of corporal punishment may have greatly diminished in education, Skinner (1965) cites the "astonishing list" of noncorporal punishments such as ridicule, scolding, sarcasm, and incarceration (being kept after school) which are commonly accepted. Such punishments, as contrasted with the negative consequences following a reading error mentioned in the case of Lee in Chapter I (teacher frowning, classmates giggling, and withholding of teacher approval) may produce many undesirable side effects including fear, tenseness, avoidance, and withdrawal, particularly when the punishment is not clearly related to a specific act on the child's part.

Just when a negative consequence becomes a true punishment is extremely difficult to determine since it relates to the degree of the consequence, the nature of the situation in which it occurs, and how it is perceived by the child. This problem will not be taken up in the present discussion in detail. In general, though, negative consequences following an incorrect response will cause the child to change his behavior in a predictable manner to avoid such consequences in the future, while punishment may exert complex effects upon his behavior going far beyond the teacher's expectation and control (Haring and Lovitt, 1967). Whelan (1966) has commented on these effects, such as only temporary suppression of undesirable behavior and increase in frequency of maladaptive behavior including escape and avoidance.

As a result the author views punishment as having little value in the education of emotionally disturbed children. Teaching children to behave in certain ways and to acquire complex skills such as reading because they are afraid not to represents an educational "dead end" since our major goal is to make appropriate behavior and acquisition of reading eventually rewarding in and of themselves. Structure in the teaching situation, however, may have to involve the use of negative consequences, particularly the withholding of a reward if the child fails to respond correctly to a task the teacher has every reason to believe is appropriate to expect of him.

Structure for the teacher of the emotionally disturbed child must be defined differently. In addition to an understanding of tasks appropriate to getting the child ready for learning and school and receipt of rewards for teaching efforts, the teacher needs the structure of a theoretical orientation including delineation of educational goals and methodology in order to be effective. A major purpose of this text is to provide this structure for teachers of emotionally disturbed children.

The role of structure is well illustrated in the NPI School's early program with Louis. This boy probably represented the most self-structured and controlled individual who will ever be found in a classroom. His extreme withdrawal and failure to respond to even minimal requests for feeding and self-care are examples of a total rejection of all outside control. Had the environment allowed this seriously ill boy to set all of his own limits, he may well have died of starvation. There was no time to try to uncover the deep-rooted emotional conflicts underlying his bizarre behavior. A strict demand that he swallow some nourishment each day had to be made in order to keep him alive. This demand was enforced by his doctor, who demonstrated to him that either he swallow some minimal amount of food or he would be fed through a tube inserted down his throat into his stomach. The reward of avoiding the unpleasant tube-feeding experience appeared initially responsible for getting Louis to undertake the task of eating.

In the classroom Louis had resisted all attempts to get him involved in learning. It was only when the clearly structured task of lever pushing, in order to obtain the colored slide reward, was undertaken that he became a participant in learning rather than a self-contained isolate. The lever had to be pushed or the slide did not come on. This was the "string" attached to Louis' task. All of the waiting and resisting in the world would not have made the simple electrical connection between switch and projector. Lever pushing was a simple act, and since no strings were attached regarding the time allowed, Louis was able to tolerate this environmental limit and take a significant step in the direction of rehabilitation. When Louis responded in the classroom, he committed himself to interacting with the environment and gave up a measure of the total state of withdrawal into which he had regressed. He therefore made a highly important start toward recovery. Eliciting similar "commitments" from all emotionally disturbed children in the classroom through careful selection of tasks, provision of rewards, and establishment of structure may also serve to initiate improved attitudes toward school and more adaptive and successful learning. For once the child who is fearful, negative, and resistant is drawn into a learning situation in which he succeeds and is rewarded, he can no longer as easily retreat to the level of "non-learner" or "failure."

This section has discussed the significance of the three sides of the learning triangle—a suitable task, meaningful learner reward, and degree of structure for both the teacher and the child.

Two examples from the research literature will further illustrate the relationship of the learning triangle to the problems displayed by emotionally disturbed children in school. Although these examples do not involve school age children they will demonstrate why emotionally disturbed children are "not ready" to learn, the fact they are "ready to learn something," and finally how to "get them ready to be in school while they are actually there."

Peter was a three-year-old participant in a well-known experiment done by Jones (1924) several decades ago. He was a normal, healthy preschooler with one exception. Peter had an aversion toward rabbits. This aversion was so strong that it had generalized to all white furry objects. Whenever a rabbit or one of these objects was brought near him, Peter exhibited extreme distress and avoidance behavior. At such times he was not ready to pay attention, respond, order his behavior, explore his environment, or function appropriately in relation to others, much less master intellectual tasks. Under such stress Peter's readiness for learning was reduced practically to zero.

Emotionally disturbed children often develop an aversion to the school setting which, like the rabbit for Peter, reduces their readiness for learning to a near zero level. School has become a great noxious "rabbit" which when brought too close elicits distress and avoidance behavior.

The school, however, is not a discrete stimulus but a collection of physical, emotional, social, and intellectual stimuli which converge on the child simultaneously. Johnny must arrive in the classroom before nine o'clock in order not to be tardy, hang his coat on the hook with his name on it, place his lunch directly overhead, walk in an orderly manner to his desk, sit quietly, ignore the teasing and poking of Charles, his classmate, who sits behind him, and pay attention to the teacher as she starts the reading lesson, for he may be called on to recite without warning.

The aversive "rabbit" of school may generalize to the classroom environment, rules, other children, or teacher and actual teaching materials in much the same way Peter's fear of rabbits generalized to a variety of white, furry objects.

The author has worked with two adolescent boys with severe reading problems who became so upset when given a book to read that they broke out in giant hives all over their bodies, in one case so severely that hospitalization was required. A ten-year-old girl, admitted to the Children's Service of the Neuropsychiatric Institute with severe school phobia, related pleasantly to the author during their first meeting but promptly began to hyperventilate (breathe rapidly) to such a degree that she fainted when he introduced himself as the "Principal" of the hospital school.

While normal children manage to take the stresses and expectations of school in their stride, the emotionally disturbed child may not be ready to deal with them. When the teacher arbitrarily imposes demands on such children without any consideration of their lack of readiness to be in school in the first place, the same insensitivity that might have been shown by an individual directly confronting Peter with a rabbit and impatiently glaring at him as he became upset is demonstrated.

How can a child like Peter be helped to overcome his fear of rabbits, and how can emotionally disturbed children be aided in getting ready for school while they are actually in school? Despite the apparent dissimilarity of problems, the measures taken to help Peter have direct relevance in the classroom.

Peter was seated in a high chair. On the high chair tray were many of his favorite foods, including ice cream and a selection of toys which appealed to him. He was immediately drawn to the food and toys, sat quietly, and apparently was quite happy eating and playing. In fact, Peter was so content that he hardly noticed when a door, some distance away, was opened and someone stood there holding a rabbit. The rabbit was in the general vicinity of Peter but so rewarding and positive were the activities in which he was engaged that these positive stimuli dominated whatever negative stimuli might have been associated with the rabbit. The animal, however, was not brought in and given to Peter at this time. No doubt, had this occurred, Peter would have become upset, ice cream or no ice cream; but a starting point was established in a program to help Peter overcome his aversive reaction to rabbits, and he was being helped to get ready to tolerate rabbits while this one was actually in his presence.

On subsequent days the rabbit was moved closer and closer but never at a rate which upset Peter. In fact if Peter had displayed discomfort, despite the rewarding objects on the tray, the rabbit would no doubt have been withdrawn a distance until he relaxed. The actual stages involved in deconditioning Peter's fear to the rabbit were as follows:

a)   Rabbit anywhere in a room in a cage causes fear reaction.
b)   Rabbit 12 feet away in cage tolerated.
c)   Rabbit 4 feet away in cage tolerated.
d)   Rabbit 3 feet away in cage tolerated.
e)   Rabbit close in cage tolerated.
f)   Rabbit free in room tolerated.
g)   Rabbit touched when experimenter holds it.
h)   Rabbit touched when free in room.
i)   Rabbit defied by spitting at it, throwing things at it, imitating it.
j)   Rabbit allowed on tray of high chair.
k)   Squats in defenseless position beside rabbit.
l)   Helps experimenter to carry rabbit to its cage.
m) Holds rabbit on lap.
n)   Stays alone in room with rabbit.
o)   Allows rabbit in playpen with him.
p)   Fondles rabbit affectionately.
q)   Lets rabbit nibble his fingers.[3]

The case of Peter well illustrates the learning triangle in operation. First a suitable *task* was selected—sitting in a high chair in a room with the rabbit initially out of sight. While this represented but a "thimbleful" of the eventual goal for Peter (i.e., overcoming his aversive reaction toward rabbits) it was a significant start and like the lever pressing response for Louis had important implications. Next a meaningful *reward* was presented by means of the table heaped with his favorite food and toys. Finally *structure* was imposed by gradually introducing the feared rabbit and not moving it any closer than Peter could tolerate on a given day. The balance between making demands on the child while

[3] M. Jones, "A Laboratory Study of Fear: The Case of Peter," *Pedagogical Seminary,* 1924, 31, pp. 310–311.

carefully assuring him of success and rewarding consequences is the essence of the model which should be followed in all special education programs for children with learning problems.

In another study, Ayllon and Haughton (1962) aided institutionalized, psychotic adult patients with severe eating problems. In most mental hospitals patients who refuse to eat present serious difficulties. A great deal of staff time and effort must go into coaxing and supporting them during mealtimes. In some cases, spoon-feeding is required to get them to eat. The investigators in this study decided that patients who refused to eat but who had no physical problems which precluded them from feeding themselves could be helped to improve their level of functioning. A group of patients with serious eating problems was placed together in a ward. With the cooperation and participation of the medical staff a program was instituted that required all patients to enter the ward dining room in order to be fed. There were to be no exceptions. The initial *task* was to go to the dining room, the *reward* was the obvious receipt of food, and the *structure* imposed was that food would only be available during specific times in the dining room itself. Despite initial reluctance most patients responded. The steps in the program designed to help these patients paralleled the levels of the developmental sequence (although this was not the purpose of the study) and demonstrated how gradual introduction of increasingly complex demands can bring about dramatic changes in behavior.

Step one involved the patient's being told when it was time to eat and then being allowed an hour to get to the dining room. Each patient was expected to *attend* to the nurse's announcement and the clock and *respond* by going to the dining room. Step two required entrance into the dining room during shorter and shorter periods of time following the nurse's announcement—a half hour, then 15 minutes, and finally five-minute intervals were imposed. At this step the task and reward remained the same but the structure was increased and a greater degree of *order* introduced. Step three required that the patient stop by the nurse's office and pick up a penny to deposit in a can at the door to the dining room in order to gain admittance. This step involved the *exploratory* motor behavior of picking up a coin and placing it in a designated place. Step four was at the *social* level. Each patient had to get the assistance of a fellow patient in order to obtain a penny. A device was placed in the ward with two buttons on it some seven feet apart. Pennies were available only when the two buttons were pushed simultaneously. The patients quickly adapted to this increased demand, and the degree of interaction among them increased considerably as a result.

Had the investigators imposed step four initially it probably would have been unsuccessful with these patients. The fact that they reduced the task assigned to a minimal level (e.g., getting up and going to the dining room within a long time period) provided a meaningful reward immediately following the accomplishment of this task (e.g., food) and finally increased the structure or "strings" attached to accomplishment of the task before the reward was provided in such gradual steps (e.g., dining room open during shorter and shorter periods, required tokens to be picked up, required cooperative behavior before tokens given) that success was assured.

The case of Peter is an example of the deconditioning of involuntary behavior such as that associated with classical or respondent conditioning, while the work of Ayllon and Haughton represents the use of operant conditioning to promote acquisition of behavior under voluntary control. Such behavior modification methodology is extremely useful in education because it focuses the teacher's attention on small increments of learning and stresses the importance of rewards and systematic structuring in the learning process.

This chapter has been concerned with an introduction to the methodology utilized by the developmental strategy in the education of emotionally disturbed children. Selection of the task which moves the child toward a goal on the developmental sequence, providing him with a reward for his efforts, and making demands with relation to accomplishment of the tasks which are gradually and systematically increased, have been presented as sides of a learning triangle, and these will be further developed in later chapters of this book.

IV EDUCATIONAL ASSESSMENT OF EMOTIONALLY DISTURBED CHILDREN

This chapter will review current diagnostic and assessment procedures with emotionally disturbed children, relate the developmental sequence of educational goals to educational assessment of the disturbed child, and provide two examples of its use.

Case studies of emotionally disturbed children, prepared for the school by consultants in medicine, psychiatry, social work, and clinical psychology, may be elaborate and comprehensive under such headings as "Physical Development," "Personality Assessment," "Family Background," and "Intelligence," but often quite sparse when the final heading, "Implications for Classroom Instruction and Management," is reached.

The medical and neurological report may describe "immature skeletal development," a "questionable" electroencephalographic wave pattern, or suggest the possibility of "minimal cerebral dysfunction" or "specific dyslexia." Despite the authoritative ring to such medical terminology, it has little direct usefulness to the teacher in the classroom.

Psychiatric diagnostic terminology often reflects an adherence to Freudian psychoanalytic theory. The teacher may find the psychiatrist's observations centering around interpersonal behavior of the child and inferences regarding its origin. Terms such as "ego defect," "Oedipal fantasy," and "transference relationship" may appear in the case study and be of educational significance in direct relation to the teacher's sophistication with psychoanalytic theory. Psychiatric diagnostic labels including "primary behavior problem," "childhood schizophrenia," and "adjustment reaction of childhood or adolescence" have in common with other medical terms the specificity of diagnosis but limited implication for treatment.

The observations of the social worker reveal to the teacher the nature of the family milieu from which the child emerges as he enters school each day. The occupational status of the parents, ages, special characteristics of siblings, and information regarding the family interactional pattern provide the teacher with clues regarding the basis for the child's behavior. But exactly how to utilize such information in putting together a more suitable educational program for an emotionally disturbed child may be difficult to determine.

Clinical psychologists base their observations of the child on psychological test findings. A standardized intelligence test may reveal that the child's "verbal" functioning is superior to his "performance" level. Psychological evaluations may also include perceptual-motor and projective test information. Perceptual-motor tests give indications of the child's ability to discriminate and his spatial orientation, while projective tests provide a glimpse into his fantasy and emotional life. Some clinical psychologists are more adept than others in relating test findings to educational programs, but all too often statements such as "inability to separate figure from ground" and "poor reality testing" are presented to teachers who may say, "Fine, but now what do I do?"

Schwitzgebel (1965) has likened this dilemma to that faced by a newcomer to a large city who must find his way through unfamiliar territory. If during the course of his attempts to locate a particular destination he is offered a geological map, he is provided with accurate and interesting information about this strange environment but still left stranded in relation to his goal of reaching a destination. In the same manner, if a topographical or political map is provided, his knowledge of additional dimensions of the environment increases but his crucial immediate problem is largely unsolved. What he needs is a street map with directions which are related to his problem of the moment.

It is not that the multi-disciplinary maps or viewpoints of psychiatry, clinical psychology, or neurology are inaccurate or irrelevant but that they seldom are truly useful in bridging the gap between description and diagnosis and practical classroom application that is a major concern of this text.

Redl (1966) has commented on the unfortunate gap often existing between terms and concepts used to describe children's problems and specific techniques for attacking them.

> The concept of the "ego" and the functions it has to perform has grown in complexity over the years—so much that nothing but a book in its own right could do justice to all that has been described, postulated and said about it. The complexity of the job of the adult who meets the child

in the role of therapist, nurse, teacher, or parent has grown proportionally too. Yet—and this is a most deplorable state of affairs—the specificity with which we can advise that adult on what to do has in no way kept pace with the increase in complexity of the concept itself. In short, I can give long lectures on the concept of ego and impress my psychiatric trainees no end with the wisdom packed into them. But when they ask me, "Listen, you said we were supposed to give 'ego support' at times— *Just what are we supposed to do?*"—they catch me with my consultative pants down.[1]

The author is reminded of the true story of a young man who sought help because of recurring anxiety attacks. After three interviews with a therapist, he was told the cause of his difficulties had been uncovered. In the therapist's words, the anxiety attacks were the result of "premature narcissistic dethronement." The young man paid for the interviews but later confided to another therapist, "I was glad to find out what my problem was, but I'm still anxious most of the time."

Despite the limitations discussed, medical, psychiatric, social work, and psychological data can be extremely valuable in the overall assessment of the emotionally disturbed child. They should be used by teachers in an effort to better understand the strengths and weaknesses, assets and liabilities of their students. A natural next step, however, is to utilize this information along with observations of the child as he functions in school for a truly educational diagnosis.

Various approaches have been utilized for screening and identifying emotionally disturbed children in schools, including behavior check lists (Quay, Morse, and Cutler, 1966; Kough and Dehaan, 1955), teacher, peer, and self-ratings (Bower, 1961), and sociometry (Cunningham, 1961). Rather than survey these screening procedures the author would like to share a unique educational assessment device based on the developmental sequence of educational goals. This device was constructed by the staff of the NPI School to facilitate the use of the developmental sequence in a continuous program from assessment through classroom practice. Psychosis, neurotic traits, behavior problems, and other social-emotional difficulties can be viewed as failures to pay attention, respond, follow directions, explore, function appropriately in a social context, acquire intellectual and adaptive skills, and develop a self-motivation for learning.

It is to the child within the learning triangle that we now turn. To introduce the use of the developmental sequence as an educational assessment device, the type of emotionally disturbed child commonly having difficulty at each level will be considered and the kinds of learner

[1] F. Redl, *When We Deal with Children* (New York: The Free Press, 1966), p. 125.

reward and degree of structure implicit at each level discussed. Assessment of a child is made by first considering whether or not he has attained the goals at each level, next by selecting the rewards which are meaningful to him, and, finally by deciding on the structure or degree of teacher control which will assure successful learning.

ATTENTION

Does not pay attention to learning tasks	1.	Prefers fantasy to reality	2.	Repetitive behavior interferes with learning	3.	Beliefs and interests inappropriate	4.	Does not pay attention to teacher	5.	Does not profit from instruction	6.	Not rewarded by tangible reward ($, food) in learning	a.

FIGURE IV-1

One characteristic common to many emotionally disturbed children in school is failure to pay attention. Preoccupation with irrelevant stimuli, daydreaming, withdrawal, and inability to recall what has been presented often eliminate these children from participation in the learning process.

The most seriously emotionally disturbed children display the most serious attention problems in learning. The autistic child is a case in point. From early infancy these children often fail to pay systematic attention to their environment. Instead, they seem to prefer attending to themselves and to certain selective stimuli around them, to which they respond in bizarre and inappropriate ways. Rimland (1964) has summarized much of what is known about autistic children. In addition, other information about these children may be found in the writings of Kanner (1949), Bender (1956), Mahler (1952), and Bettelheim (1967). Despite normal or superior intellectual potential, they are often highly resistant to learning on the teacher's terms.

Children with schizophrenic and other psychotic disorders readily retreat into fantasy and attend to internal rather than external stimuli. Descriptions of these children may be found in the writings of Ekstein, Bryant, and Freedman (1958), Bender (1953), and Mahler (1949). Along with autistic children, they may engage in repetitive behavior, such as rocking, head-banging, twirling, flapping of the arms, and other ritualistic behavior which occupies their attention and interferes with learning. They may hallucinate and develop delusions or false beliefs about the real world around them. The autistic child may be totally oblivious to the teacher's presence, and other psychotic children may withdraw actively from any teacher contact. Needless to say this degree of inattention to the teacher and environmental stimuli may well preclude the autistic and psychotic child's learning adaptive behavior.

Less severely disturbed children may only intermittently pay attention to the environment; occasionally retreat from reality through daydreaming; display compulsive, ritualistic behavior, such as sharpening their pencil before each problem is attempted or making constant trips to the bathroom or drinking fountain; maintain immature, inappropriate beliefs for their age and sex; and regularly avoid paying attention to the teacher.

While these children can be labeled autistic, schizophrenic, psychotic, and atypical, a fundamental characteristic they share in common which has educational significance is inattention. Figure IV-1 (Boxes 1-6) summarizes the type of attention problems which must be considered before any systematic teaching in school can take place. Each of the numbered boxes at this level and those to be presented at succeeding levels attempt to provide examples of behaviors which prevent the child from attaining the goal being considered. The remedying of the problems stated in Boxes 1-6, Figure IV-1, then, constitutes the educational task at the attention level.

The problem of providing a meaningful learner reward is dealt with in Box a, Figure IV-1. Often children with severe attention problems are not susceptible to any of the conventional rewards for learning (e.g., sensory, social, and task success) and must be given more primary rewards, such as food, candy, and other tangible items. Since some type of reward is essential in learning, the teacher cannot overlook the possibilities offered by extrinsic motivators, even though this runs counter to traditional practices. Emotionally disturbed children are often far from traditional learners, and a unique and innovative educational scheme may have to be developed for them if they are to be taught.

The same type of flexibility may be necessary with regard to the third side of the learning triangle—structure. In order to get the child to pay attention, considerable care and ingenuity may have to be exercised by the teacher with respect to selecting what the child does and when, where, how, and how well he does it.

Since paying attention to the teacher and the learning task is fundamental if any child is going to learn in school, describing emotionally disturbed children as having severe (e.g., autistic child), moderate (e.g., borderline psychotic), or mild (e.g., child with learning disability) attention problems or in terms of frequency of occurrence of such problems rather than borrowing secondhand diagnostic labels from medicine, psychiatry, and clinical psychology has direct implications for classroom procedures.

Table IV-1 presents an Attention Level Inventory, which can be used by teachers to qualify the frequency of inattention displayed by a given child and his receptivity to tangible rewards. The use of this Inventory and the boxes which appear in Figure IV-1 in an overall assessment of the child will be discussed in a later section of this chapter.

TABLE IV-1

ATTENTION LEVEL INVENTORY

TASK

Attention

1. Child does not pay attention to learning tasks.

□ (ALWAYS)	□ (SOMETIMES)	□ (RARELY)
Child never pays attention to learning tasks	Child often does not pay attention to learning tasks	Child occasionally does not pay attention to learning tasks

2. Child prefers fantasy to reality.

□ (SEVERE)	□ (MODERATE)	□ (MILD)
Child out of contact with reality	Child often day-dreams	Child occasionally daydreams

3. Child engages in repetitive behavior which interferes with learning.

□ (SEVERE)	□ (MODERATE)	□ (MILD)
Child preoccupied with constant self-stimulation	Child preoccupied with rituals or other compulsive behavior	Child preoccupied with neatness, cleanliness, or correctness

4. Child's beliefs and interests are inappropriate.

□ (SEVERE)	□ (MODERATE)	□ (MILD)
Child has extremely bizarre beliefs and interests	Child has distorted beliefs about his environment	Child's beliefs and interests immature for sex and age

5. Child does not pay attention to teacher.

□ (ALWAYS)	□ (SOMETIMES)	□ (RARELY)
Child never pays attention to teacher	Child often does not pay attention to teacher	Child occasionally does not pay attention to teacher

6. Child does not profit from instruction.

□	□	□
(ALWAYS)	(SOMETIMES)	(RARELY)
Child never retains and uses instruction he has been given	Child often does not retain and use instruction he has been given	Child occasionally does not retain and use instruction he has been given

REWARD

a. Child not rewarded by tangible rewards (e.g., food, money) in learning.

□	□	□
(ALWAYS)	(SOMETIMES)	(RARELY)
Child's responses never controlled by tangible rewards	Child's responses often not controlled by tangible rewards	Child's responses occasionally not controlled by tangible rewards

It can be anticipated that teachers will ask at this point: "So I can describe the child as having an attention problem, what can I do about it?" The answer to this question, with reference to attention problems and problems at the other six levels of the developmental sequence, will be dealt with in Section 2 of this text, Chapters V–IX.

RESPONSE

Does not respond to learning tasks	7.	Perform- ance level constricted	8.	Exhibits narrow range of learning interests	9.	Withdraws from teacher and peers	10.	Cannot function in regular classroom	11.		Not rewarded by social attention	b.

Figure IV-2

In the introduction of the developmental sequence in the last chapter, it was pointed out that getting children to attend or to notice something was just the beginning. Once they are paying attention, the teacher must get them to respond or to do something. Emotionally disturbed children are often unpredictable and highly selective responders. Refusal to accept any assignment, cautious and constricted performance in school, immobilization in the presence of the teacher or other classmates are problems seen in children who are having difficulties at the response level.

Psychotic or borderline psychotic children are often constricted responders. In the classroom they may only respond to subject matter that falls within a particular area. History, higher mathematics, and biology are examples of subjects that have appealed to certain constricted adolescent students in the NPI School. As long as their assignments were restricted to these areas they would respond, often prodigiously, but when attempts were made to involve them in other activities they withdrew and refused to work. The case of Louis, cited earlier, provides an example of a strong interest that was utilized by the teacher to elicit a response in school.

Perhaps the classic example of a response problem with educational implications found among emotionally disturbed children is school phobia. Some children experience such anxiety separating from their family, particularly their mothers, that they cannot function in a school setting. Children with school phobia have been subjects of considerable literature in the field, and information regarding the problem can be found in the writings of Eisenberg (1958), Johnson, Falstein, Szverk, and Svendsen (1941), Davidson (1961), and Coolidge, Hahn, and Peck (1957). Although they are often bright and capable learners, their inability to function in school becomes a serious limiting factor in their psychological and educational development.

Children with less serious emotional problems may exhibit shyness, extreme self-consciousness, or a high anxiety level when called on to recite in a classroom setting. Since the structure of the school is highly social such children may be constantly in a state of distress. Children with response problems have been labeled psychotic, neurotic, phobic, and excessively shy. Figure IV-2 (Boxes 7-11) summarizes some of the kinds of difficulties they present in the classroom. The problem for the teacher becomes one of getting them to respond, increasing their response repertoire, and helping them adjust to the social milieu of the school.

At the response level, the rewards available for the child are largely social in nature as stated in Box b in Figure IV-2. It is getting the child to make a variety of responses, respond in the presence of others, develop trust and acceptance in relation to the teacher and peers, and finally be rewarded by social attention and contact that are major tasks.

The degree of structure imposed on the child at the response level is still subject to the same flexible handling as was the case at the attention level. In order to gain the child's attention and to involve him as a responder in the learning process, the teacher must carefully gauge his capacity for limits. In the case of Louis no demand was made that he push the lever at any specific time. This choice was up to him.

Table IV-2 lists the Response Level Inventory to aid the teacher in assessing the extent of the child's problem.

TABLE IV-2

Response Level Inventory

TASK

Response

7. Child does not respond to learning tasks.

☐ | ☐ | ☐
(ALWAYS) | (SOMETIMES) | (RARELY)
Child will never undertake a learning task | Child often will not undertake a learning task | Child occasionally will not undertake a learning task

8. Child maintains a constricted level of performance.

☐ | ☐ | ☐
(ALWAYS) | (SOMETIMES) | (RARELY)
Child always controlled and rigid with learning tasks | Child often controlled and rigid with learning tasks | Child occasionally controlled and rigid with learning tasks

9. Child exhibits a narrow range of learning interests.

☐ | ☐ | ☐
(ALWAYS) | (SOMETIMES) | (RARELY)
Child will never try a new or different learning task | Child often will not try a new or different learning task | Child occasionally will not try a new or different learning task

10. Child withdraws from teacher and peers.

☐ | ☐ | ☐
(ALWAYS) | (SOMETIMES) | (RARELY)
Child always avoids contact with teacher and peers | Child often avoids contact with teacher and peers | Child occasionally avoids contact with teacher and peers

11. Child cannot function in a regular classroom.

☐ | ☐ | ☐
(SEVERE) | (MODERATE) | (MILD)
Child does not respond to tasks in individual tutoring | Child does not respond to tasks in a special class or program | Child does not respond to tasks in a regular classroom except for brief periods of time

REWARD

b. Child not rewarded by social attention in learning tasks.

☐ | ☐ | ☐
(ALWAYS) | (SOMETIMES) | (RARELY)
Child's responses never controlled by social attention | Child's responses often not controlled by social attention | Child's responses occasionally not controlled by social attention

ORDER

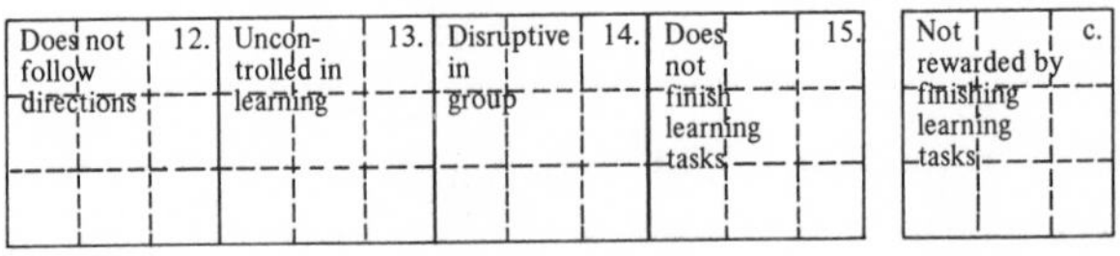

Does not follow directions	12.	Uncon-trolled in learning	13.	Disruptive in group	14.	Does not finish learning tasks	15.	Not rewarded by finishing learning tasks	c.

FIGURE IV-3

Of all the problems manifested by emotionally disturbed children in the classroom, none has been of more concern to teachers than order problems. Despite ready attending and responding, the child who does not follow directions and attend and respond in an orderly manner is a poor candidate for learning. Uncritical, haphazard approaches to assignments, uncontrolled and disruptive behavior in the classroom, and incompletion of work, commonly found among children with order problems, consistently tests the teacher's patience and endurance. In fact, the ability to follow directions, obey rules, adapt to routines, and respect the working rights of others is so basic to the level of socialization expected of all children before they enter school that teachers often view nonconforming children as the most seriously disturbed.

The early study of Wickman (1928) revealed that teachers rated order problems as indicative of more serious disturbance than attention and response problems, in direct contradiction to ratings of mental hygienists, who saw the withdrawn, shy child as being more disturbed. Bower (1957) and Beilin (1959) have obtained evidence that teachers at the present time are more aware of the significance of withdrawn behavior than their earlier counterparts, but the fact remains that children with order problems are far more difficult to tolerate in a program of group instruction.

Children who display order problems in school may be psychotic, but, more commonly, they are individuals with poor control of their impulses, who act out their feelings, and who appear driven to coerce the environment and others in it into doing things their way. While their behavior is often destructive, it may be less indicative of serious psychopathology than the retreat from reality seen in children with marked attention and response problems. The child with order problems is central to the writings of Redl and Wineman (1951, 1952), Newman (1956), and Adams (1960). These children have been described as acting out, as hyperaggressive, and/or as exhibiting conduct disturb-ances, primary behavior problems, and adjustment reactions, but from the teacher's point of view, it is their inability to follow directions and function according to limits set for the group that is the main problem. Figure IV-3 (Boxes 12-15) summarizes the types of order problems displayed by these children in school.

Box c in Figure IV-3 alludes to the learner reward operating at the order level. Before the child can proceed with learning he must find completion of the task rewarding in itself.

Structure emerges as a far more important factor at the order level. The very essence of this level is the establishment of fixed environmen-tal limits, in marked contrast to the more flexible structure at the attention and response level. The teacher is concerned with getting the child to start, follow through, and finish assignments as directed, to function within the limits of time, space, and activity, and to come to respect the working rights of the other children in the classroom. Table IV-3, the Order Level Inventory, presents frequency descriptions of order problems.

TABLE IV-3

ORDER LEVEL INVENTORY

TASK

Order

12. Child does not follow directions.

□	□	□
(ALWAYS)	(SOMETIMES)	(RARELY)
Child never follows directions when doing learning tasks	Child often does not follow directions when doing learning tasks	Child occasionally does not follow directions when doing learning tasks

13. Child is uncontrolled in learning.

□	□	□
(ALWAYS)	(SOMETIMES)	(RARELY)
Child always approaches learning tasks in an impul-sive, uncritical manner	Child often approaches learning tasks in an impulsive, uncritical manner	Child occasionally approaches learning tasks in an impulsive, uncritical manner

TABLE IV-3 *(Continued)*

14. Child is disruptive in group.

☐   ☐   ☐
(ALWAYS)   (SOMETIMES)   (RARELY)
Child always is   Child often is   Child occasionally is
disruptive in group disruptive in group   disruptive in group

15. Child does not finish learning tasks.

☐   ☐   ☐
(ALWAYS)   (SOMETIMES)   (RARELY)
Child never   Child often does not   Child occasionally
finishes learning   finish learning tasks   does not finish
tasks   learning tasks

REWARD

c. Child is not rewarded by finishing learning tasks.

☐   ☐   ☐
(ALWAYS)   (SOMETIMES)   (RARELY)
Child's per-   Child's performance   Child's performance
formance never   often not controlled   occasionally not
controlled by task   by task completion   controlled by task
completion   completion

EXPLORATORY

Does not adequately explore environment	16.	Dependent on others for interests and activities	17.	Motor, physical, sensory, perceptual, or intellectual deficits	18.	Not rewarded by multisensory experiences in learning	d.

FIGURE IV-4

Assessment of the emotionally disturbed child on the exploratory level actually is an extension of consideration given at the attention, response, and order levels. Because of their preoccupation with fantasy, inappropriate beliefs, lack of attention in the classroom, constricted range of interests, and uncontrolled behavior, many emotionally disturbed children are inadequate explorers and do not have an accurate knowledge of their environment. This limited knowledge and understanding may be due, in part, to their being overprotected by their parents, being unable to attend school, being disinterested in exploring the world around them, through looking, listening, touching, smelling, and tasting, or being afraid of unfamiliar experiences. For some children considered emotionally disturbed, actual physical deficits, such as visual or hearing problems or neurological impairment, may markedly interfere with exploration. As a result, they operate under a considerable handicap with respect to achieving independence. They may have to be carefully supervised by others to protect them in a basically unfamiliar environment. They may also be continually dependent on others for choice of interests and activities.

A child with an exploratory, as well as an order, problem who has received increasing attention in special education, is one with perceptual-motor difficulties, possibly related to neurological impairment. He is of particular concern to special educators focused on the sensory-neurological strategy discussed in Chapter I. In addition to difficulty in motor coordination and spatial and temporal orientation, this child may exhibit extreme restlessness and be oversensitive to stimulation. As was suggested, this problem spills over on both the order and exploratory levels. While not always seen as emotionally disturbed, these children's difficulties with control, coordination, and orientation place them under considerable stress in a learning situation. A further discussion of this type of problem may be found in the writings of Strauss (1947), Kephart (1960), Cruickshank (1961), and Birch (1964).

For the teacher, however, the child described is an order and exploratory problem in the classroom. Figure IV-4 (Boxes 16-18) summarizes the educational problems found at the exploratory level.

Learner rewards at the exploratory level are multisensory in nature, as stated in Box d Figure IV-4. At this point it is the child's experience of moving, looking, listening, touching, smelling, and tasting that motivates him. Those children with sensory or neurological deficits will be limited in the extent to which these experiences are rewarding, but they may be fully rewarded on the lower and remaining levels. It is obvious that exploratory goals and sensory rewards are also a part of the attention, response, and order levels. At these lower levels, however, it is more sensory stimulation than multisensory involvement which is stressed.

Structure considerations at the exploratory level are similar to the order level, as it is systematic, orderly exploratory activity that relates to efficient learning; however, the child needs to be encouraged to develop interests on his own and be allowed some freedom of choice. The Exploratory Level Inventory is found in Table IV-4.

TABLE IV-4

Exploratory Level Inventory

TASK

Exploratory

16. Child does not adequately explore his environment.

☐ (SEVERE)	☐ (MODERATE)	☐ (MILD)
Child's exploration of his environment extremely limited	Child's exploration of his environment moderately limited	Child's exploration of his environment limited in a few specific areas

17. Child overly dependent on others for choice of interests and activities.

☐ (ALWAYS)	☐ (SOMETIMES)	☐ (RARELY)
Child completely dependent on others for choice of interests and activities	Child excessively dependent on others for choice of interests and activities	Child usually dependent on others for choice of interests and activities

18. Child cannot do learning tasks because of motor, physical, sensory, perceptual, or intellectual deficits.

☐ (SEVERE)	☐ (MODERATE)	☐ (MILD)
Child severely impaired by motor, physical, sensory, perceptual, or intellectual deficits	Child moderately impaired by motor, physical, sensory, perceptual, or intellectual deficits	Child mildly impaired by motor, physical, sensory, perceptual, or intellectual deficits

REWARD

d. Child not rewarded by multisensory experiences in learning.

☐ (ALWAYS)	☐ (SOMETIMES)	☐ (RARELY)
Child's responses never controlled by multisensory rewards	Child's responses often not controlled by multisensory rewards	Child's responses occasionally not controlled by multisensory rewards

SOCIAL

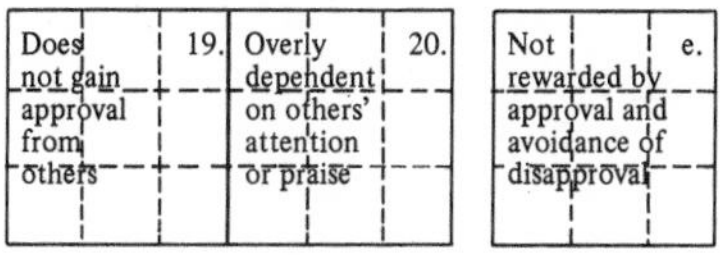

Does not gain approval from others	19.	Overly dependent on others' attention or praise	20.	Not rewarded by approval and avoidance of disapproval	e.

FIGURE IV-5

Educational assessment of the emotionally disturbed child on the social level is an elaboration of that done on the response and order levels. The major consideration at this level is the child's development of appropriate social behavior, rather than his merely functioning in a social setting as a participant. In this text, appropriate social behavior is defined as being exhibited when the child gains the approval of others and avoids their disapproval.

All children must not only learn to accept others and respect their rights but also to develop an understanding of standards of appropriate social behavior. This may sound redundant, but there is a difference between participating and conforming as opposed to understanding what others expect of you. Eisenberg (1950) reports the case of a very intelligent, schizophrenic young man, who had maintained a borderline adjustment and entered college. At a football rally one night, when his classmates were, one by one, extolling the virtues of the school team and expressing confidence that it would win the next day, the young man took his turn, stood up, and calmly stated that the team would lose, as it was obviously inferior to its opponent. The group reaction and rejection which followed was totally incomprehensible to him. He had gone to the rally and was conforming to the student participation rules but was most inadequate in understanding standards of appropriate social behavior in this setting.

Emotionally disturbed children vary with respect to the social behavior difficulties they exhibit. Some are oblivious to social standards, others so painfully aware of them that they live in constant fear of offending someone. Some are driven to gain attention and approval at all costs. Others go out of their way to displease everybody. Regardless of the underlying reasons for this behavior, the teacher's concern is in helping the child learn to gain social approval and to avoid disapproval. Figure IV-5 (Boxes 19-20) summarizes the problem at this level.

The rewards for learning at the social level are obvious and have been stated several times in this section—social praise and approval and avoidance of disapproval. These are stated in Box e of Figure IV-5.

Structure at this level is based on standards of appropriate social behavior, and limits are firmly set for the child.

Table IV-5 lists the Social Level Inventory.

TABLE IV-5

Social Level Inventory

TASK

Social

19. Child does not gain approval from others.

☐	☐	☐
(ALWAYS)	(SOMETIMES)	(RARELY)
Child never gains approval from others	Child often does not gain approval from others	Child occasionally does not gain approval from others

20. Child overly dependent on attention or praise from others.

☐	☐	☐
(SEVERE)	(MODERATE)	(MILD)
Child will only work with constant supervision and attention from the teacher	Child will only work for brief periods of time without attention and praise from others	Child often seeks attention and praise from others while doing learning tasks

REWARD

e. Child not rewarded by gaining approval and avoiding disapproval for learning tasks.

☐	☐	☐
(ALWAYS)	(SOMETIMES)	(RARELY)
Child's responses never controlled by social approval and disapproval	Child's responses often not controlled by social approval and disapproval	Child's responses occasionally not controlled by social approval and disapproval

MASTERY

FIGURE IV-6

The inability of the child to utilize his intellectual capacity to care for himself and to develop basic intellectual skills constitutes a mastery level problem and is commonly seen among children with emotional problems.They may be unable to assume responsibility for their own care and safety, and dependent upon adult assistance in handling such problems as toileting, bathing, dressing, eating, crossing the street, and making simple purchases at the store. Disturbed children also may fail to learn to read, write, spell, and do arithmetic in keeping with their chronological age and intelligence. These failures more often than not are the result of attention, response, order, exploratory, and social problems, which have kept the child out of the mainstream of socialization in the community and school. Intellectual skills, such as spoken language, ability to deal with abstractions, and concept formation, are also considered at the mastery level. Where the child builds a fund of knowledge regarding the environment at the exploratory level through sensory-motor experiences, at the mastery level he must accumulate information intellectually, using tool skills such as reading.

Accurate mastery level assessment of the disturbed child is difficult because of the questionable validity of both intelligence and achievement tests with children who pay little attention, often do not respond even though they may know the answer, have difficulty following directions, and are uncomfortable in the presence of an adult examiner and other children taking the test.

The author designed a two-year reading and written language program for an autistic boy of 12 who had never learned to speak, read, or write (Hewett, 1964). Before the program the boy was seen as severely mentally retarded (IQ—38). Working daily with this boy, it was soon apparent he had far more intellectual ability than expected, and as he began to learn to attend, respond, and follow directions and to read, master the alphabet, and write simple phrases, this was confirmed. After two years he was again given the Performance Section of the Wechsler Intelligence Scale for Children. His overall IQ score on this section was 79, and he obtained a scale score of 14 on the Block Design Sub-Test, which suggested superior visual-motor ability.

Figure IV-6 (Box 21) summarizes the major considerations at the mastery level. Box f in Figure IV-6 implies that the reward available at this level is "doing learning tasks correctly." In the area of self-care, it is tying shoe laces in the correct manner, crossing the street when the signal turns the right color, and being able to correctly recall your address and phone number that constitute examples of mastery level functioning. Thus, correctness becomes a source of reward when it gets the job done for the child. Obviously, many of the other rewards on the lower level, such as social attention, task completion, multisensory experience, and social praise, may also be operating. In the area of intellectual skills undertaken in school, it is the number of questions or problems done correctly, and perhaps the eventual grade given for the child's efforts, that is the mastery level reward. It is at the upper levels of the developmental sequence that more traditional educational rewards become meaningful. In assessing the child on a mastery level, the teacher must determine if the reward of correctness exerts a positive effect on his performance in learning.

Structure at the mastery level is defined by the specific requirements of the tasks undertaken. There is only one correct way to cross the street and to read the word "house."

Table IV-6 provides the Mastery Level Inventory. It will be noted that self-care and intellectual skills receive separate consideration.

TABLE IV-6

Mastery Level Inventory

TASK

Mastery

21. Child's functioning level in self-care and intellectual skills below capacity.

(self-care)

▽	▽	▽
(SEVERE)	(MODERATE)	(MILD)
Extreme discrepancy between child's capacity and functioning level in self-care	Considerable discrepancy between child's capacity and functioning level in self-care	Slight discrepancy between child's capacity and functioning level in self-care

(intellectual skill)

△	△	△
(SEVERE)	(MODERATE)	(MILD)
Extreme dis-crepancy between child's capacity and functioning level in intellectual and academic skills	Considerable dis-crepancy between child's capacity and functioning level in intellectual and academic skills	Slight discrepancy between child's capacity and functioning level in intellectual and academic skills

REWARD

f. Child not rewarded by doing learning tasks correctly.

□	□	□
(ALWAYS)	(SOMETIMES)	(RARELY)
Child's responses never controlled by knowledge of results	Child's responses often not controlled by knowledge of results	Child's responses occasionally not controlled by knowledge of results

ACHIEVEMENT

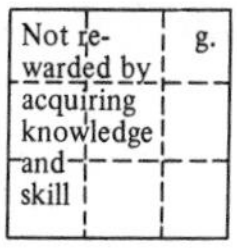

FIGURE IV-7

Assessing the child on the achievement level involves determining whether or not acquisition of knowledge and skill provides its own reward. Some emotionally disturbed children are so self-oriented, so preoccupied with fantasy, so constricted in their interaction with their environment that they avoid learning anything. For others, intellectual functioning is relatively unimpaired by their emotional problems, and they lose themselves in reading and studying. Indeed, for some, the pursuit of knowledge and acquisition of skills, such as reading and arithmetic, appears to offer a kind of refuge. The intellectual world may seem a far safer place than the world of people. Because of this fact, teachers may be misled by the child's performance in school. If the criterion for a successful educational program is the number of pages read and understood or problems done correctly by a given student, then the schizophrenic adolescent who functions five years above grade level in reading, vocabulary, and comprehension, and whose mastery of trigonometry is far beyond that of his own teacher, is gaining all that is necessary in school. This criterion, however, may be wholly inadequate. The teacher will not only consider the achievement level, but will look carefully at such a child's functioning on the exploratory and social levels, where he may compare unfavorably with what is expected of a normal first grader.

The achievement level completes the developmental sequence, because self-motivation in learning is a desired end product of all education. Its significance in the education of emotionally disturbed children, however, may be very minimal in comparison to the more fundamental readiness levels below it.

The reward at the achievement level constitutes the level itself and is stated in Box g of Figure IV-7.

Structure is largely intrinsic, and the child operating on the achievement level sets his own limits with a minimum of outside direction and control.

Table IV-7 states the criteria for assessing the child at the achievement level.

TABLE IV-7

Achievement Level Inventory

REWARD

    g. Child not rewarded by acquiring knowledge and skill.

☐	☐	☐
(ALWAYS)	(SOMETIMES)	(RARELY)
Child's performance never controlled by acquisition of knowledge and skill	Child's performance often not controlled by acquisition of knowledge and skill	Child's performance occasionally not controlled by acquisition of knowledge and skill

The developmental sequence of educational goals has been reviewed as an assessment device with emotionally disturbed children. Table IV-8 summarizes the task, reward, and structure provisions at all seven levels.[2]

---

[2] From F. Hewett, "Educational Engineering with Emotionally Disturbed Children," *Exceptional Children*, 1967, 33, pp. 459–467.

TABLE IV-8

SUMMARY OF THE DEVELOPMENTAL SEQUENCE OF EDUCATIONAL GOALS

Level	Attention	Response	Order	Exploratory	Social	Mastery	Achievement
Child's Problem	Inattention due to withdrawal or resistance	Lack of involvement and unwillingness to respond in learning	Inability to follow directions	Incomplete or inaccurate knowledge of environment	Failure to value social approval or disapproval	Deficits in basic adaptive and school skills not in keeping with IQ	Lack of self motivation for learning
Educational Task	Get child to pay attention to teacher and task	Get child to respond to tasks he likes and which offer promise of success	Get child to complete tasks with specific starting points and steps leading to a conclusion	Increase child's efficiency as an explorer and get him involved in multisensory exploration of his environment	Get child to work for teacher and peer group approval and to avoid their disapproval	Remediation of basic skill deficiencies	Development of interest in acquiring knowledge
Learner Reward	Provided by tangible rewards (e.g., food, money, tokens)	Provided by gaining social attention	Provided through task completion	Provided by sensory stimulation	Provided by social approval	Provided through task accuracy	Provided through intellectual task success
Teacher Structure	Minimal	Still limited	Emphasized	Emphasized	Based on standards of social appropriateness	Based on curriculum assignments	Minimal

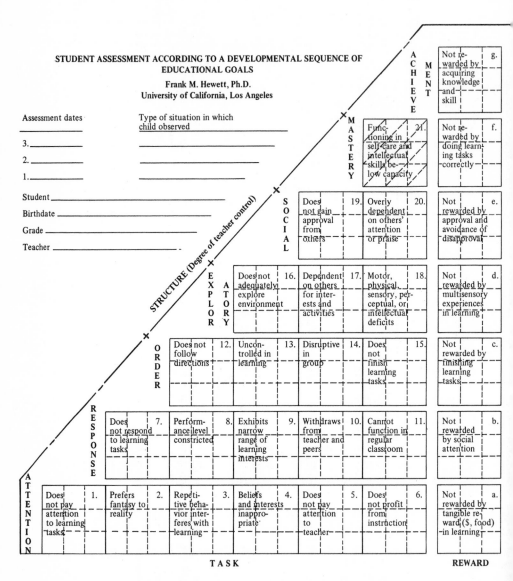

FIGURE IV-8. Composite developmental sequence form.

Additional Information	Instructional Implications
Ach. test data:	
Med./diag. data:	

The result of such an assessment will provide answers to the following questions for the teacher:

1. Which educational goals has the child failed to attain and which are most basic to his getting ready to learn in school?
2. What does the child find rewarding in learning? What possibilities exist for assuring that some meaningful reward is present for him in the classroom?
3. In terms of the degree of structure suggested at each level, can the child tolerate limits of what, where, when, how, and how well?

In actual practice, the developmental sequence is used in composite form. Appendix I contains the complete Inventory for all seven levels. The teacher completes the entire Inventory, considering the child's problems at each level and where they apply, checking the ratings which describe the frequency or degree of the problem. If the problem described on the Inventory does not apply, no rating is checked.

The next step is to utilize the composite developmental sequence form illustrated in Figure IV-8. Here, the boxes presented earlier have been combined to provide a graphic picture of the levels in sequence. Each box is divided into nine squares, three squares horizontally, in three horizontal segments. The boxes are numbered or lettered to correspond to the descriptive statements and ratings found in the Inventory.

The three horizontal segments in each box are utilized for three different assessments of a given child. The bottom segment is for assessment one, the middle segment for assessment two, and the upper segment for assessment three. Usually, assessment one is made three or four weeks after the teacher begins work with the child and is based on previous records and observations made by the teacher during that period. Assessment two is made five to six weeks later, and assessment three, five to six weeks after that. This spacing of the assessments permits the developmental sequence to be used over a standard school semester as a means of recording changes in the child's behavior during that time.

During each assessment the teacher transfers the Inventory ratings to the corresponding horizontal segment in each box on the composite developmental sequence. If a given rating is "severe" or always," the far left square is filled in with a colored felt pen, if it is "moderate" or "sometimes," the middle square is colored, and if it is "mild" or "rarely," the far right square is filled.

For example, in Box 1 of the developmental sequence at the attention level, suppose the teacher considers the statement "child does not pay attention to learning tasks" and decides it "always" applies, that is the "child never pays attention to learning tasks." Since this rating corresponds to the far-left square and since it was made during the initial assessment the box would be filled in as shown in Figure IV-9.

Suppose at the time of the second assessment the appropriate rating is "rarely" applies as the child now only "occasionally does not pay attention to learning tasks." This rating corresponds to the far right square. Since this is the second assessment, the middle segment is utilized to record the child's functioning level as shown in Figure IV-10.

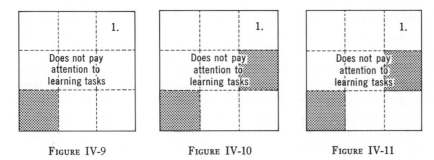

FIGURE IV-9   FIGURE IV-10   FIGURE IV-11

If at the time of the third assessment, the child was seen by the teacher as no longer manifesting any problem of attention in relation to learning tasks, no rating on the Inventory would be checked, the top segment would be empty, and the box would look like Figure IV-11.

At the end of the school semester, a glance at the box would reveal that the child was initially seen as never paying attention, later as occasionally not paying attention, and finally as not exhibiting the problem at all. A graphic picture, then, is provided of the child's progress over the semester in school. With each box on the developmental sequence considered in the same manner, a complete picture of the child and his learning problem in terms of the developmental sequence is available.

Box 21 of the mastery level refers to both self-care and intellectual skills. In order to separate ratings of the child's functioning in each of these areas, the squares within the box are divided diagonally. The upper portion of each square is utilized for self-care ratings, the lower portion for ratings of intellectual skills. The Inventory also separates these two portions, and once the ratings are made for the two areas covered by Item 21 they are transferred to the appropriate portions of the squares in Box 21.

The developmental sequence form in Figure IV-8 is organized to provide information regarding the child which has reference to the learning triangle. The 21 numbered boxes refer to behavioral characteristics which describe the child's functioning on six levels of the developmental sequence and which have implications for specific task assignments. The seven lettered boxes in the far right column describe the child in terms of his responsiveness to various rewards which can be provided in the classroom setting. As can be seen the achievement level is considered in this column. The degree of structure or teacher control implicit at each of the seven levels is suggested by the minus and plus signs appearing along the diagonal line above these levels. As was stated earlier in this chapter, structure may be minimal at the attention and response levels, emphasized at the order, exploratory, social, and mastery levels, and minimal again at the achievement level.

The two columns in the right of the developmental sequence form shown in Figure IV-8 provide space for specific comments by the teacher and data from the child's previous records. These columns "Additional Information" and "Instructional Implications" correspond horizontally to the seven developmental sequence levels and three assessment periods. Achievement test data are recorded at the mastery level and medical and other diagnostic data at the exploratory level.

Two examples of the use of the developmental sequence form will be given. The first example describes Louis, the seriously emotionally disturbed boy cited in Chapter III, and the second, Mark, a less seriously disturbed boy enrolled in a public school program for emotionally disturbed children.

Louis' degree of withdrawal and inattention is clearly seen in the first assessment on the attention level of Figure IV-12. He "never" paid attention, apparently was "out of contact with reality," "never" paid attention to the teacher, "never" retained instruction given him, and was "never" rewarded by tangible rewards. At the response level, he "never" undertook a learning task, was "always" controlled or rigid, "never" tried to do anything new or different, "always" avoided contact with others, and did not respond to tasks even during individual tutoring. Social attention was apparently no reward at all for him. Louis would not follow directions, and consequently, never finished any learning task. He was not, however, uncontrolled or disruptive in his classroom behavior, as can be seen by empty Boxes 13 and 14.

Louis' lack of demonstrated interest in the environment is seen at the exploratory level. Box 17 indicates that during the initial assessment he was totally dependent on others with respect to choice of activities. Box d was left blank by the teacher because his eyes were seen to move from time to time. Evidently to some minimal degree, Louis was re-warded by visual stimuli. Indeed, this observation led to the establish-ment of the lever pushing response given him in the initial stages of his educational program. At the social level, Louis' complete detachment and withdrawal often did not gain approval. He was also in no way controlled by others' approval. Despite his previous adequacy in self-care and intellectual functioning, at the time of admission to the NPI School, he was operating severely below his capacity. This is further indicated at the achievement level, where his almost complete lack of involvement with the environment restricted his undertaking any as-signments at all.

Additional information the teacher obtained on Louis from outside sources, as well as that obtained through classroom observation, is listed at each level. The formulation of the simple lever pushing response as the initial task and the fact that the first four levels—attention, response, order, and exploratory—were involved is seen in the "In-structional Implications" column. Louis' progress can be followed by referring to the middle and upper horizontal segments of each level in the "Additional Information" and "Instructional Implications" col-umns.

During the first five weeks of the program, his attention to tasks and teacher improved markedly, as did his level of responding and direction-following. As he began to respond, Louis' behavior earned him the approval of others, and he appeared slightly more responsive to such social approval. Reward of correctness in learning also became much more important.

Some seven weeks later, at the time of the final assessment, Louis' functioning level improved dramatically. Attention problems all but disappeared. His level of responding increased, although he remained fairly constricted and withdrawn in the classroom. Louis consistently followed directions and regained much of his former efficiency on the mastery level. Despite these latter gains, the teacher cautioned, under the "Instructional Implications" section of the upper level, against emphasizing intellectual and academic aspects of the program at the expense of lower levels and allowing him to "retreat" into mastery and achievement assignments.

Overall, Louis can be described as a severe attention and response problem in school and as such, an extremely difficult child to teach. These fundamental problems initially had to be given priority, and as has been described, the teacher had to demonstrate considerable re-sourcefulness and ingenuity in getting this very disturbed boy started up the ladder of learning again.

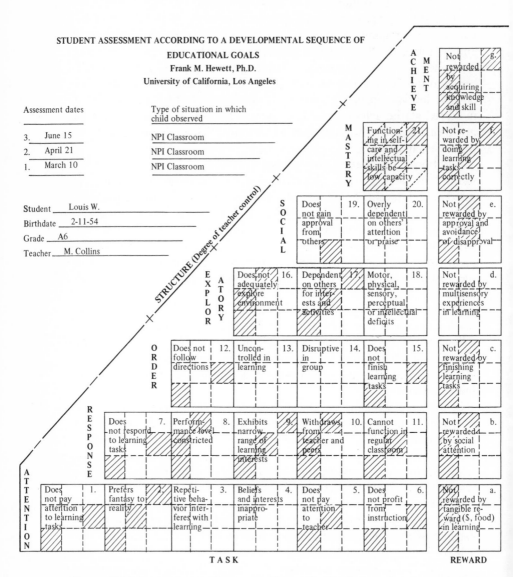

FIGURE IV-12. Assessment of Louis according to the developmental sequence of educational goals.

Additional Information	Instructional Implications
Now displays interest in doing more than assignments call for	Provide stimulating academic assignments but do not allow him to retreat into them
No change	Offer him open-ended assignments
Outstanding student in public school. Received all A's	Not applicable now
Uses pencil readily in doing sixth grade work	Maintain at grade level program but not at expense of lower levels
Does arithmetic by pointing to correct answers. Also does silent reading	Increase time in classroom to two periods. Get to write with pencil
No speech at present. Ach. test data: Was doing reading and arithmetic on 7-8th grade level	Not applicable. Program must start on attention, response, explor. levels
Will speak now in low voice	Pair him with stable, outgoing classmates for interaction
No change	Increase teacher verbalization but do not pressure him
Always has been a shy, withdrawn child. Now no eye contact at all	Do not approach too quickly. Try to establish teacher as positive
More general interest in environment. Will hold earthworm and frog	Expand program of science. Use listening post
Looks intently at slides. Appears to like them. Will also look at book	Continue use of prehistoric life in stories and pictures
Disinterest in environment. Has liked science and pre-historic life. Med./diag. data: Physical exams normal. Binet IQ 130	Use dinosaur slides in projector. May serve as adequate reward
Stands and follows flag salute with class	Don't impose rigid limits. Don't force speech. Focus on response level
Willingly moved lever to see slides. Will point to answers in book now	Increase complexity of directions given in reading and arithmetic
Highly conforming in past. Now extremely overcontrolled	Moving lever to turn on projector will get him responding
Walks unaided to class. Will catch ball. Walks in room like robot	Give tasks involving movement in room. Let select own activities
Slight smile while teacher reads aloud with slides. Long delays with lever	Increase types of responses expected. Give pencil. Have walk to class
Does not move any part of body. Must be carried into classroom	Construct lever box for projector. Try to get him to move lever
Continual improvement. Little problem here now	Continue focus on response and exploratory levels
Pays attention quite regularly to teacher direction and tasks	Emphasize response level
Appears to be aware of others but resists paying attention	Since eyes seem to move, use visual stimuli for attention

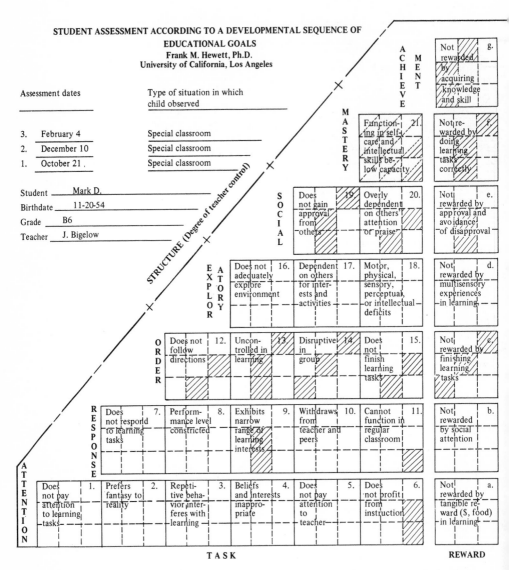

FIGURE IV-13. Assessment of Mark according to the developmental sequence of educational goals.

Additional Information	Instructional Implications
Slow but readily observable interest in learning, acquiring knowledge	Provide research, discussion, and projects when he is ready
Evidence of self-motivation in learning more about ships	Encourage independent free reading in areas of his interest
Claims no interest in learning	Not applicable

Additional Information	Instructional Implications
Much more willingness to do reading, writing, arithmetic assignments	Maintain routine, academic program. Give enrichment when ready
Does minimal academic work. Some outside reading on ships in relation to model construction	Maintain routine academic program with flexibility
Extremely careless in work. Many errors. Functioning level very sporadic	De-emphasize academics. Main focus on order and social levels
Ach. test data: Capable of functioning two years above grade level	Consider pairing less able children with him for reading, arithmetic help.
Works appropriately with others	
Incident when other boy started fight. Mark blamed, sent to office. Others defended him. This provoked his crying	Leadership potential evident. Pair other children with him during model building.
Demands attention. Bullies others. Boasts he "raped" girl in last class	Rearrange seat so removed from smaller children

Additional Information	Instructional Implications
Model building interest has run course. Move to mastery focus as possible	Expand exploratory interests through general science
Model building a success. Surfing magazines less motivating	Continue program emphasis here and at order level
Claims no interest but seems to like model construction, ships, surfing	Allow time to build ship model when does minimum mastery assignments
Med./diag. data: Physical exams normal. Large for age. WISC IQ (Full Scale) 103	Still will have bad days but not as often. Maintain expectations
Only one suspension last six weeks.	
Sent home once weekly up to 3 weeks ago. Quieter but sullen and angry	Limits must remain. No physical or verbal threats to teacher or he goes home
Main problem here. Impulsive, rude, hostile. Shakes fist at teacher	Don't lecture. Set firm limits. Send home at once for threats to teacher

Additional Information	Instructional Implications
Wrote story about ships. Less defensive about academic assignments	Continue emphasis on responding more at mastery, less at exploratory levels
Likes model. Brags to class about his skill in model building	Don't push too quickly. Try to move ship interest to reading and writing
Responds readily but on own terms. Likes others' attention. Resists tasks	Have build ship model. Use for later discussion with class

Additional Information	Instructional Implications
No problem now	Continue with simple, direct, specific directions
Some success putting schedule on card on his desk. He checks as done	Keep demands simple. Continue with card for assignments
Appears to pay attention but does not retain directions or facts	Appears primarily an order problem. Give few directions. Make them clear

Mark represents a different type of emotionally disturbed learner. In contrast to overcontrol and immobility, he presented problems of impulsivity and acting out. Figure IV-13 presents the teacher's assessment of Mark over a 13-week period.

Initially he demonstrated mild attention and response problems, but moderate to severe problems at the order level. He only "sometimes" followed directions, was impulsive and uncritical in learning, "always" was disruptive, and only "sometimes" finished assignments given to him. No problems were seen at the exploratory level, but at the social level Mark's behavior often did not gain him approval; he "frequently" sought teacher and peer attention, and his behavior was not readily controlled by social approval and avoidance of disapproval. Mark was seen by the teacher as functioning slightly below expectation in academic skills at the mastery level. According to the teacher's comments during the initial assessment, Mark displayed marked disrespect for authority and assumed the role of bully and terrorist with the other children. These problems were so severe that expulsion from class was frequently necessary. A model-building project was used to capitalize on one of Mark's exploratory interests and to help him achieve minimum conformity. This project lent itself to appropriately providing Mark with attention and status, which he so inappropriately sought in the classroom.

At the time of the second assessment some six weeks later, Mark's order and social problems had generally improved and he was gradually led toward more typical mastery assignments. The final assessment seven weeks later reveals no attention or response problems and only a mild degree of difficulty on the order level. He was also much more readily controlled by approval. The teacher's program from this point on was to maintain the minimum expectations of no physical or verbal abuse from Mark in the classroom and to try to channel his interests into an academic program of enrichment.

In reviewing the assessment of Mark, he can be described as a severe order and social problem in the classroom. In keeping with the philosophy of the developmental sequence, the teacher went to work selecting educational tasks related to goals he needed to attain and which held promise for success in the classroom. The teacher concentrated initially on appealing to his exploratory interests as a source of reward yet maintained the considerable degree of structure necessary to assist this boy in functioning effectively as a student in school.

Whatever advantages the developmental sequence may possess in the educational assessment of emotionally disturbed children, the real test of its worth comes as the teacher attempts to translate it into a classroom program. Once an initial assessment has been made as outlined in this chapter, the teacher will be confronted with a myriad of shaded boxes describing the child's deficits on the developmental sequence. Keeping in mind that every child is a candidate for learning "something" in school and that a great deal of individualization in the classroom is possible if the teacher really believes in it, the child's program is planned as follows:

1. Consider the entire assessment according to the developmental sequence in an effort to select the type of assignments and activities most appropriate for the child, the kind of rewards most meaningful, and the degree of structure necessary to insure learning. It is important not to restrict consideration to a single level in overall planning.
2. Once an overall review has been made, focus on the lowest level where problems exist. Consider each box which has been shaded and pay particular attention to "severe" or "always" ratings. Give priority to helping the child with his most basic learning problems and decrease emphasis on higher level problems.
3. Since most activities and assignments teachers can offer children in a classroom contain aspects of several, if not a majority, of the levels on the developmental sequence, a problem arises creating "pure" attention, response, order, exploratory, or social tasks. When the teacher holds up a picture and asks "What is this?" the child must pay attention, make a verbal response, follow the teacher's direction, and visually "explore" the picture. As a result the teacher should:
    a. Emphasize the aspect of the activity or assignment which represents the child's most basic learning problem. Getting the child to look at the picture may be all that is initially required, with the teacher deemphasizing verbal responding, direction following, and visual exploration.
    b. Reward the child for accomplishing that aspect of the task which represents his most basic learning problem. This is extremely important and is analogous to Peter's being highly rewarded while tolerating the feared rabbit when it was almost out of sight as described in the last chapter. The child whose eyes attend to the picture for a fraction of a second may have made an important step toward learning—by paying attention. Raymond, the "careless" third grader in Martin and Stendler's example, presented in Chapter I, was soundly criticized for poor functioning at the order and mastery level, when the teacher probably should have rewarded him for attending to the class assignment in general, getting his name on the paper, and trying to write a letter.
    c. Settle for the child's minimal accomplishment in line with his most basic learning problem and consider such accomplishment indicative of a teaching success. It is doubtful that a teacher as rigid and "mastery" oriented as the one in Raymond's classroom could ever feel personally rewarded when children with learning

problems made minimal progress on the lower levels of the developmental sequence, and it is equally doubtful that she would ever be an effective teacher of the emotionally disturbed. Such a teacher would most likely have directly confronted Peter with the rabbit and would have become critical and frustrated with his inability to handle the situation.

4. Be prepared to reassess the child at any given moment and drop back to a lower level expectation to insure his success.

5. Increase demands for functioning at higher levels gradually and systematically.

Once Louis' teacher had made the initial assessment seen in Figure IV-12, his program was planned according to the considerations just discussed.

1. An overall review of the developmental sequence revealed serious problems at most levels although the records available on this boy described him as an excellent student in the past. Selection of a task was most difficult because of this boy's total withdrawal. The right hand column of the composite developmental sequence states the types of rewards for learning which the teacher can provide (Boxes a, b, c, d, e, f, g). In Louis' case all but one reward appeared inappropriate. Even tangible rewards, such as food and candy, were useless with this severely disturbed boy. Because Louis' eyes had been seen to move, the teacher hypothesized that visual stimulation might be rewarding to him. In addition, his previously demonstrated interest in prehistoric life suggested that an exploratory reward in this area might prove effective. As far as structure was concerned, only minimal external controls were desirable because of this boy's extreme overcontrol.

2. The attention and response levels both reflect severe problems, and it was readily apparent that getting this boy to notice something and do something in school was far more important than considerations on higher levels. The most minimal task the teacher could devise was the simple lever pushing response. This became the task which also facilitated attention. The reward was selected from the exploratory level because of considerations previously discussed. The structure was minimal. Louis could or could not push the lever. It was up to him. In addition, he was given unlimited time to make his response.

3. Louis' initial program was an example of the first four levels on the developmental sequence being combined. He was only expected to attend, respond, follow directions, and explore in a very limited and specific manner, and he was immediately rewarded by the colored slide flashing on when he pushed the lever. The teacher was highly satisfied when this beginning step was accomplished, although as was described in Chapter III, another teacher who viewed Louis' efforts apparently only considered mastery accomplishments personally rewarding.

4. The fact that Louis' program was initiated on such an extremely basic level made dropping to a lower level unrealistic. However, if at any time

during the following stages Louis had been unable to function, he would have quickly been moved back to the starting point.

As was discussed in Chapter III, demands that Louis engage in more complex motor tasks, solve problems, and finally verbalize to the teacher were steadily but very gradually introduced.

In the case of Mark, whose assessment according to the developmental sequence is seen in Figure IV-13, the teacher planned his program as follows:

1. A review of Mark's developmental sequence form revealed problems primarily at the order and social levels, although he appeared to have moderate difficulties with retention and involvement with learning tasks. Selection of a task would have to take into consideration Mark's serious control and social behavior problems. Several rewards appeared feasible to provide this boy with in the classroom, including tangible rewards, social attention, and multisensory experience. Structure would have to be a most important consideration, for the developmental sequence reflects Mark's inability to tolerate controls imposed by others and his attempts to set his own limits. As can be seen, Mark's behavior made it necessary for him to be excluded from class a number of times during the assessment period. This was considered a negative consequence for his unacceptable behavior (e.g., physical and verbal abuse) rather than punishment. It was accomplished in a matter-of-fact manner with no scolding or threatening on the part of the teacher. Mark was told that "only students can remain in the classroom" and when it appeared he was unable to meet the minimum expectations for a student he would have to leave. When he returned, no grudges were held by the principal or teacher. He was readily accepted back into the class and nothing more said about the episode. In Mark's case such negative consequences were effective in getting him to modify his behavior, and he was only sent home once during the last six weeks of the assessment period. The "student role" and use of negative consequences following unacceptable behavior will be further discussed in Chapter VII.
2. The order level appeared most basic to Mark's problems and the teacher decided to set firm limits regarding verbal and physical abuse in the classroom, provide simple and clearcut expectations and directions, and reduce academic demands to a minimum in an effort to limit conflict in the classroom. The reward selected for Mark was at the exploratory level, and he was given time to build a ship model in hopes he might eventually be able to develop more appropriate social relationships with his classmates in connection with this project.
3. In all of the work given Mark, it was the order component that was primarily stressed. Establishment of a routine, direction following, and respect for the rights of others took precedence over assignments that might more fully have taken advantage of his intellectual and academic potential.

4. The teacher moved slowly enough with Mark to make dropping back generally unnecessary, although from time to time academic demands had to be modified in favor of more rewarding exploratory activities.

5. The gradual and systematic increase in demands made on Mark in the classroom is clearly illustrated in the teacher's comments during the three assessment periods covered by the developmental sequence form.

This chapter has attempted to move assessment of emotionally disturbed children a step closer to actual classroom practice. The limitations of medical, neurological, social work, and psychological evaluations for direct application were briefly considered and the importance of describing emotionally disturbed children in terms of their educational disabilities stressed. The 21 numbered boxes used as the basis for task assessment each contain a description of one or more of the major maladaptive behaviors contributing to a child's dysfunction at six levels of the developmental sequence. The seven lettered reward boxes describe the child on the basis of his responsiveness to rewarding consequences in the classroom. Implications for structure appear as plus and minus signs over the seven goal levels.

The overall goal is to offer the teacher a device to describe emotionally disturbed children with reference to behavior which has direct relevance to the operations of an educational program. The accompanying Inventory further defines each maladaptive behavior in terms of severity. The statement made in the last paragraph, that the attempt of this procedure is to move a "step closer," bears repeating at this point. It would be satisfying to report that all problems of semantic confusion had been solved by this approach and that assessment of emotionally disturbed children by means of the developmental sequence had closed once and for all the gap between diagnosis and classroom practice.

As inviting as such a sweeping claim may be, the author is aware that understanding and translation of the behavioral characteristics on the developmental sequence into specific courses of action will cause some teachers difficulty and that this will result in the sequence's being useful to varying degrees. In addition, the assessment procedures described in this section have not been subjected to extensive inter-rater reliability studies and as such must be considered "working" hypotheses.

Over a two-year period of actual use in hospital and public school classrooms, however, assessment using the developmental sequence has moved many teachers "a step"—often a sizable one—closer to devel-

oping a sounder and more effective educational program for emotionally disturbed children. Beginning with the next chapter the remainder
of this text will be devoted to helping the teacher translate assessments
according to the developmental sequence of educational goals into such
educational programs.

2 Specific Classroom Practices

V ATTENTION LEVEL

The preceding chapters have introduced the developmental strategy which embodies a developmental sequence of educational goals and the methodology of the learning triangle. This strategy attempts to get emotionally disturbed children ready for school while they are actually there and suggestions for assessing the learning deficits of such children were presented in the last chapter.

This chapter begins a second section in the text which is devoted to specific classroom practices and elaboration of the three sides of the learning triangle, particularly the side concerned with a "suitable educational task." Once the teacher has assessed the child according to the developmental sequence and has located his educational goal deficiencies the selection of specific tasks to aid in remedying these deficiencies is of major concern. In addition, determining the type of rewards and the degree of structure to insure accomplishment of the task by the child is important.

We turn now to consideration of tasks to help the child achieve the goal of paying attention. First general characteristics of these tasks will be considered, and second specific examples will be given. Finally rewards and structure will be discussed.

Task characteristics which are useful in getting the emotionally disturbed child to pay attention in learning fall into at least four categories:

1. Removal of distracting stimuli.
2. Presentation of small, discrete units of work.
3. Heightening the vividness and impact of stimuli.
4. Use of concrete, rather than abstract, tasks.

117

Some emotionally disturbed children may be easily distracted in classrooms where a high degree of visual and auditory stimulation is produced by the movement and noise level of other students, assignments are complex, and teacher demands frequently shift. Strauss (1947) and Cruickshank (1961) recommend careful control of distracting stimuli for brain-injured and hyperactive children as an aid to getting them to pay attention for longer periods of time.

Just how far the teacher should go to reduce such stimuli is debatable, particularly with emotionally disturbed children who may be given to more fantasy and self-stimulation when placed in drab, sterile surroundings. But assisting disturbed children in paying attention to specific tasks may well involve clearing their desk of clutter, providing a quiet work area when needed, and presenting them with clearly defined units of work.

Vague, open-ended assignments often overwhelm the emotionally disturbed child, who cannot focus his attention on a whole page of problems at one time. For some children, presentation of a single problem on a page may be necessary so that "the end is in sight." For others, pages may have to be torn out of workbooks one by one, rather than assigning the entire book and expecting the child to work systematically through it.

Teaching machines and programed instructional materials are often very useful with inattentive children. Single units of work are presented frame by frame, and no long-range demands are made for accomplishment. Provision for immediate knowledge of results and a gradual increase in level of difficulty are also advantages offered by programed instruction. Reading materials such as the Sullivan program (1966) and the Science Research Associates (SRA) Reading for Understanding Series (Thurstone, 1958) have proven successful with emotionally disturbed children who have short attention spans.

Increase in the vividness and impact of instructional materials is generally seen as an aid to increasing attention and retention. Riggs (1956) investigated the learning of nouns associated with violence and found increasing configural emphasis of these words during learning trials (from arsenic to arsenic to arsenic!) increased the efficiency of recall.

Bousfield (1957) has presented similar evidence with respect to the addition of pictures to stimulus words. He observed that words accompanied by descriptive uncolored pictures were recalled more efficiently than words presented alone and that words accompanied by descriptive colored pictures were recalled best of all. This should come as no surprise to educators because of the common practice of enhancing the content of basal readers with colored illustrations. A great number of such illustrations with their prominent page after page displays, however, may actually provide a source of distraction for children with learning problems. This possibility has been taken into consideration in the construction of at least one remedial reading series (Berres, Coleman, Briscoe, and Hewett, 1958).

The author (Hewett, 1961) found that the nature of the pictorial context within which words appear had a highly significant effect upon rate of learning and immediate recall. Underachieving adolescent boys learned a phrase such as "swallow this gradually" far more efficiently when it was accompanied by a picture of a bottle of poison complete with skull and crossbones as compared to a picture of a tempting ice cream soda. Several examples of the phrase-picture combinations used in this study are found in Figure V-1.* In each case, the violent, more vivid pictorial context enhanced learning rate and immediate recall.

With many emotionally disturbed children, concrete experiences are superior to assignments which rely on abstract symbols and a high degree of verbal instruction by the teacher. Early learning in school is accompanied by many concrete experiences in language and number development. By the upper elementary grades, however, children are expected to function on a much more symbolic level through reading, discussion, and listening. The emotionally disturbed child may find it difficult to pay attention when primarily presented with symbolic assignments, and teachers should investigate the use of concrete aids normally emphasized only in the primary grades.

The author (Hewett, 1964) undertook a two-year reading and writing program with Jimmy, a twelve-year-old, nonverbal, autistic boy who had failed to profit from a series of earlier attempts to teach him, largely because he never paid attention to either teacher or tasks. Jimmy's attention was initially gained through the use of a tangible reward (e.g., candy gumdrop) and maintained through a systematic program which moved from concrete to symbolic tasks. The use of tangible rewards in initiating learning will be discussed in a later section of this chapter.

In the process of learning to read and write, Jimmy was first expected to hand the teacher three objects, differentiated by shape and color—a red ball, yellow box, and blue cross. These objects were placed on a table, first one at a time, then paired, and later all together. Jimmy's task was to pick up the object called for by the teacher.

The next step was to get Jimmy to copy the teacher's two-dimen-

---

* Drawings in Figure V-1 by Vladamir James.

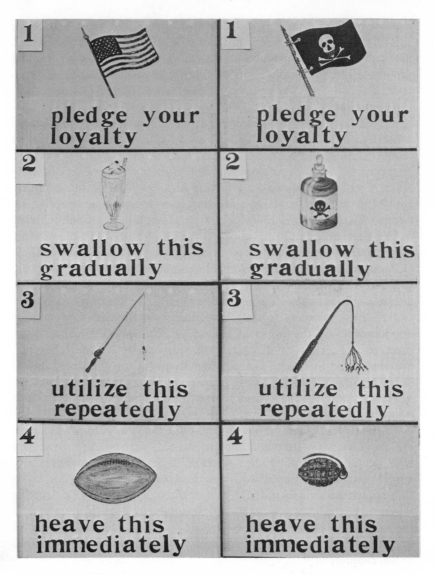

FIGURE V-1. Phrase-picture combinations (Hewett, 1961).

sional drawing of a ball, box, or cross and then draw these objects on verbal command. During this stage, the concrete objects were also present.

Once this copying task was mastered, colored pictures of the objects were introduced, along with their concrete counterparts, and Jimmy had to pick up the pictures according to the teacher's instructions.

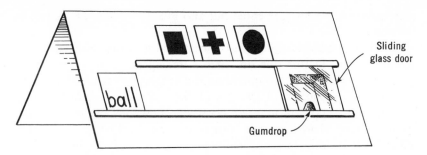

FIGURE V-2. Word board used in reading program with Jimmy.

Finally, these colored pictures were presented alone, and word cards matched with them. The word board shown in Figure V-2 was used in the reading program.

First, the picture of the ball would be placed on the upper rail alone with the word card "ball" at the far left on the bottom rail. Jimmy's task was to slide the word card directly underneath the picture. Next, two picture cards were placed on the upper rail and Jimmy had to discriminate between them when he slid the word card "ball" into place. Finally three picture cards were placed on the upper rail and Jimmy had to correctly match word and picture. All words taught Jimmy were introduced in this way, first with word and picture alone, then with two and later three picture cards placed on the top rail to foster visual discrimination. The position of the picture cards was regularly changed to prevent Jimmy's responding on the basis of card placement alone. Following each correct matching, the glass door at the far right of the board would be slid open by the teacher and a candy gumdrop which had been in plain sight all the time was made available to Jimmy. The door was then closed and another gumdrop placed in the box behind it through an opening under the word board.

From this introduction of the relationship of word symbols to objects, Jimmy went on to learn and label many objects in his environment, to master the alphabet, and later to write simple phrases indicating his needs ("I want candy," "I want school," etc.). The transition from concrete to symbolic learning in Jimmy's program utilized the shaping procedures or "thimbleful" approach discussed earlier in relation to Peter and the rabbit and the psychotic patients in the study by Ayllon and Haughton.

Teachers of emotionally disturbed children should be aware that the words they use in the classroom may be far removed from the understanding level of their students. Frequent use of concrete illustrations in teaching may increase not only the probability of the child's understanding what is being presented but also greatly increase his degree of attention.

The developmental sequence of educational goals has evolved over a period of years. During this time it has undergone continual modification, largely because of the questions and suggestions provided by institutional and public school teachers of the emotionally disturbed who have tried to apply it in their classroom programs. Many of these teachers have shared specific procedures and activities they have utilized successfully to assist children at each level of the developmental sequence. In the following section on attention level tasks and in similar sections throughout the next several chapters, the author will present some of their suggestions, as well as those he has utilized in teaching emotionally disturbed children. These suggestions will be organized with reference to the descriptive statements found in the individual boxes on each level of the developmental sequence (Figure IV-8 in Chapter IV) and are only examples of the many types of activities teachers can adapt.

ATTENTION LEVEL TASKS

1. Child Does Not Pay Attention to Learning Tasks

A useful device for preparing the child for paying attention in learning is the tachistoscope. Tachistoscopes are available as overhead projectors for group presentation and as individual units. They provide controlled exposures of geometric designs, pictures, digits, words, and phrases which may vary from a full second to 1/100 of a second. The simplest targets are line drawings of familiar objects which the child is asked to recognize as they are flashed before him for a fraction of a second. Later, these objects may be shown in an incomplete form (e.g., table without a leg, clock without hands) and the child given the task of locating the missing part. Various symbols may be flashed in pairs, with the child expected to determine if the two symbols are the same ($\triangle$ $\square$), facing the same direction ($\_|\_$), or the same size (o O).

Digits varying in length from three to ten numbers are conventionally used as targets on tachistoscopes to foster widening of eye span and accuracy of visual perception. Words and phrases can also be flashed, although these defeat the purpose of the attention level if reading is difficult for the child.

If a tachistoscope is not available, a substitute activity used successfully by Jensen (1966) with children with attention problems may be prepared with numbers and words as follows:

687	786	867	687
495	459	495	549
821	821	812	182
saw	was	saw	aws
girl	gril	gilr	girl
smile	smile	simle	smeli

The child is instructed to look at the number or word in the left-hand column and then cross out the number or word in the right-hand columns which is identical. Sheets of these tests can be mimeographed and then inserted in plastic covers. The child can use a black crayola to make his marks, which can be wiped off following use. In actual practice, the sheets might contain a series of three-digit numbers followed by a series of longer digits and words. The same sheet may be used several times with a given child and a record kept of the time it takes for him to complete it, as well as the number of errors he makes. Self-timing and competition with one's own record in activities such as this are often appealing to children who balk at time pressure for academic accomplishments.

"What's missing?" work sheets and games which present the child with incomplete drawings of animals, people, and objects such as cars and trains are also useful in getting the child to pay attention, identify the missing part, and possibly draw it in himself.

A flashlight which has been extended by a roll of cardboard tubing to provide a sharp, circular area of light is useful to get young children to attend to objects in the classroom. The lights in the room are turned off and the teacher flashes the light around the room, stopping at various places (e.g., the clock, flag, pictures) and the children are asked to identify the objects aloud.

Older children and adolescents can be encouraged to pay attention to directions given by the teacher when these are prerecorded on tape and imbedded in a popular musical sequence. The music starts playing and at various times the volume diminishes and the teacher's directions are given (e.g., "Take out your math books"). Later directions, such as specific page references to individual students, may also be given. This approach has been effective in getting children to settle down and get to work the first thing in the morning or after recess.

2. Child Prefers Fantasy to Reality

Heightening of vividness and impact in teaching and use of concrete multisensory experiences are helpful in getting the emotionally disturbed child who engages in a great deal of fantasy to pay attention to reality. In fact all of the exploratory activities to be discussed in Chapter VIII provide strong reality emphasis.

While for normal children, and some mildly disturbed students, assignments emphasizing fantasy are highly motivating, these should be avoided with children who have difficulty discriminating what is unreal from what is real. In story-writing activities teachers may be successful stimulating normal children's creative thinking by asking them to finish such sentences as "If I were on the moon and a two-headed green monster came after me I would—" and then write a story. For children preoccupied with fantasy, however, story topics should focus on the here and now and might include, "If I were going on a camping trip the five most important things I would need to take with me would be—." Jacobson and Faegre (1959) have discussed the usefulness of "neutralizing" subject matter used with emotionally disturbed children in order to limit conflictual and distracting fantasies.

Extremely disoriented and delusional adolescent students have been successfully engaged in simple labeling and coloring activities with drawings of fish and cars. First assignments involve copying a single label for an entire drawing, and then gradually spaces are drawn by the teacher alongside individual parts. At this point the student is directed to label each part with the aid of reference materials. Map copying, coloring, and labeling also provide a type of activity where attention can be directed toward specific reality tasks.

Younger children enjoy sorting actual objects into categories of "real" and "not real." Objects including flying horses and space creatures may be mixed in with toy cars and furniture and a child asked to sort them out.

Activities such as having the child shut his eyes and try to describe as many objects in the room as he can in terms of their location, size, color, and use also helps develop an awareness of the real environment.

3. Child Engages in Repetitive Behavior which Interferes with Learning

The child who leans back in his chair, rocks back and forth, drums his fingers on his desk, makes constant trips to the bathroom, pencil sharpener, or nurse's office, starts his work over and over because the paper is smudged or he has made a mistake often fails to pay attention in learning because of constant interference.

Problems of pencil sharpening may be quickly resolved by providing a constant source of sharpened pencils for exchange, and chair tipping may be prevented by bolting the chair and desk to the floor. Such anticipatory actions on the teacher's part may reduce the frequency of interfering behaviors, but others are more difficult to eliminate. Constant trips to the bathroom and drinking fountain by some emotionally disturbed children have been controlled by use of a pass system. The child is given a number of passes to keep at his desk. Each time he needs to go to the bathroom he stops by the teacher's desk and deposits a pass. The number of passes initially given the child may be equal to the number of trips he usually makes, and over a period of time he may be given fewer and fewer passes with the understanding that he can only go to the bathroom or drinking fountain the number of times equal to the number of passes which he has. It is obvious that this procedure is not appropriate to use unless the teacher is certain there is no organic basis for the child's bathroom or drinking fountain needs.

The study by Zimmerman and Zimmerman (1962) cited earlier demonstrated how ignoring a child's inappropriate behavior when it appears directed toward getting teacher attention can cause it to dramatically diminish. A boy who constantly misspelled his spelling words and consequently obtained a great deal of teacher time and attention became a much more accurate speller when the teacher turned from him when he made errors and lavished praise and attention on him for correct spelling. Simply not rewarding the child when his behavior is inappropriate may cause the frequency of such behavior to markedly diminish.

An emotionally disturbed second grader who almost always tore up his work after encountering the least bit of frustration was effectively helped by his teacher to reduce and finally eliminate this behavior. A stuffed toy tiger which sat on the teacher's desk was a great favorite of the children in the class. Whenever the teacher observed this boy appropriately starting an assignment, she would place the tiger on his desk without saying a word. When he "blew up" the tiger was removed with nothing said. In a short while the boy "got the idea" that his behavior while working controlled the presence or absence of the tiger and without any verbal instruction his behavior greatly improved.

The principle of providing the child with a reward at the moment his behavior approximates the teacher's expectation is another example of the use of methodology included in the behavior modification strategy. Rather than wait for the child to engage in inappropriate, interfering behavior, the teacher moves in and rewards him during the time he is appropriately behaving and often does not have to verbalize the reason. The child soon learns that he controls the consequences provided in the classroom. It is important, initially, to provide such a "surprise" reward systematically and frequently, and the use of this technique will be discussed several times in the text.

4. Child's Beliefs and Interests are Inappropriate

Emotionally disturbed children may develop very distorted beliefs about themselves, bodily functions, and their environment. Some of these, such as the delusion sometimes found among female adolescents with anorexia nervosa (refusal to eat despite severe weight loss) that eating will cause pregnancy, are inappropriate to directly deal with in the classroom and are more properly taken up in psychotherapy. Classroom activities can, however, reinforce appropriate interests and beliefs.

An NPI School teacher assigned one female adolescent suffering from anorexia nervosa the responsibility of caring for a vegetable garden in a large window box. In addition, a study of the type of vegetables that would best grow, chemical additives which would promote growth, and the nourishment properties of the vegetables was encouraged. While this did not cure her, the classroom program supported the therapist's efforts to help this girl develop more accurate beliefs about food, eating, growth, and nourishment.

Other emotionally disturbed children may only want to attend to rather bizarre subjects and activities. The author has worked with boys who were fascinated with such topics as tattooing, instruments of torture, and bodily mutilation. Whatever the origin and meaning of these preoccupations, when they precluded the child's paying attention to more varied subject matter, they constituted a serious problem.

The author has known teachers who indulged such children in their bizarre interests by providing reading material and emphasizing research and projects in these areas, on the pretext that a valuable source of motivation for increasing reading and written language skills was available. However, before following such a course, the teacher should weigh the risks and consequences with the individual child very carefully. Here is an example of the clinical judgment necessary when using the developmental strategy. If increased reading and writing performance is the sole objective, one might assume any means would be appropriate to attain these mastery goals. In such cases, however, the child's development of truly adaptive interests and skills on lower levels of the developmental sequence is of greater importance.

A more constructive approach and one that holds promise for assisting the child in paying attention to more useful subject matter is to gradually shape his interests. A sixteen-year-old boy fixated on tattooing was led into a study of Oriental art, a boy who had acquired a vast amount of knowledge regarding torture devices was encouraged to study social problems of medieval times, and a third boy who professed interest in body mutilation was provided a basic program of human physiology.

With regard to the study of physiology and biology in classrooms of emotionally disturbed children the question often arises as to whether dissecting animal specimens is an appropriate activity. No absolute policy can be stated, for the author has seen both positive and negative results from such an activity. In a rural community where children were intimately acquainted with animal reproduction and the slaughter of animals for food, the dissection of a stillborn calf in school was seen as a valuable learning experience by a teacher of emotionally disturbed children. In a city school setting for the emotionally disturbed, the class dissection of a frog was highly upsetting to several children and had very negative consequences. Again, the importance of teacher judgment in assessing the child's readiness for such an activity cannot be overemphasized.

5. Child Does Not Pay Attention to the Teacher

Getting emotionally disturbed children to look at the teacher and pay attention to verbal direction in a classroom is often a difficult task. Teachers have found speaking softly and using simple terms and phrases often increases the degree of attention they can elicit from their children. Excessive verbalization and the use of vague or complex terminology probably constitutes one of the more common errors made by teachers of emotionally disturbed children.

A one-to-one teaching situation, while unrealistic in many classrooms, is valuable in helping the child pay attention to the teacher, and having the same teacher regularly in the classroom is also a useful aid.

Younger children have increased their degree of visual and auditory attention to the teacher through participation in various games and activities. One teacher used a colored stick which had been established as the "attention wand." Whenever she used it to point to an object in the room or written work on the blackboard the children were expected to give their full attention.

An "attention mask" may be useful in getting severely disturbed or very young children to establish eye contact with the teacher. The teacher puts on a rectangular mask cut from construction paper which provides a one-inch wide frame around her eyes. The children may also be given similar masks to put on. While teacher and pupils are wearing these "attention masks" the task is for the child to look directly at the teacher's face while the teacher looks directly at each of them in turn. Candy, or other tangible rewards may be distributed to those children looking at the teacher for periods of ten seconds or more.

Teachers have also successfully used a "drum echo" procedure which requires the child to tap out the same number of beats on a drum at his desk which the teacher taps out on a drum at the front of the room.

Young children who do not pay attention to teacher direction may initially be reached with a hand puppet which the teacher controls and which "speaks" to the child, giving him his assignment. The teacher may also pantomime group instructions with no verbal explanation and obtain more attention from the class.

Older elementary-aged children can be given mirrors at their desks which they hold up in front of them to view the teacher standing in the back of the room. The teacher displays various familiar objects which they must identify during this unique teacher attention activity.

Rolled paper telescopes may also be given students with instructions to keep the teacher in view when directions are being given.

Having the teacher draw objects on the blackboard, work simple arithmetic problems, or spell basic words and make obvious errors in the process which the children must "catch" also have been found to elicit teacher attention from children with problems in this area.

One teacher of adolescents found that kicking over the wastebasket and sending it noisily across the floor quickly drew his class to attention during times when it was difficult to get them to settle down. He also found dropping coins one at a time in a jar on his desk was effective in getting his class to pay attention since few individuals fail to respond to the sound of clinking money.

Another teacher used a loud ticking clock for the same purpose. When she wanted to get the attention of her students she started the clock ticking and waited quietly until all eyes were on her desk.

6. Child Does Not Profit from Instruction

The value of removing distraction, heightening impact of teaching materials, presenting small units of work, and emphasizing concrete experiences is obvious in helping emotionally disturbed children retain what is presented in the classroom. It also is relevant to assisting children with problems of mental retardation and sensory and neurological impairment which often restrict attention and retention.

Task repetition aids children with retention problems, but such repetitions must be varied in order to maintain the child's interest. Frequent checks for recall also may have to be made, rather than relying on weekly or monthly tests. Teachers of emotionally disturbed children who observe a given child's failure to grasp a concept or retain a fact or process must quickly move back and review previous material. This technique is one of the advantages of programed instruction on teaching machines where "branching" from the regular program is often provided to give slower learners a chance to "brush up" before continuing on.

An activity in the classroom which has been found to appeal to emotionally disturbed children with attention problems is the familiar "memory for objects" game. The teacher exposes a picture of various items, or an actual assortment of objects on a tray, for a brief period of time and the children are instructed to try to remember as many items shown as possible. For younger children, such an activity may use animals and toys, but for adolescents car parts, Army, Navy, and Marine insignia, or radio and television components may be utilized. Variations include the teacher removing an object behind a screen and then asking the children to identify what is missing.

An inventive teacher of adolescents who was concerned with their paying attention and recalling events they had seen arranged several impromptu "incidents," in which strangers would walk into the room, often carrying unusual items, (e.g., fruit, hardware, etc.) and briefly talk to the teacher. The teacher would instruct the class to keep their eyes on the front of the room while the stranger was there and when he left various questions regarding his age, size, and the objects he was carrying would be asked.

A variation on the old "shell game" has proven useful with emotionally disturbed children who will not pay attention or who have difficulty retaining information. The teacher hides a piece of candy or a penny under a paper cup which is one of three in front of the child. As the cups are interchanged a varying number of times, the child is instructed to watch carefully. After the teacher stops the child is to point to the cup covering the desired object, and if he chooses correctly, it is his to keep. For children with extreme attention and retention problems the cups may be different colors. The desired object is then always put under the cup of a specific color, and after the interchange, the child has the color cue to aid him in his selection.

While some may comment at this point, "these are hardly *educational* tasks" the author must disagree and continue his plea for flexible, creative, innovative additions to classrooms where emotionally disturbed children must be helped to get ready for school while they are in school.

ATTENTION LEVEL REWARDS

Box a on the composite developmental sequence shown in Figure IV-8 alluded to the most basic reward possible for use with children in school —a tangible reward. Although certainly not necessary for enlisting many emotionally disturbed children's participation in learning and not effective in reaching some (e.g., the case of Louis) the fact remains that a tangible piece of candy, a coin, or desired toy is both the most primitive and often the most powerful reward that can be offered. For this reason tangible rewards cannot be overlooked in special education.

Educators have a well-known aversion toward "extrinsic" motivators, and some may consider use of such rewards an unwholesome compromise with basic educational values. Even though most children attending school can be reached using the traditional rewards of grades, task accomplishment, and social praise, educators cannot afford to neglect the small percentage, including many children labeled as emotionally disturbed who do not obtain or who are not gratified by these traditional rewards.

Levine and Simmons (1962) have investigated the relative effectiveness of food and social praise as rewards for emotionally disturbed boys who were given the task of dropping marbles into a box. The food reward alone, in this case peanuts, proved superior to social praise alone or social praise in addition to peanuts in maintaining both response rate and duration of performance.

Ferster and DeMeyer (1962) investigated the performance of several autistic children who could obtain tokens by pressing a bar in an experimental room. Once they had obtained these tokens they were given free choice in "spending" them in various devices which would deliver the use of a pinball machine, a glimpse of a pigeon and trained monkey, activation of a color kaleidoscope, television viewing, music, access to an electric train, candy, trinkets, food, and projected color slides. For the two experimental subjects the tangible rewards of candy, trinkets, and food were selected far more frequently than any of the others.

While these studies included a limited number of subjects and somewhat extreme problems not usually found in the classroom, they illustrate the effectiveness of primary or tangible rewards in controlling the emotionally disturbed child's behavior. Jimmy, the autistic boy discussed earlier in this chapter, was viewed as an inaccessible learner because he would not attend to either teacher or task for even brief periods of time. In the initial stage of the reading and writing program designed for him the teacher got him to sit down in a chair and to tolerate brief periods of attention by controlled provision of candy gumdrops. This reward was provided Jimmy on the word board illustrated in Figure V-2 following his fulfillment of simple demands for attention such as eye contact with teacher or task. The candy, while in sight all of the time, was only provided for him when the teacher slid the glass door open and allowed him to take it out of the box. Getting Jimmy to pay attention to a task and the teacher provided the cornerstone upon which the subsequent program of reading and written language was based.

The Ferster and DeMeyer study illustrated the use of token rewards which in and of themselves have little value but which can be exchanged for food and other rewards. Tokens are a form of tangible rewards and have had their counterpart in classrooms for years in the form of gold stars, although the latter normally constituted the end reward itself.

Staats, Staats, Schutz, and Wolf (1962) observed that the continued use of trinkets, food, and small toys was ineffective for holding children at a reading task for any considerable length of time because of satiation. Similar observations have been reported by Long, Hammack, May, and Campbell (1958). In a later study Staats, Minke, Finley, Wolf, and Brooks (1964) found token rewards (marbles which could be later "spent" for toys, etc.) effective for maintaining the performance of four-year-olds in a reading task.

Birnbrauer and Lawler (1964) found token rewards (poker chips) successful in replacing actual candy units in the development of controlled behavior and academic skills with institutionalized retarded children.

Hewett, Mayhew, and Rabb (1967) utilized candy rewards in a reading program with mentally retarded, neurologically impaired, and severely emotionally disturbed children, and while the satiation effect reported by others was not observed, except with two autistic children, token rewards in the form of check marks on a card which could later be converted to candy and trinkets were equally effective.

Classroom use of check-mark token rewards for behavior in academic accomplishment has been employed by the author (Hewett, 1966) in a pilot project in the Tulare County Schools in California. A more systematic use of check marks was employed in a demonstration project in the Santa Monica Unified School District and a detailed explanation of this appears in Chapters X–XII. Birnbrauer, Bijou,

Wolf, and Kidder (1965) have also described the use of check marks as token rewards with retardates.

Quay (1966) has used light flashes as token rewards for appropriate attention behavior with emotionally disturbed children. Candy units were later provided as an exchange for the number of light flashes occurring during a period of time in the classroom.

In this section the intent has been to establish the premise that many emotionally disturbed children do not pay attention because there is nothing rewarding in the act of attending for them. Just as attention is the most basic of all learning competencies, so tangible motivators constitute the most basic of all rewards. A myth sometimes promulgated by educators is that use of tangible rewards dooms the child to long-term dependence on them. In the author's experience nothing could be further from the truth. During some 15 years of work with severely disturbed children there has never been a case where rewards of task involvement and completion, sensory experience, social praise, and knowledge of results did not eventually become major sources of learning gratification.

ATTENTION LEVEL STRUCTURE

Imposing some degree of structure or attaching some strings to tasks given the child has been presented as essential in helping him learn. A purely self-demand educational program in which the child makes all the decisions regarding what, when, where, how, and how well is not likely to teach anything efficiently or well.

The shaping of behavior through reducing structure to a "thimble-ful" in order to establish a starting point and then gradually but systematically increasing demands is basic to the behavior modification strategy and the educational methodology presented in this text. It has been illustrated in the cases of Louis and Peter and the work of Ayllon and Haughton.

At the attention level the goal is to establish contact with the child and initiate learning. In order to accomplish such a goal it may be that few quantitative or qualitative strings can be attached. Louis was given a program on the attention, response, order, and exploratory levels simultaneously. The structure imposed on him dictated the "what," "where," and "how," but not "when" or "how well." The same apparatus used with Louis was later used with an immobilized schizophrenic adolescent in the hospital ward. In this boy's case it was not deemed appropriate to impose the "where" on him so rather than expecting him to come to the classroom the teacher set up lever box, projector, and screen by his bed and only expected him to conform to a specific task ("what" and "how").

Another NPI School student was allowed to come to school any time during the day when he wished. A teaching machine with several instructional programs was available in a separate room where he could work "when" he pleased, learning "what" he pleased as long as he pleased.

In public school classrooms some hyperactive and inattentive children may be initially allowed to freely change their activity and only held to the structure of work area ("where") and nondisruptive behavior ("how"). This initial step in making contact with such children is analogous to the beginning stages of the program designed to help Peter overcome his aversive reaction toward the rabbit. In that example, Peter was only expected to stay in the room ("where") and maintain appropriate behavior in his high chair ("how").

Severely autistic children are sometimes only introduced to learning with the two strings of "when" and "where" attached. The child may be allowed to do whatever he pleases in a classroom or playroom and receive a continual reward of candy or food just for tolerating the surroundings. At this level the distinction between education and psychotherapy is less than at any other point on the developmental sequence.

As can be seen from these examples some degree of structure was maintained, and rewards which were available were contingent on the child's ability to function within this structure. It should also be apparent that the reward side of the learning triangle was often emphasized at the expense of the type of task presented or the criteria for successful accomplishment.

It is not possible to present specific rules for establishing the appropriate degree of structure with every child. In actual practice this may have to be done on a trial and error basis. The NPI School student who was allowed complete freedom in choosing the time of day to work with a teaching machine made much faster progress when limits of time ("when") were imposed and he only had access to the reading program during a specific period each day. The other student who was worked with in his hospital room with the same apparatus used with Louis was initially held for limits of work area ("where") and was brought into the classroom. It was soon apparent that this was an inappropriate demand to make on him so a change in the structure was made and the demand of "where" withdrawn.

In this chapter examples of tasks which lend themselves to assisting children attain the goal of paying attention in learning have been presented. Since this level is the most fundamental on the developmental sequence, rewards used to foster attention may have to be most basic in nature, and the use of tangible rewards has been discussed. Structure is conceived of as necessary at this level but subject to considerable flexibility. In general, leverage in learning is best provided through emphasis on rewards rather than structure.

VI RESPONSE LEVEL

It will readily become apparent that the task characteristics discussed at the attention level are equally applicable at the response level. Reducing distraction, heightening vividness, presentation of limited assignments, and emphasis on concrete, rather than abstract, approaches increase the probability of the emotionally disturbed child doing something, as well as noticing something in learning. Therefore, some of the examples to follow will overlap with those presented earlier. Actually this overlap will exist throughout the discussion of the first four levels of the developmental sequence, and aspects of these levels will apply cumulatively. After a discussion of general response level task characteristics, specific examples will be presented, followed by reward and structure considerations.

Two task characteristics deserve particular emphasis at the response level:

1. Reduction of criteria for correctness.
2. Guaranteeing the child success in learning.

One of the most commonly found differences between classes for children with emotional and learning problems and regular classes is the absence of a traditional letter grading system in the former. If an individualized educational program is being undertaken with the child, then the grade he earns should reflect his individual progress rather than grade level expectations appropriate for his chronological age. As a result children in special classes are often graded merely as making "satisfactory" or "unsatisfactory" progress in relation to their individual learning problems.

While removal of the pressure of grades is often a source of relief for many emotionally disturbed children, it can create problems for others. Some consider school without grades not school at all and become frustrated and unhappy when each unit of work they accomplish is not graded in a conventional manner. Often this seems related to the child's awareness of the parents' academic aspiration level for him. The teacher therefore is faced with a dilemma: no grade at all and the child is unhappy, a letter grade truly reflecting his accomplishments according to chronological grade level expectation may be a devaluating "F" for failure, a complimentary "A" given on the basis of individual effort and progress may set up a false standard of accomplishment that will be entirely unrealistic when the child returns to a regular classroom.

Despite such problems with emotionally disturbed children and with their parents who also may demand a report card with "genuine grades," the author has found that "satisfactory—needs to improve" grading is the most successful. Its use often entails individual conferences for both the child and his parents in order to explain the purpose of the special classroom—helping the child "catch up" as quickly as possible. The teacher points out that since each child in the classroom has unique learning problems and is progressing at an individual rate, he really represents a separate class by himself. Therefore, traditional grades are meaningless. In actual practice most emotionally disturbed children who have failed in regular classrooms are helped to respond and to become involved in learning by the removal of grades, although some type of progress reporting is important.

Public school teachers who have two or three children with emotional problems in their regular classroom are often forced to assign these children letter grades based on group and grade level expectations. The futility of this practice is seen in the report card of David, a grossly psychotic boy of 11, who sat in a regular classroom in a compliant and passive manner, seldom interacting with the teacher or the other children and who daydreamed his way through most of the fifth grade. An actual copy of David's card is seen in Figure VI-1. Although he was rated as doing very poorly in most academic subjects the teacher awarded him an "A" for behavior. It can be argued that David really should have been given an "F" for behavior and more individualized grades for academic accomplishments, but in the framework of a traditional grading system the teacher had little choice. The emphasis on compliancy and passivity even to the obviously unhealthy degree seen in this case is often found in public school classrooms and is reflected in David's "A" for behavior.

In addition to removal of letter grades teachers wishing to encourage

A - Markedly Above Average
B - Above Average   D - Below Average
C - Average   F - Markedly Below Average

In the subheadings, a check (✓) indicates an area where improvement is needed.

PUPIL'S NAME _David F._

	First Quarter	Second Quarter	Third Quarter	Fourth Quarter
READING *read during level group*				A-
Interest				
Understanding				
Development of Skills				
ARITHMETIC				F
Number Skills				✓
Measurement				✓
Problem Solving				✓
ENGLISH				A-
Oral Expression				
Written Expression				
SPELLING				A-
Assigned Words				
Accuracy in Written Work				
HANDWRITING				C-
Neatness				
Legibility				
SOCIAL STUDIES (History, Geography) and SCIENCE				A-
Participation				✓
Use of Information				
ART				B
Participation				
Development of Skills				
MUSIC				C
Participation				✓
Development of Skills				
INSTRUMENTAL MUSIC				F
PHYSICAL EDUCATION				✓
Sportsmanship				
Participation				
Development of Skills				
Health Practices				

	First Quarter	Second Quarter	Third Quarter	Fourth Quarter
BEHAVIOR AND ATTITUDE				A
Self-control				
Cooperation				
Courtesy				
Dependability				
Respect for Propterty				
Respect for Rights of Others				
WORK AND STUDY HABITS				A
Initiative				
Listening Habits				
Response to Directions				
Use of Time				
Neatness				
Safety Practices				
Independent Work Habits				
Acceptance of Suggestions				

4/9 P.E. Will not participate in any games.

FIGURE VI-1. David's report card.

children to respond in learning can reduce emphasis on such skills as handwriting, mechanics of English, grammar, and spelling. For the child who does not respond in school, who is constricted, and who readily withdraws, the crucial task is to establish contact with him and start him functioning. For that reason getting the child to express himself in writing may be a highly significant event, although his writing is barely legible, his sentences run together, and his spelling is extremely poor. Allowing children to initially copy compositions or encouraging them to dictate stories aloud to the teacher who writes them down also promotes responding to written assignments.

The author has observed programs for mentally retarded and emotionally disturbed children that placed great emphasis on handwriting perfection. Long periods of tedious drill in making letter forms were imposed on the children in what seemed an activity designed to stifle responding and communication.

Guaranteeing the child's success in school may well be the theme of this text, and it is most important in initiating learning. While the ability to "profit from one's mistakes" may aid the individual at the higher levels of the developmental sequence, at the response level this is not the case. Bateman (1967) has commented on the possibility that some teachers may view an assignment that guarantees the child success and which rules out the possibility of errors as educational "cheating" because of a commonly held belief that some anxiety and frustration is a necessary part of the learning process. Without delving into whether or not this is so with normal children, it must be emphasized that the major concern of the response level is with children who are "standing still," not those engaged as "active participants" in learning. Therefore, guarantee of success is essential.

An intriguing and exciting approach for guaranteeing success is found in the work on "errorless training" pioneered by Terrace (1963) and by Moore and Goldiamond (1964). The latter authors presented normal preschool children with a difficult discrimination task involving matching triangles on the basis of degree of rotation. For example, a rotated triangle would be presented and then withdrawn. The child was then shown three triangles, only one of which matched the original sample. Most of the children could not correctly select the previously shown sample from the three rotated triangles. But by initially illuminating the correct choice with a light the child was "given the answer" and engaged in a sequence in which he made few if any errors. Gradually the illumination of the light under the correct choice was decreased and finally deleted, and it was found that the children could then discriminate accurately on the basis of degree of rotation alone.

Acker (1966) utilized the prompt of size difference in teaching color and form discrimination to young normal and autistic children. His subjects learned to respond to the "smaller" of two color plates or letter pairs and eventually to respond to color and letter form alone when the size differences were gradually eliminated. Learning under such errorless conditions was superior to that obtained during more conventional training when subjects were rewarded for making correct choices and nonrewarded for making errors.

Holland (1960) has pointed out that a basic goal of programed instruction is to preclude the individual's making errors by very gradually increasing the difficulty level of successive items which are presented.

The author has applied the principle of errorless training to the teaching of reading to autistic and other severely disturbed children (Hewett, Mayhew, and Rabb, 1967). A program was developed for use on a simple, manually operated teaching machine (Grolier Min/Max II), and in addition to prompts of color and geometric form the child was immediately rewarded for correct responses with a small bit of candy. Kate was an eleven-year-old autistic girl who was given the errorless training program at the NPI School because of her previous failures to learn by a more direct programed instructional approach.

The program designed for Kate and presented frame by frame on a teaching machine with confirmations of correct choices immediately appearing after her response was in three phases.[1] Phase I emphasized consistent discrimination of solid colors, solid forms, and later color and form outlines.

PHASE I: COLOR AND FORM

a) Color Only

F<small>IGURE</small> VI-2

---

[1] Figures and material in the following section copyright, The American Orthopsychiatric Association, Inc. Reproduced by permission. Mrs. Irene Kassorla served as teacher for Kate during the errorless training program.

Teacher: "Find the red box"

b) Solid Form Only

Figure VI-3

Teacher: "Find the red box"

c) Color Outline Only

(red)   (blue)

Figure VI-4

Teacher: "Find the red box"

d) Form Outline Only

(red)   (red)

Figure VI-5

Teacher: "Find the red box"

A similar series in which the discriminations centered around finding a blue ball was also used. Many repetitions of each item were presented and placement of correct choices alternated to control position effects.

Phase II presented the words "Tom" in the red box and "ride" in the blue ball and offered the color and form cues as aids in making the child's choices "errorless."

PHASE II: TWO WORDS WITH
COLOR AND FORM CUES

a) Matching

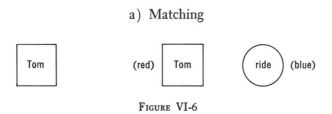

FIGURE VI-6

Teacher: (points to box on left) "The word in the box is 'Tom.' Find the word 'Tom' in the red box over here" (points to choices)

b) Directed Choice

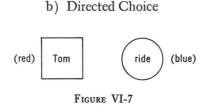

FIGURE VI-7

Teacher: "Find 'Tom' in the red box"

The same sequence was followed for matching and choosing "ride" in the blue ball.

This series was intended to introduce the word "Tom" in association with the red box and "ride" in the blue ball and the teacher's color and form cues were utilized to make it virtually impossible for Kate to fail and to initially relieve her of the responsibility of any actual word discrimination or retention skills. In addition Kate received continuous tangible reinforcement by means of tiny bits of chocolate placed in her mouth by the teacher following each correct response.

Phase III was the final stage in the errorless training program and involved gradual fading of the color and form cues used in Phase II.

PHASE III: FADING OF COLOR
AND FORM CUES

a)

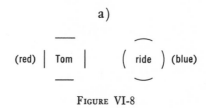

FIGURE VI-8

Teacher: "Find 'Tom' in the red box"

b)

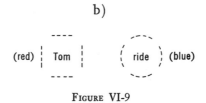

FIGURE VI-9

Teacher: "Find 'Tom' in the red box"

c)

Tom   ride

Teacher: "Find 'Tom.' "

The actual program also used the matching items and included presentation of "ride" and the blue ball.

Kate readily responded to the color and form errorless training although she took almost two months to achieve consistent functioning on a 75 per cent correct response level. While during the reading program attempted earlier she had regressed and been inattentive she now cooperated well and appeared to thoroughly enjoy her guaranteed successes. Figure VI-10 Section A shows Kate's correct response rate during the color and form training in Phase I. Section B of Figure VI-10 reports her rate during Phases II and III and illustrates her consist-

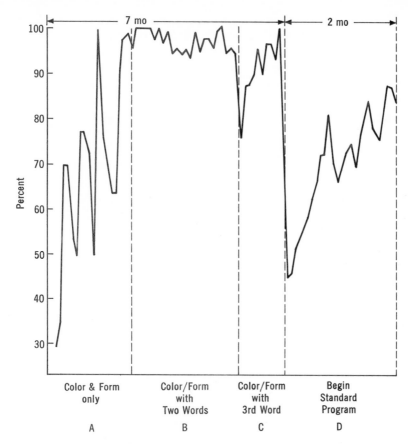

FIGURE VI-10. Kate's correct response rate for errorless training and standard program.

ently high level of correctness which was maintained even when the color and form cues were gradually removed.

Where initially Kate had been unable to discriminate these words she had learned them even though color and form cues were utilized much of the time. This incidental learning of complex discrimination during errorless training is extremely interesting. Rather than merely relying on color and form supports indefinitely to the exclusion of any attention to the word symbols inside, Kate and other autistic children enrolled in the NPI School program definitely acquired word discrimination skills.

Section C of Figure VI-10 represents Kate's correct response rate when a third word "Betty" was introduced in a cross. No color cues were utilized at this point and the form cues were quickly faded. The three errorless training phases including the introduction of a third word consumed some seven months. While only 48 sessions are reported in Figure VI-10 and Kate was actually scheduled on a three times a week basis, interruptions due to illness, teacher absence, school vacations, and the like extended these sessions over a seven-month period.

The most dramatic portion of Kate's reading program is illustrated in Section D of Figure VI-10. Following the seven months of errorless training Kate was reintroduced to the reading program unsuccessfully attempted earlier. This program presented her with some six new words each week none of which were introduced with color or form cues. While her overall correct response rate initially dropped during the program she steadily improved and was soon efficiently learning twice as many new words each week as she had been able to acquire during the entire previous seven months.

Reading for Kate provided many opportunities for increased reality contact. Once she was able to read in a basal primer she engaged in discussions of the pictures, names of characters, and events described. She took the book home with her and willingly read for members of her family in what was one of her first appropriate interactions with them. It was evident they were extremely impressed by her newly-developed skill and the opportunities it provided for interaction and genuine praise.

Rabb and Busch (1968) have extended the errorless training reading techniques used in the program with Kate, and have found them effective in initiating and improving speech in nonverbal, autistic children enrolled in the NPI School. This extension was prompted by observations of autistic children placed in the reading program. Kate and other autistic children became far more accessible to instruction, were more responsive to the teacher, and spoke with greater willingness and clarity when reading than in social verbal interactions. The authors of this study reason that perhaps printed word stimuli provided clearer and less conflictual cues for eliciting vocalization than the verbal stimuli of the teacher.

In the initial portion of this speech-through-reading approach, certain words were selected for each child which were readily transferred to meaningful conversation in daily life. The words related to objects or events in the life of the child which were positive, such as "ball" or "cookie." The words were introduced to the child in a two-part puzzle within a 5 x 8 inch masonite frame. At first the cues of form (puzzle shape), background color, picture and word were all available to aid

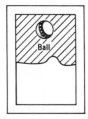

FIGURE VI-11. Level 1 task in errorless matching of word-picture puzzle.

the child in responding, and to maximize the probability of his success. Figure VI-11 shows the Level 1 task. The teacher pointed to the framed puzzle segment on the left and said "Ball," then she pointed to two choices on the right and said "Where is the ball?" If the child selected the correct puzzle segment on the right he was encouraged to place it in the frame and complete the puzzle; if he selected the incorrect segment the teacher immediately said "No" and picked up the correct piece herself and placed it in the insert. During each insertion of the correct puzzle piece the teacher verbalized the word and asked the child to repeat it. The child received one candy reward for selecting the correct piece and an additional reward for attempting to say the word after the teacher. Initially, approximations of the word were credited as correct and then gradually the criteria were made more exact.

Figure VI-12 illustrates the gradual fading of the prompting cues of picture, puzzle form and color background (faded in two steps) until in Level 6 word matching alone constituted the task. Following this initial phase, the program went on to include the errorless training procedures used with Kate and vocabulary building and book reading phases described in detail in Chapter IX. Preliminary results of the study designed to investigate the effectiveness of this approach with nonverbal autistic children have established it as a useful aid in initiating and improving speech.

It is the author's contention that further development of instructional programs utilizing principles of errorless training will constitute an extremely important contribution to special education in the future and may result in a breakthrough for teaching seemingly noneducable exceptional children.

Specific examples of tasks useful in getting the child to respond in learning will now be considered. These will be organized with reference to the descriptive statements in the boxes on the response level as shown in Figure IV-8 in Chapter IV.

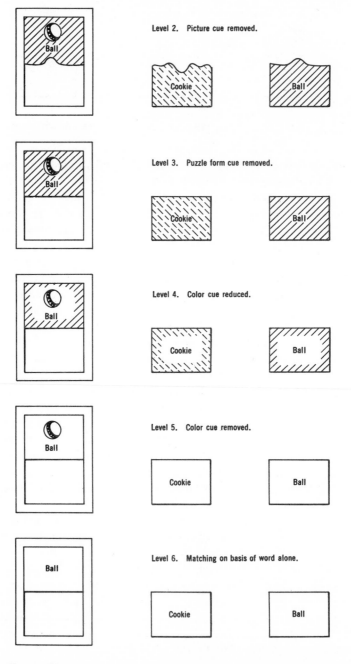

FIGURE VI-12.   Levels 2-6 in errorless matching of word-picture puzzle.

RESPONSE LEVEL TASKS

7. Child Does Not Respond to Learning Tasks

The elimination of letter grades and reduction of a demand for perfection in certain skills such as handwriting, mechanics of English, and spelling have already been discussed as aids in getting the emotionally disturbed child to respond in school. Assignments of tasks which practically guarantee success have also been suggested. When it becomes necessary to confront the child with an error, teachers (Douglas, 1961) of disturbed children have found elimination of red pencil marks useful, since such red pencil "correcting" of schoolwork may be associated with previous failure.

Use of question marks next to incorrect answers is seen as an aid in communicating to the child the acceptability of making errors yet the importance of checking over work. With children who have continuously failed in school and who may resist responding because of fear of further failure, considerable reassurance may be necessary to establish the point that mistakes are essential to make if areas for remedial help are to be uncovered.

Offering the child who fails to respond in learning a variety of short tasks rather than single longer assignments also encourages increased responding. The author has found that giving at least three different activities to children with learning problems each hour is useful in this respect. For some children twice that number may be necessary, while for others a single task may be profitably pursued for the entire period. It is also important that the teacher of emotionally disturbed children have a ready supply of new and different assignments available so that children may be reassigned as often as necessary.

Giving the child an assignment which draws upon information he has readily available and which capitalizes on his major interest also helps initiate responding. Work sheets asking no more than a list of three telephone numbers the child recalls, the names of several friends, one or more street addresses, and the title of a few television programs or movies he has recently seen have been used successfully with emotionally disturbed children. Providing the surfing enthusiast with a series of surfing pictures to caption or describe or a story title such as "My Biggest Wave" may get him started writing in the class. In the NPI School individual programs centering around rockets and electricity helped initiate learning with two highly resistant adolescent boys.

Younger children may be engaged in simple social imitation activities involving handclapping or touching parts of their bodies in response to the teacher's cue. The author (Hewett, 1965) undertook a year long individual training program with Eddie, a nonverbal four-and-one-half-year-old autistic boy. The program was designed to initiate speech, but the first activities were simple, hand imitation games. Following each imitation (e.g., touching an ear in imitation of the teacher) Eddie was rewarded by a spin in a revolving chair or a short sequence of a color cartoon movie. Each time he touched the teacher's face as directed, music was provided from a children's record and continued as long as Eddie maintained physical contact with the teacher. From these attention and response level tasks, Eddie went on to learn to follow more complex directions (e.g., assemble simple puzzles), approximate the teacher's vocalization, and later imitate actual words. Many of these latter tasks used social praise alone (e.g., "Good boy!" said by the teacher) without any other form of reward.

Musical games in which the child scribbles continuously in a circular motion on a piece of paper as long as music from a record player continues also may be used for young emotionally disturbed children Whenever the teacher stops the music the child is to stop scribbling.

8. Child Maintains a Constricted Level of Performance

The child who will seldom attempt more than an absolute minimum assignment (e.g., one problem on a page, a one-sentence story) can be helped to increase his responding by means of several of the approaches already discussed. In addition the introduction of a personal work record in the form of a graph may be useful. This work record may be kept on the basis of time or units of work. For some children who resist doing assignments, setting goals such as "See how long two problems take you to do" or "See how many problems you can do in five minutes" may increase their response rate. They may later graph the time or number of problems completed on a chart and compare records day by day. With such a procedure it is important that the teacher accurately time the child or possibly have him use a timer at his desk and that problems are selected which are well within the capability of the child.

As with the other examples presented, there is no guarantee that timing and graphing will be effective with all children who resist responding. In fact the increase of time pressure may be extremely upsetting to some. With these children rewarding each problem attempted or each additional word placed in a story with a tangible or token reward as discussed on the attention level may be useful. This approach has been especially successful with older elementary age children in the NPI School who resisted reading. Giving the child several token rewards, such as check marks which can later be exchanged for candy or trinkets for each page of reading he does has dramatically increased the amount of free reading attempted. Of course receipt of the reward is contingent upon the child's being able to answer simple comprehension questions about what he has read.

The author has known parents of children with reading problems who have attempted to use this procedure in an effort to encourage the child's free reading at home. In general it has failed miserably, largely due to the failure of the parents to systematically reward the reading, ask appropriate comprehension questions, and refrain from getting into an "emotionally loaded" discussion with the child regarding his reading ability and attitude toward learning. The teacher can use this approach much more successfully in a task-oriented classroom where the child systematically "earns" his reward.

Again, it should be pointed out that in order to initiate attending and responding it may be necessary to utilize an unconventional reward system. Such a system serves "launching" purposes only. It can be discarded as the child begins to respond to more traditional rewards of accomplishment, exploration, and praise. Unfortunately educators have allowed far too many children with emotional and learning problems to deteriorate on the "launching pad of the classroom" rather than boost them into the "orbit of learning" through creative and innovative procedures.

9. Child Exhibits a Narrow Range of Learning Interests

Some emotionally disturbed children do not demonstrate any clear-cut interest in particular subject matter or activities in school. Others may have a single interest which they pursue to the exclusion of everything else. Helping both types of children broaden their interests is an important goal at the response level.

While literature, history, geography, and social studies may be highly stimulating to some children when presented in traditional curriculum form, these subjects often have limited appeal to children who are poorly motivated to learn and who have had previous failure experiences with them. In order to get these children to pay attention, respond, and become involved in learning, it may be necessary to present subject matter in unique and fascinating form.

For some as yet undetermined reason the vast majority of learning, behavior, and emotional problems seen in school are found among boys rather than girls (Durrell, 1940). Several authors have suggested that the traditional curriculum material of the school is more feminine than masculine in appeal and as such contributes to a distinterest in learning on the part of the boys. Harris (1950) concluded girls show a greater preference for the content of basal reading books, even in the early grades. Mazurkweitz (1960) polled eleventh-grade boys and found a majority considered reading a feminine activity. Lecky (1945) has discussed the inadequacy of basal reading content for boys within the framework of his theory of self-consistency. According to Lecky, the content of basal reading books is inconsistent with a boy's striving for masculinity. There is, Lecky maintains, obvious inconsistency between a boy's attempts to be a "little man" on the playground and his participation in an oral reading lesson centering around talking animals and the antics of baby brothers and sisters.

Stanchfield (1961) has found boys lose interest in animal stories, fairy tales, and stories of family life characteristically found in traditional reading programs. She observed a diminishing interest in such content among boys from grades four to eight and an increasing interest in stories containing unusual experiences, suspense, action, and surprise.

During World War II a large scale literacy program conducted by the U.S. Army (Witty, 1943) was designed to bring nonreading soldiers up to fourth-grade reading level in six weeks using "highly diversified reading material, richly illustrated." Affectively potent pictures (e.g., hissing snake) were paired with consonant letter sounds (e.g., "s" sound) as a means of providing emphasis.

Over a several-year period teaching adolescent boys with learning and mild emotional problems the author conducted an informal study of the types of subject matter which were successful in getting students to ask questions, engage in discussion, and do follow-up reading and writing assignments. Several units of study were undertaken with the class and were ranked as follows with respect to eliciting the interest and involvement of the class:

1. Deep sea diving and study of marine life.
2. History of the development of the submarine.
3. Knighthood.
4. History of the development of communication techniques.
5. Tunnel building and famous tunnels built around the world.
6. History of the development of kites and balloon aircraft.

During each of these units, projects were undertaken which included conducting science experiments illustrating principles of deep sea diving, building model submarines, constructing a complete suit of armor from brown paper tape pasted in layers over newspaper forms fitted on one of the boys who served as a model, developing skill in sending secret and Morse code messages, creating an actual miniature tunnel in a model mountain, and constructing large French war kites which were later flown by members of the class.

The marked interest of this class and others similar to it in deep sea adventure led the author to collaborate in writing a series of remedial reading books based on this theme (Berres, Coleman, Briscoe, and Hewett, 1958). Several boys in the class could be characterized as having a "narrow range of interests," and these units of study and projects were of definite value in getting them to more actively participate in the class.

Another example of the type of subject matter which appeals to boys was provided following an elaborate lesson on the history of Paris given by the author. Incidentally, during the course of the presentation, it was mentioned that while the Germans were occupying Paris in World War II, Hitler had considered dismantling the Eiffel Tower and converting the scrap metal to the building of tanks and weapons. During the follow-up story-writing period every single member of the class focused on this incident to the complete exclusion of other carefully researched facts and historical material!

Jay, a nine-year-old schizophrenic boy enrolled in the NPI School, appeared his first day in the classroom loaded down with well-worn maps. He spread these out on the desk and immediately began naming cities, highway numbers, and freeway systems. He would only draw maps and refused to take part in any other activity. The teacher began working with Jay by allowing him a period of time to look at and talk about his maps—nothing else was asked of him. Gradually, however, the teacher initiated discussion and presented reading materials regarding the cities on the maps—what they produced and what could be seen if you visited them. From this point Jay was encouraged to draw pictures of signs that might be seen along the roads and later buildings, airports, and railroad stations. Finally people were introduced and Jay was asked to draw pictures of them and write about what they did in the cities. Through this individualized program utilizing reading, writing, and art, Jay's narrow range of interests was considerably broadened. The program used with Jay was yet another example of the shaping process which moved him, "thimbleful by thimbleful" toward desirable goals on the response, exploratory, and social levels.*

---

* Miss Janice Seigel, formerly on the staff of the NPI School, devised this and several other programs for disturbed children cited in this text.

10. Child Withdraws from Teacher and Peers

The social nature of the classroom is upsetting to the emotionally disturbed child who is not comfortable functioning as a member of a group. Removal of competition with other children, including in some cases individual tutoring, is a helpful first step with such a child. Once the child is assured that he is only competing with his own record and will not be graded or judged in comparison to others, the special or regular classroom becomes a safer environment. All recitation and forced participation in group activities should be avoided at first.

Allowing the child to initially withdraw in the classroom may help him get started. Study booths which are visually screened off from the rest of the class, providing privacy, are often useful with emotionally disturbed children. Steve, an eleven-year-old, hostile psychotic boy entered the NPI School elementary classroom determined not to interact with either teacher or peers. His defiance was also expressed in his refusal to have his hair cut or to remove a red jacket which he kept tightly buttoned up the front. The teacher avoided any discussion of the haircut or jacket problem and allowed Steve to withdraw to a study booth where work was waiting for him once he entered school. He was told in a matter-of-fact manner that if he needed help he could come to the teacher's desk.

Steve never initiated contact with the teacher or any of the other children during the first week. After this time he allowed the teacher to come to the study booth and give him new assignments, a process which was conducted with a minimum of verbal interaction on the teacher's part. Steve was an intelligent boy, capable of doing work on his grade level, so this presented little problem. It was the involvement with teacher and peers that he avoided at all costs. Over a period of time Steve ventured out of the booth to bring his work to the teacher and responded to requests to go on simple errands. It was a while before he could be assigned a desk in the classroom but the teacher waited until it appeared he was ready. At first he was told he could take his work back to the study booth any time he wanted, and while Steve did occasionally retreat he spent longer and longer times in the classroom itself. In six months he was participating in group discussions and assisting less able classmates with their work.

Assigning the socially withdrawn yet academically strong child responsibility for tutoring others less capable also has been very effective in initiating social contact between students. Mayhew and Ferjo (1968) have explored the use of in-patient adolescents as teacher assistants with in-patient elementary children in the NPI School. Their study was prompted first by the fact that the elementary children actually needed individual help with certain academic subjects, and that many NPI adolescent students were very competent in these subject areas; second, the role of assistant-teacher offered the adolescent a degree of prestige; third, and perhaps most significant, in the process of assuming responsibility for teaching the younger child, the adolescent might observe the younger child's problems and ways of handling them, and, perhaps, gain insight into his own difficulties. Adolescents selected as teacher-assistants evidenced a "nonpathological" interest in the younger group, displayed empathy in relation to the children, had scholastic ability which qualified them to assist the elementary group, and, finally, manifested a degree of commonality of symptomatic behavior with the child to whom they were assigned.

Mayhew and Ferjo described two individuals in their study who were severe response problems. They also contributed observations following a one-month period pairing of this adolescent and elementary-aged child.

Kathy and Margaret

Kathy is a tall, gawky, fifteen-year-old girl whose admitting diagnosis was anorexia nervosa. She was alienated from her peer group by her physical looks and social ineptness. She was above average in height and far below average in weight. She was 5'9" tall and on admission to the hospital weighed 78 pounds. She further "enhanced" this emaciated, rather macabre appearance by allowing her fingernails to grow an inch beyond her fingertips. Her peers shyed away from personal contact with her, nicknamed her "Spider" and made her the ward scapegoat, and although Kathy had a frightening quality about her, it suddenly became abundantly clear that she, herself, was an extremely frightened girl.

In school, she would literally hide in her work. She would turn out reams of written work which in terms of learning were valueless. The sole purpose of her "busyness" was to hide from her peers and distance herself from her teacher. When asked to explain some facet of her studies she would look startled, stammer, offer her notebook with the explanation— the answer was within—or look completely bland and turn mute.

Initially, she never volunteered a question or answer in class discussion and when called upon to answer would squirm, fidget, and shrug or say "I don't know."

Margaret is a small, blonde, thin, eight-year-old who never smiled, wore a permanent frown and was extremely fearful. She was phobic about many things—animals, new people, new places. She had no friends among her peers who were either frightened by her terrified shrieks or who would tease her by saying "A rabbit will get you," to watch her hide under the desk or run to a far corner weeping. When calm at her desk she did superficial academic work and would always appear to be reading her book or writing out her assignments. When questioned about her work she showed little comprehension or would begin to cry. Margaret could not tolerate praise from the teacher, and would tear up her work if the teacher complimented her. She actively resisted all attempts by others to show friendship toward her.

Results following one-month pairing

Kathy was a quiet, withdrawn adolescent. Margaret was a frightened and shy eight-year-old. Both were shunned by their peers. Both hid in their academic work. When Kathy was initially assigned to work with Margaret the younger child ignored her and the teacher had to reassure timid Kathy of Margaret's fright. Then as the situation relaxed Kathy could talk more freely to Margaret, and Margaret could respond to the interaction. Because both Kathy and Margaret were perfectionistic and showed little comprehension, it was impressed upon Kathy that Margaret could read well as long as she did not have to recall details but that this was not "true reading"; therefore, it would be necessary for Kathy to structure questions to help Margaret understand the material. In the beginning the teacher wrote out questions for Kathy to ask of Margaret. Gradually the older girl was able to develop her own questions from the academic material and discuss these with Margaret. This did not appear to generalize to Kathy in her own academics, but she gradually became more communicative and talkative in her own classroom.[1]

11. Child Cannot Function in a Classroom Setting

Despite individualized assignments and lack of pressure to participate as a member of a group, some emotionally disturbed children are too upset to even set foot in the classroom. With these children, individual tutoring at home or in an outside area in the school may have to take place initially. Home teaching is provided in many school districts for children who are too disruptive to be tolerated in a classroom or who are so frightened of attending school that they refuse to leave home. While it may be necessary at the very beginning, teaching the child in his home when he is physically able to work elsewhere is probably undesirable. Parents are seldom able to remove themselves completely from such an arrangement, and it requires an objective and firm teacher to deal with the barrage of questions, complaints, and bits of advice which parents offer. The home setting is also not conducive to a work orientation on the part of the child. Distractions, interruptions,

---

[1] D. Mayhew and J. Ferjo, "The Use of In-Patient Adolescents as Teacher Assistants in an Elementary Classroom in a Psychiatric Setting," paper presented at the Forty-Fifth Annual Meeting of the American Orthopsychiatric Associataion, Chicago, 1968.

and attempts at manipulating teacher assignments are all too frequent. For this reason getting the child to come to school even if only to work in a separate room with a home teacher is more effective. Increased positive results are apt to ensue when teacher and child interact in school and parental influence is removed from the teaching situation.

Systematic inclusion is the next natural step to get the child into a classroom. In contrast to systematic exclusion which involves removing the child for periods of time because of misbehavior this procedure involves gradually introducing a child into the class for increasing periods of time until he can tolerate a full day.

Spencer was an eight-year-old emotionally disturbed boy whose lack of control in public school had made home teaching necessary for one year. With the cooperation of the teacher an attempt was made to systematically include him in a special class for emotionally disturbed boys which used a check-mark system to acknowledge appropriate behavior and accomplishment. The check marks were given on a card, and cards filled with checks could later be exchanged for tangible rewards of toys and candy. This system was introduced by the home teacher for several days while Spencer worked at home. For the next several days he worked with his home teacher in the classroom after the regular group had been dismissed. Use of the check marks was continued, and finally he was brought into the classroom with the home teacher for 15 minutes a day while the regular class was present. During this time he was tutored individually in the back of the room.

The length of time he spent in the class was gradually increased, and eventually the home teacher withdrew altogether. At this point, Spencer became part of the regular group. Although this procedure was ultimately successful in getting Spencer back into a regular classroom, it would have proceeded more smoothly had the home teacher not worked with him in the room with the other class members present. It appeared that introduction of a new boy and his own special teacher at the same time drew undue attention to Spencer and some resentment was expressed by the other boys.

RESPONSE LEVEL REWARDS

In Box b on the composite developmental sequence form presented in Figure IV-8, Chapter IV, the response level reward was described as "social attention." It has already been stated that rewards of social contact and attention from others may be next most effective in controlling the child's responses in learning as compared with tangible rewards. This statement, however, is admittedly open to challenge, for conclusive evidence regarding a possible "hierarchy of rewards" which controls human learning is yet to emerge in the scientific literature. Indeed, the idiosyncratic nature of the human organism may preclude the development of a hierarchy that specifies the relative effectiveness of various types of rewards for all individuals. The motivational hierarchy of Maslow briefly introduced in Chapter II has attempted this in more general terms than those used in the developmental sequence of educational goals. But it is obvious that some individuals forego the meeting of primary drives and maintenance of self-preservation (Maslow's two most basic motives) in order to obtain approval and esteem (higher motives on Maslow's hierarchy).

Schwitzgebel (1965) has speculated that the idiosyncratic nature of what is rewarding in learning for one individual as compared with another is probably a guarantee that a society of conditioned human automatons will never develop. What is presented in ascending order in Boxes a, b, c, d, e, f, and g in Figure IV-8 as the major sources of reward available to the emotionally disturbed child in the classroom is largely the result of the author's experience working with such children. In the light of these considerations the various rewards presented in the developmental sequence of educational goals are to be viewed collectively rather than in rigid hierarchical order.

Social contact or attention has been found to provide an important reward for emotionally disturbed children although as was found in the Levine and Simmons (1962) study it is not always as powerful as tangible rewards of food.

The author (Hewett, 1966) in a preliminary study with Jimmy the twelve-year-old nonverbal autistic boy engaged in the reading and written langauge program described earlier obtained evidence of the effectiveness of social attention for increasing response rate. Jimmy was taught a task which involved dropping a marble into a box mounted on a wall panel. The marble rang a bell and then was deposited in a cup below the box ready to be picked up and dropped in again. For each marble drop, Jimmy received some type of reward. Candy units were first used continually, and a consistently high rate of marble dropping was maintained. As various other rewards were introduced (e.g., exposure of an animal picture, various animated hand puppets, music played from behind the panel) his rate of responding dropped noticeably. Only one other type of reward competed favorably with the candy although it very definitely was second best. This reward was provided by opening a large door in the panel and exposing the smiling face of a variety of individuals, some familiar, some unfamiliar, to Jimmy. Jimmy "worked" harder to maintain the presence of a human face (no

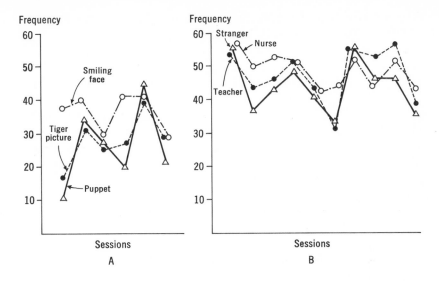

FIGURE VI-13. Jimmy's comparative response rates to obtain rewards of animal picture, exposure of puppet, and smiling human face.

significant difference between familiar or unfamiliar individuals) than for any of the other rewards except candy. Figure VI-13 Graph A summarizes the frequency of marble drops during three-minute intervals for the various rewards except candy. Graph B reflects Jimmy's response rates in order to obtain the exposure of the smiling faces of three individuals.

Zimmerman and Zimmerman's (1962) study already summarized illustrates the significant control social attention exerted over academic performance in the spelling of an emotionally disturbed boy. As long as the teacher gave him extra attention and individual drill when he made errors the boy's spelling performance did not improve. Once teacher attention, which consisted of smiling, chatting, and physical proximity, was withheld, except for correct spelling responses, the boy's performance dramatically improved.

The reward of social attention is familiar to teachers of all children because it is so commonly used in the classroom every day. The child who puts extra effort into an assignment or who remembers to put his book away on a shelf as directed may be the recipient of an approving nod from the teacher. A problem may arise, however, when the teacher lacks understanding of how attention may serve to reward deviant behavior as illustrated in the Zimmerman study. The classroom clown whose strange noises, grimaces, and impulsive physical behavior always draw the attention of the teacher away from others to himself may be unwittingly rewarded for such behavior.

The reward of social contact or attention overlaps the reward of social approval or avoidance of disapproval specified in Box e on the social level of the developmental sequence. The reward being considered at the response level is merely making contact with the child socially and giving him attention. The reward of the social level implies a verbal interaction and the gaining of praise or the avoiding of disapproval. Emotionally disturbed children may be initially rewarded more effectively by attention than social praise. As the latter reward begins to exert control over their behavior such children are apt to be functioning more adequately in school.

Of course, tangible rewards discussed at the attention level also may be utilized to foster responding in learning. At each level on the developmental sequence, rewards associated with either higher or lower levels may be useful. The use of a higher level reward (multisensory stimulation) to foster attention and response behaviors was illustrated in the case of Louis.

RESPONSE LEVEL STRUCTURE

Structure at the response level is still subject to the same flexibility that was described at the attention level. In the initial stages of introducing the emotionally disturbed child to learning it is the reward dimension of the learning triangle which is emphasized sometimes at the expense of maintaining fixed environmental expectations. The child-centered structure associated with the psychodynamic-interpersonal strategy may be more applicable at the attention and response levels. The goal of these two lower levels is to initiate the learning process and to get the child involved in learning. It is at the order level to be discussed in the next chapter that the child is more directly confronted with fixed environmental expectations and the limits or "strings" which determine the consequences of his behavior.

This chapter has elaborated the general characteristics of tasks designed to help the child achieve response goals and has cited a variety of examples of activities, assignments, and approaches which have proven useful in getting the child to respond in learning, become less constricted in his performance, broaden his learning interests, and function more adequately in a classroom setting with teacher and peers. The reward of social contact or attention has been introduced and the similarity of structure at the response and attention levels discussed.

VII ORDER LEVEL

The order level of the developmental sequence emphasizes the structure side of the learning triangle in contrast to the attention and response levels which focused on the task and reward dimensions. This shift in focus between levels is the sharpest made at any point on the developmental sequence. However, structure is imposed on the child gradually and always with concern for assigning a suitable educational task and providing a meaningful reward for learning.

In this chapter we will review general characteristics of order tasks, consider specific examples of tasks for dealing with order problems, and discuss the nature of rewards and significance of structure at the order level.

Order tasks aim at helping the child learn to adapt to routine, follow directions, complete assignments, and control his behavior. Task characteristics at the order level include:

1. Maintaining a structured learning environment based on fixed environmental expectations.
2. Defining a specific starting point and a series of steps leading to a conclusion which is scorable as complete or incomplete.
3. Requiring "student" behavior.

Although many special educators agree that a structured learning environment assists emotionally disturbed children in learning, they do not always agree on just what constitutes such an environment. Differences of opinion exist with respect to size and composition of the class group, length of the daily program, and physical arrangement of the classroom itself.

For some teachers one severely disturbed child is a handful, while for others, two or three such children can be taught at the same time. For others, a reasonable class size might be six, eight, or ten children. Finally, for a few select teachers, 15 or 20 emotionally disturbed children may comprise an acceptable group. Factors which obviously enter into the feasibility of a particular size group are teacher's skill, degree of disturbance of the children, resources available, and number of hours of the daily program.

The author has visited institutional and public schools where a supervisor will explain with delight as he leads the way to a classroom of emotionally disturbed children: "Wait until you see *our* Mrs. Green. She has 20 of the most severely disturbed children in the entire school and never has any problems with them. She doesn't ask for expensive teaching materials and is loved by all of the students and staff."

As the door to Mrs. Green's room is opened this rare individual comes into view, calmly and collectively keeping her eye on 20 problem children who for some reason are all sitting at their desks working diligently. If you ask her how she does it she may smile and state: "I love the children" or "They know exactly what I expect." But it is doubtful she really knows herself why she is so successful.

While the author never ceases to be amazed that such gifted teaching artists exist, he has come to the conclusion they are few and far between and probably will never be able to accurately transmit to other teachers exactly why they are so successful against such overwhelming odds.

Twenty emotionally disturbed children in a class is far too many for most teachers. The appropriate number is probably closer to from six to ten. Where a teacher aide is available in the classroom, ten children can usually be adequately handled by an average teacher. Without an aide, the teacher must be more skilled and devote more time to dealing with problems of classroom management. The classroom design to be presented in Chapter X of this text includes a class size of nine students along with a teacher aide.

Regardless of the size of the class group, the type of emotionally disturbed children present in it is an important consideration. Redl (1949) has discussed the problem of "group contagion" and how no group can tolerate more than a certain degree of disruptive elements. For that reason a class of nine emotionally disturbed children should probably contain no more than one-third order and social problems, although in making this statement the author is reminded of several children whose behavior was so unmanageable that they could not be tolerated in any group, no matter what the size. An additional third of the class might be children with attention and response problems and, if possible, the remaining third composed of children with mastery and exploratory problems who are not behavioral extremes at either the attention-response or order-social levels. As has been suggested specific guidelines are hazardous to offer because of the great variability found among emotionally disturbed children.

While Mrs. Green, cited earlier, may never request teaching materials and this may be considered a "blessing" by her supervisor, the truth remains that providing the "something" which emotionally disturbed children need to learn in school requires a great many teaching supplies, remedial materials, games, art supplies, and the like which will be discussed in greater detail later. Mrs. Green may be able to teach reading to emotionally disturbed children without anything more than a telephone directory but the practicability of such martyrdom is highly questionable.

Several of the issues raised in this section will no doubt provoke concern, if not outright anger, from teachers who are faced with 20 or more emotionally disturbed children, a class full of severe order and social problems, extremely limited funds with which to obtain teaching materials, and no prospect of having a teacher aide. One such teacher approached the author after a lecture during which some of the points covered in this section were raised. He was shaking his fist and exclaiming, "What do you mean taking my time telling me what to do with my children when I can't do any of the things you suggest?"

This teacher was in a frustrating and unfortunate situation, but the position is taken in this text that certain standards and guidelines must emerge in the field of education of the emotionally disturbed child. Hopefully, application of some of the approaches and suggestions presented will be possible in even the most difficult classroom situations.

The length of the classroom day for emotionally disturbed children is an important consideration in establishing a structured learning environment. In California there is a state requirement for a minimum 240-minute day when the child attends public school. Therefore most public school programs cover a full four hours. In some schools where special classes are not available a child must remain in school a full day. The NPI School maintains a maximum school day of three hours and provides flexible scheduling from five minutes a day for some children to the full three hours for others. This flexibility is possible because of the highly individualized educational program in the institutional setting.

As most educators who have worked with emotionally disturbed children are aware, four hours is often far too long a time for all children to remain in school. Flexibility of scheduling is essential. How much more useful it is for a child to experience a successful 30- or 40-minute period in school each day than to have to remain in the classroom for four hours until his problems force him to face failure or possible exclusion.

The importance of a controlled physical environment has been stressed by Strauss (1947), Cruickshank (1961), and Haring and Phillips (1962). Strauss and Cruickshank's concern with limiting classroom stimulation has already been discussed in Chapter I. Haring and Phillips, while recognizing that Strauss and Cruickshank were primarily concerned with brain-injured children, view a controlled physical environment as useful for the emotionally disturbed child.

Whether "controlling classroom stimulation" should go as far as to include removal of all bulletin boards, covering of windows with opaque material, and placement of each child in a separate study booth is debatable. Cruse (1962) in a study comparing brain-injured and familial mentally retarded children's performance on a reaction time test under varying levels of distractibility failed to demonstrate that brain-injured children are detrimentally affected by extraneous stimuli, such as toys, moving balloons, and mirrors. While our present concern is with emotionally disturbed children and reaction time tests cannot be equated with complex learning in the classroom, the study suggests that more research needs to be done before legislating extremely drab classroom environments for all distractible children.

The appeal of such specific structuring of the classroom to teachers of the emotionally disturbed has already been discussed. The author takes the position that the importance of reducing classroom stimulation to near zero has been overemphasized, particularly with regard to the emotionally disturbed. It is not surprising, however, that this has occurred. At our present state of knowledge there are very few specific guidelines available in the field and painting a classroom battleship gray is a concrete act that seems to make sense. Extreme application of the principle of stimulus reduction to the classroom may, then, be more a reflection of the teacher's rather than the emotionally disturbed child's need for structure.

A structured learning environment can exist in a classroom with colored walls, bulletin boards, and activity centers with stimulating displays. What may be more important than the physical arrangement is the manner in which assignments are made and expected behavioral standards presented to the student. However, physical considerations which have been found by the author to be important are room size, student desk arrangement, and provision for various activity centers including study booths.

Because special classes for the emotionally disturbed usually have far fewer children than regular classrooms the assumption may be made that the room size can be reduced accordingly. Such an assumption is erroneous and a contradiction to a structured learning environment if an individualized program for each child is to be established. Emotionally disturbed children need to be seated further apart than in regular classrooms, given larger desk areas on which to work, and have various centers available in the room where they may work individually or in small groups on order, exploratory, and social tasks. For this reason at least 100 square feet per child is recommended and classrooms providing 1200 square feet of floor space for ten emotionally disturbed children are seen as ideal. The advantage of a large classroom with adequate space for varied activities in programs for emotionally disturbed children has also been recognized by Hay (1953).

Small student desks or armchairs with limited storage space are not as desirable as large tables 2 x 4 feet in size. The latter are sometimes used in regular classrooms for two students to share, but in the case of the emotionally disturbed child a separate table is recommended for each student. There are several advantages to such an arrangement. The first is that the child is separated from other students by virtue of the size of his desk and physical and verbal contact with others is more difficult to initiate. The second advantage is that the student is provided with a large surface on which to spread out materials and work. The third and perhaps most important advantage is that a large desk permits the teacher to sit down next to the child at a respectful distance and work with him in a businesslike manner. It is difficult to work with a student seated at a small desk without "closing in" or "hovering" over him. Since physical contact with the teacher may produce a variety of reactions from an emotionally disturbed child ranging from obvious satisfaction to aversion, it is probably best avoided in the classroom. The author has observed teachers of older elementary and secondary age emotionally disturbed children who frequently put their arms around students, pat them on the back, playfully nudge them, or even in some cases hold them on their laps. The results of such physical contact have included the immediate calming down of an upset student to the angry striking of one teacher in the face when a hand was placed on the student's shoulder in what appeared to be a friendly and supportive gesture.

Without speculating as to the "meaning" of such physical contact to the child, in the author's experience a more productive work orientation is maintained in the classroom when teachers avoid touching their students. No hard and fast rules are intended, however, for again consideration of the individual case is required. Young children in pre-school, kindergarten, and primary grade programs may be approached much differently from older children. And in the case of assaultive behavior on the part of the child the teacher may have no choice but to directly intervene with physical restraint.

As part of the discussion of a classroom design for emotionally disturbed children to be presented in Chapter X the setting up of a center for order activities as well as an exploratory-social center will be described. Each of these centers needs two to four large tables included in it and can best be established in a large classroom.

Study booths have been referred to previously on several occasions. In some programs each child may be assigned to a booth and screened off from his classmates for the major part of the day. In others, the booth may be used to help particularly distractible students work more efficiently for a limited period of time. The author has found at least two study booths extremely valuable in classrooms for nine or ten emotionally disturbed children. These are simple structures usually four feet square with six foot high partitions across the back and on two sides. One end is open so that the teacher can observe the child. The booths are used on a selective basis only with the child expected to work at his desk for as much as a day if possible. In the classroom design to be discussed later the booths are presented as highly desirable working areas with carpets on the floor and upholstered chairs. The child may request to go to a booth or "office" whenever he feels he can work more efficiently there or the teacher may assign him in an effort to reduce distraction.

The setting-up of a structured learning environment includes consideration of class size, group composition, length of the school day, and planning for physical arrangement of bulletin boards, desks, centers, and study booths. Suggestions made in this section are directed toward establishing an "ordered' environment with enough flexibility to provide for work-efficiency differences among students.

The second major characteristic of ordered tasks is that they have a fixed starting point and a series of steps that leads to a conclusion which is scorable as complete or incomplete. The tasks should minimize conflict and confusion and maximize follow-through and completion. For this reason academic skills such as reading and spelling generally should not be emphasized at this level; however, for those students who are functioning adequately at the mastery level but who have order problems, these two levels may be combined.

While it is difficult, if not impossible, to separate concepts of "completion" and "accuracy," the intent at the order level is to help the child finish what he starts, stressing his following through the steps necessary for completion without undue emphasis on the quality of his results.

The type of task which lends itself best for use at the order level is one that is simple enough to do so that when completed, it is also accurate. Picture puzzles are used as order tasks and it is obvious that a complete puzzle with all the pieces in place is also an accurate one. For students who are uncritical and uncontrolled in learning, it is extremely important to assign tasks with a high probability of successful execution and which involve them in a satisfying and novel activity. If this is done the concepts of completion and accuracy are practically synonymous.

Visual-motor training materials such as those found in the Continental Press Reading Readiness Series (Maney) and the Frostig Program for Development of Visual Perception (Frostig) are useful at both the order and exploratory levels. Such tasks as matching similar forms and reproducing designs are neutral and nonscholastic. The emotionally disturbed child who solves a simple maze or copies the teacher's pegboard design is operating outside the often emotionally loaded area of a "school assignment."

In this text the position is taken that perceptual motor training techniques such as those developed by Strauss (1947), Cruickshank (1961), Kephart (1960), and Frostig (1964) for brain-injured children are very useful at the order and exploratory levels for the emotionally disturbed regardless of whether or not such children suffer from sensory or neurological impairment.

In summary, the type of activity useful for the development of order with emotionally disturbed children should:

1. Have a well-defined beginning and end and a systematic series of steps leading to completion.
2. Be graduated in difficulty so that at even the simplest level probability of complete and accurate execution is high.
3. Involve the child in a novel and satisfying activity appealing to his interest level.

The third major characteristic of the order level, that is, requiring "student" behavior, will be discussed under the "structure" section of this chapter.

We turn now to consideration of specific examples of tasks at the order level. Following this, a discussion of rewards and a further consideration of the importance of structure will be presented.

ORDER LEVEL TASKS

12. Child Does Not Follow Directions

All of the tasks to be suggested in this and the other three sections have been selected because of their usefulness in assigning the child a specific starting point and a series of steps which lead to completion.

The direction box assists emotionally disturbed children in following both written and spoken directions. It is based on an activity developed by Birnbrauer, Bijou, Wolf, and Kidder (1965) for use with institutionalized retarded children. Each direction box is filled with familiar objects such as model cars, airplanes of various colors, miniature animals, toy soldiers, small plastic scuba divers, and colored poker chips. Accompanying each direction box is a 6 x 16 inch card with three numbered squares 4 x 4 inches printed on it. For the box of cars the squares are labeled "lots," for the airplanes "airports," for the animals "corrals," for the soldiers "forts," for the divers "tanks," and for the poker chips "boxes." A series of direction cards accompanies each box. The cards are graduated in difficulty starting with Step I—e.g., "Put two red cars in Lot 1; put 6 blue cars in Lot 2; put 4 yellow cars in Lot 3." This step is illustrated in Figure VII-1 along with the direction box and cars. At the Step I level the child's task is to merely put the assigned number of cars in the designated boxes. Later steps involve moving the cars from box to box—e.g., "Put one red car from Lot 1 in Lot 3; put 4 blue cars from Lot 2 in Lot 1; put 2 yellow cars from Lot 3 in Lot 2." These tasks are scored by use of answer cards given fo the student. The answer card states the exact number of cars which should be in each box at the completion of the task. The sequence used in the construction of steps for the activity is as follows:

Step I   —Place a designated number of objects in each box.
Step II —Same as Step I with the addition of a single transfer of objects from one box to another.
Step III—Same as Step II but adds an additional transfer of objects.
Step IV—Same as Step III with one additional transfer.

The steps can be increased in difficulty indefinitely but one to five steps have been found most suitable for elementary age children. Adolescents can be given different objects such as electrical and radio parts and military insignia (e.g., "Put four corporal stripes in Box 1," etc.).

In the creation of this direction box material a very simple reading vocabularly was used. With some children, however, reading introduces such resistance that the activity is unsuccessful. For these children the

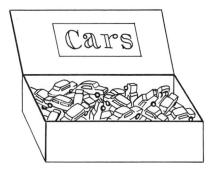

FIGURE VII-1. Direction box.

directions can be tape-recorded on Language Master cards. A strip of recording tape affixed to the bottom of the card records each step, and as these are played back on the Language Master the child arranges the objects as directed. Visual cues can also be utilized by having drawings of the exact number of objects to be put in each box on a card. It is important that the materials (e.g., model cars) in the direction boxes be used only for the assigned order task and not free play. Use of such materials in a more informal and creative manner is provided for at the exploratory level, next on the developmental sequence.

Secret code writing has a fascination for most children and can be used to foster direction following. A code that has been used successfully with emotionally disturbed children is illustrated in Figure VII-2. The teacher may have the child first write his own name in the code and then names of other children in the class. Longer coding assignments can be given in a variety of ways and the teacher can write messages to the child in code which he must decipher. Older students

(A)	(H)	(O)	(V)
(B)	(I)	(P)	(W)
(C)	(J)	(Q)	(X)
(D)	(K)	(R)	(Y)
(E)	(L)	(S)	(Z)
(F)	(M)	(T)	
(G)	(N)	(U)	

FIGURE VII-2. Symbol code.

may be given messages written in other codes without a deciphering key and assigned the task of "breaking" the code. This activity has been very successful with adolescent students in the NPI School.

The International Signal Flag Code System can also be used. A key with the 26 colored flags used to send messages between ships printed on it is provided the child. Several masts may be mimeographed on a sheet of paper with four or more blank flags suspended from each mast. At the bottom of the paper spaces are provided for a simple message (e.g., "SEND US FOOD"). The child must refer to the key and translate the message by coloring the blank flags with the appropriate colored insignia. An example is shown in Figure VII-3. Since "coloring" may be tedious or distasteful to some children because of association with primary grade activities, a set of flags can be printed on cards in advance and sorted into boxes or envelopes according to the letters they represent. The child's task is to select the appropriate flags and arrange them properly in order to put the message into code.

Direction-following tasks which involve reading should only be used with students well able to read at the level required. Some examples of order tasks which require reading are paragraph puzzles, ordering of events in a paragraph into a logical sequence, and spotting obvious errors in written material.

Paragraph puzzles engage the child in following printed directions, step by step. An example of such a paragraph puzzle is as follows:

Read this entire paragraph carefully. Put a red line under all four and five letter words. Next draw a blue circle around all words ending with "e." Write your name in each blank space on the paper. _____. Cross out all words that start with the same letter as the first letter in your name, etc.

This activity can be shortened or lengthened, simplified or increased in difficulty, according to the attention span and reading level of individual students.

Simple stories may be typed on cardboard and cut up so that one line of the story is on each of several cardboard strips. The story should involve a clearly understandable sequence of events such as the following:

John's Day

John got up in the morning.
He ate his breakfast.
In school he learned a new song.
On the way home from school he met Tom.
John and Tom played until time for supper.

Message: ___Send___   ___us___   ___food___

FIGURE VII-3. International Flag Code activity.

The child is given the cardboard strips, each with a sentence of the story on it, in random order. The task is to organize them, one under another, so that the story makes sense.

Again, length and level of complexity are subject to change. For adolescents a more suitable theme would obviously have to be chosen.

Inserting errors (e.g., illogical statements) in reading paragraphs and assigning the child the job of locating them has also been used by Jensen (1966) with institutionalized delinquent boys.

Simple direction-following tasks not involving reading are provided by sorting and pencil and art activities. Sorting objects (e.g., skeins of yarn and commercial paint chips) on the basis of color alone is perhaps one of the simplest order tasks. Classifying such items as geometric cutouts and nuts and bolts according to form and size is a related activity.

Stan, an adolescent boy in the NPI School, frequently became extremely restless and distractible in the classroom. He often had to be removed from class because he could not be engaged in any activity. One day the teacher brought a large box of assorted nuts, bolts, and washers to school and gave Stan the job of sorting them into different piles according to size. The boy quickly settled down and began sorting. Although he tired of this after a while, he then was able to respond to another assignment. After that, the box of nuts and bolts was used regularly by the teacher to help Stan "settle down" during periods of distractibility.

Dot-to-dot number-connecting pictures are also useful since most children are motivated to work until a recognizable picture emerges. Painting-by-number art kits which require that the child paint a specific color in a specific area in order to complete an oil painting are readily available. Although these are too complex and tedious for many emotionally disturbed children, they have been useful with some.

13. Child is Uncontrolled in Learning

According to the Inventory introduced in Chapter IV, children rated as "uncontrolled" in learning approach their work in an impulsive and uncritical manner. As a result, tasks given them should be well-defined and lead to a conclusion that is clearly in sight for the child at all times.

In assigning order tasks to the impulsive, uncritical child, the teacher does not permit free choice. Allowing the child some freedom of choice was encouraged on the response level, but at the order level it is completion of an assigned task that is of primary concern. In cases where the child is highly resistant to teacher direction he may be presented two activities and told he may do one or the other.

Jigsaw puzzles, differing in complexity, are widely available and encourage orderly completion of a task. These puzzles range from simple form boards which involve inserting geometric shapes into matching openings to picture puzzles with subjects which are appealing to children (e.g., sports figures, comic strip heroes). Obviously, the complexity of the puzzle needs to be matched to the ability and frustration tolerance of the child. A puzzle table may be set up in the room and members of the class periodically assigned to add pieces to a puzzle on which the entire room is working. The author has been surprised at the patience and care exhibited by children working on such puzzles when their typical behavior patterns in the classroom are highly erratic.

Paper and pencil maze activities are also successful in eliciting interest and a more critical approach to problem solving from such children.

14. Child is Disruptive in Group

The child with an order problem is never more visible or difficult to deal with than when he is defying the teacher's request and engaging in a power struggle while his classmates look on. When such a crisis arises, teachers often make the mistake of primarily relying on increased verbalization and, unwittingly, actually reward the child's misbehavior.

Haring and Phillips (1962) have considered the problem of increased verbalization as a control technique.

> As a general rule, teachers talk a great deal more than is necessary. Verbalizing is the most abstract method of getting across a point. Whenever possible, *show* the child instead of telling him. Excessive talking on the part of the teacher often seems to condition children not to listen. Set the precedent of giving instructions once. Be sure the instructions are well organized, clear and to the point. After the instructions have been given and understood, it is reasonable to expect the child to get the job done without having to repeat the instructions. When the child will not face up to his fair share of the responsibility, urging and coaxing as influence techniques are usually futile. A good rule to follow is to do at first, what you would have to do later in order to get over to the child the consequences facing him. This attitude on the teacher's part saves a lot of time and avoids encouraging the child to play the game of testing the firmness of the educational requirements.[1]

[1] N. Haring and E. Phillips, *Educating Emotionally Disturbed Children* (New York: McGraw-Hill Book Company, 1962), p. 140.

Increased verbalization on the part of the teacher often reflects anxiety and anger, as seen in this example cited by Martin and Stendler (1959):

> Lawrence is a large, overweight boy in the first grade. He stands out, not only because of his size, but also because of his actions. During an observation lasting one hour, Lawrence stuck a pin into the boy in front of him and pretended he knew nothing when the boy squealed with pain; he "accidentally" knocked against a neighbor's crayons as he swaggered down the aisle, and then proceeded to step on them when they fell to the floor; he used Bobbie's miniature projector against Bobbie's better judgment and held on to it for ten minutes, although four boys were lined up waiting for it; he snatched a film from one of the boys and kept it until the boy appealed to the teacher; he crowned his accomplishments by spilling a jar of paint on the floor.
>
> At this point the group turned on Lawrence and poured out their wrath to the teacher. Terribly angry, the teacher told Lawrence that he couldn't be trusted, that he was a "mean person," that nobody liked a mean person, and that he'd have to work in a corner by himself until he learned to get along with other children. Lawrence stared straight into the teacher's face; unashamed and apparently unmoved by his tirade, he insolently and noisily moved his seat into the corner and sat facing his peers with a look of defiance, indeed, almost triumph on his face.[2]

For some children who are disruptive in the classroom, simply ignoring the behavior will cause it to diminish in frequency. Theoretically, if the child is seeking social attention through misbehavior, not rewarding him at such times will cause the frequency of this maladaptive behavior to diminish. While this may be sound theoretically, in a group setting, particularly in the public school, it is often not practical because of the price which must be paid by the other students. Nevertheless, teachers should be aware that the child who always gets the teacher's attention through his antics, brings the entire class to a halt, gains a large audience as a result, provokes the teacher into repetitive lecturing, and eventually gets sent to the principal's office where he may view the passing parade of fellow students and receive attention from secretaries and clerks may have discovered a very predictable means for obtaining rewards in school.

A more practical and effective approach to such a student is to try to make school and learning more rewarding during times when his behavior approximates the desired standard. Selection of tasks the child

[2] W. Martin and C. Stendler, *Child Behavior and Development* (New York: Harcourt, Brace & World, 1959), pp. 355–356.

can do and enjoys doing is of utmost importance as is providing social attention and approval at moments of appropriate behavior. Teachers and parents alike may fail to notice a child unless there is a problem. They may overlook the importance of rewarding his attempts at conformity because "that's only what's expected."

Some teachers have provided rewards for children with order problems by giving them a poker chip or gold star periodically during the day at times, brief as they may be, when the child is following directions. These "token rewards" may be exchanged for some tangible reward or privilege at a later time.

A series of classroom interventions for dealing with disruptive behavior is presented as part of the total classroom design discussed in Chapter X.

Exclusion from a classroom when necessary should occur as a predictable consequence rather than an arbitrary exercise of the teacher's authority. Ott (1958) has described the use of a warning system with emotionally disturbed adolescent students which gets them ready for the possible consequences of having to leave the room.

To deal successfully with the everyday disciplinary problems that crop up with normal as well as disturbed youngsters, it is essential that the parent or teacher have an intelligent plan that is generally able to meet all situations. If the authority's methods are inconsistent and confused, we can expect no more from the youth. I have found a four-step plan to be particularly successful. With modifications to fit one's personality, this plan can be a valuable asset to the teaching day.

Step 1. The youngster violates a rule. The teacher (dean, parent, etc.) explains in clear language what the rule is and, if need be, why the act is unacceptable to society. If the rule is generally known and accepted by all, then this step is not necessary.

Step 2. Again the rule is violated. The youngster is given a choice. He can choose between adequate disciplinary action now or no disciplinary action now. If he chooses to be disciplined now, the action is carried out and the sequence of discipline is closed. If he chooses to try to solve the problem on his own, it is made clear that the next time he will be a three-time loser, and he is told exactly what action will be taken. (I have never experienced a youngster asking for immediate discipline. This natural reaction is good, for it allows the youth an opportunity to look at himself and the immediate problem realistically. This also gives him a well-controlled setting in which he may rebel or test if his personality demands these reactions to a firm control.)

Step 3. Again a violation. Without hesitation and in no uncertain terms, the promised discipline is used. It is well to point out to the youth that this discipline was his choice.

Step 4. After the youngster has "paid," forget about it. Of course consistent violation in specific areas (i.e., chronic lying, stealing, etc.)

indicates a behavior pattern that will require help from a specialist in human behavior. But throwing specific "paid-up debts to society" back into the youngster's face time and time again will wreck any child-adult relationship.[3]

Whelan and Haring (1966) have been cited earlier with respect to their usage of a time-out area for the emotionally disturbed child who is unable to control himself in the classroom. The assignment to such an area places the child in isolation for a specified period of time. The author has uitlized this approach, which will be discussed in greater detail in Chapter X. At present it is important to stress that removal of a child to a time-out area (e.g., principal's office, hall, bench outside the room) when he is unable to control himself should be done with the following considerations:

1. It should occur only after the child's behavior has exceeded the limits of the classroom which have been clearly stated to him previously.
2. It should occur matter-of-factly, rather than as a result of teacher exasperation.
3. It should be presented to the child as a constructive aid to learning rather than arbitrary punishment (e.g., "It seems you are having trouble working in the class right now. Perhaps you can work better if you have a chance to sit by yourself for a period of time.")
4. It should involve a specific period of time (e.g., a specified number of minutes) and not be open-ended with the child spending hours in isolation until the teacher "gets around" to checking with him.
5. Once the specified period of exclusion from the class has passed, the child should be immediately returned without any attempt on the teacher's part to get him to promise "to be a good boy from now on."

Removal of the child from the classroom is often necessary when he cannot fulfill the "student" role expected at the order level. This will be discussed in further detail in the "structure" section of this chapter.

15. Child Does Not Finish Learning Tasks

Besides concern with helping the child learn to follow directions, the order level attempts to assist him complete tasks which he undertakes. Direction-following activities with unique rewarding consequences, model copying, timing, and record-keeping have proven useful in this regard.

---

[3] J. Ott, "Teaching the Emotionally Disturbed Teenage Student," *Bul. Nat. Ass'n. Sec. Sch. Prin.*, 1958, 42, pp. 180–181.

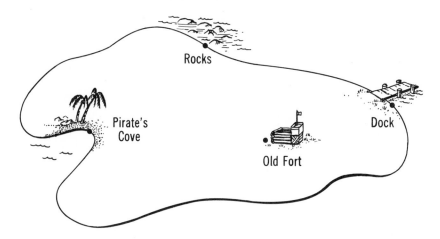

Figure VII-4. Treasure map direction following activity.

Treasure maps which require simple following of arrows, reading of directions, or computations of arithmetic problems in order to locate the "treasure" are intriguing to children. The complexity of the map assigned again depends on the functioning level of the individual child. A sample map (not to scale) with directions used with one child is seen in Figure VII-4. The child was given a special ruler with ¼" spaces marked off on it. The scale on the ruler read "Each mark is equal to ten paces."

The directions accompanying the map read as follows:

1. Mark off 50 paces from Pirates' Cove toward the Old Fort.
2. Now mark off 70 paces toward the Rocks.
3. From this point mark off 100 paces toward the Dock.
4. You have just found the treasure. Mark the spot where you think the treasure is located.

This is only an example and many variations are possible. Once the child has "searched" for the treasure, the teacher checks his calculations and if he is correct he is allowed to pick out a reward (e.g., candy bar) from a "treasure chest" kept in the teacher's desk for such purposes. Such assignments cannot produce miracles and guarantee the child will never leave an assignment incomplete again, but they can be helpful in initiating an interest in pursuing tasks to completion in school. Obviously the teacher's skill and ingenuity will have to be relied on to round out an educational program for a student with problems at the order level.

Model-copying tasks which do not depend on academic ability but rather on hand-eye coordination and attention to detail have been successful in encouraging the child with order problems to complete assignments. Toy construction kits are readily available commercially and can be utilized to make such objects as small rocking chairs, toy trucks, and miniature buildings by assembling wood and plastic units according to pictorial diagrams. The teacher can mount each diagram on a card and assign the child the task of building the object illustrated from an assemblage of parts. Once the model is copied the parts can be dismantled for future use.

Car, airplane, and ship models can be permanently constructed with commercial kits but are more difficult and often frustrating to the child who is not adept at fine motor tasks. However, these can be used effectively in the classroom with some children.

Pegboard designs can also be copied by the child who inserts colored wood or plastic pegs into a board in order to match a model design given him by the teacher. Similar model copying can be done with colored beads, blocks, and plastic units available commercially. The teacher can also assemble several painted washers and nuts on a bolt and give it to the child as a model. The child's task is to assemble as many similar units as possible from a supply of painted washers, nuts, and bolts.

Some children who have difficulty completing assignments are highly motivated if timed records are kept of their work. The child is given an individual timer and a page of arithmetic problems to do. The timer, which may be one commonly used in the kitchen, is set by the teacher when the child starts, and the child is given the responsibility for stopping it when he is through. Of course, such time pressure may create frustration and an uncritical approach to the assignment with some emotionally disturbed children and therefore has to be used advisedly.

Record-keeping, mentioned earlier at the response level, may also contribute to the child's desire to complete his assignment. A daily or weekly schedule written down by the teacher, with a box opposite each assignment to be checked off following completion, may serve as an incentive. Graphs recording number of problems done, pages read, and spelling words reviewed are also useful with some children, although it should be recalled that task completion is the focus of the order level, not academic achievement level. For children with problems at the order level such records should reflect work accomplished which is well within their functioning level rather than emphasize academic progress.

The specific tasks which have been suggested in this section are designed to help the child start, follow through, and complete assignments according to a set of directions. The reward operating at this level and a further discussion of the significance of structure will now be considered.

ORDER LEVEL REWARDS

Box c on the composite developmental sequence form in Figure IV-8 in Chapter IV refers to the order level reward as "finishing learning tasks." The hypothesis here is that task completion provides a reward in itself and aiding the child in developing motivation for finishing learning tasks is an important goal in the education of emotionally disturbed children.

Supporting evidence that task completion may indeed function as a source of reward must be drawn largely from Gestalt psychology. According to the Gestalt conception of motivation, if an individual is motivated toward success in a task, a specific tension system is aroused which persists during the time he is undertaking the task and only is resolved by its completion. The classic study which investigated this premise was done by Zeigarnik (1938), and the tendency for individuals to recall incomplete tasks better than completed ones has come to be known as the "Zeigarnik effect."

In her study, Zeigarnik found that incompleted tasks were recalled almost twice as often as completed tasks. Since this study a number of attempts have been made to verify her findings. The results of these studies indicate that several factors influence whether or not the Ziegarnik effect occurs, including the attitude of the subject toward the task, stress associated with the task, and the length of time which elapses between a task and a recall test.

Martin and Davidson (1964) compared underachieving and achieving children with respect to occurrence of the Zeigarnik effect and report that it occurred only with achievers operating under an "achievement orientation."

Cartwright (1942) found that incompleted tasks were rated as "more attractive" following their interruption than they had been rated previously.

The author has observed numerous autistic children who had a great fondness for putting jigsaw puzzles together and "getting everything back in its proper place." One of Kanner's (1951) criteria for the diagnosis of autism is a preoccupation with sameness. With these severely disturbed children task completion may be a powerful reward, although it may only serve to maintain rigidity of functioning rather than aid in the developing of adaptive behavior.

For purposes of the present discussion, a more important consideration is the effect of interruption on the subject's preference for resuming a particular task. Rosensweig (1933) found that crippled children varying in ages from five to 14 years differed with respect to preference for returning to incompleted as compared with completed tasks. The younger subjects preferred to resume completed tasks, while the older subjects stated a desire to return to incompleted tasks. In a later study Rosensweig (1936) interpreted the tendency of the older children to prefer incompleted tasks as a function of increased "pride," "self-criticalness," and a "certain sensitivity to failure."

The evidence available from this area of research is far from conclusive, but it suggests that children who expect success when undertaking a task may be motivated by a desire to complete the task and in a sense task completion functions as a positive consequence or reward for their efforts. Since it would appear that many emotionally disturbed children expect to fail in the classroom, it is not surprising that some of them do not appear motivated to finish assignments.

The negative attitudes children have toward themselves and their chances of success in school cannot be overlooked. Selection of suitable tasks to assign these children then becomes an extremely important consideration for the teacher, and guaranteeing success appears crucial for developing motivation for task completion.

ORDER LEVEL STRUCTURE

In the early part of this chapter mention was made of the role of a structured learning environment in helping emotionally disturbed children learn in school. Part of such an environment included the fostering of "student behavior." The problem of dealing with children who are not under the control of the teacher and who are disruptive in the classroom has also been discussed.

If the child is to function in the classroom setting, he must fulfill the minimum requirements of the "student role." This role includes reasonable tolerance for limits of time (when), space (where), and activity (what) and a reasonable respect for the working rights of others (how). "How well" assignments are done is a concern for the mastery level. While children with severe attention and response problems can not always be held for this role, it is one of the major goals of the order level.

In the NPI School, children are generally only permitted to remain in the classroom when they can function as "students." The message is "schooling for everyone," but "school only for students." When it is apparent that a given child cannot control himself, he is immediately returned to the hospital ward. If the expectation for student behavior is seen as inappropriate because of his emotional problems, he is provided with individual tutoring until such time as it is felt that he can function as a member of the class group again. In setting up a program of individual instruction the child is not rejected or criticized for his inability to fulfill the student role. His education is of vital concern to the teacher, and every effort will be made to continue it. But inclusion in a class group carries with it the responsibility for being a "student," and this is made very clear to all of the children.

The author has been impressed by the discrepancy sometimes seen between severely disturbed children's behavior on the hospital ward during nonschool hours and what is seen in the classroom. Once the child understands that "only students come to school," it is surprising how appropriate his behavior becomes once he walks through the classroom door.

As was mentioned in Chapter VI, Mayhew and Ferjo have assigned adolescents as teacher assistants with younger children in the NPI School. The effect of this arrangement on both the older and younger students is quite remarkable. Adolescents with severe order problems themselves often demonstrate a patience and understanding in marked contrast to their more typical behavior. In addition they make it clear to the child with order problems whom they are helping that he must conform to certain limits such as not leaving his seat and not disrupting the class. The reactions of the younger children are also interesting to observe. They often settle down and work prodigiously, apparently anxious to please their individual "teachers."

The maladaptive behavior of children with order problems is perhaps the easiest to identify. The environmental factors which support it, however, are not always readily apparent. The possibility that teachers may unwittingly reward such behavior has already been pointed out. Another possibility which bears mention at this point is that the child never has had the teacher's expectations clearly and firmly spelled out for him, and as a result he continues to "test the limits." Therefore the environmental change of greatest usefulness in bringing about more adaptive behavior may involve careful delineation of the "student role." It is the author's contention that such a role can be successfully assumed in the classroom by more emotionally disturbed children than often thought possible. The fact is that with only rare exceptions all children with serious order problems hospitalized on the Children's Service of the Neuropsychiatric Institute are successful "students" in NPI School classrooms.

In this chapter we have considered examples of order tasks, the type of reward operating at the order level, and the significance of establishing a structured learning environment. In contrast to the attention and response levels, the order level emphasizes the structure side of the learning triangle and holds the child for maintenance of a "student role."

VIII EXPLORATORY AND SOCIAL LEVELS

At the exploratory and social levels the child applies the basic tools of attending, responding, and direction-following which he has acquired at the first three levels of the developmental sequence in activities involving multisensory experience and social interaction. In this chapter we will examine the types of tasks which foster accurate exploration of the environment and which aid the child in developing appropriate social behavior, the nature of rewards, and the degree of structure suggested at the exploratory and social levels.

EXPLORATORY LEVEL

There are three major characteristics of tasks associated with the exploratory level. Exploratory tasks provide:

1. A wide range of multisensory experiences.
2. An emphasis on reality.
3. Predictable outcomes.

Children learn about the world in which they live through looking, listening, touching, moving, tasting, and smelling. The stove may be labeled "hot" by a parent, but it is often the experience of touching the hot stove that teaches the meaningful lesson. Emotionally disturbed children may have a fragmented knowledge of the environment because of constriction and fearfulness, discussed as problems of the attention and response levels. What will be discussed in this section is an extension of some of the same problems considered earlier.

181

The curriculum area of science holds excellent promise for successfully engaging the emotionally disturbed child in multisensory exploration of his environment. It also provides a significant emphasis on reality and experiences with predictable outcomes.

As children undertake simple science experiments with air, heat, light, sound, magnetism, color, and various chemicals, they are exposed to a multitude of sensory stimulation. The elementary and secondary science curriculum has been rapidly developed and emphasized since the launching of the first Russian Sputnik, and a great many materials are available for adaptation in the special classroom for emotionally disturbed children.

At the exploratory level the goal is to get the child involved in learning with his hands, eyes, ears, nostrils, and taste buds, not to focus on underlying scientific principles or theories. This does not mean that simple explanations of science activities should not be given, but rather that they should not become tedious or overdrawn.

A fascinating, simple science experiment which appeals to all children involves a demonstration of air pressure, utilizing a milk bottle, a peeled, hard-boiled egg, and a burning piece of paper. The egg will not go through the neck of the bottle initially, but when the burning paper is first placed in the bottle using up the air inside, the egg "pops" through the neck as a result of external air pressure. One teacher of the disturbed using this experiment and attempting to adhere to the exploratory emphasis of the developmental sequence avoided any discussion of the reason behind the egg's descent into the bottle. One child decided on his own that the neck of the bottle had "stretched," and the teacher let his comment go unchallenged because of her conviction that the purpose of the experiment was only to get the child involved in a multisensory experience.

Such literalness is undesirable and a simple explanation that the fire used up the air inside the bottle so that the air outside pushed harder on the egg is most appropriate. Here is an example of the unavoidable overlap between levels of the developmental sequence. Certain mastery considerations will be essential at even the attention level. It is the emphasis placed on the task at various levels that determines its usefulness, not its complete isolation from all other levels.

However, a long and complicated verbal explanation of the properties of air would also have been inappropriate. In this regard, the author is reminded of the story of the little boy who saw a penguin for the first time at the zoo. When he got home he described it to his father and asked what it was. The father, obviously delighted at his son's inquisitiveness, took out the encyclopedia and obtained several reference books from the library. After a lengthy lecture on penguins the father noticed the troubled look on his son's face. "What's the matter," he asked, "didn't you want to learn about penguins?" His son looked up and said slowly, "Yes, but not that much."

At the exploratory level the goal is to maintain the child's interest and provide him with intriguing information and experiences through exploration of the environment, not to overwhelm him with information in depth.

In the classroom design to be discussed in Chapter X an exploratory center is set up in one area to include a variety of science equipment, materials for performing simple experiments, microscopes for looking at tiny organisms, small telescopes for looking out the classroom windows at birds and other objects of interest, and kaleidoscopes for exploring a myriad of colors and forms. A projector for viewing color slides and a collection of magazines such as *National Geographic* provide additional visual experiences. A listening post consisting of a record player and tape recorder allows the child to hear stories and music and to play back recordings of his own voice. A shortwave radio will provide fascinating experiences for children as they hear programs from all over the world, keep track of the locations picked up, and perhaps plot these on a map.

Carrot tops and avocado seeds in water can be watched day by day until they begin to grow. A class-garden in a window box or perhaps in a plot of ground outside provides many tactual-exploratory experiences. A terrarium in which exotic and unusual plants will grow is of special interest to children. Carnivorous plants such as Venus-flytraps are particularly fascinating.

The presence of animals in the room provides many opportunities for exploration through physical contact, feeding, care, and cleaning of cages. Over a period of years the author has observed with interest the kinds of animals best suited for inclusion in classrooms for emotionally disturbed children. The indestructible turtle is ideal for younger children, and large rabbits can be fed and petted with few problems. The NPI School located on the UCLA campus in the same complex of buildings housing the University vivarium is in the fortunate position of having a "traveling zoo" visit the younger children each week. Frogs, monkeys, sheep, birds, dogs, and kittens are a few of the creatures brought in for short visits which allow each child an opportunity to examine and in some cases touch or hold them.

Tame white rats have been particularly popular with older elementary age children and appear more appropriate than hamsters. Guinea pigs have also been housed with few problems. Snakes and lizards have

been successfully kept, although how appropriate they are in the classroom may well depend on the teacher's comfort in handling them. A
fish tank is commonly present and provides children with a constant
source of changing movement and color. Caged birds such as para-
keets, canaries, and pigeons have been less successful due to the fact
that they can seldom be handled.

In selecting animals the teacher of the disturbed child should avoid
those which are extremely fragile. The author has known of two instances where the killing of a baby rabbit by disturbed children in
school had unhappy consequences for all concerned. In one case a
thirteen-year-old boy with severe order problems in a public school
class for disturbed children was inappropriately given responsibility for
caring for several baby rabbits. When one of the rabbits was killed
through careless handling the teacher was visibly shaken, the other
members of the class very upset, and the boy himself expelled for his
display of aggression. In the other case a seven-year-old psychotic child
was excluded from a residential treatment center because he purposely
killed a small baby rabbit in front of his classmates. Both of these
instances probably could have been prevented had the teacher exercised
better judgment in advance.

Just what constitutes an "attractive nuisance" or "genuine hazard"
in classrooms for disturbed children is by no means an easy question to
answer. While exposure to fragile animals is probably best avoided,
allowing emotionally disturbed children to use gas burners, delicate
scientific instruments, and sharp objects in science experiments has
never proven a problem in either the NPI School or public school
programs with which the author has been associated. One important
point, however, must be made. In all cases the classrooms were well-
structured, and the student role described in the last chapter was expected of all the children.

The use of art, music, dance, and dramatic play provides additional
exploratory activities for the emotionally disturbed child. Painting, clay
modeling, drawing, crafts, and creative activities associated with music,
dance, and drama offer opportunities for self-directed exploration by
the child and can be a useful part of the educational program. The
author is aware that art, music, dance, and dramatic play activities are
seen as valuable by some because of the self-expressive and psychotherapeutic aspects they bring into classrooms for emotionally disturbed children. In the context of the developmental sequence, however, they are significant because of the opportunity they afford for
exploration of the outer rather than the inner world.

In addition to a variety of multisensory experiences the area of
science offers a distinct emphasis on reality. For this reason it was

important for the teacher who demonstrated the "egg in the bottle" experiment mentioned earlier to call attention to the causal factors involved. This was an opportunity to emphasize the real existence of air and the fact that it takes up space and has weight.

Emotionally disturbed children may have superstitions and fears which inhibit their exploration of the environment. Susan, an eight-year-old child in the NPI School, with severe attention, response, exploratory, and social problems, entered the classroom for the first time and screamed with terror at the sight of a caged white rat. She immediately sat down on the floor by the door, curled up, and covered her eyes. The teacher calmly stated that the rat was a part of the classroom, that it would remain in the cage, and that it would not bother her at all. Susan was not about to take the teacher's word for this at first and remained huddled on the floor. She was allowed to stay in the room, as the teacher immediately recognized her attention and response problems and decided it would be inappropriate to hold her for the "student role" initially. For several days Susan would enter the classroom, see the rat, and huddle on the floor, while the rest of the children went to their desks and began work. Not a great deal of attention was paid to her; the teacher only briefly explained that the rat would not harm her and pointed out that a desk was waiting when she was ready to take her place with the other children. There was not a great deal of verbalization on the teacher's part, and she purposely avoided rewarding Susan's maladaptive behavior with attention. Her message to Susan was simply: "That's just the way it is in this classroom. The rat belongs here. But you do not have to go near it, if you do not wish."

It was not long before Susan voluntarily went to her desk where she readily undertook assignments on the mastery level. She was a bright and capable learner, functioning well in all academic areas. She was, however, a good example of a child who had not mastered tasks on the lower levels of the developmental sequence. Problems with Susan and the rat were not over by any means, for she screamed loudly when any of the other children went to play with the animal and took it out of the cage. Again, this behavior was largely ignored and it soon diminished. After several weeks Susan was observed to be quietly watching the other children play with the rat. Whatever the basis for her fear of rats, the fact that the other children readily picked one up, fondled it, and let it crawl on their shoulders seemed to interest her. Susan never progressed to the stage where she joined them, but watching her classmates from a distance provided an important "reality" lesson regarding rats.

The controlled use of fire and simple science experiments demonstrating the properties of heat also can provide valuable reality experiences for disturbed children. One teacher devised a unit demonstrating the three essential requirements for fire—heat, oxygen, and fuel—in a number of clever experiments which the children could replicate on their own. Snipping off the wick of a burning candle illustrated the importance of a source of heat, and covering the candle with a glass provided an example of the necessity for oxygen. A simple fire extinguisher which could be used to put out the flame was later constructed with vinegar and baking soda. While children may be trained "never to play with matches" they do need to know something about fire, why it occurs and how it can be controlled, in order to function adequately in their environments.

Both science and art activities are useful in getting emotionally disturbed children to freely explore with their hands. Some disturbed children display discomfort in "making a mess" or "getting dirty." Whatever the basis for this aversion they can be aided in becoming more complete explorers through participation in activities involving touch and manipulation. Cleaning a fish tank, feeding animals and cleaning their cages, tending a garden, working with clay, papier-maché, or plaster of Paris, and finger painting are examples of tasks which promote manual exploration of the real world.

The predictability associated with science demonstrations and experiments is seen as very valuable in classrooms for emotionally disturbed children. For this reason every effort should be made to select activities that are simple yet intriguing to children and which have a high probability of success when undertaken in the classroom.

Some science demonstrations can involve complex preparation and exacting maneuvers before they "work." When they do not it is both frustrating and disappointing. The author recalls a craft and science project he utilized in a classroom with emotionally disturbed adolescent boys. The task was to construct tin-can submarines which operated on calcium carbide. The submarines filled with water and sank when placed in the tub. The water eventually overflowed into a container of the chemical inside the submarine and a gaseous reaction occurred. This reaction was supposed to close several intricate valves in the submarine and force the water out through a propulsion tube, moving the submarine through the water and eventually raising it to the surface. At least, that was the intention. But the sad truth was that after several months of cutting metal and shaping and soldering various parts of the submarine, not one functioned according to plan. While the entire project was an interesting exploratory activity in itself, it was somewhat defeated by the "letdown" experienced when the submarines failed to operate.

Other such examples which the author recalls involved constructing metal pinwheels which were supposed to rotate when held over a flame, but which could not be balanced with precision so that they would turn, and a candle-making project which resulted in disaster because the wicks could not be centered during the process. Suffice to say teachers are advised to try out exploratory activities before presenting them to their students so that frustrating failures like this can be avoided for all.

Sanford was a fifteen-year-old boy in the NPI School who spent long hours designing mathematical formulas, computers, and elaborate electronic devices which were based more on fantasy than on fact. He refused to participate with the class in simple science experiments because he felt they were too elementary. His resourceful teacher, however, gradually got him interested in constructing a simple buzzer which operated on a dry cell battery. Despite Sanford's preoccupation with electronic wizardry, he was led patiently through the buzzer-making project and actually finished it. When a "loud buzz" ensued on the day of completion, the boy was obviously very delighted. He displayed the buzzer with pride to his classmates and later confided to the teacher, "Do you know that this is the first thing I ever planned and made that actually worked!"

Exploratory tasks are designed to engage the child in a variety of multisensory experiences, put him in maximal contact with reality, and guarantee him a predictable outcome. Science is seen as particularly useful at the exploratory level, although a variety of other activities that involve the child in visual, auditory, and tactual exploration of his environment are also valuable.

We turn now to consideration of the task boxes at the exploratory level, as stated in Figure IV-8.

EXPLORATORY LEVEL TASKS

16. Child Does Not Adequately Explore His Environment

The characteristics of exploratory tasks discussed in the previous section are directed toward aiding the child in more adequately exploring his environment and increasing his knowledge of it. At the exploratory level it is direct knowledge obtained through sensory and motor experience that is of concern as compared with information obtained through more symbolic exploration at the mastery level.

Multisensory exploratory tasks are commonly emphasized in preschool and primary educational programs. Once the child acquires reading competency he is expected to acquire knowledge more and more through symbolic means, although social studies and science units in the later grades are often accompanied by demonstrations and projects which involve visual, auditory, and tactual exploration.

Classrooms for emotionally disturbed children at upper elementary and secondary levels must operate as "camouflaged kindergartens" in certain respects. This fact has been suggested by the nature of various attention, response, and order tasks illustrated earlier. The goal for the teacher is to assist the child in acquiring skill and knowledge which has already been mastered by normal children during their earlier learning experiences.

Children can be encouraged to visually explore their environments through periods of observation outdoors. Trees, plants, flowers, and other objects can be described in terms of color, size, shape, and location. Drawings can be made during such observations or material gathered for later story writing. Art work offers a more direct exploratory experience and does not involve translation of description into words.

Some emotionally disturbed children, such as Jay described in Chapter VI, may engage in constantly drawing the same object to the complete exclusion of anything else. The author has observed Tom, a deaf eight-year-old boy with severe order, exploratory, and social problems who, left alone, would draw one fluorescent light tube after another. If not interrupted, Tom covered sheet after sheet of drawing paper with carefully drawn and spaced fluorescent tubes. Because he was generally disruptive in school but remarkably calm and controlled while drawing fluorescent lights, the teacher encouraged him to sit and draw for much of each day. His most prized possession was a fluorescent desk lamp which his mother had purchased for him.

Tom was a real exploratory challenge, but unfortunately the teacher did not attempt to get him involved in other types of art activity which might at first have focused on different kinds of light fixtures such as neon signs and later on the variety of shapes (geometric designs, letters, and finally human forms) which are often made with neon tubing.

One institutional teacher in a state hospital who worked with a boy who only would draw airplanes was successful in getting him to begin drawing the pilots who flew the airplanes, paying particular attention to the insignia they wore in different countries and the branches of service which they represented.

Visual exploratory activities on the order level were suggested in the last chapter. Sorting objects according to size, length, width, color, and shape provides both a specific assignment with directions and also a task of visual exploration.

Mixing food coloring in glasses of water to provide an assortment of hues also provides an interesting visual exploratory task. Tempera paints, when mixed to match color samples, can be the basis for teaching the child about primary colors and the combinations involved in creating the full range of colors for art work. Older children may be intrigued with the principles of mixing lights to obtain different shades and colors.

An auditory exploratory task that has proven appealing to children involves tapping glasses filled with varying amounts of water and listening for the differences in pitch. Rubber bands stretched with different degrees of tightness across the open top of a cigar box can be plucked and compared for sound.

A "mystery box" has been used successfully by some teachers. Each week a closed shoebox was presented to the children. An object (e.g., pencil, eraser, tennis ball) had been placed inside, and members of the class attempted to "solve the mystery" by shaking the contents of the box and listening for clues that might disclose the object's identity.

Tactual exploratory tasks include a familiar guessing game which involves reaching in a paper bag containing such objects as a piece of fur, a sponge, and buttons and attempting to identify these objects from touch alone. One teacher has given students the task of matching adjectives describing tactile qualities of objects which the child is familiar with in the environment. A list of such words as hot, warm, cold, freezing, gooey, sticky, slimy, slippery, slick, smooth, hard, brittle, soft, spongy, bouncy, rough, coarse, bumpy, uneven, cracked, sandy, firm, taut, slack, and wet may be printed on a work sheet and the child given the task of writing in the names of objects with each characteristic.

Science experiments offer many tactual experiences. The child may be given an assortment of objects to explore one-by-one to see if they float or can be picked up by a magnet.

Experiences of tasting and smelling can also be offered the child to increase his awareness and knowledge of the environment. Substances which are sweet, sour, and bitter can be sampled and described. Containers of familiar household substances such as vinegar, perfume, and iodine can be smelled, described, and identified as to the nature of the contents.

The use of science in providing multisensory experience with the child has been discussed in this section. A few additional comments at this point will serve to elaborate on its usefulness. One of the most successful science exploratory activities with older elementary and secondary age children is a weather station. Commercial kits are available with inexpensive devices for measuring wind speed and direction. Thermometers, hydrometers, and barometers can also be obtained from science supply houses. Reference material describing types of cloud formations, their scientific labels, and their relation to various weather conditions are also readily available for the teacher. A large weather chart can be maintained in the classroom with the children given various responsibilities for taking readings describing each day's weather conditions, noting them on the chart, and attempting to predict the following day's weather.

Small incubators for poultry eggs are available commercially or can be constructed as a class project. Maintaining the appropriate degree of temperature, taking periodic readings of the temperature inside the incubator, and keeping track of the time elapsing before the eggs hatch are intriguing exploratory activities. Of course, watching the baby chicks emerge from their shells provides the highlight for children. The author has observed that this activity is even very popular with children who live in rural areas where eggs and chickens are most commonplace.

One teacher made a large chart divided into two sections. One was labeled "Bird of the Day" and the other "Mammal of the Day." Each day a different bird or animal picture was placed in each section. The children were either given the name of the bird or animal or asked to identify it from various reference sources. In this way the exploratory or mastery emphasis of the activity could be manipulated.

Invisible ink made with milk or lemon juice seldom fails to be of interest to children of all ages. Messages can be prepared in advance by the teacher and given to children who "discover" what they are by holding them over an electric light bulb or candle flame. Children can also write their own messages and exchange them with their classmates.

17. Child Overly Dependent on Others for Choice of Interest and Activities

Some emotionally disturbed children appear to have no clearcut interests and activities of their own. Others may have a greatly reduced number, and still others may always adopt the role of the "follower" and only select what someone else has selected first.

As we near the upper levels of the developmental sequence, the types of problems described are by no means as serious as those on the lower levels, but they still represent learning deficits in children. Although these problems may be found to some degree among relatively normal children never labeled "emotionally disturbed," when seen by the teacher they should be recognized and dealt with insofar as it is possible in the classroom.

While on the order level such concern with self-selection was eliminated in favor of getting the child to conform to teacher-directed tasks, at the exploratory level an attempt is made to get the child to take some responsibility for selecting tasks himself.

Teachers have encouraged children who display little interest in anything or who always follow others to express themselves through forced-choice situations. Such children may be asked to select a task, book, or activity from one of two or three possibilities. These possibilities are clearly presented to the child and he is told he must make a choice.

In the area of reading, teachers may make a mistake by taking dependent children to the school library and directing them to "find a book" they like. Confronted with the dozens of possible selections available on the shelves, such a child may balk, pick a book similar to one a classmate has chosen, or randomly pick up the first one he sees. In such cases, if the teacher will take the time to study interests which the child overtly or covertly expresses, preselect two or three books in these areas, present them to him, and state he must choose from these, some degree of independent choice may be fostered.

The author has observed tutors working with emotionally disturbed children who sat down with a child and, in an attempt to establish rapport, a nonthreatening atmosphere, and some degree of self-expression on the part of the child, cheerfully exclaimed, "Well, what shall we do today?" Often, in such an open-ended situation, the child becomes confused and changes his mind again and again; as a result a great deal of time is wasted. If the teacher feels the child should be encouraged to function more independently in his choice of interests and activities, it is usually wisest at first to set definite limits within which a choice must be made.

In the classroom, when it is appropriate for children to select their own activities for a period, the dependent child may be given first choice so that he does not merely fall in line with his classmates. Of course, the advisability of putting the child "on the spot" has to be weighed carefully beforehand by the teacher.

Mail-order catalogs have been utilized in an interesting exploratory activity designed to encourage some independent selection on the part of children. The child is told he has a certain amount to spend (e.g., $500) and is shown a section of the catalog which displays a specific type of merchandise (e.g., camping equipment). His task is to "spend" the money to outfit himself for a camping expedition, keeping in mind all of the requirements of a trip to a familiar camping area in the locale. This activity also lends itself to the building of addition, subtraction, and decimal skills.

18. Child Unable to do Learning Tasks Because of Motor, Physical, Sensory, Perceptual, or Intellectual Deficits

The child who is emotionally disturbed and who also is physically handicapped, has visual or auditory problems, or who is chronically ill, neurologically impaired, or mentally retarded, may have serious additional restrictions as to the kind and degree of exploration of the environment in which he may engage. Such handicaps also compound the emotionally disturbed child's problem on the other levels of the developmental sequence. With these children, the teacher should first concentrate on assisting the child at the attention, response, and order levels using sensory modalities and perceptual motor tasks in keeping with the child's capacities. While the focus of this text is on "what" behavior the child exhibits in school, not "why" it occurs psychologically, the importance of "how" it is related to motor, physical, sensory, perceptual, or intellectual factors cannot be minimized at this point on the developmental sequence. Therefore, medical and psychological test data are particularly important here.

Emotionally disturbed children with particular sensory handicaps are traditionally aided in compensating for their deficits by reliance on sense modalities which are intact. The blind child may become primarily an auditory and tactual explorer, while the deaf child may come to rely on visual knowledge about the environment. Thus, the nature and type of task assigned is manipulated. As with other emotionally disturbed children, the reward and structure dimensions of the learning triangle may also be very significant.

The author has served as consultant for a pilot project at the California State School for the Deaf in Riverside, California. The project was set up in an attempt to develop an educational program for deaf boys from eight to eleven who also demonstrated severe attention, response, and order problems and who previously had not been considered educable in a classroom. The severity of these boys' problems was readily apparent from their records. Some were preoccupied with fantasy, some were almost totally withdrawn from contact with others, some never paid attention to any teacher-directed tasks or directions, and some were so uncontrolled and assaultive in their behavior that they could never be left alone.

Four class groups with four students in each were set up and all 16 boys placed under 24-hour residential care in the School for the Deaf. The four teachers assigned to the pupils were all highly skilled in conducting traditional educational programs with the deaf. They had, however, only had limited experience with children with such serious problems on the lower levels of the developmental sequence.

The boys were first assessed according to the developmental sequence, and individual programs were established for each. A wide variety of attention, response, order, and visual-exploratory activities were provided in the classroom. Visually oriented mastery training in word recognition, word concept understanding, and basic arithmetic also was given. A check-mark system was utilized to reward the children periodically for appropriate behavior and work accomplishment. The system involved the use of individual cards ruled with squares which were carried around the classroom throughout the day. Following each 20 minutes of class work, the teacher gave each child a possible ten check marks, five black check marks for the work he had accomplished and five red check marks for his behavior. The check marks were given in different colors to visually emphasize their meaning. Each day the boys could exchange several completed rows of check marks for soft drinks and candy.

The pilot project also extended to the boys' dormitory. Check marks were first used to acknowledge the boys getting up on time, dressing, cleaning their rooms, washing, brushing their teeth, and lining up for breakfast. They also were given in the dining room for appropriate behavior while eating. In addition, they were used during periods of walking from the dormitory to the dining room and back and then to the school. A separate check-mark card was utilized by the dormitory staff. On the card were printed the various responsibilities which the boys had, such as "brushing teeth" and "dressing." These duties were printed within the actual squares on the card in which the boys would receive their check marks so that it would be very clear exactly for what the checks were given or withheld.

Since the dormitory environment was less structured than the school and many different things were going on at the same time for practical reasons the check marks had to be given after considerable periods of delay. As a result, their initial overall effectiveness, as meaningful rewards and as consequences for specific behavior, was minimal. In an effort to make the reward dimension of the learning triangle more immediate and concrete, cardboard milk bottle caps with holes punched in them were given to the boys "on the spot" following successful completion of dormitory tasks. These were saved by each boy on a metal shower ring attached to his belt. Later the cardboard bottle caps were converted to check marks and exchanged in the usual manner.

The pilot project illustrates the role increased visual and concrete tactual experiences can assume in assisting severely disturbed deaf children to master attention, response, order, social, and mastery tasks. Stanley was an eight-year-old deaf child brought into the project at California School for the Deaf from a neighboring state hospital for the mentally ill. He had never been given any formal schooling because of his violent, uncontrolled behavior. A special visually oriented reward procedure was utilized to bring him under control and establish him as a student in one of the project classrooms.

Stanley was first brought into the classroom by a teacher aide designated to work solely with him for very brief periods of time (e.g., five to ten minutes). In order to get Stanley to sit in a chair, he had to be forcibly held in place by the aide who knelt beside the chair and put his arms around him. The boy resisted in every way possible but he was finally held firm.

The teacher in the classroom placed a piece of candy on the desk in front of Stanley and quickly covered it with a clear plastic cup. Stanley could see the candy and knew what it was, but his access to it was prevented by the teacher who held the cup in place. The moment Stanley stopped resisting and relaxed, the aide released him and the teacher lifted the cup, making the candy available to him. This procedure only had to be repeated a few times before Stanley was a willing "chair-sitter" and physical restraint was no longer necessary.

From the shaping of this first necessary order behavior, Stanley's program went on to include simple form discrimination and puzzle-making tasks. Before each activity was presented to him, a piece of candy was placed under the cup in plain sight. Following his completion of a simple response, the cup was lifted by the aide, who now could work with Stanley alone since the boy did not have to be held in his chair any longer. In two weeks Stanley was able to tolerate more extended periods of time in the class and such immediate tangible reinforcement was no longer necessary.

Emotionally disturbed children with minimal neurological problems which interfere with their accurate perception of time, space, and form and whose motor skills are limited are of particular concern to the proponents of the sensory-neurological strategy discussed in Chapter I. Individuals such as Fernald (1943), Strauss (1947), Cruickshank (1961), Kephart (1960), and Frostig have devised specific training procedures for helping these children become more adequate and accurate explorers of the environment. Their teaching techniques and materials are also often useful in increasing the child's competency at the first three levels of the developmental sequence—attention, response, and order.

EXPLORATORY LEVEL REWARDS

Box d in Figure IV-8, Chapter IV, refers to the reward operating at the exploratory level as multisensory experience. The assumption is that sensory stimulation of any modality is rewarding and that it can be used to motivate children in learning.

Evidence indicating sensory stimulation is rewarding, including curiosity, manipulation, locomotion, and activity, was first provided by animal studies. These have been summarized by Kish (1966) and Glanzer (1958).

In human studies most research has been done with normal children who were presented with a simple bar-pressing task. These children soon discovered that the rate and duration of their pushing down on a bar or lever positioned in front of them controlled the presentation of certain visual and auditory stimuli. As they continued to "work" through bar pressing in order to obtain such sensory stimulation, evidence was provided that looking and listening provides a form of reward that can be utilized in learning.

Stevenson and Odom (1961) found exposure of colored animal pictures effective in eliciting bar-pressing behavior with kindergarten and elementary age children.

Antonitis and Barnes (1961) rewarded lever pressing by preschool children with both turning on and turning off a light in front of them. While this visual reward was effective at first in getting the child to increase his rate of response, it diminished over time but was reinstated when exposures of various cartoon cutouts were added.

Hayes (1958) demonstrated that three- and four-year-olds would "work" by pushing buttons in order to get a glimpse of a picture of a cat presented on a screen in front of them. In addition, he found simple one-person games involving dropping a marble in a box and awaiting its return and pushing a bar that delivered a clicking sound also provided rewards which controlled response rate.

Frey (1960) observed that garbled sounds or recorded phrases, such as "That's good" or "That's bad," increased bar pressing by nursery school children. The two phrases were also found to be equivalent in their effectiveness for maintaining bar pressing, and apparently the children responded to the auditory stimuli alone rather than the positive or negative implications of the words.

Rheingold, Stanley, and Doyle (1959) successfully used motion pictures and music to reward a young child's touching of a ball. The author (Hewett, 1965) provided music, a ride on a spinning chair, and colored cartoon movies as rewards following nonverbal and verbal imitations from autistic children and observed that these were effective in controlling their behavior.

Kish (1966) has alluded to the everyday observation that children appear to gain pleasure from stroking and touching material such as fur and concludes that such tactual stimulation may well be rewarding for them.

Although gustatory studies have not been reported with children, Pfaffman (1960) presents evidence suggesting tasting may in itself be a rewarding experience irrespective of the hunger drive with which it is usually associated.

The Premack (1959) principle introduced earlier in connection with the behavior modification strategies of Whelan (1966) and Whelan and Haring (1966) relates to the use of exploratory rewards to strengthen and accelerate low-frequency behaviors such as pursuit of academic subjects. Teachers in programs using the Premack principle observe a given child for a period of time to determine his interests as expressed through behaviors occurring with a high frequency (e.g., model building). They also determine behaviors occurring on a low frequency basis (e.g., reading). By making the exploratory reward (model building) contingent on accomplishment of a reading assignment the child's functioning in reading may be expected to improve.

Evidence from research investigations, then, tends to support the notion that children may indeed derive definite sensory rewards from exploration of their environment. In fact, this should come as little surprise to teachers who constantly observe how children are drawn to activities and games which they pursue for considerable periods of time apparently motivated by the visual, auditory, and tactual pleasure they receive.

EXPLORATORY LEVEL STRUCTURE

Exploratory activities allow some freedom of choice for the child, but they are considered learning tasks rather than free play. The exploratory level on the developmental sequence follows the order level and as such exploration is done within limits and involves definite assigned tasks. Open-ended exploratory type activities are probably more appropriate on the attention and response levels where the goal is to stimulate the child, get him started exploring his environment, and involved in learning. At the exploratory level the child is expected to explore as a "student" and in relation to an assigned learning task.

This section has described the characteristics of tasks on the exploratory level and the types of rewards which may be obtained. Structure maintains the importance given at the order level, and it is the undertaking of an assigned exploratory task rather than free play which is stressed.

We turn now to a discussion of the social level of the developmental sequence.

SOCIAL LEVEL

The social milieu of the classroom within which learning takes place becomes a major concern at this level on the developmental sequence.

General characteristics of social tasks will be described and then the specific task boxes on the developmental sequence considered. Following this, rewards and structure related to the social level will be discussed.

The goal of the social level is to help the child learn to obtain the approval of others and to avoid their disapproval. It is an extension of the response level where getting the child involved in learning in a social setting and working for social attention was stressed. It also relates to the order level concern of bringing the child's behavior under control so it is not disruptive to the class group. At the social level these earlier goals are augmented with an attempt to establish the child as an acceptable member of the class group and engage him in appropriate working relationships with his teacher and peers. Toward this end the task characteristics at the social level require that the child:

1. Communicate with the teacher or one or more peers.
2. Maintain appropriate social behavior.
3. Tolerate periods of delay, during which time he must "wait his turn."

Emotionally disturbed children are often "loners." They may prefer to select and pursue activities without including others, or they may demand that others immediately conform to their wishes. Such interpersonal problems are of primary concern to the psychodynamic-interpersonal strategy discussed in Chapter I, which probably emphasizes aspects of the response and social levels before the attention, order, and exploratory levels. This strategy may attribute a lack of responding or appropriate social behavior in the classroom to feelings of mistrust and nonacceptance on the part of the child. The developmental strategy presented in this text does not attempt to interpret the levels of the developmental sequence in terms of such feeling states. Rather, it suggests that in the course of undertaking suitable educational tasks which guarantee success, receiving meaningful rewards for learning, and being given appropriate demands for efficiency and accuracy, the child's attitudes and feelings toward learning and others will be modified along with his behavior.

All social tasks given to emotionally disturbed children in a classroom should be communication-oriented. Getting the child to listen to others, appropriately express himself, and contribute as a member of a group toward attainment of a mutual goal are prerequisites if he is to receive social approval and to avoid disapproval.

Perhaps the most fundamental communication task which can be given the child is that of listening. In both the NPI School and in public

school classrooms for the emotionally disturbed the author has observed the obvious satisfaction children derive from listening to the
teacher read aloud. Such a group-listening period can be incorporated
into the daily schedule of the class, and a portion of a book read each
day by the teacher. In this way several books may be read to the class
over the course of the school year. While "far out" science fiction tales
may be too stimulating for children with tendencies to dwell on fantasy,
real life adventure stories from both fiction and nonfiction have been
used with marked success. The author has found books such as *The
Pearl Lagoon* by Nordhoff and Hall and stories by Meader and Pease
particularly appealing to older elementary and secondary level boys.

A period of 15 to 20 minutes may be profitably used by the teacher
to read from a book, and this activity may be followed up by class
discussions, story writing activities, and various projects. Of course, at
the social level, reading aloud to the students and expecting them to
listen to the story constitutes the essential task, and follow-up work at
the exploratory or mastery level should be recognized as such.

Reading aloud to children with reading problems in school has been
criticized by some "authorities" in the reading field because it is seen as
promoting passive listening rather than independent reading on the part
of the student. From the author's experience it is seen as a valuable
activity for assisting children at the attention, response, order, exploratory, and social levels. These are the essential levels to consider in
learning before concern with intellectual and academic mastery accomplishments.

A social task similar to listening to teacher-read stories as a member
of the class group is listening to a story record with one or more
classmates at a listening post. Use of the listening post as an independent exploratory activity has been discussed in the previous section of
this chapter. Placing the child in such a situation with other classmates
makes it a simple social communication activity. In fact, any of the
exploratory activities described earlier can be used as social tasks by
assigning two or more children to work together on them.

Code activities, described as order tasks when pursued by the child
alone, are intriguing social communication tasks when undertaken by
children in pairs. The Morse Code is intriguing to many children. Two
telegraph keys which utilize flashing lights can be arranged as shown in
Figure VIII-1. One child sits on each side of the screen in order to send
and receive messages. The teacher may provide a word or simple
phrase to be sent at first, and later, the children may devise their own
messages. The symbol code and International Flag Code discussed in
Chapter VII may also be used in a similar manner.

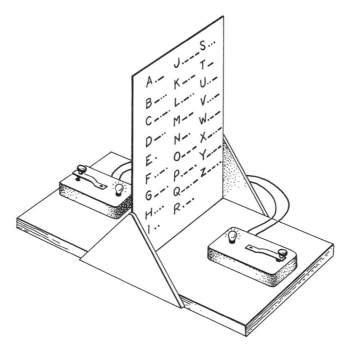

FIGURE VIII-1. Morse Code communication task.

Inexpensive "walkie-talkies" are available commercially. These sending and receiving sets permit children to be separated across the room or even at some distance from each other outside the class. The children may not only engage in spontaneous conversation but also work on assigned tasks. One such task that may be used involves direction-following. A simple street map of the immediate area around the school may be given both children. One child's map is blank but the other has a route drawn on it that covers several blocks. The children are separated and each given a walkie-talkie. The child given the map with the route drawn on it "sends" the other child the directions (e.g., "Start at the corner of Maple and Elm Street, go north three blocks to Main Street, turn left, and go four blocks left to the City Hall, etc."). The child receiving the directions attempts to duplicate the route on his map, and later the two maps are compared. A variation of the treasure map order task described in Chapter VII may also be utilized in this manner.

In addition to promoting communication between children, social tasks should encourage appropriate social behavior, including "waiting for a turn." There are numerous games available for use in the classroom which can be used toward this end. Some commercial games are quite elaborate with complicated directions, rules, and countless goals, and they require long periods of time for completion. These games probably should be avoided because of the frustration often experienced by children who do not clearly understand what to do and who cannot finish playing them in a limited period of time. The author observed one institutional teacher of severely emotionally disturbed children, who presented such a game to two children with order and social level problems. In a very short time one child was loudly accusing the other of cheating and was in tears, while the other child began tearing up the game materials in an angry outburst.

Simple paper and pencil games like "Battleship" are more successful. In this game the child draws a fleet of ships among printed coordinates on a paper without letting his game partner see the position of his fleet. The children take turns naming coordinates to see if they can score a "hit" on the other child's ships. Despite the competitive aspects of this game, the author has observed its success with many emotionally disturbed children.

The place of competition in a classroom for emotionally disturbed children bears consideration at this point. At the attention, response, order, and exploratory levels, avoidance of competition was stressed as an important step in getting the child functioning in the classroom and involved in learning. At the social and mastery levels, however, the reality of competition in the society, in general, and in the school, in particular, cannot be completely overlooked. This is not to say that comparisons must be drawn between various children's performances and a competitive atmosphere established in the classroom. Such an emphasis on competition is probably undesirable in any classroom, whether or not the students have special learning problems, but it is unrealistic to legislate out all aspects of competition in classrooms for students who are functioning adequately on the first four levels of the developmental sequence. In the process of learning to gain the approval and avoid the disapproval of others, the child inevitably must deal with winning and losing, coming in first and coming in second, and possessing more ability than his classmates in some areas and less in other areas. It is important to stress that the type of competition being discussed here is nonacademic. Until the child is functioning at grade level in school subjects, such competition in academic areas (e.g., spelling bees) is inappropriate, but in the undertaking of social tasks with other children, it is necessary for the child to learn not to always have to win as well as to observe principles of good sportsmanship such as waiting for his turn.

Teachers of emotionally disturbed children who utilize the composite developmental sequence assessment form usually comment on the child's capacity to handle competitive aspects of social situations under the "Additional Information" heading and carefully gauge the type of social tasks which are assigned. Group listening, message sending, and exploratory tasks assigned children in pairs minimize competition. Games in which one child is the obvious winner and the other the loser are a different matter. In selecting games which minimize competition for use as social tasks the author has observed that those depending more on "luck" (e.g., "Battleship") than "skill" (e.g., checkers or chess) are viewed by children as less competitive. Selection of more skill-oriented and competitive social tasks will not prove difficult for the teacher because of the large number of commercial games which are available. In summary, games assigned two or more emotionally disturbed children should involve the level of competition which each can handle comfortably, and while the reality of competition should be recognized by the teacher its pitfalls must also be appreciated.

Working on a class project with emotionally disturbed children, in which each child must assume independent responsibility for its successful completion, may be viewed with trepidation by the teacher. While group projects are admittedly a great deal of work and involve careful preparation and supervision, they often provide excellent opportunities for emphasizing the goals of the social task level—communication, appropriate social behavior, and learning to take turns.

One Christmas season the teacher of ten junior high students in the NPI School decided he would attempt a class drama project, using a radio script version of Dickens' "Christmas Carol." The story was read to the class and they expressed varying degrees of interest in the project. Two students with serious response problems claimed they would have no part of it since they would have to perform in front of an audience, but these were the only strong dissenters. The teacher was particularly concerned with one child who had a serious reading problem and who was unable to read the script. This boy, he decided, could work on sound effects, where accurate reading would not be necessary. One of the reluctant response problems was assigned as "engineer" to control the volume on the loudspeaker. He was assured he could perform his duties off stage, away from the audience. The other response-problem child loved to play the piano. She finally agreed to play a few bars of Christmas music at the opening and closing of the program, although in situations of stress she frequently fainted. The other children were assigned parts in the play which they practiced, and the whole class was "standing by" when the show went "on the air" in an auditorium filled with doctors, nurses, and other staff members of the NPI. The performance was flawless. Nobody fainted, ran away, made serious mistakes, or for that matter, displayed much stage fright. The class had functioned as might have been expected of any group of junior high children in a public school setting.

Success of this project was largely due to the enthusiasm and extreme patience of the teacher, as well as his skill in viewing each child as a candidate for "doing something" and making wholly individual assignments based on the child's readiness for participation on the social task level. Radio plays offer ideal group experiences for emotionally disturbed children. There is no memorization of lines to worry about and no fussing with costumes or scenery. Radio plays can be of any length and obtained from the library or written by the teacher or students. The variety of jobs available ranges from the nonverbal level (e.g., engineer, sound effects, musician) to the highly verbal level (e.g., actor, director, announcer), and as a result, even the most serious attention and response problem can usually do something (e.g., putting a record on the turntable). This type of activity is ideal for emphasizing all levels of the developmental sequence in a single project.

The NPI School version of the "Christmas Carol" was tape-recorded and played back several times not only for the class but for other people. The group satisfaction and cohesiveness, which was promoted by this project, was readily recognizable and a Radio Club was formed, which produced other programs and received technical consultation from the Radio Division of the UCLA Theater Arts Department.

Social tasks place the child in an interaction with the teacher and his classmates and focus on promoting attention, response, order, and exploratory behavior in a social setting. The two descriptive boxes at the social level on the composite development sequence form illustrated in Figure IV-8 will now be considered.

SOCIAL LEVEL TASKS

19. Child Does Not Gain Approval from Others

Emotionally disturbed children who seldom gain the approval of others and who often receive disapproval can be helped at the social level of the developmental sequence through assignment of tasks which promote group approval, selective rewarding of desired behavior, and role playing.

The child who is ignored or rejected by his classmates may have problems on the response and order levels. He may also fail to understand standards of appropriate social behavior for his age group. The child who whines, complains, refuses to share or wait his turn, alibis, and blames others for all problems which arise is seldom a candidate for "the most popular student in the class." In order to help such a child gain increased acceptance the teacher may utilize some skill or interest which the child possesses in such a way that it benefits the entire class. The child who excels in science may be given responsibility for preparing science materials for the rest of the class. The artistic child may be given the job of mixing and caring for paints and art supplies. The strong reader may be made library monitor and asked to keep a supply of free reading books available for the class. Each of these tasks is not without potential hazards, for making a child who is a social misfit more visible in the classroom can produce an avalanche of criticism and disapproval from the peer group. However, under careful teacher supervision, children with problems at the social level can often be directed toward more appropriate behavior in areas related to their particular skills and interests.

Selective rewarding of appropriate social behavior is useful in calling the child's attention to acts which will gain him increased approval from others. Glen had earned a solid reputation as the "class pest" in the NPI elementary classroom. He spoke loudly all the time, demanded more than his share of materials and attention, and appeared oblivious to the rights of any other child in the classroom. The rule in the class was that students obtained teacher help or permission to move from their seats by raising their hand. Glen apparently did not consider this rule as applying to him, for he always spoke out and freely left his seat. The teacher had attempted to ignore him on most occasions and quietly restructured the hand-raising expectation. One day Glen surprised everyone by sitting in his seat and raising his hand. He raised it only for a split second and was about to embark on one of his loud demands for help when the teacher immediately approached him, lavishly praised his attempt at conformity, and gave him the help he needed. The problem with Glen did not miraculously disappear, but more and more often the teacher found opportunities to praise his approximations of appropriate behavior (e.g., picking up a classmate's paper, which had fallen to the floor, and returning it).

Role playing, in which members of the class take turns demonstrating classroom and social etiquette (e.g., asking for help, lining up for recess, table and telephone manners) may be useful with some emotionally disturbed children although a given child's capacity to succeed in such a group activity should be carefully weighed in advance. Often role playing by students who are free from problems at the social level may provide an example for imitation by the less able child, who may only participate as a spectator.

20. Child Overly Dependent on Others' Attention or Praise

In marked contrast to the child with problems at the attention and response levels who avoided interaction with teacher and classmates, children with social level problems may seek a disproportionate amount of attention, recognition, and praise. Suggestions for aiding such children in the development of more appropriate social behavior include providing an adequate number of opportunities for deserved recognition, encouraging independent assessment of assignments, and selective rewarding for independent behavior.

A teacher of children with emotional problems who is particularly concerned with social level tasks (although she was not oriented in terms of the developmental sequence) claims success with children having problems described in this section with the use of the following technique:

> Tom is given to sudden outbursts of "clowning" in order to get the attention of the class. He frequently grimaces, purposely falls off his seat, and makes silly noises, all in an apparent attempt to get his classmates and the teacher to notice him. When the teacher sees such a bid for attention about to emerge, she stops the class, comments that "Tom seems to need our attention right now," and encourages Tom to "perform" for two or three minutes, doing anything he wants. At the end of this time, the teacher leads the class in a round of applause for Tom, who bows and returns to his seat with, according to the teacher, "his need for social recognition apparently out of his system for the moment."

This illustration will undoubtedly be appalling to many teachers of the emotionally disturbed because of its artificiality and suggestion of veiled hostility on the part of the teacher toward Tom. The author was also appalled when it was described to him, and it is presented in this text as an example of "what not to do."

It is difficult to see how Tom could maintain any vestige of dignity or self-respect when his problems were treated in such a patronizing manner by the teacher. However, providing opportunities for children such as Tom to gain recognition through assigning them tasks which make them highly visible in the classroom may be very useful. Puppet shows, class plays, and radio productions, as described earlier, offer constructive outlets in this regard. A class bulletin board displaying examples of each child's "best work" during the week and arts and crafts displays of student creations also serve the same purpose.

Children who request teacher evaluation of each step they go through in solving an arithmetic problem or each word they write in a story can be helped to assume more independent responsibility for their work by being given an answer book to check arithmetic problems or a dictionary in which to look up unfamiliar words. They can also be expected to maintain daily records of tasks accomplished and keep graphs of the number of problems they do correctly.

Since a constant demand for teacher and peer recognition is closely related to a problem considered at the order level (Box 14. *Child disruptive in group*), the overly dependent child may have to be seated in an inconspicuous place in the room and even sent out of class when his behavior exceeds tolerable limits. The teacher may also find that simply ignoring excessive demands and selectively rewarding independent accomplishments will aid the child in maintaining more appropriate social behavior.

SOCIAL LEVEL REWARDS

The rewards available to the child at the social level of the developmental sequence are the approval of others and the avoidance of their disapproval. At this level, avoidance of a negative consequence (disapproval) is added to receipt of a positive consequence (approval) as a source of reward for learning. Social level rewards are perhaps the most powerful and commonly relied on rewards present in any classroom. Teachers of normal children, such as Miss A., in the example cited in Chapter I, depend on controlling the attending, responding, direction-following, exploring, social behavior, and academic accomplishments of their pupils largely through approval, recognition, disapproval, and the withholding of praise. Of course, the other rewards, with the possible exception of tangible rewards, discussed to this point in the text are in existence in classrooms for normal as well as disturbed children. But social rewards probably predominate in the former.

In classrooms for emotionally disturbed children, it may be wise to use social rewards sparingly with some children and initially rely more on rewards on the lower levels of the developmental sequence. The teacher who indiscriminately showers all children with lavish praise may quickly alienate the suspicious or hostile child whose previous experience with inconsistent, untrustworthy adults may lead him to label the teacher a "phony." For such a child, a task-oriented teacher who is fair and predictable in letting the child know where he stands on a largely nonverbal level using tangible rewards may be more readily accepted initially. Eventually, however, the goal is to get the child working to gain approval and to avoid disapproval, for this will be required if he is to eventually function adequately in a regular classroom.

Evidence supporting the effectiveness of social rewards in controlling the behavior of adults and children is provided by the following studies among others:

Ayllon and Michael (1959) trained psychiatric nurses to record and selectively provide social rewards for severely emotionally disturbed adults in an institution. It was found that withholding social rewards following such maladaptive behaviors as excessive demands for attention, delusional verbalizations, and assaultive behavior caused these behaviors to dramatically diminish. Lovaas, Freitag, Kinder, Rubenstein, Schaeffer, and Simmons (1964) have demonstrated that control over autistic children's behavior can be established by social-verbal ("good") and social-physical (a pat on the shoulder) rewards, which, while initially paired with tangible rewards of food, eventually proved controlling in their own right.

A shy, withdrawn preschool girl was rewarded with teacher attention for interacting with other children and greatly increased her participation in group activities in a study by Allen, Hart, Buell, Harris, and Wolf (1964). In this study, and the two previously cited, the behavior elicited through selective rewarding was maintained for long periods of time.

Rowley and Keller (1962) have obtained evidence that social approval is an effective controller of verbal behavior in both elementary and junior high normal children. Rowley and Stone (1964) found that the reward of an adult saying "good" every time one group of fourth-grade normal children started sentences with the pronouns "I" or "we" accounted for an increasing number of sentences starting with these words over time. A significantly greater number of such sentences were obtained under these conditions than from a similar group which was not rewarded for this pronoun usage.

Page (1958) undertook a large-scale study with 74 randomly selected secondary teachers and some 2,139 unknowing students in their daily classes to investigate the effectiveness of written teacher comment on test papers given back to the students. For some students, no comments were written next to the letter grade received, for others a free comment, left up to the teacher was made, and for the remainder specified comments were written in accord with the experimenters' direction to the teacher (e.g., all students receiving an "A" on a test would automatically receive the written comment "Excellent! Keep it up."). Students receiving free comment and specified comment did better on subsequent tests than those receiving no comment and the author concludes "when the average secondary teacher takes the time and trouble to write comments (e.g., to be 'encouraging') on student papers, this apparently has a measurable and potent effect upon student effort, or attention, or attitude, or whatever it is which causes learning to improve. . . ."

This study lends additional support to the notion that social approval, even in written form, is a source of reward for learning.

Dunn-Rankin (1967) has developed a rating scale for assessing children's preferences for various rewards available in the classroom. He categorized rewards used by teachers into five classes: (1) adult approval, (2) peer approval, (3) consumables, (4) competition, (5) independence. The rating scale was administered to 200 upper elementary age children in regular classes and the results obtained indicated that adult approval was most preferred, consumable rewards, least preferred. This study illustrates the powerful reward value which teacher praise and approval provides in the classroom with normal children. It also suggests that such children have attained a higher level of socialization (social level of the developmental sequence) as compared to that attained by the emotionally disturbed boys in Levin and Simmons' (1962) study who responded more positively to consumable rewards (attention level of the developmental sequence) than social praise.

SOCIAL LEVEL STRUCTURE

Structure at the social level is emphasized as it was at the exploratory and order level. The *student role*, described as a major goal of the order level, becomes the *social role* at the social level and includes more than minimal control of behavior and a reasonable respect for working rights of others. At the social level, standards of social appropriateness extending beyond those covered at the order level are of concern. The standards are operationally defined as referring to behaviors which elicit teacher and peer group approval and restrict disapproval. The child then moves from a parallel social relationship at the response and order levels, involving reasonable and tolerable behavior, to an interacting social relationship at the social level, where his behaviors must include appropriate communication and understanding of the expectation of others.

This chapter has discussed the nature of tasks at the exploratory and social levels of the developmental sequence. Specific examples have been cited and types of rewards and degree of structure associated with exploratory and social tasks considered.

IX MASTERY AND ACHIEVEMENT LEVELS

The mastery and achievement levels complete the developmental sequence of educational goals. Once the child possesses the ability to care for himself independently, is able to meet the intellectual and academic expectations for his chronological age, and has acquired a self-motivation for learning, the basic goals of education have largely been attained. Since opportunities for formal education in the American society can never truly be said to end, these two levels as well as those presented earlier may continue to be refined and developed throughout the individual's life. For purposes of this text and in relation to the education of emotionally disturbed children, however, aiding the child in achieving competence at the attention, response, order, exploratory, and social levels; bringing him up to a level commensurate with his chronological age and ability in self-care and intellectual and academic skills; and helping him acquire intrinsic motivation in learning complete the educational task of the school. Because of the primary concern of the developmental strategy with readiness for learning (first five levels), the final two levels (mastery and achievement) are not considered as relevant to the education of emotionally disturbed children.

In this chapter, as was done with the previous five levels of the developmental sequence, we will consider the nature of mastery and achievement tasks, rewards, and structure. Chapter XI is devoted to specific curriculum considerations at the mastery level.

MASTERY LEVEL

At the mastery level, attention is given to helping the child attain the following:

1. A level of self-care enabling him to function independently in his environment.
2. Cognitive development in such areas as speech, concept formation, and problem solving within the limits of his intellectual potential.
3. His expected achievement level in basic school subjects.

Since these goals are linked closely with the descriptive box (Box 21) at the mastery level on the composite developmental sequence form in Figure IX-8 discussions of them will be presented in relation to the general problem of the mastery level—*child functioning in self-care and intellectual skills below capacity*. For purposes of assessment, the "self-care" and "intellectual skill" aspects of the mastery level were separated in Table IV-6, and are considered separately at this point.

MASTERY LEVEL TASKS

21. Child Functioning in Self-Care Below Capacity

Because of problems at the attention, response, order, exploratory, and social levels, emotionally disturbed children may remain helpless and dependent on others when exposed to the dangers and demands of the larger environment. The child may fail to learn to cross streets, obey traffic rules, make simple purchases, and maintain appropriate conduct in public places. More basic self-care skills of personal hygiene, toileting, eating, and dressing also may be limited.

The teacher in the institutional school encounters such self-care deficiencies more often than the teacher in the public school. Children enrolled in public school programs cannot be given continual individual supervision, and hence placement in a public school class for several hours each day is usually contingent on the child's having attained self-care skills, particularly in the area of toileting. When the child runs away or cannot function on the playground or in the cafeteria without supervision, a parent may be required to assume responsibility periodically during the day. Despite problems which might result from such parental involvement, providing needed supervision at critical times may allow the child to participate in classroom experiences which he otherwise would be denied.

In including self-care training in the classroom, the teacher of the emotionally disturbed is concerned with accomplishing the same goals as many teachers of the mentally retarded. In fact this was also the case at the preceding levels of the developmental sequence. It is when consideration on the mastery level is given to development of intellectual and academic skills that the two become more clearly separated.

21. Child Functioning in Intellectual Skills Below Capacity

In Chapter VIII mention was made that the emphasis at the exploratory level was on sensory experience and perception rather than cognition. While a discussion of the discrete aspects of these processes and their points of overlap is beyond the scope of this text, it is important to establish that one of the goals of the mastery level is to stimulate cognitive development in the child, including language and speech.

In introducing the notion of the "educability of intelligence" another major issue with implications beyond the realm of the present discussion arises. Environmental experiences have been shown to exert a definite influence on the rate of mental growth in children. A dramatic example of this has been provided by Skeels (1966) who reported the results and follow-up studies with both normal and mentally retarded children exposed to differing degrees of environmental stimulation. Adopted normal children have been found to be achieving as adults at levels consistently higher than would have been predicted from the intellectual, educational, or socio-economic levels of their biological parents. Mentally retarded children moved from a nonstimulating institution to one with considerably more stimulation displayed a marked increase in cognitive development as compared with those left in the nonstimulating environment. The latter group showed progressive mental retardation.

Environmental contributions to the improved functioning level of children in this study undoubtedly included the attention, response, exploratory, order, and social as well as mastery levels and were provided from a variety of sources other than the school. But whether the child is normal, retarded, or emotionally disturbed the stimulation offered by the school will be an important determinator of his adequacy in cognitive areas such as concept formation, problem solving, and language. These become of concern at the mastery level.

In the case of Louis, presented in Chapter III and referred to several times in the past several chapters, mention was made of the visiting teacher who questioned the simple lever-pushing program for him because she did not know of "any science curriculum in the sixth grade which included the study of dinosaurs." The inappropriateness of her "mastery" concern for this severely inattentive and withdrawn boy was very apparent. Curriculum considerations at this initial stage of the educational program for Louis were unimportant, and all the efforts of the NPI School teacher went into reaching him on the attention, response, order, and exploratory levels.

There are other emotionally disturbed children, however, who are excluded from mastery training because of the conviction of a therapist and/or teacher that they need extended periods of self-expression and relationship-building before being exposed to formal mastery training. Such exclusion may be unnecessary, and when it delays training in such skills as speech beyond what may be critical periods for cognitive development it can contribute to the child's failure to improve in his general adjustment.

Evidence for this has been cited by Eisenberg (1956) who reported on a group of 63 autistic children followed into adolescence and reevaluated. Three of the group had achieved a "good" adjustment (functioned well at an academic, social, community, and communication level and accepted by peers although perhaps still somewhat "odd"). Fourteen of the children followed were categorized as making a "fair" adjustment (able to attend regular classes in public or special school yet obviously deviant in personality). The remainder of the children (46) had made only a "poor" adjustment (not having appreciably emerged from autism and manifesting behavior so maladaptive that they required continual care at home or in an institution). A striking finding, however, was that presence of useful speech by age five appeared to have important prognostic implications. Thirty-two of the group had such speech at age five while 31 did not. Of the 31 with speech three were later classified as having made "good" adjustments, 13 as "fair" and 16 as "poor." The 32 without speech at age five were classified as follows: one "fair" and 30 "poor." Thus, 16 of 32 children with speech at age five achieved a "fair" to "good" adjustment while only one of the 31 without speech could be comparably classified. Eisenberg also found that there was no correlation between formal psychiatric treatment and eventual outcome. Similar findings have been reported by Kanner and Eisenberg (1955) and Brown (1960). If acquisition of useful speech before age five does increase the probability of a better future adjustment for autistic children it would seem logical that every effort be made to introduce such training as early as possible. Long periods of psychotherapy which delay such training are hardly justifiable from observations reported in the literature.

A speech training program was undertaken by the author with Eddie, an autistic boy of four-and-one-half years of age (Hewett, 1965). The program utilized the task-reward-structure model and the concept of the developmental sequence of educational goals.

Eddie, like most autistic children, was a highly selective "attender," "responder," "direction-follower," and "explorer." He avoided eye contact, resisted efforts of others to direct his attention, and continually pursued repetitive mechanical activities such as water pouring and tinkering with mechanical gadgets. He followed few directions given by others and was an insatiable explorer of certain features of his environment (e.g., water faucets, cabinet hardware, and appliances). Socially, Eddie was totally aloof from concern with approval and disapproval and he had never developed speech, although the words "da-da" and "ma-ma" appeared briefly during his first year and a half and then disappeared.

Eddie entered the NPI Children's Service ward when brought for admission by his parents without so much as a glance back at them as they withdrew. He showed no awareness of being left by them in this new setting although the period of hospitalization brought about his first separation from his family.

While the program designed for Eddie had mastery level goals (e.g., the initiation of speech) it had to focus on initially helping him at the first five levels of the developmental sequence. As in the program designed for Louis, several levels were introduced concurrently. A special teaching booth illustrated in Figure IX-1 was constructed to facilitate the teaching of attention, response, order, exploratory, social, and later mastery skills.* Eddie was seated as shown in one side of the booth, the teacher in the other.

The booth was divided into two sections, joined by a movable shutter (2 x 2½ feet) which could be raised and lowered by the teacher. Each section of the booth was 4 feet wide, 3½ feet in length, and 7½ feet high. The only source of light came from the teacher's side and was provided by two spotlights which were directed on the teacher's face. When the shutter was down, Eddie's side of the booth was dark; when it was raised, light from the teacher's side flooded through the opening and illuminated a shelf in front of Eddie. To the left of the shelf was a ball-drop device with a dim light directly above it. This device consisted of a box into which a small wooden ball could be dropped. The ball rang a bell as it dropped into the box and was held inside the box until released by the teacher. When released, the ball rolled out into a container at the bottom of the box where it could be picked up. This ball-drop device was Eddie's "key" for opening the shutter. When the ball was released into the container he picked it up and dropped it into the box. At the sound of the bell, the teacher raised the shutter and initiated contact between the two of them.

The task of "attention" was presented Eddie when the ball was released and it rolled into the container in front of him. The shutter was down, the booth dark, the ball-drop device the only lighted stimu-

---

* Mr. Frank Langdon, Principal of the NPI School, made a major contribution in the design and construction of this teaching booth.

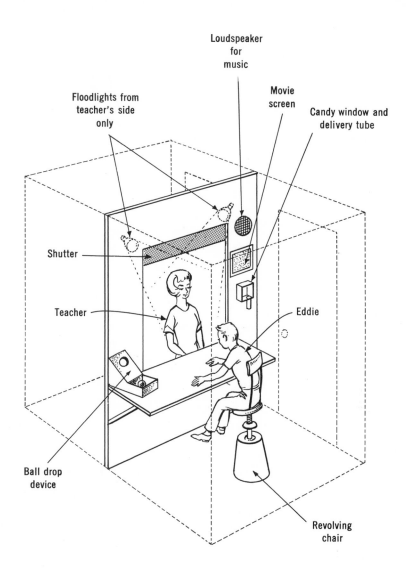

FIGURE IX-1. Teaching booth.

lus. When Eddie picked up the ball and dropped it into the opening, ringing the bell, he had accomplished a task at the response level. Following accomplishment of these two tasks, Eddie was rewarded by having the shutter raised, a mouthful of food provided, the teacher's face brought into view, the booth lighted, and the words "Good boy!" spoken by the teacher. These rewards (food, social attention, task completion, sensory stimulation, and social approval) have previously been described as associated with the first five levels of the developmental sequence. The structure involved in the teaching situation was provided by the operation of the booth itself. Eddie had to attend, respond, and follow directions in the manner described before he received available rewards. The first week of the program was devoted to introducing Eddie to the learning routine in the booth. Following this the attention, response, order, exploratory, social, and mastery tasks given Eddie were as follows over a one-year period:

1. Eye contact with teacher expected before reward of food given (attention, response, and order levels).
2. Imitative hand movements involving "patty-cake," handclapping, and touching various parts of his body in imitation of the teacher (e.g., head, eye, ear, nose, mouth, stomach) required in order to get his motorized chair to spin one revolution and the teacher to say "Good boy!" (attention, response, order, and social levels).
3. Touching the teacher's face as a means of keeping music playing (attention, response, order, exploratory, and social levels).
4. Cupping his face in his hands to get a colored cartoon movie segment to show on screen (attention, response, order, exploratory, and social levels).
5. Humming a few bars of a children's song in imitation of teacher in order to obtain candy reward and "Good boy!" (attention, response, order, exploratory, social, and mastery levels).
6. Providing shrill undifferentiated vowel sound (ē-oö) in imitation of the teacher for candy reward and "Good boy!" (all levels).
7. Giving successive approximations of the word "go" in imitation of the teacher who gradually moved from (ē-oö) to "go-o-o" for candy reward and "Good boy!" (all levels).
8. Using word "go" to command teacher to start spinning chair, turn on music, and open door (all levels).
9. Produce word "my" in imitation of teacher in order to get Bingo markers to place on numbered squares (all levels).
10. Use word "my" to denote possession and to obtain desired objects (e.g., puzzle pieces, toys) from teacher (all levels).
11. Produce words such as "high," "see," "yes," "no," "shoe," "key," "mama," "daddy," "water," "toilet," "food," "eye," "ear," "nose," "mouth," "Eddie," "please," "juice," "cracker," "milk," "school" in

response to pictures or objects held up by the teacher for reward of "Good boy!" alone (all levels).

12. Use simple phrases ("I want toilet," "I want water," "I want candy," "I want school") in order to have needs met by ward personnel throughout the day (all levels).

13. Practice and expand verbal repertoire with parents and siblings acting as teachers for various tangible, sensory, and social rewards (all levels).

This summary of stages in the speech training program designed for Eddie omits many details. All of the training except the transfer phase, when ward personnel and later parents worked with him, was undertaken in the teaching booth. During the period of booth training, the structure side of the learning triangle was emphasized whenever Eddie refused to obey the teacher's requests for imitative responses. Usually five seconds would be allowed following each request and three separate requests given. If Eddie withdrew or did not comply during this time the teacher lowered the shutter and he was penalized with a five-second period of isolation and darkness. After this period, the ball was released by the teacher and when Eddie dropped it through the opening in the ball-drop device, the shutter was raised, and the training continued. This added structure was rarely used after the first few months.

While such limit-setting and imposition of a penalty involving isolation and darkness has alarmed some individuals because of the inferred "meaning" such rejection by the teacher was felt to have for the child, the author never found its use with Eddie or some five other autistic children "traumatic" or "upsetting." Few children ever cried after the shutter was lowered for brief periods, and most quickly modified their behavior in order to keep the rewarding consequences of tangible rewards, social attention, light, and social approval forthcoming. It appeared they were "bored" in the stimulus-free, closed-shutter environment and were willing to "work" in order to obtain the rewards which were available when the shutter was up.

Eddie's program illustrates the use of the task-reward-structure model and the levels of the developmental sequence to effect learning of mastery tasks with often inaccessible and highly resistant learners. Tasks given Eddie were gradually increased in complexity, a variety of rewards offered, some alone, others in combination, and a predictable learning environment and routine established with him. This program further illustrates the nondiscrete nature of the levels of the developmental sequence and how types of tasks and rewards overlap from one level to the next. When the mastery task of vocal imitation was given Eddie, candy was introduced for the first time. This reward was known to be the most powerful of all for Eddie and so was reserved for the most crucial stage in the training program. It can also be seen that the higher level reward of social approval alone was eventually effective in maintaining his newly acquired behavior. This reward was paired with most other rewards given from the very beginning in an effort to establish it as a controlling consequence in its own right.

Eddie's use of speech for labeling purposes as well as for simple requests does not constitute true language. Weiss and Born (1967) have called attention to the distinction between speech acquired through operant conditioning (a series of vocal utterances) and genuine language (capability of generating and understanding novel utterances). While there can be no doubt that the level of speech development obtained experimentally was limited, the secondary gains were significant. Eddie became more aware of his social environment and also was viewed differently by others. Members of the NPI nursing staff sought him out frequently for verbal interactions, aided him in practicing his speech, and held him for verbal requests before granting his wishes.

Eddie's increased social awareness was well demonstrated when his parents would leave following a visit to the hospital. In marked contrast to his apathy and seeming unawareness when they left him upon admission to the hospital, Eddie now cried and clung to his mother and was visibly very upset when she departed. As unpleasant as it is to see a child so distressed upon separation from his parents, the author and ward staff were delighted with this family interaction.

Goldfarb (1956) has suggested that the responses of others to the speech defects of schizophrenic children actually may reinforce such defects. Thus, the nature of the relationship between the nonverbal schizophrenic child and the environment may not be conducive to improved socialization. Meeting the needs of such a child by responding to his primitive and often bizarre attempts at communication may merely make an unsocialized existence more rewarding. In addition, the nonverbal schizophrenic child may be perceived as so atypical and difficult to reach that others develop less personal and involved means of relating with him.

Clearly, the acquisition of beginning speech skills places the child in a position to interact more favorably with his environment. Eddie left the hospital, was enrolled in a private nursery-kindergarten, and later a public school class for the educationally handicapped.

His vocabulary grew considerably and he quickly learned to read, write, and to master written number concepts expected for his age.

Three years after the initial speech training program, Eddie's speech was still restricted and mechanical. He was generally echolalic (re-

FIGURE IX-2. Eddie's drawings.

peated exact phrases and questions spoken to him rather than giving appropriate answers) and had little understanding of pronoun references. Since almost no formal speech training was continued after Eddie's discharge from the NPI, the growth of his vocabulary and improvement in articulation was due to experiences he had at home and at school.

At least one significant occurrence suggests the merging of speech and true language in Eddie's case. Following a severe spanking by his mother, he withdrew to his room and later appeared with the drawings presented in Figure IX-2. These drawings are of a "broken dryer" and "broken washer," two of Eddie's favorite appliances in the home. He actually drew and labeled them as shown. The figure drawing was verbally labeled by him as "Eddie."

Here appears to be an attempt on quite a primitive level to convey an emotional state of distress through written and spoken communication.

Five other nonverbal autistic children participated in speech training programs similar to the one designed for Eddie. Their ages ranged from three to five years. Three approached Eddie's level of speech development and two never progressed beyond simple one-word repetitions, although in the case of these latter children, training had to be terminated because of lack of personnel for the program. One notable change was made in the program for these other five children. Their mothers were involved in the training program from the very beginning and proved effective teachers in the booth and at home. Additional examples of speech training programs similar to the one discussed in this section may be found in the work of Lovaas, Berberich, Perlaff, and Schaeffer (1966) and Jensen and Womack (1967).

Related to the goal of assisting children with speech and cognitive skills at the mastery level of the developmental sequence is academic training in reading and arithmetic. Such academic training may be unnecessarily delayed or neglected with emotionally disturbed children in much the same manner as speech training. This is not to support the position of the visiting teacher who observed Louis (Chapter III) and who could only see his problems in terms of academic training, but attention, response, order, exploratory, and social tasks may be incorporated within a mastery program of reading instruction and the child assisted in getting ready to learn to read while he actually is learning to read.

The unique reading program developed for Jimmy, the twelve-year-old nonverbal autistic student in the NPI School, was introduced in Chapter V. The word board utilized to present words and pictures during the matching phase of his program was illustrated in Figure V-2.

Once Jimmy mastered some 75 word-picture combinations presented on the word board, he had acquired characteristics of a true mastery learner, although periodic tangible rewards of candy were used to keep him functioning on the attention, response, order, exploratory, and

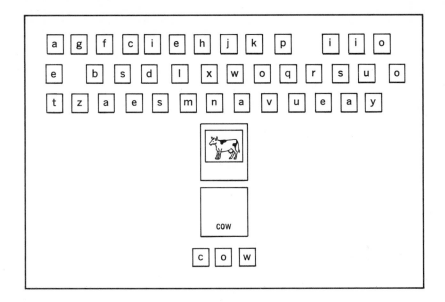

FIGURE IX-3. Flannel board used with Jimmy.

social levels. But gaining the approval of the teacher and accurately accomplishing tasks given him were by and large the only rewards he needed at this point. Therefore, a mastery program of spelling and handwriting was undertaken so that he might communicate through writing. The four phases of this program will be briefly described.

Phase I. Letter-By-Letter Spelling and Alphabet Mastery

A large flannel board was set up in place of the word board on Jimmy's work table. Alphabet letters which had been printed on small squares of tagboard with flannel backing so that they would adhere to the board were affixed to the surface. A picture of an object (e.g., cow) which Jimmy had learned to label earlier was also affixed to the board and the card with the name of the object printed on it placed below. While Jimmy watched, the teacher took the letters "c," "o," and "w" from those on the board and placed them one at a time below the picture and word in proper order, saying aloud "c-o-w." The teacher then took the three letters and randomly affixed them to the side of the board and directed Jimmy to replace them in correct order, using the word card below the picture as a model. This was not difficult for Jimmy and he quickly responded. The next step was to go to a regular classroom blackboard and practice one of the letters in a handwriting exercise. In the case of "cow" the letter selected was "c" and the teacher drew a "c" on the board, naming it aloud for Jimmy. Jimmy was then instructed to copy a row of "c's" and as he did, the teacher named each letter aloud. The flannel board and arrangement of teaching materials is shown in Figure IX-3.

By referring to word-picture combinations he had learned previously in a similar manner, all 26 letters of the alphabet were presented to Jimmy. Candy rewards were reserved for every 10 to 15 minutes and on some occasions Jimmy worked for 45 minutes without any tangible reward. It should be pointed out that no attempt was made to foster handwriting perfection at this point. A legible manuscript alphabet was the only goal.

Phase II. Auditory Discrimination

In this phase Jimmy was presented with a large assortment of randomly assembled letter squares on the flannel board. On the teacher's command, he was to take off all the squares containing the particular letter (e.g., "Jimmy, give me all the "e's"). Since there were several duplicates for each letter, particularly for commonly used vowels, Jimmy had to practice in both auditory and visual discrimination of the alphabet. This he mastered quickly and with few problems.

Phase III. Spelling and Beginning Phrase Writing

Once Jimmy was familiar with letter names, he could spell any word dictated letter-by-letter to him by the teacher. Shortly thereafter, he acquired skill at reproducing complete words dictated to him without letter-by-letter spelling. Figure IX-4 presents a sample of Jimmy's writing of the word "cow" and his accompanying spontaneous drawing. At this stage a most significant communication and mastery task was introduced. Jimmy would no longer be given any candy without a written request. In one session he correctly learned to write, "I want candy" and thereafter was only given the candy reward when he presented the teacher with such a written request. While Jimmy did not understand the meaning of "I" or "want" and possibly not "candy," he had been introduced to an appropriate means of communication which was in marked contrast to the "grunting," pointing, and primitive coercion he had used previously in order to get others to satisfy his wants. An interesting communication between Jimmy and the author took place one day when Jimmy assembled all of the animal pictures used in the training program, along with the pictures of "mama" and "daddy," and then wrote the word "zoo." He was telling the author of a weekend trip to

FIGURE IX-4. An example of Jimmy's writing and drawing.

the zoo taken with his parents which he apparently enjoyed very much.

Phase IV. Phrase Writing Transfer

As Jimmy was able to write more and more words, he appeared to become fascinated with this symbolic means of referring to objects and events with which he was familiar. In a short while he was writing "I want school" in order to be allowed to accompany the teacher for his daily lessons, and "I want water," "I want to eat," "I want pool," "I want a walk," "I want toilet," and other phrases on the ward in order to express his wants to the staff. Jimmy took great delight in offering these written communications to the ward staff and carried a pad of paper around with him for this purpose. The reciprocal reactions displayed on the part of the staff when Jimmy appropriately communicated with them through writing can be likened to those experienced when Eddie used his conditioned speech for such communication.

It would be satisfying for the author to report that twelve-year-old Jimmy went on to expand his mastery of written communication so that he functioned on a fairly high level in relation to his environment.

Unfortunately, this cannot be done. Shortly after completion of the reading and written language program, Jimmy was transferred to a private school for mentally retarded children. Although he was diagnosed as autistic, this was the only long-term residential school placement his parents could obtain for him. Despite the author's plea that the school continue the written communication program and despite sending the school complete records of Jimmy's program along with actual materials for continuing the work, the new school decided that speech was the most essential skill to develop with Jimmy and completely neglected any continuation of the NPI School program. Three years later, the author had occasion to again see Jimmy. He had been engaged in an entirely futile program of speech development which had not helped him at all. His written language skills had deteriorated almost to zero during this time and he was again dependent on "grunting" and pointing in order to communicate his wants to others.

The author was struck with the difference in orientation between himself and those who worked with Jimmy in his new school. Certainly spoken language would have been desirable but at age 12 its development was highly unlikely and hence written language skills should have been encouraged in an attempt to realistically compensate for his lack of speech.

An elaboration of the reading program prepared for Jimmy has been developed by the NPI School staff (Hewett, Mayhew, Rabb, 1967).[1] It is directed toward verbal children who are diagnosed as severely emotionally disturbed, mentally retarded, or brain-injured and who have serious problems at the attention, response, order, and exploratory levels. Of particular concern are children who have failed to learn by more traditional approaches and who are often considered noneducable. This program is a modification and elaboration of one developed by Birnbrauer, Bijou, Wolf, and Kidder (1965) at the Ranier School in Buckley, Washington, for institutionalized retardates.

The basic goal of the NPI School Experimental Reading Program is to get the child ready to read while he actually is learning to read. Toward this end the following general principles are adhered to:

1. Present the child with small increments of learning which gradually increase in difficulty based on principles of programed instruction.
2. Initially immediately reward each correct response the child makes; use social praise and tangible rewards and withhold these rewards for incorrect responses. Later reward the child on an intermittent basis.

---

[1] The figures and material in the following section copyright, The American Orthopsychiatric Association, Inc. Reproduced by permission.

3. Use systematic word review, discrimination exercises, and comprehension questions to consolidate learning.
4. Provide the child with an actual reading experience in a real book in addition to programed learning of words on a teaching machine.
5. Freely adapt the steps, structure, and type of rewards used in the program to insure continued success for each individual child.
6. Maintain detailed records of each of the child's responses to follow his progress, determine his need for program modification, and provide teacher feedback.

Words to be learned in the program were taken from the 155-word basic sight vocabulary contained in the three preprimers and primer of the Ginn Basic Readers (Russell, 1957). This vocabulary was presented to the child in a series of programed lessons involving use of a teaching machine (Grolier Min/Max II) and supervision of an individual teacher. While "word calling" or reading of word symbols without full comprehension of their meaning is in disfavor in the field of reading instruction, it is tolerated and even encouraged in the experimental program. There is no alphabet, verbal fluency, or word concept training, and development of handedness and laterality are incidental aspects of the program.

Thirteen emotionally disturbed children have been included in the program. A normal subject was also included for comparative purposes.

A five-part lesson based upon words introduced in each chapter of the Ginn Basic Readers was developed. This program was administered by the teacher in a one-to-one relationship with the child. Each child was given a pretest of words used in the part of the program to which he was assigned. While pretest scores varied, no child generally was enrolled in a part of the program if he knew more than 50 percent of the pretest words. In most cases the program took from 25 to 35 minutes a session and was offered to the child three times a week in a partially screened off booth in a classroom.

Responses to the entire five-part program were recorded by the teacher on a data sheet, as well as the amount of time taken for completion of the session. A check mark card also was available to record for the child the number of correct responses he made. For each of these correct responses tangible rewards (e.g., candy, money) were first used on a continual and then a periodic basis. These rewards later were replaced by the check marks on the card, and completed cards with 200 checks could be converted to prizes after several days' work.

Part I of the five-part program was an Oral Reading Review of the chapter in the Basic Reader containing the words learned on the previous day. The child read the chapter aloud and immediately was given any unfamiliar words—without encouragement to sound them out. The teacher recorded missed words on the data sheet.

Part II consisted of Vocabulary Building using a systematic presentation of new words on the teaching machine controlled by the teacher. In this phase of the program, words were introduced and reviewed in the following manner:

1. *Visual Discrimination of the new word.* To introduce new words, a simple visual-matching task was used. The new word appeared on the left enclosed in a box and again on the right, with two different words which served as distractors. The child's task was to match the word in the box with the same word on the right. This he did by pointing, drawing a line under it, or placing a marker on it, depending on his level of functioning.

Item: | Tom | ride   Tom   fast

Teacher: "Find a word just like the one in the box."
Immediate confirmation of the correct response was given as the machine was turned to the next frame and the correct choice appeared directly beneath it.

Confirmation: | Tom | ride   Tom   fast
                        Tom

Teacher: (if correct) "That's right!" (if incorrect) "No, (points) this word is like the one in the box. Say 'Tom.'"

2. *Auditory Discrimination of the new word.* The next frame presented the same word with two distracting words and the teacher verbally directed the child to find it. This task involved auditory and visual matching and the correct response was again confirmed as the machine was turned to the next frame.

Item: Tom   fast   ride

Teacher: "Find Tom."

Confirmation: Tom

Teacher: (if correct) "That's right!" (if incorrect) "No, (points) this word is 'Tom.' Say 'Tom.'"

3. *Readback of the new word.* In this frame the new word appeared alone and the subject was asked to read it. Confirmation was given verbally by the teacher.

Item: Tom

Teacher: "What is this word?"

Confirmation: (if correct) "Yes, that word is 'Tom,' " or (if incorrect) "No, this word (points to Tom) is 'Tom.' Say 'Tom.' "

4. *Visual Recall of the new word.* In the next frame the new word appeared alone and the subject was asked to look at it. The machine was rolled to the following frame where the word appeared with two distractors and the subject was asked, "Find a word like the one you just saw." The subject therefore was asked to remember the word over a short time.

Item 1: Tom

Teacher: "Look at this word."

Item 2: fast ride Tom

Teacher: "Now find a word like the one you just saw."

Confirmation: Tom

Teacher: (if correct) "That's right!" (if incorrect) "No, this word (points to Tom) is like the one you saw. The word is 'Tom.' Say 'Tom.' "

5. *Phrase Reading.* Next, the new word appeared in a phrase taken from the book. This was done to promote transfer of reading skill to Part III of the lesson, New Oral Reading. The child merely was asked to read the words and the teacher immediately provided miscalled words.

Item: Ride, Tom

In the Vocabulary Building section of the experimental program, words were introduced into the program in the same sequence as they were introduced in the book. Review words were systematically introduced into the program along with the new words. For each new word introduced, two review words appeared as Auditory Discriminations, a third review word appeared as a Visual Recall item, and from five to ten review words appeared as Readback and Phrase Reading items. The program thus provided for retention of words previously learned.

The actual format followed in a single lesson during the Vocabulary Building section was as follows:

Visual Discrimination	(new word)
Auditory Discrimination	(new word)
Readback	(new word)
Auditory Discrimination	(review word #1)
Readback	(review word #1)
Auditory Discrimination	(review word #2)
Readback	(review word #2)
Readback	(new word)
Visual Recall	(new word)
Visual Recall	(review word #3)
Readback	(new word)
Readback	(review word #4)
Readback	(review word #5)
Phrase Reading	(new words)
Phrase Reading	(new and review words)
Phrase Reading	(new and review words)
Phrase Reading	(new and review words)
Phrase Reading	(new and review words)

Part III of the lesson was New Oral Reading. The child was given a Basic Reader and asked to read the new chapter containing the words just learned during the Vocabulary Building section. When he failed to read a word correctly within a five-second period, it was immediately given to him by the teacher who asked him to repeat it aloud. No attempt was made to build phonic skills in this part of the program.

Part IV consisted of a Comprehension section involving questions about the content in the new chapter. In the first Primer the subject was asked to respond verbally to simple questions (e.g., "What was the boy's name?"). In later readers the child was asked to read comprehension questions presented in simple multiple choice and true-false form. This part of the program was eliminated for some of the autistic and severely disturbed children because of the confusion which existed regarding social objects and concepts. As these children became more familiar with the basic vocabulary, however, a surprising degree of comprehension of content and pictures developed.

Part V, the Follow-Up phase of the lesson, consisted of discrimination exercises with the newly learned words. These exercises emphasized initial, medial, and final word completions and discriminations in an effort to focus attention and offer additional cues for recall.

a) Initial completion item: Tom   L   T
                                 _om

The child was asked to select the missing letter and the teacher confirmed the response by writing the correct letter in the appropriate blank. Medial and final completion tasks were presented in similar fashion with middle and final letters missing.

b) Initial word discrimination item: Tom   Lom   Rom   Tom

The child was directed to choose the correct matching word from two distractors which varied in initial, medial, or final letters. Confirmation appeared in the next frame underneath the correct choice.

Data collection included recording the child's responses in all five parts of the lesson and calculating the percentage of his correct responses. A 75 percent correct response rate was set as a criterion for moving the child ahead in the reading program since it was found that progress could be achieved with most children even though they made a 25 percent error rate. If this standard were not achieved, the program would be repeated. If a series of repetitions did not appear to move the child on to criterion performance, the errorless training sequence described in Chapter VI was introduced.

Rewards for giving correct responses (e.g., reading a single word, answering a comprehension question, selecting a missing letter) were provided on a continual basis (one correct response earned one unit of reward) for all subjects during their first three lessons. Candy, in the form of readily dissolvable fruit drops, was deposited into a small cup beside the subject each time he responded correctly. Older subjects were rewarded with money, and pennies were dropped into the cup rather than candy.

According to the standard procedure, after the first three lessons each subject would have to make five correct responses before having one candy or money unit placed in his cup. In addition to actual receipt of a tangible reward, the subject was given a token reward in the form of a check mark on a card ruled off with 200 squares. These check marks always were given on a 1:1 basis, and later exchange was delayed until an entire lesson was completed. At this point the recognition of the value of the check marks increased with all subjects. Eventually a 1:200 schedule for tangible rewards was established with the child being given his choice of one five-cent prize (e.g., balloon, whistle, package of candy or gum, etc.) for each full card of check marks he accumulated. These full cards also could be saved, and two could be exchanged for a ten-cent prize. The total number of possible responses varied somewhat from lesson to lesson but it usually took two days for a subject to accumulate a full card of 200 check marks.

Subjects were moved through the different reward schedules at individual rates, and nine of the subjects had progressed from a continual schedule by the end of the first 12 lessons.

The normal subject was only given social rewards during her lessons which included the teacher's smiling, nodding approval, and commenting, "Good girl!" The removal of tangible rewards made possible establishment of a normal developmental baseline for the first part of the reading program.

Figure IX-5 illustrates the correct response rate and learning efficiency (number of responses per minute) of the normal subject, a four-year, eleven-month-old girl, during her learning of the 19 basic words which made up the vocabulary of the first Ginn Basic Pre-Primer. As is readily apparent, this subject had little difficulty reaching an almost perfect correct response level and steadily increased her learning efficiency. This type of data is what one might expect to obtain with a normal first grader of superior intelligence in a typical public school basal reading program. In such a program it is the social reward of conformity, teacher and peer approval, and mastery of a highly valued skill which provide all the necessary rewards for learning.

Figure IX-6 shows the progress in correct response rate and learning efficiency (number of responses per minute) for a four-year, ten-month-old emotionally disturbed boy for the same portion of the program undertaken by the normal subject. This boy was highly distractible and poorly motivated in the learning situation, but the provision of candy rewards gained his attention and cooperation. He maintained a correct response rate that was lower than the normal subject's, and he also was less efficient in his rate of responding. While this boy's intelligence was estimated below that of the normal subject's, the variability displayed

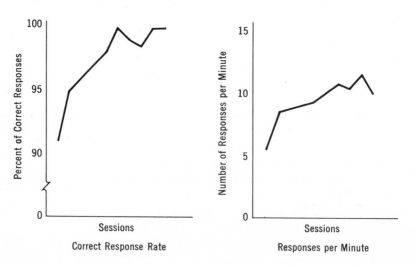

FIGURE IX-5. Correct response rate and responses per minute for normal girl.

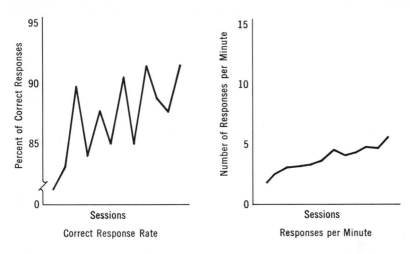

FIGURE IX-6. Correct response rate and responses per minute for emotionally disturbed boy.

may be viewed as an indicator of his emotional problem. Although there was much variability in the correct response rates and learning efficiency of the other subjects, the overall effectiveness of the experimental program was similar for all, and no subject failed to maintain progress for the period of time he was enrolled in the program. Because of differences in length of hospital stay and availability as outpatient participants, the range of participation in the program was from eight to 137 sessions.

The reading program emphasizes tasks at the attention, response, order, exploratory, social, and mastery levels and relies on a variety of rewards in a manner similar to that demonstrated in the speech training program with Eddie. Provision for the task and reward levels of the developmental sequence can be summarized as follows:

Task Level	*Reward*
1. Attention	
a) Removal of distracting stimuli (one-to-one teaching situation)	Tangible (can be money, candy, check marks)
b) Presentation of small discrete units of work	
2. Response	
a) Active participation of learner	One-to-one teaching situation with individual attention to the child at all times
b) Guaranteeing child success	

Task Level	*Reward*
3. Order	
a) Program organized in small discrete steps, each providing the child an opportunity to complete a task	Task completion
b) Structured learning environment (teaching machine, controlled presentation, program systematically organized and reviewed)	
c) Specific directions must be followed in answering each item	
4. Exploratory	
a) Visual and auditory discrimination emphasized in program items	Visual-auditory stimulation
5. Social	
a) Teacher directs child in all phases of program	Gaining social approval
6. Mastery	
a) Building a basic reading sight vocabulary	Knowledge of results through confirmation of items and teacher comments

The reading program was designed to be used on the multi-level basis illustrated above. The errorless training sequence described in Chapter VI is an adaptation which emphasizes all but the mastery level. In its emphasis on the lower levels, however, it is less complex and more concrete.

Since consideration of curriculum for emotionally disturbed children at the mastery level is the subject of Chapter XI, a more complete discussion of reading, written language, arithmetic, and other curriculum areas will be delayed until then.

MASTERY LEVEL REWARDS

The reward stated in Box f on the mastery level (Figure IV-8) is "doing learning tasks correctly." This reward is related to the traditional grading system relied on in education to inform students of the teacher's and school's rating of their academic and behavioral performance, and it is of particular concern to both the child and his parents.

The reward of "grades" or "knowing where you stand" has been investigated for several decades in experimental psychology under the heading "knowledge of results." Arps (1917, 1920) found that providing subjects engaged in a tedious experiment involving lifting weights with their index fingers with constant feedback regarding their functioning was a great help in holding their attention, aiding them in resisting fatigue, and increasing their output of muscular work.

Target practice studies were undertaken at Cambridge University by Elwell and Grindley (1938) and MacPherson, Dees, and Grindley (1948, 1949) and revealed that subjects who could see their errors and hence try to correct them on the next trial improved rapidly and maintained a higher interest in the task than those who were not permitted knowledge of results.

Woodworth and Schlosberg (1954) conclude: "It seemed that knowledge of results was a reward and that lack of this knowledge, like the discontinuance of reinforcement in conditioning experiments, led to extinction. Knowledge of results had a directive or corrective function and it also had incentive value."[2]

Wallen and Travers (1963) have reported that comparisons a learner makes between his behavior and some standard associated with attainment of a goal may function as rewarding consequences.

The finding that knowledge of results exerts a positive effect on learning rate and performance has been incorporated into the programed instruction field where teaching machines keep the student constantly infomed of his correct and incorrect responses and overall progress.

This principle is extremely useful for teachers of emotionally disturbed children, particularly when the knowledge of results given a child is positive. Assuring the child success, and hence receipt of positive consequences, has been stressed a number of times in the text as vital to an effective educational program. If we are successful, manipulating the task and structure dimensions of the learning triangle according to the readiness level of the child, we are in a position to provide him with a powerful reward—knowledge of positive results.

But learning is not all sweetness and light, and knowledge of results may not always be positive. Holding the emotionally disturbed child responsible for his behavior, for specific task assignments and consid-

---

[2] R. Woodworth and H. Schlosberg, *Experimental Psychology* (New York: Holt, Rinehart and Winston, 1954), p. 687.

erations of structure, may result in his occasionally being confronted with negative consequences. The use of the lowered shutter and darkened teaching booth in the speech program with Eddie provided just such a knowledge of results with an extremely inattentive and resistant learner. The fact that it had to be used very sparingly is evidence that the knowledge which it provided was meaningful and was utilized by Eddie to modify his subsequent behavior. For Jimmy, merely withholding the candy reward following incorrect responses served the same purpose and alerted him to pay closer attention and follow directions.

MASTERY LEVEL STRUCTURE

As was shown in Table IV-8 the emphasis on structure—on attaching strings to tasks given the child and expecting him to perform according to considerations of what, when, where, how, and how well—is maintained following the order level. At the mastery level the structure of the task is largely determined by the operations associated with the task itself and focuses on the "how" and "how well."

For example, reading the word "house" requires that the child say or understand "house." Spelling this word also requires that the letters h-o-u-s-e be correctly arranged. Four plus four equals eight and there are no two ways about it. The expectation of correctness in reading, spelling, and arithmetic and other school subjects imposes rigid demands on the child, and many emotionally disturbed children refuse to pay attention, respond, follow directions, or explore in learning because of the risk of failure inherent in undertaking a mastery assignment. Therefore, mastery level assignments must often be presented using the "thimbleful" approach and various props or supports in learning as was illustrated in the section on errorless training in Chapter VI.

Encouraging correctness is a mastery level goal, however, and sooner or later, if the child is ready to learn, he must acquire the ability to respond correctly. It will eventually be this ability that will determine whether or not the consequences will be an "A" or "F" since structure at the mastery level emphasizes "how well" the task is done.

ACHIEVEMENT LEVEL

At the achievement level we reach the final goal on the developmental sequence. Here the distinction between the three sides of the learning triangle diminishes. The task is to get the child to efficiently pursue learning in breadth and depth on a self-motivated basis, the reward is the pursuit of learning, and the structure is largely determined by the child himself as he seeks to gain knowledge and skill.

ACHIEVEMENT LEVEL TASKS, REWARD, STRUCTURE

The goal of the achievement level is more to foster an approach to learning rather than a specific competency such as attending, responding, direction following, exploration, self-care, and proficiency in academic subjects. However, in assisting the child to develop self-motivation in learning it is important to increase the stimulation of materials and subject matter, offer him opportunities for independence and creativity, and help him develop certain learning tools in order to increase his efficiency. These considerations, then, become the characteristics of tasks at the achievement level and can be stated as follows:

1. Presentation of an enriched curriculum.
2. Allowing the child freedom in selection of learning tasks and encouraging creativity.
3. Stimulating critical thinking ability, strengthening study and reference skills, and increasing proficiency in such areas as power and speed reading.

In the process of getting any child truly involved in learning, teachers know the value of supplementing traditional textbook presentations of subject matter with class projects, group discussions, and various audiovisual aids, such as records, tapes, filmstrips, and motion pictures. In addition, when a particular child shows interest in the unique aspect of the social studies or science curriculum, he may be allowed to undertake study in this area rather than be held for rigid adherence to the standard course of study. For example, the Civil War period may be of great interest to a child studying U.S. history, and the political issues, geographical locations, critical battles, and key figures of the time may offer many possibilities for independent research and study. In science, areas such as astronomy or space biology may hold fascination for a child, and if given the opportunities and resources, he may very willingly go beyond the minimum requirements of an assignment on his own.

In large, regular classrooms such individualization and enrichment of curriculum is difficult, but in smaller classes for children with emotional and learning problems teachers often have the opportunity for channeling a particular student's interest along certain lines. However, it has been mentioned earlier, some emotionally disturbed children with severe response, exploratory, and social problems prefer to withdraw intellectually into one narrow curriculum area such as higher mathematics or physiology rather tuan to involve themselves in a broad range of interests and studies. For such children, the most important considerations are their problems on the lower levels of the developmental sequence.

Where emphasis on the achievement level is appropriate, it is important to introduce the child to library facilities including types of reference materials available. In addition, he should learn how to use an index and obtain information from graphs, maps, charts, and tables. The teacher should engage in discussions with the child about what he is studying, have him report to his classmates, and possibly participate in discussions and debates with them. He should be helped to formulate critical questions, recognize basic issues, and organize the knowledge he has obtained so that he can write about it and discuss it clearly and succinctly.

Music, art, and drama, while mentioned as examples of exploratory interests, can be pursued far beyond this level in breadth and depth by the artistic, creative child on the achievement level.

Development of power and speed reading skills may greatly increase the child's effectiveness as a learner. Since reading is such a critical skill for knowledge acquisition, the child who reads inaccurately or laboriously seldom reaches the achievement level of the developmental sequence. There are many commercially available power reading programs designed to aid the child in becoming a more thorough and careful reader, enlarge his reading vocabulary, and increase his comprehension. Programs to increase reading also have received increased emphasis, and in addition to the tachistoscope and various reading pacing devices which have been available for some time, special approaches to the reading process have been developed which make possible, according to their originators, the doubling or tripling of basic reading rate.

The author has successfully taught speed reading to emotionally disturbed children when their basic vocabulary and comprehension skills were strong and when they were motivated to increase their reading efficiency. However, it should be kept in mind that teaching children with weak basic reading skills to be fast, poor readers is most undesirable. In addition, pressure for speed in reading is often a source of frustration and anxiety and hence not appropriate with many emotionally disturbed children.

The achievement level of the developmental sequence probably does not have as much relevance to the education of emotionally disturbed children as the lower six levels. Its presence, however, is necessary to call attention to the ultimate goal in education—that of aiding children in becoming efficient learners and assisting them in developing a true self-motivation for learning.

One of the topics found in most works on the education of emotionally disturbed children and not discussed in detail in this text is the characteristics of successful teachers of these children. Such qualifications as "tender without being sentimental," "tough but not callous," "sensitive but not irritable," "possessed by conviction," "profoundly aware without loss of spontaneity," "trusting in the intuitive humane responsiveness of one's self and one's colleagues," and "self actualized" may be recommended in the literature (Rabinow, 1955; Mackie, Kvaraceus, and Williams, 1957; and Haring and Phillips, 1962) and imply a saintliness and degree of perfection somewhat unrealistic to expect from most teachers who work with disturbed children. During the course of some seven years training teachers of the disturbed, the author has selected seven characteristics which appear important (Hewett, 1966). These can be stated in relation to the developmental sequence, although no exact parallel is intended.

1. *Objectivity:* knowledge of normal and deviant psychosocial development and professional literature in special education; ability to communicate with other disciplines and define educational goals in understandable terms; concern with objectively evaluating teaching successes and failures and capacity to separate own emotional needs from those of the students.
2. *Flexibility:* ability to shift teaching goals easily and instantly in line with the student's capacity for learning of the moment.
3. *Structure:* capacity to set and maintain reasonable behavioral and academic expectations.
4. *Resourcefulness:* ability to formulate innovative, meaningful and impactful approaches to learning.
5. *Social Reinforcement:* capacity to establish one's self as a positive social reinforcer in the classroom.
6. *Curriculum Expertise:* thorough knowledge of all basic curriculum content and methods.
7. *Ability to Function as an Intellectual Model:* skill to stimulate student's creativity and pursuit of learning in breadth and depth.

While these are presented with an implied priority ranking, certain teachers effectively compensate for weaknesses in one area with strengths in another. As a result, these characteristics should be viewed collectively as a total statement of desirable teaching competencies seen as related to overall teaching success with disturbed children.

This chapter concludes the section of the text devoted to the review of the levels of the developmental sequence and their relation to classroom programs for emotionally disturbed children. The mastery and achievement levels are of primary concern to education since this is where most learning takes place with normal children in regular classrooms from the upper elementary grades on. The fact that emotionally disturbed children are often not ready to function effectively on these levels and need programs emphasizing attending, responding, direction following, exploring, and socializing is the major tenet of this text.

3 Total Classroom Design

X A CLASSROOM DESIGN FOR EMOTIONALLY DISTURBED CHILDREN

This chapter introduces the third and final section of the text. Section 1 (Chapters I–IV) introduced the goals and methodology of the developmental strategy. Section 2 (Chapters V–IX) elaborated on the goals and methodology through discussion of attention, response, order, exploratory, social, mastery, and achievement tasks, rewards, and structure. This section (Chapters X–XII) is concerned with translation of the goals and methodology of the developmental strategy into a classroom program. Toward this end, a specific classroom design has been developed and will be described in detail in this chapter. Thus it is hoped that the interrelated and continual sequence of development of the approach presented in this text—from goals to methodology, to assessment, to classroom implementation—will become apparent.

This chapter will first discuss the models which have been used in the creation of the classroom design, provision for each side of the learning triangle—task, reward, and structure—in the design itself, and a brief historical account of its development in public and hospital school settings. Chapter XI will elaborate on curriculum and operational aspects of the design, and Chapter XII will report on a demonstration project undertaken to assess its effectiveness in the public schools.

The design to be discussed in this chapter has been referred to as the "engineered classroom." Such a label has caused concern among some educators because of its mechanistic, nonhumanistic overtones, and its origin in the physical rather than social sciences. Some who abhor the idea of teaching machines replacing teacher instruction may view an "engineered classroom" as one step closer to a totally nonpersonalized level of education. While the author recognizes the disadvantages associated with "secondhand labels" originating outside the field of education, since this was discussed in an earlier chapter, he is impressed with the advantages inherent in communicating to teachers the necessity for manipulating a classroom environment and the three sides of the learning triangle so that efficient learning and continued success may be experienced by the emotionally disturbed child. For that is the real implication behind the term "engineering." The teacher is urged to determine "what" the child's deficits are according to the developmental sequence of educational goals and then "engineer" a successful program of remediation through manipulation of the three sides of the learning triangle—task, reward, and structure. It is hypothesized that a natural consequence of such an approach will be the improvement of psychological and perceptual-motor difficulties. And it will engage the teacher in the role of learning specialist rather than educational therapist or diagnostician—a role far more consistent with the teacher's preparation and one which no other professional person is as well qualified to fulfill in the classroom.

The model for the engineered classroom is taken directly from the examples of classical and operant conditioning provided by the studies of Jones (1924) and by Ayllon and Haughton (1962) cited in Chapter III. These two studies shared in common application of the educational methodology stressed in this text:

1. Start where the child is and get him ready for more complex tasks through assignment of basic readiness tasks.
2. Settle for "thimblesful" of accomplishment and resist preoccupation with a "bucket" orientation in learning.
3. Once you have established contact with a child gradually increase demands and expectations at a pace which the child can tolerate.
4. Attempt to guarantee that the child will experience continual success in the classroom.
5. Create a predictable learning environment for the child in which he is rewarded for his accomplishments, nonrewarded if he fails to meet demands which, according to everything known about him, are reasonable to expect of him.
6. Be prepared to back up, modify tasks, and reset expectations if the child fails.

In addition, the two studies complement each other with respect to goals. Peter was helped to overcome a maladaptive fear or attitude, while Ayllon and Haughton's patients were assisted in developing specific adaptive skills for coping with their environment. Both goals are essential in aiding the emotionally disturbed child in school. He must first be deconditioned to the negative, aversive aspects of learning, teachers, and school and then be provided with a program designed to get him ready for learning. This will involve emphasis on the attention, response, order, exploratory, and social levels of the developmental sequence as a prelude to success on the mastery and achievement levels.

The engineered classroom attempts to achieve these goals through assignment of suitable tasks, provision for meaningful learner rewards, and maintenance of an appropriate degree of teacher structure. Such goals are best pursued, at least in the initial phases of an educational program with emotionally disturbed children, in a self-contained classroom. It is in a totally unique learning environment which does not "fit" with the child's previous negative experiences in school that the highest probability for changing attitudes and "launching" him into learning exists. In this environment it is hoped the child will find himself learning and enjoying his successes before he is actually aware that it is all part of "school." The engineered classroom attempts to create such an environment and build a foundation for learning through establishment of attending, responding, direction following, exploring, socializing, and academic skills. Once this foundation is firmly established, the child may be placed back in the regular classroom for varying periods of time. Transitional programs have been explored and found to be surprisingly uncomplicated for most children (such as the educationally handicapped children included in the Santa Monica Project and described in Chapter XII) if they are near their grade level in academic areas and competent on the lower levels of the developmental sequence.

The emphasis in this text will be on the beginning phase—a self-contained approach. This will be thoroughly discussed here and in the final two chapters. Use of aspects of the engineered classroom design in the regular classroom or specific discussion of reintegration of children back into regular classrooms will not be dealt with in detail. It is hoped however that all teachers will recognize the implications of this approach for use in classes for exceptional children in general as well as those for normal children.

Charters (1945, 1948) in the forties asked the question, "Is there a field of educational engineering?" and contrasted the "idea men" in education with the "engineers." According to Charters, the latter are concerned with planning, organization, and execution, while the former are "bored" by these activities. The "engineer" is "well grounded in information," has a "passion for efficiency," and possesses a "patient thoroughness." Charters also described the "inferior professional status" given individuals concerned with making ideas work and the fact that those who concentrate on offering techniques and practical suggestions "sit just below the salt at educational banquets." Skinner (1965) has also commented on the "extraordinary neglect of method" reflected in current efforts to improve education.

The field of education of the emotionally disturbed has had its share of "idea men" who have been more concerned with theory and formulation of goals than with the development of teaching techniques and specific curriculum approaches. The developmental strategy presented in this text and related to a total classroom design in this chapter attempts to achieve a balance between "ideas" and "engineering," goals and methods.

CLASSROOM TASKS

The keystone of the engineered classroom is assigning the child tasks he needs to learn, is ready to learn, and with which he can be successful —the first side of the learning triangle. These tasks will be related to his deficits on the developmental sequence of educational goals and determined through the assessment procedures discussed in Chapter IV. In order to accomplish this, a classroom environment must be provided in which floor plan, facilities, and program support the goals of the developmental strategy. The floorplan of the engineered classroom is illustrated in Figure X-1.[1]

It can readily be seen that the room is arranged so that specific areas are available for work on various levels of the developmental sequence. Starting with the upper two levels, the mastery and achievement area includes the student desks where assignments in reading, written language, and arithmetic are given. Adjacent to the desks and part of this area are two study booths or "offices." The offices are primarily used with students undertaking mastery assignments but who need a more secluded working environment. These study booths are not included in the design because of the conviction that emotionally disturbed children are so stimulus-prone that they must be isolated in drab, sterile surroundings. To the contrary, it is the author's contention that reality and environmental stimulation is essential in reducing the self-stimulation and fantasy preoccupation often demonstrated by emotionally disturbed children with problems on the attention and response levels. The "offices" may be carpeted and they contain large work tables and upholstered easy chairs. The teacher attempts to make these specialized work areas as glamorous and acceptable as possible for students who

---

[1] From F. Hewett, "Educational Engineering with Emotionally Disturbed Children," *Exceptional Children,* 1967, 33, pp. 459–467.

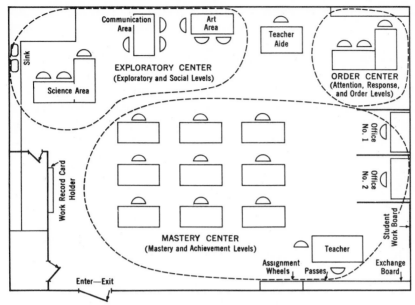

FIGURE X-1. Floorplan of an engineered classroom.

are not able to work comfortably on mastery assignments at their regular desks.

All student desks in the room are tables providing a desk top working area 2 x 4 feet in size. The desirability of such tables and the recommendation of 100 square feet of classroom space per student have been discussed in Chapter VII. Needless to say, such space allocation is not always available in existing schools. The author has implemented the engineered classroom design in rooms with only 40 square feet per student and although the programs have been successful they have not been as effective as those in larger rooms. Utilization of large tables, separation of students, and provisions for distinct classroom work areas require at least twice as much space. Teachers, however, are usually "reality compromisers," and it is the author's hope that many of the "ideal" recommendations made in this text, including provision for a spacious classroom, will not deter them from at least considering adaptations which might be possible even in the most limiting situations.

The teacher's desk is normally at the front of the mastery and achievement area (called the Mastery Center) and adjacent to a blackboard. In this respect, the area represents a traditional classroom arrangement. What is not so traditional, however, is a class size of nine students and the inclusion of a teacher aide. There is no magic in the number nine. Depending on the types of problems exhibited by students and the competencies of the teacher, an additional two or three children have been included in a successful class group. Once the number increases past 11, however, there is a definite price to pay in terms of the amount of individual time which can be spent with each student. A group of nine permits the class to be organized into smaller groups of three students each, and this has been found particularly useful in implementing the program to be described in detail in the next chapter.

Provision for a teacher aide may seem an extravagance beyond the means of many school programs for emotionally disturbed chldren. Aides, however, have been commonly used in preschool and kindergarten classes but are not found as often in the upper elementary and secondary grades. If the emotionally disturbed child is conceived of as an individual in need of learning experiences often as fundamental as those provided much younger children, the logic of not only utilizing the same tasks (e.g., attention, response, order, exploratory, social) but the assistance of an aide as well is clear. The aide need not be a credentialed individual; PTA volunteers, parents (usually of children not assigned to a particular class, although success has been reported by some teachers with parents of children in their classrooms), college and high school students, and even mature children from slightly older grade levels have all been found by the author to adequately fulfill the role. Of course the advantages of a salaried individual, who maintains a regular schedule, who is dependable, and who accepts a defined responsibility cannot be ignored. However, rather than dismiss provision for a teacher aide as impossible when funds are not available, some of the alternatives mentioned above are worth exploring.

The presence of an aide in a classroom increases the probability that a child's request for assistance will be met in a far shorter time than is normally possible when only the teacher is available. Provision for such "instant" assistance when needed may greatly reduce the incidence of maladaptive behavior and frustration commonly seen when emotionally disturbed children are subjected to long waiting periods. The teacher aide's desk is placed at the back of the room near the two other centers so that supervision for these areas is provided.

The Exploratory Center is the second major classroom area. It is usually set up in the vicinity of the sink and work counter, toward the back of the Mastery Center so that it will not distract students working at their desks. Here science, art, and communication activities are undertaken, each at a different table. The use of science as an exploratory activity has been discussed in Chapter VIII and examples of art and communication activities provided. Art activities engage the child in less well-defined and more self-expressive experiences, and the communication area offers two or more children opportunities for cooperative behavior, interaction in simple games, and group listening activities at a listening post. Although both exploratory and social activities are undertaken at this center, it is referred to as the Exploratory Center.

The Order Center is the third major defined area in the classroom. It includes two tables and a storage cabinet set up in a corner of the room so as not to be distracting to students working in the Mastery Center. The purpose of this center is to provide activities for the child emphasizing active participation, direction following, and task completion. This area is referred to as the Order Center in the classroom even though attention and response activities are included there. Examples of order activities assigned at this center are given in Chapter VII.

The floor plan, physical arrangement, and possible activities may be likened to the setting provided Peter during the deconditioning phase of Jones' study. In this setting he was offered positive, intriguing activities totally removed from association with the rabbit, and a starting point was established for gradually helping him overcome his fear. While the engineered classroom is still a part of school and not an example of as complete a separation from the problem as in the case of Peter, the underlying rationale is similar. As the operation of the classroom is described in the next chapter, this rationale will become more apparent.

There are four bulletin board areas in the room. One area is designated as a "Student Work Board" and used to display assignments done by students each week. A second bulletin board area features assignment wheels for use in assigning students in groups of three to various classroom activities. A third and fourth board are used in connection with the check-mark system which represents the second side of the learning triangle—meaningful learner rewards—in the engineered classroom.

CLASSROOM REWARDS

As has been stressed several times up to this point in the text, an effective learning situation must include some form of meaningful learner reward. In the discussion of the developmental sequence, possible rewards available in the classroom were listed as tangible rewards, social attention, task completion, multisensory experiences, social approval, task accuracy, and acquistion of skill and knowledge. For any given child, the effectiveness of each of these rewards may vary greatly, and they cannot be conceived in a rigid hierarchal order with universal application. But the most basic of those cited above and the most likely to be effective with children for whom few more traditional rewards have been forthcoming in school are tangible rewards.

In an attempt to provide a program with "something for everybody" the engineered classroom in its initial phase utilizes a tangible reward system consisting of check marks which have an exchange value for such items as candy, toys, and trinkets. Modification of the reward system in subsequent phases will be discussed at the close of Chapter XII.

By introducing the use of tangible or extrinsic rewards into the classroom, the author is fully aware of the Pandora's Box which is opened. "Children should not be enticed to learn." "Paying the child for learning will certainly doom him to the expectation of 'getting something' for any school work he does and probably precludes development of intrinsic motivation." "Tangible rewards are in effect bribes and represent an unwholesome compromise with educational values." One county business office, upon receiving a teacher's request for a purchase order to buy candy for use in a classroom for emotionally disturbed children, responded with the terse reply, "No candy bait with county funds." And so it goes.

Rewards of any type, if used systematically in school, represent consequences and acknowledgments of accomplishment. The use of letter grades constitutes such a system of acknowledgment and is generally acceptable in all educational programs. Grades, however, are not called "rewards." They are considered traditional acknowledgments of progress and achievement. In actuality a grade of "A" is a powerful reward and one which motivates many children to study, do their homework, and keep alert in the classroom. It is, however, a somewhat abstract reward, available to those select children who function well on the attention, response, order, exploratory, social, and mastery levels and who are susceptible to fairly sophisticated long-range rewards in learning.

Just as many emotionally disturbed children are often not susceptible to rewards of social attention, task completion, multisensory experience, and social approval, they are often not motivated by letter grades. This may largely be due to the fact that they have never functioned adequately enough in regular class programs to deserve or to obtain them. The use of tangible rewards is viewed by the author as a logical and temporary extension of the traditional reward system including social attention, task completion, multisensory experience, social approval, and grades generally relied on by educators. The term "temporary" is used advisedly, for in the author's experience use of such rewards is unnecessary after a short period of time. Once the child is engaged in a consistently successful learning experience, he naturally moves toward the seeking of these more traditional rewards. This is constantly seen with autistic and other severely disturbed children as well as less severely disturbed children in the public school.

Bribery is an unpleasant word with many unpleasant connotations. The fact that it is often associated with dishonest transactions makes it particularly offensive. Yet the fact remains many "honest transactions" may be interpreted as involving "bribes." Depending on how the word is defined, letter grades and diplomas may be viewed as "bribes" to get children to learn in school. Outside school, anyone who holds a regular job may be seen as only working to obtain the "bribe" of a regular paycheck. The author takes the position that systematic consequences or acknowledgments in a learning or working situation are a necessary and natural part of the honest transactions which occur between teacher and child, employer and worker.

The major problem in using tangible rewards in the classroom is that the concrete and primitive nature of such rewards is so alien to traditional practices that there are some who hasten to label them inappropriate when in truth they constitute a natural point on the continuum of consequences which are essential in the learning and working process.

The check-mark system in the engineered classroom is a temporary extension of the traditional system of acknowledgments used in regular classrooms. It is designed to guarantee that even the most disinterested and resistant learner will be rewarded for his efforts. It is also designed to create a wholly unique system of immediate consequences consistent with the novel and intriguing nature of the total classroom environment and program. In this way, the child who negatively views school is provided with one more positive experience in the classroom, further enabling the teacher to gradually introduce what may be the "noxious rabbit" of learning.

The engineered classroom day revolves around the child's receiving check marks for various accomplishments. Each morning as he enters the door the child picks up a Work Record card from the Work Record holder nearby. The bulletin board area utilized for this holder is illustrated in the photograph and an actual Work Record card partially filled with check marks is shown in Figure X-2.

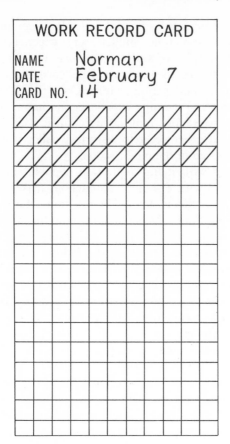

FIGURE X-2. Work Record card.

As the child goes through the day he is given check marks reflecting his task accomplishments and classroom functioning. Cards filled with check marks can later be exchanged for tangible rewards such as candy and trinkets. The criteria for receipt of check marks are presented on the Work Record card holder (see opposite page). Usually a possible ten check marks are given by either the teacher or aide following each 15-minute work period in the classroom. During the time devoted to giving check marks (usually five minutes) all work done within the preceding work period is corrected and the new assignment for the next 15 minutes is given. This allows three 15-minute work periods and three five-minute check-mark-giving periods during each class hour.

Two check marks are given if the child started his work, three if he "followed through" on an assignment, and a possible five bonus check marks are administered for "being a student." In the engineered classroom "being a student" refers basically to the student role described

Work Record card holder. (Photography in Chapters X and XI by José Lucero.)

earlier. That is, it refers to how well the child respected limits of time, space, and activity and the working rights of others. But, for the student with no problems on the order level of the developmental sequence, the five bonus check marks reflect his functioning on the levels most critical to his learning needs. For some extremely inattentive children, the bonus check marks may be given "Because you put your name on the paper and paid attention to your work," even though no actual work was accomplished. For those children with response problems, the five check marks may be given "Because you tried to do the assignment," regardless of the number of problems correct. Children with exploratory problems might receive their five bonus check marks for "Trying to do more of the assignment than usual." The child who is functioning well at the attention, response, order, and exploratory levels but who has trouble getting along with others may be given his check marks largely for his social behavior—"Because you worked well without bothering anybody else" or "Because you worked well with Johnny" on a cooperative task or "Because you did the assignment just as I (the teacher) wanted you to." The mastery learner may receive his bonus check marks as letter grade equivalents and be told "You earn five bonus check marks for getting all the problems correct."

In the giving of check marks, the teacher or aide takes time to explain why the child either receives or does not receive the possible ten. This transaction between child and adult is viewed as most significant and is not brushed over mechanically or carelessly. The check marks must reflect what the child has actually earned in terms of the teacher's expectations of him according to his functioning on the developmental sequence of educational goals. Since selection of suitable educational tasks aimed at attaining these goals is the most important aspect of the engineered classroom, each child should be receiving the majority of the ten possible check marks each 15 minutes. When he has not earned these, the teacher needs to reconsider the type of task assigned the child. If, however, in the teacher's judgment, the task was appropriate and the child needs reminding of the expectations for him, reduction of the number of check marks given is essential. This is not done punitively but in a matter of fact manner. "Here are your two check marks for starting, three for working and following through but you have only earned two bonus check marks because you did not . . . , etc."

Those who might view the check-mark-giving responsibility of the teacher in the engineered classroom as "technicians duty which anybody, including a robot could carry out" should reflect on the considerable degree of awareness of the appropriate educational goals for each child which is necessary in order to truly individualize the check-mark-giving transaction. The 15-minute, fixed interval basis for awarding the check marks may also seem mechanistic, but its very regularity guarantees that each child will be visited by either teacher or aide at least three times an hour, have his work corrected, and find out where he stands. This routine is in marked contrast to the inconsistent and often infrequent teacher-pupil contact, reliance on group-directed teaching, and the long delay in receiving grades, or teacher appraisal of work accomplishments in the regular classroom. Here again we have a unique program aspect designed to reorient the child more positively toward school and help him learn more efficiently.

The role of the teacher during the check-mark-giving process and in the engineered classroom in general is also unique. Words are used sparingly. Verbal contact with students is largely restricted to individual conversations during the correcting of assignments, giving check marks, and assigning of tasks during the five-minute check-mark-giving periods. Of course, verbal contact is also established whenever the student asks for help during a work period. This verbally limited role is probably the most controversial innovation in the engineered classroom, next to the use of the check-mark system. The rationale for a controlled verbal "task oriented" rather than highly verbal "interpersonal" relationship stems from recognition of the negative associations many emotionally disturbed children with school problems have with teachers who "talk too much." Rather than intended as a harsh criticism the author views this as a simple statement of fact. Teachers who are confronted with resistant, noncooperative, and seemingly inaccessible students often remind, lecture, and resort to long-winded verbal discourses in an attempt to "bring such children into line." Without dwelling on why this occurs (e.g., teacher anxiety), the fact remains that such verbal excess is probably one of the most prominent characteristics of school and classrooms which negatively orient children toward learning. Temporary removal of this characteristic is yet another move in the direction of creating a unique classroom environment for the child.

In the engineered classroom, the teacher attempts to establish a working relationship with each child. An effort is made to convey the notion that the teacher "works" in the classroom too and that his job is assigning tasks that the child needs to learn, is ready to learn, and can be successful in learning. Part of the teacher's job is also administering check marks which the child has earned as a result of task accomplishments. In this regard, the teacher may be viewed as a "shop foreman" or "working partner" who credits workers for actual accomplishments yet who is also a worker in the school setting. Check marks are presented as objective consequences of the child's efforts and literally part of a reality system in the classroom over which the teacher has little subjective control. The teacher's message to the child is, in essence, "That's just the way it is. I work here too." The check-mark system, then, serves as a neutral nonconflictual meeting ground for teacher and student devoid of the connotation that acknowledgment of the child's accomplishments is based on the fact that the teacher is a powerful adult, bigger and smarter than the child.

Viewing emotionally disturbed children as workers and paying them what they have earned rather than as helpless individuals and pitying them is seen as valuable in giving such children self-respect. By placing definite responsibility which he can assume on the child's shoulders and by providing predictable consequences for his behavior, it is his strengths that are being appealed to rather than weaknesses. The entire concept of being preoccupied with emotionally disturbed children as "sick" and totally unable to care for themselves denies them the self-enhancement and dignity which comes from being given responsibility and successfully carrying it out.

Despite the "work" and "task" orientation of such a teacher-pupil relationship, very definite interpersonal aspects are present. Without always having to tell the child "I like you. You did exactly what I asked" or "I want to help you" the fair and predictable administration of check marks soon establishes the teacher as a classroom ally who has the child's best interests at heart, accepts him as he is, and wants more than anything else to assist him in learning and achieving success. In engineered classrooms which have abruptly removed the check-mark system and then relied on the more traditional rewards of teacher attention, praise, and grades, there has been little noticeable change in the children's cooperation and learning efficiency. Teachers in these rooms apparently had become far more than mere purveyors of check marks and had acquired secondary reward value of their own through association with the primary check-mark reward system.

While the check-mark system may appear to some as contrived and totally devoid of warmth and personal interest, it is the author's contention that attempting to guarantee the child's success through assigning tasks he needs to learn, is ready to learn, and then providing fair, predictable, and systematic consequences related to his accomplishments is the greatest expression of "teacher love" which can be given in the classroom. Despite the seemingly mechanical routine involved in the giving of check marks, most teachers the author has observed who have utilized the check-mark system are warm and personal in their manner although expression of these attributes does not necessarily occur verbally.

The use of the check-mark system can enhance the good teaching qualities of any teacher through providing regular contact with pupils and constant assessment of progress. In the engineered classroom there is still plenty of room for teachers to be themselves and to create and innovate despite the highly structured nature of design. In addition, the teachers appear to find frequent contact with students and opportunities for continuous assessment of progress personally rewarding.

On the first day of school, children enrolled in an engineered classroom are greeted outside the room by the teacher. They are lined up and each handed a Work Record card with his name on it. With no more explanation than "This is going to be a different classroom from any you've ever been in before" the teacher instructs them to go inside the room and sit down at the desk with their name on it. Immediately after they are seated at that desk, the teacher and aide circulate and give each child ten check marks, "Five because you were on time, and five because you found your desk and are ready to go to work." In addition, a candy unit is placed on top of each check mark to establish the card and checks as important and rewarding. The children are told that they can eat the candy whenever they wish, and the first assignment is also given the child during this initial check-mark-giving period.

Questions inevitably arise regarding children who have dental problems, who are allergic to chocolate, or who have diabetes. In this regard, sunflower seeds, popcorn, raisins, and peanuts have proven just as effective as candy.

For the first two hours of the first day, a candy unit is placed over each check mark given. Following this time the children are told that they will receive a candy exchange for all check marks earned at the close of the day. Before dismissal the teacher and aide provide a candy unit for each check mark on each child's card including those previously accompanied by candy units during the first two hours. The second day the children receive check marks but no candy and are told that they will receive the exchange at the end of the day. This approach may be carried out on the third day but by the fourth day the children should be held to having an entire card filled with checks before being allowed to turn it in.

By the end of the second week, cards should only be exchanged twice weekly at designated times, regardless of when the child completes them, and after the third week only a weekly exchange time is provided on Friday. The process of having the child exchange his completed check-mark card for tangible rewards can become unnecessarily elaborate. The author visited one classroom in which the teacher allowed each child ten minutes to "shop" from five tables covered with items available for one, two, or three completed cards. In another program, exchange items lined the walls of the hall leading to the classroom. The items ranged in value from fifty cents to ten dollars and involved a complicated exchange procedure. In still another classroom, each completed check-mark card was worth a dollar and fifty cents and parents of the students in the class objected because their "problem" children brought home costly toys which they displayed with pride before their "nonproblem" siblings, creating a somewhat confusing situation regarding rewards, learning, and school.

In the engineered classrooms the author has supervised, the cost and nature of an exchange item is generally unimportant, particularly with elementary age children. What does matter, however, is that it was "earned" in school. Children with enough money in their pockets to buy the equivalent of the teacher's entire supply of exchange items at the local five-and-ten-cent store display delight with a five-cent item earned with check marks. One teacher who used miniature candy bars as exchange items had one student who would bring a regular-size bar of the same candy to school in hopes he could "trade" his larger bar to some classmate for a more valued "school" candy bar that was used as an exchange item.

It is not *what* you give the child in exchange for his check marks, *how much* you give him, or its *monetary value* that is the crucial determiner of its real worth. These considerations constitute the "small idea" inherent in the check-mark system. The "big idea" is that the child's accomplishments are being acknowledged in a systematic fashion and that he comes to recognize that his behavior controls certain consequences. Despite the author's plea for such placement of "big" and "little" ideas in perspective, some teachers upon reading this text will undoubtedly rush out, buy a large stock of candy, begin to pass it out rather haphazardly in the classroom, and then wait for a teaching miracle to occur. Such an approach may produce results initially, but it can be predicted with some certainty that its effectiveness will diminish fairly quickly. There is no magic in giving tangible rewards, including gold stars, which have been used in education for years. It is the system with which such rewards are associated that will guarantee their success. Knowledge of the relationship of rewards to learning is ancient, but their systematic usage to help foster more adaptive behavior in the classroom is new and relatively unexplored in special education.

In the engineered classroom evaluated in Chapter XII, each completed Work Record card with some 200 check marks on it could be exchanged for one item costing no more than five cents. The child was given the choice of exchanging each card for a five-cent item, saving two cards for a ten-cent item, or three cards for a 15-cent item. In general, children were not allowed to save more than three completed cards, and the number of check marks possible to earn each week usually made it possible for a child to complete two-and-one-half cards. One of the classroom bulletin board areas is devoted to displaying exchange items; an example of this is shown in the following photograph. It has been found useful to vary the exchange items and add at least one new item to each of the three choices each week.

In addition to giving check marks following 15-minute work periods, the teacher may use a "surprise" bonus when a given child is displaying some behavior close to one of the teacher's goals for him (e.g., keeping all four legs of his chair on the floor, not disturbing others, raising his hand to request assistance). He may be "surprised" and be given five or ten extra check marks on the spot. At other times when the class is having difficulty settling down, the teacher may announce, "Each student who is ready to work and who has followed my directions will receive five extra check marks." These are then immediately given out to those students who have fulfilled the teacher's expectations, and no additional comment is made about the children who were "not ready" and who did not receive bonus check marks.

Exchange board.

Check marks are also given first thing in the morning following the flag salute and after recess and the nutrition and physical education periods. The complete breakdown of the number of check marks given following various periods of the day appears in Table XI-1 in the next chapter.

At the close of the day, each child totals up his check marks, and these are graphed on a Work Report fixed to his desk. This is illustrated in Figure X-3 and allows the child to compare his individual progress day by day.

While some children may become preoccupied with the number of check marks given their classmates and become competitive regarding comparisons, it has been found a reminder that "In this room every student receives check marks for doing what he needs to do. Since everyone is working at his own level, check marks are given to different children for different reasons" causes such behavior to rapidly diminish.

The check-mark system actually encompasses all of the rewards stated in Boxes a, b, c, d, e, f, and g in Figure IV-8. Tangible rewards are provided by both the actual check marks and the exchange items; social attention is given in the very act of administering the check marks after each work period. Task completion, multisensory involve-

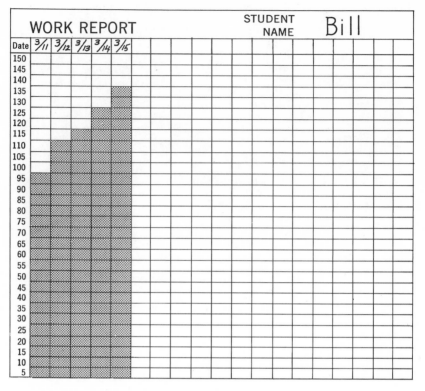

FIGURE X-3. Work Report.

ment in learning, behavior gaining social approval, and task accuracy are selectively rewarded by the five bonus check marks given at the discretion of the teacher. In addition, the actual centers themselves in the room provide rewards associated with mastery, exploratory, social, attention, response, and order activities.

CLASSROOM STRUCTURE

From the description of the floor plan, arrangement of various centers, check-mark system, and the task-oriented role of the teacher, it is obvious that the engineered classroom is "highly structured." At first glance it may appear that the child is introduced into a learning situation with a minimum of flexibility and a maximum number of fixed environmental expectations. Despite this seeming rigidity of the classroom design as presented up to this point, every effort is made to balance "fixed environmental expectations" with "child-centered considerations."

It may be recalled in Chapter III how the term "structure" was an issue of debate between the behavioristic classroom approach described by Haring and Phillips and the interpersonal approach taken by Bettelheim. While Haring and Phillips described their approach as "the structured classroom" and alluded to the lack of structure in Bettelheim's program, the point was made that providing for the educational needs of individual children in any classroom usually involves considerable structuring.

The author has defined structure in an educational program as referring to the "strings" the teacher attaches to assigned tasks which determine whether or not the rewards present in the classroom will be made available to the child. These "strings" involve dictating "what" the task will be, "when" and "where" it will be undertaken, "how" it will be done, and "how well" it must be accomplished. In the engineered classroom these aspects of structure are provided for in the following ways:

What

The schedule and curriculum of the classroom is discussed in detail in the next chapter. Five main periods devoted to order, mastery (reading, written language, and arithmetic), and exploratory tasks constitute the class day. During each of these periods the entire class is assigned to scheduled tasks. However, when it is apparent from the initial assessment of the child according to the developmental sequence that he cannot successfully undertake a particular task (e.g., reading) or if it appears on a given day that an assignment of a particular type of task is likely to end in frustration and failure, the teacher immediately alters "what" the child is asked to do. Therefore, while the fixed environmental expectations of a schedule activity exists at all times, the specific task assigned a child will be determined by his readiness to undertake it. The child is not given free choice in deciding "what" he does, but the teacher's selection of "what" is assigned will be based on the child's functioning according to the developmental sequence.

When

The engineered classroom schedule dictates certain time blocks for various activities. If the child is viewed as unable to successfully undertake a scheduled activity, he will be reassigned as described above. Therefore, "when" a child does a given task will also be determined by his functioning of the moment.

Where

The engineered classroom is divided into three major centers. When the teacher determines "what" task is appropriate to assign the child and "when" it may be assigned, the child is expected to undertake it in a specific area. Therefore, attention, response, and order tasks are undertaken at the Order Center; exploratory and social tasks done at the Exploratory Center; and mastery tasks at the Mastery Center either at the child's desk or in one of the offices or study booths. The child is not allowed to choose "what" he will do or "when" he will do it, and he must also conform to the teacher's assignment of "where" he is to work. Children in the engineered classroom are not permitted to crawl under their desks to do arithmetic assignments, climb up on the filing cabinet to put a puzzle together, or to sit on the sidewalk in front of the school to do their reading. Except during special intervention procedures to be discussed later, structure is defined as "teacher selected strings" and does not include the child's selection of what, when, where, how, and how well.

How

An arithmetic assignment in addition requires that the numbers be added, not subtracted. If such an assignment is considered appropriate for a child he is expected to try to do it, not fold the paper into a glider and sail it through the room, draw pictures on it, or crumple it up and stuff it inside his desk. When any of these inappropriate behaviors occur, the teacher needs to consider the rationale for assigning the child the task in the first place. As was discussed in the "what" section, the task assignment must be something the child needs to do, is ready to do, and can succeed at. If he cannot or will not do an assignment, the teacher must move quickly to reassign him. For the moment, the reward of the check marks may have to be withheld, but before another activity is given the child, careful attention must be paid to his chances of succeeding at it. In the description of classroom interventions, which appears later, procedures for such reassignment are presented in detail.

How Well

Of all the considerations of structure, "how well" the child accomplishes a task is probably least important for the emotionally disturbed child, particularly if he has problems on the first five levels of the developmental sequence. Task accuracy is a mastery level consideration, and more significant concerns are task attention, response, completion, and exploration. Before any child is assigned a mastery task during the reading, story writing, or arithmetic period, the teacher must be certain he possesses the academic competency to do the assignment correctly. The teacher must also recognize that for some withdrawn children with response problems, getting their name on the paper and completing half of one problem may be more than enough to earn them the full complement of check marks. For an acting-out child with problems at the order level, sitting quietly at his desk may constitute the most significant task for him at the time, and the number of problems he has correct is of minimal importance.

In summary, the structure in the engineered classroom is both child-centered and based on fixed environmental expectations. "What" the child does and "when" he does it depends on his functioning level of the moment and his deficits according to the developmental sequence of educational goals. "Where," "how," and "how well" he must do it are determined by the teacher and the design of the classroom once an appropriate task has been selected.

Selection of an appropriate task is both the most essential and the most difficult consideration in the engineered classroom. If the teacher is always accurate in determining what a child needs to do, is ready to do, and can be successful doing, things can be expected to run along smoothly. But despite a commitment to individualization of instruction and careful planning, no teacher can expect such success with emotionally disturbed children because of their day-to-day, moment-to-moment variability.

In an effort to assist teachers in the engineered classroom with those inevitable times when the child does not "take" to an assigned task even though thoughtful consideration of his learning needs went into its selection, a series of interventions has been formulated. These interventions involve descending the developmental sequence of educational goals until a level is reached where the child can be successfully engaged in a learning task, receive meaningful rewards, and operate within the degree of structure imposed on him.

Interventions

As long as the student can function with an assignment at any of the levels on the developmental sequence he continues to earn his full complement of check marks. There is no penalty attached to reassignment at lower level tasks. Just as the rabbit occasionally had to be moved back from Peter when it was brought too close during deconditioning, so the teacher must be prepared to reduce school expectations when an emotionally disturbed child cannot handle the structure being imposed on him.

The interventions will be discussed one by one. In actual practice the teacher may try them one at a time or, most likely, select the one that appears to be most appropriate for a given child at a given time. The ideal time for initiation of an intervention is in anticipation of the actual problem or very shortly after the first sign of inability or unwill-ingness to do an assigned task. The first seven interventions are consid-ered "student interventions" because they involve the child's continuing to earn check marks at all times. Interventions 8 and 9 are "nonstudent interventions" and do not enable the child to continue earning check marks.

1. *Send Student to Study Booth. (Mastery level)*

   The first intervention involves sending the child to work on an assigned mastery task in one of the study booths or "offices." It has been pointed out that these booths are presented to the children in a positive manner and as a result they are desirable working areas. In being sent to the booth the child picks up a "pass" (cutout yellow wooden key) from the teacher's desk and hangs it on the wall inside the booth. This signifies his assignment to the study booth for a period of time. It has been observed that merely allowing the child to change position and move around in the room often appears to interrupt effectively a period of boredom or resistance.

Study booth intervention.

2. *Modify Assignment. (Mastery level)*

   The next logical intervention in terms of the developmental sequence and the engineered classroom philosophy is to change the mastery task given the child, either making it easier, different, or perhaps more difficult in an effort to get him involved. Sending the student to the study booth with a modified assignment may also be used at this time.

3. *Restructure Verbally. (Social level)*

When the mastery interventions described above are not successful or appear inappropriate, an intervention at the social level is next in line for consideration. This intervention involves verbal restructuring on the part of the teacher, using social approval or disapproval as leverage. The child is reminded of the teacher's expectation for him in relation to the assigned task and his behavior. It has been previously mentioned that interactions between teacher and child in the engineered classroom are largely task-oriented because of the poor relationships with adults previously experienced by many emotionally disturbed children. Nevertheless, with some students a reminder by the teacher regarding what is expected may be all that is necessary to help them improve their behavior. This intervention is perhaps most often used by teachers in regular classrooms with children who display problem behavior and often reinforces the child's negative concept of school and teachers. Therefore, it should be used only after careful consideration, and it is often deleted in the intervention process.

4. *Send to Exploratory Center. (Exploratory level)*

The next intervention reassigns the child to another task center in the room. Upon direction the child picks up a blue pass key from the teacher's desk and goes to the exploratory center where he hangs it on the wall, signifying reassignment to this area. The teacher selects a previously demonstrated science, art, or in some cases, communication task and assigns it to the child, making sure all the materials are available and that he understands what to do. Assignments at the Exploratory Center are always teacher-selected. In practice the teacher should always have one or two exploratory tasks set up in advance for "instant" use as interventions.

5. *Send to Order Center. (Order level)*

Since the Exploratory Center involves a high degree of stimulation, it may not be as appropriate for some disturbed children at a given time as the Order Center. After picking up a red pass key at the teacher's desk, the child hangs it on the wall by the Order Center and is given a simple direction-following task such as making a puzzle, copying a pegboard design, stringing beads, deciphering a secret code with the aid of a key, or constructing a model of plastic or metal components.

6. *Take Student Outside Classroom and Agree on a Task. (Response level)*

In an effort to maintain contact with the student and keep him earning check marks, an intervention at the response level may be undertaken outside the room. Both student and teacher (or aide) go out of the class-

Mastery intervention.

Social intervention.

Exploratory intervention.

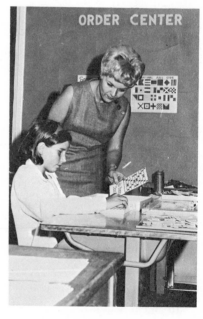

Order intervention.

room and agree on some task the child will undertake, such as turning somersaults on the lawn, swinging on a swing for 15 minutes, punching a punching bag, or even resting in the nurse's office for a period of time. If the student successfully completes the task, he is given his full complement of check marks and returned to the room. Following a response intervention the teacher attempts to select some assignment in the classroom to insure the student's success upon his return.

Response intervention.

7. *Provide Individual Tutoring and Increase Check Marks. (Attention level)*

The intervention corresponding to the lowest level on the developmental sequence involves the teacher or aide devoting full time to individual instruction with the student. Such individual tutoring is not always possible for extended periods of time because of the needs of the other students, but it is the next logical step to take in order to help the child. It may also include doubling the number of check marks given the child during a 15-minute period or in some cases going back to placing a candy unit on top of each check mark.

8. *Time Out. (Nonstudent)*

Interventions 8 and 9 are nonstudent interventions and require that the child give up his Work Record card and the opportunity to earn check marks for a time. During the time-out intervention the child is told that he cannot earn check marks for a five-, ten-, or 15-minute period, during which he must sit in isolation, usually in the principal's office. Following this time-out period the child is immediately returned to the class with no questions asked. As long as he sat quietly during the time-out period he is able to return to the classroom and begin earning check marks again. In returning the child to class the teacher will select an intervention level which seems to hold promise of successfully re-integrating him back into class. There is no extracting of promises that the child "be a good boy" or statements to the effect that "you can return when you feel you can control yourself." The student's return is based solely on the clock, and there is no verbal pressuring on the part of the teacher or principal. In regard to this and the final intervention, the importance of total school support, including the office clerks and the principal, cannot be minimized.

Attention intervention.

9. *Exclusion (Nonstudent)*

When the child is unable to tolerate a given time-out period or has to be placed in a time-out intervention three times in one day, he is immediately excluded from school and if at all possible, sent home. There is no "lecture" given by anyone in the school. He is merely told he cannot remain in school because it appears he cannot "be a student." He will be permitted to return the next day "with no hard feelings." If a given student has to be sent home three times in one semester he must earn his way back into class and can attend one hour the first day, two the next, and so on.

As can be seen from the nature of the interventions, an attempt is made to move the "noxious rabbit" of school demands as far out of the picture as may be necessary in order to maintain the child in a successful learning situation. When it is apparent that no amount of task manipulation will successfully engage the student in learning, the final consequence of exclusion is the only resource left. It should be stressed again that time-out or exclusion carries no "bad boy" connotation with it but represents a "fact of life" which the student must be made aware of when he is unable to meet the school and the teacher even a small part of "halfway."

In selecting an intervention, the teacher uses the model provided by the learning triangle. When the child is unable to pursue an assigned task, it is evident that something is wrong. The engineered classroom philosophy does not dwell on "what is wrong with the student?" but rather focuses on "what is wrong with the classroom environment?" The answer to this question can usually be obtained by considering the three sides of the learning triangle. Is it the nature of the task given the child? Is it the lack of a meaningful reward for learning? Is it because the structure imposed was an excessive demand associated with the task?

Intervention 1 (send to study booth) maintains the task and reward but alters the structure by changing "where" the child does his task. Intervention 2 (modifying task) directly deals with "what" the task is and attempts to provide a more suitable assignment. Intervention 3 (verbally restructure) leaves the task alone and moves to consideration of rewards and structure. Perhaps the reward of avoiding the teacher's disapproval and working for approval will reorient the student. Perhaps the verbal reiteration of "how" the task should be done will be all that is necessary.

Intervention 4 (send to Exploratory Center) alters all three sides of the learning triangle. The mastery task is replaced by one at the exploratory level. In addition to the reward of check marks for successful accomplishment of a task at the Exploratory Center, the reward of multisensory stimulation is added at this point. Considerations of "what," "where," "how," and "how well" in terms of structure are also modified during this intervention. Intervention 5 (send to order center) approaches the three sides of the learning triangle in approximately the same manner as Intervention 4 with the exception that a more defined "what" is provided and task completion as a reward is emphasized.

At the level of Intervention 6 drastic modification of task and structure occurs. The task is ill-defined and the child is allowed some freedom now in its selection. It can be literally anything which engages the teacher and child in a task-oriented relationship. Considerations of structure on the teacher's terms diminish, and the child is a partner in determining "what," "when," "where," "how," and "how well." Intervention 7 (individual tutoring) may involve considerable modification of all three sides of the learning triangle. The task could be anything at any level on the developmental sequence. Tangible rewards may be increased if necessary and structure altered as in the previous intervention.

If Interventions 8 and 9 are necessary, the structure side of the triangle receives emphasis, the task aspects are minimized, and the rewards eliminated. During Intervention 8, the child's task is merely to sit in isolation. Although sitting quietly can be considered an order level task, since it occurs outside the classroom it is not viewed as related to the levels on the developmental sequence. The Work Record card is taken from the child and it is made clear to him that he cannot earn check marks for a specified number of minutes. "What" he does and "when," "where," "how," and "how well" he does it are arbitrarily imposed. The child is expected to sit quietly until his specified "time-out" period is over when he can return with no questions asked.

Intervention 9 is the last resort. When it must be utilized, the implication is that every available resource in the school and the classroom has failed. Despite its seeming finality, many children who are excluded "learn" something valuable about the minimum requirements for being in school and subsequently alter their behavior to avoid being sent home again. The same is true of hospitalized children and adolescents in the NPI School. When the teacher matter-of-factly points out that for the time being the child is apparently unable to be a "student" and must leave, even a severely disturbed child has been found capable of understanding "That's just the way it is," and the intervention seldom has to be used again.

A perplexing issue inevitably comes up at this point. What about the child for whom school and everything associated with it is so negative that the greatest reward of all is to escape and retreat home? Such a child normally has serious problems at the response level and is not aided at all by being excluded. Although this problem has only been seen very rarely, when it has occurred, the teacher's task is clear cut. The three sides of the learning triangle must be so altered, particularly the reward side, that the child receives more satisfaction from being in school than at home. With such children unique projects (e.g., building a model ship at the Order Center for the entire class day) may be introduced or the structure changed so that the time spent in the classroom is reduced and the child is only expected to be in school for a limited period of time which he can tolerate and which he enjoys.

Another query which arises from the use of the interventions in the manner described is "What about the child who is far more rewarded by exploratory and order tasks and who actively seeks to create problems in the classroom so he can be reassigned to a more attractive task? Doesn't such reassignment in effect 'reward' maladaptive behavior?" Viewed in the context of the operant model illustrated in the work of Ayllon and Haughton, the answer to the latter question is "Yes." But viewed in the context of the respondent model provided by Jones' study with Peter and the rabbit the answer is "Such a price is well worth paying if it preserves a link with learning at some level of the developmental sequence and maintains the child as a successful student." Therefore, freely "move the rabbit back" when you set it too close. The engineered classroom design is truest to the respondent model and is more concerned with maintenance of classroom success and changing negative attitudes toward learning than rigid adherence to the well-known principle of learning that rewarding maladaptive behavior may cause it to increase in frequency. This is an example of the statement made earlier that the developmental strategy uses the behavior modification methodology "pragmatically," and when compromises are necessary they occur in favor of the child and sound educational practices.

In actual practice, the problems created are slight. Few children persist in attempting to manipulate the teacher into assigning them to a different work area. In cases where this occurs, Intervention 8 (time out) is used directly as a negative consequence. Most children in engineered classrooms which the author has supervised "get the idea" very quickly that the class is set up to help them and they relax and fit comfortably into the routine. In addition most emotionally disturbed children, despite their avoidant behavior in relation to mastery level activities, really want to learn to read and improve in arithmetic and other skills very much. It is when we place them in a truly supportive learning environment and devise individual programs for them according to the learning triangle that their motivation for succeeding at the mastery level can be fully exploited.

This chapter has reviewed possibilities for assigning appropriate tasks, providing meaningful rewards, and implementing a flexible structure in a special classroom design for emotionally disturbed children. The suggestions offered have been found practical and useful both in public and hospital schools. Because of the great variability among

teachers of emotionally disturbed children, rigid and universal acceptance of each and every aspect of the design presented is highly unlikely.
The design, however, is consistent with the goals and methodology of
the developmental sequence which it translates into actual classroom
practice. An evaluation of a large-scale public school project involving
the engineered class will be reported in Chapter XII.

We turn now to a brief summary of the historical development of the
engineered classroom approach. In the summer of 1965 the author was
invited by the Tulare County Schools to develop a classroom design for
use with educationally handicapped children, including those with emotional disturbance, minimal neurological impairment, and learning disabilities. Eight boys ranging from nine to twelve years of age were
selected and assigned to the class which ran for five weeks during
the summer. The teacher and aide were trained during a six-hour
period prior to the start of the class. Since this project constituted the
pilot study of the design, the classroom was put together in tentative
form and changed day by day as needed. While the developmental
sequence of educational goals had been conceived earlier by the author,
the use of behavior modification methodology in a group situation had
not been explored and the guidelines for this were obtained from the
Rainier School Project for institutionalized retardates (Birnbrauer,
Bijou, Wolf, and Kidder, 1965). In this project a small teacher-pupil
ratio, study booths, a check-mark system, centers for emphasizing exploratory and direction-following activities, use of passes for assigning
children to areas, and time-out interventions had all been included.

The floor plan and physical arrangement of the Tulare classroom
was practically identical to that shown in Figure X-1, although division
of the Exploratory Center into specific science, art, and communication
areas came later. The curriculum included reading, story writing, science, and physical education, and the class was in session three hours
daily.

Evaluation data of the project were largely based on observational
records but pre- and post-parent and teacher ratings were done utilizing
the rating forms presented in Appendix II. The results of the parent
ratings are seen in Figure X-4 and those of the teacher's (child's
teacher during spring semester as compared with summer project
teacher) in Figure X-5. As can be seen parents noticed definite improvement in the children's attitude toward school and teacher as expressed at home, while the comparative teacher ratings indicated improvement in general learning and classroom behavior.

In the fall of 1965 an engineered classroom was instituted at the
elementary level in the Neuropsychiatric Institute School. Eight chil-

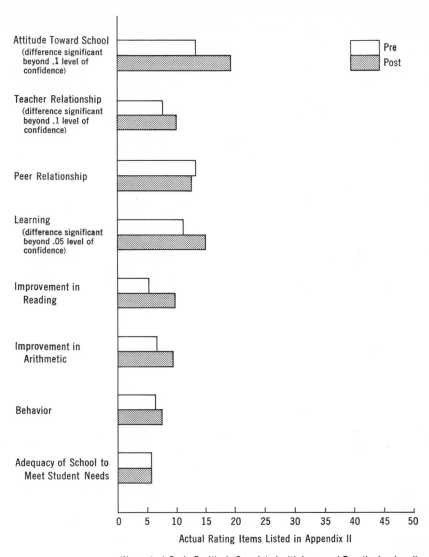

FIGURE X-4. Tulare pre- and post-program parent ratings.

dren with severe emotional problems, several with neurological impairment, were enrolled after the entire design was thoroughly discussed
with the child psychiatry staff. The children's therapists were encouraged
to visit the class and assist the teacher in selecting goals to be emphasized in the program. Because of the excellent rapport and cooperation

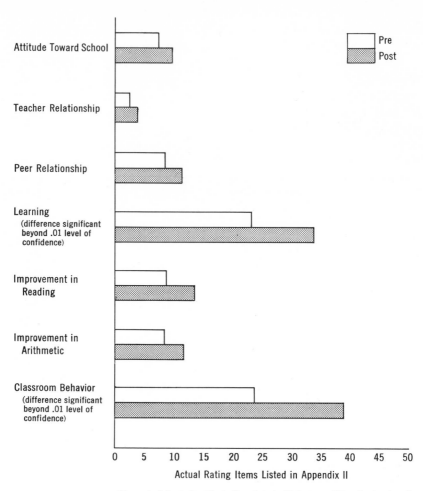

Attitude Toward School

Teacher Relationship

Peer Relationship

Learning
(difference significant
beyond .01 level of
confidence)

Improvement in
Reading

Improvement in
Arithmetic

Classroom Behavior
(difference significant
beyond .01 level of
confidence)

Pre
Post

0   5   10   15   20   25   30   35   40   45   50
Actual Rating Items Listed in Appendix II

(Numerical Scale Positively Correlated with Improved Functioning Level)

Figure X-5   Tulare pre- and post-program teacher ratings.

between members of the psychiatric staff and the NPI School teachers, the engineered design was well accepted in a hospital setting with a predominantly psychoanalytic orientation.[2] The "good teaching" aspects of the design as well as its inherent flexibility were clearly recognized

_____

[2] The author is indebted to Henry Work, M.D., Acting Chairman, Department of Psychiatry; and Edward Ritvo, M.D. and Ronald Griffith, M.D., Ward Psychiatrists, UCLA Neuropsychiatric Institute, for their strong support of the NPI School educational program.

by the staff psychiatrists. The actual engineered classroom set up in the NPI School was not an exact replica of the one described in this chapter.[3] It provided for a more child-centered structure, and the program reflected not only the teacher's but also the therapist's goals for the child. The design presented in this chapter has developed largely in the public school where such close collaboration between education and psychiatry is seldom possible.

During the summer of 1966, an engineered classroom was set up in the University Elementary School in the University of Hawaii as part of a summer session teacher training program. Ten disadvantaged and disturbed youngsters from the Palolo School district in Honolulu were enrolled in the class for a five-week period. These children had been chosen from among the most difficult learning problems in the district, and it was interesting to note the contrast between their behavior and that of their mainland counterparts in the earlier pilot program in Tulare. Instead of serious order and social problems, the Hawaiian children demonstrated response and exploratory problems. In the operation of the Hawaiian classroom, it was noted that several days passed before the children would actually eat the candy given them and that surprise bonus check marks had to be frequently given just to get the children to raise their hands, speak out, and move about from center to center in the room. In some respects such withdrawal and passivity is a more difficult problem to deal with than aggressivity. The developmental sequence supports such a view since the response level precedes the order level.

In the fall of 1965 the author was invited by the Santa Monica Unified School District to assist them in extending the engineered classroom design to the public school and during the school year two pilot upper-elementary classes with educationally handicapped boys were set up.[4] From this pilot study the Santa Monica Project developed, and it is the subject of the remaining two chapters in the text.

---

[3] Mrs. Juanita Ferjo, Elementary Teacher, NPI School, has been largely responsible for the development of the hospital engineered classroom at the elementary level.

[4] The author wishes to express appreciation to Mr. Walter Stoltze and Mr. Thomas Taglianetti, teachers of these classes.

XI THE SANTA MONICA
PROJECT*–CURRICULUM

Research investigations and public school settings are often like oil and water when mixed together. The innovative, controlled-variable orientation of the experimenter does not always blend well with the traditional methods and obligations for service of the public school educator. In the field of education of the emotionally disturbed child so little has been supported by definitive research evidence and so much is needed in order to assist the great number of disturbed children who fail to profit from traditional programs that implementation of research in the public school laboratory is essential. This chapter and the next report on a smoothly blended university and public school liaison between the University of California, Los Angeles, and the Santa Monica Unified School District directed toward assessing the effectiveness of the goals and methodology of the engineered classroom design and translating the guidelines which it offers into basic curriculum materials and sound educational practices for application to the public school.

Dr. Alfred Artuso, Superintendent of the Santa Monica Schools, and Dr. Frank D. Taylor, Director of Special Services for the district, had explored several approaches for programs for educationally handicapped children, but none had proven wholly successful. They expressed an interest in incorporating the framework of the engineered classroom in the Santa Monica Schools and offered to contribute the resources of the district and the creative talents of their staff for adapting and developing specific procedures and curriculum materials to be

* A portion of the work reported in Chapters XI and XII was performed pursuant to a grant from the United States Office of Education, Department of Health, Education and Welfare.

included in this framework. They also agreed to serve as co-investigators with the author of a demonstration project to develop and evaluate the use of the engineered classroom design in the public school. Mr. Thomas Taglianetti was appointed Coordinator of the Santa Monica Project which ensued.

In this chapter we will review the engineered classroom schedule and curriculum as it has emerged in the Santa Monica Project. While some of the materials and procedures to be described were included in earlier pilot investigations of the engineered design, what is reported in the following sections was largely developed in this project and represents contributions of the Santa Monica staff.

CLASSROOM SCHEDULE

The engineered classroom schedule operates on a 240-minute day schedule consistent with the State of California minimum requirements for special classes for educationally handicapped children. This four-hour school program has been developed so that it would meet state specifications and be applicable to other districts in California, although for some emotionally disturbed children this is far too long a time to expect them to function in the classroom. In the author's experience a three-hour day may be closer to ideal for such children, but no hard and fast rules can be established. Eventually it is hoped to establish enough flexibility to permit some children to attend school for only one or two hours daily and then extend the time as it appears the child can profit from it.

The engineered class schedule is divided into four main periods: order, reading and written language, arithmetic, and exploratory. In addition, two recesses and a physical education period round out the class day. School begins at 8:30 A.M. and students are dismissed at 12:30 P.M. Table XI-1 presents the daily schedule along with the provisions for check marks throughout the day.

ORDER PERIOD

As the students are given their initial check marks for coming in the room, taking their seats, and participating in the flag salute, the order assignment is handed out individually by the teacher and aide. The teacher avoids orienting the class as a group from the front of the room and whenever possible explains assignments on an individual basis at each student's desk.

TABLE XI-1

CLASSROOM SCHEDULE AND PROVISION FOR CHECK MARKS

Time	Activity	Possible Check Marks and Criteria
8:30 A.M.	Coming in room, taking seat, and flag salute	5 *for being ready to work* 3: Coming on time 2: Picking up card and going to seat
8:35 A.M.	Order	10 *for doing order worksheet* 2: Starting 3: Following through 5: Bonus for "being a student"
8:40 A.M.	Reading (skill reading, individual reading, work study, or story writing)	10 *check marks following each of three 15-minute work periods* (same criteria as above)
9:40 A.M.	Recess (outside room)	10 *check marks for recess behavior* 2: Leaving the room 5: Behavior during recess 3: Returning and being ready to work
9:50 A.M.	Arithmetic (skill arithmetic and individual arithmetic)	10 *check marks each 15 minutes* (same criteria as for reading)
10:50 A.M.	Recess (nutrition— inside room)	10 *check marks for recess behavior* 5: Behavior during recess 5: Being ready to return to work
11:00 A.M.	Physical Education (outside room)	10 *check marks for behavior during period* 2: Leaving the room 5: Behavior during the period 3: Returning and being ready to work
11:20 A.M.	Group listening to teacher read story or record	10 *check marks for behavior during period*
11:30 A.M.	Exploratory (science, art, and communication)	10 *check marks each 15 minutes* (same criteria as reading and arithmetic)
12:20 P.M.	Check out	Total number of check marks received for the day are graphed on the child's Work Report on his desk

Mastery Center.

Exploratory Center.

Order Center.

Initial check marks for the day.

The order period is designed to settle the students down and involve them in a short direction-following task, stressing hand-eye coordination and completion. Commercially available visual-motor training and readiness work sheets are used along with simple tracing, design copying, and visual-discrimination tasks prepared by the Santa Monica staff. Since the order period is only five minutes in length, the task is simple and short and guarantees success. While this activity is referred to as "order" it includes attention and reponse components in an effort to launch the class in learning at the basic levels of the developmental sequence.

In general, exercises involving merely coloring pictures with crayons have been used sparingly because often such an activity is viewed as "babyish" by upper-elementary age children. The task is presented to the students as a direction-following activity—one that has a specific starting point and a series of intermediate steps which lead to a conclusion scorable as complete or incomplete in line with order task characteristics. Some teachers working with younger children have used actual order-center materials (e.g., direction boxes, pegboard designs, bead stringing, puzzles, etc.) described in Chapter VII for the initial order period and have distributed these materials rather than work sheets. In this way manipulative aspects of the order assignment given the child were increased.

READING PERIOD

Before the teacher and aide circulate and give check marks for the order period, the teacher calls the class's attention to an assignment wheel mounted on the third bulletin board area in the room labeled "Work Assignments." This wheel is used for the purpose of dividing the class into three separate work groups, usually on the basis of rows, for three 15-minute work periods in reading. The wheel is presented in the following photograph, and the three reading work periods appear on it—individual reading, word study, and skill reading. The inner wheel, with the three rows printed on it, can be turned so that a given row can be consecutively assigned each of the three reading activities by one-third turns. The teacher calls attention to the row assignments: "Row one, get ready for individual reading. Row two, get ready for word study. Row three, get ready for skill reading." Following this announcement, both teacher and aide administer the order period check marks and individually lead each student into his first reading assignment.

Reading assignment wheel.

During the first two weeks of the engineered classroom, these three reading activities are introduced gradually along with the use of the assignment wheel. Various types of reading activities which are simple and intriguing have been developed to be used during this introductory period. An example of one of these activities is shown in Figure XI-1.**

This is a form of "scrabble" with words relating to each other both horizontally and vertically. The teacher completes the blank—"Use words from _____" indicating to the child the source of the words for the squares. Words the child is studying in connection with reading or spelling may be used or he may be directed to select some from the dictionary. Once the squares are filled the child calculates the number of points or "score" he has obtained for each word block by referring to the numerical equivalents for the letters at the top of the sheet. At the bottom the teacher may assign the child the additional task of alphabetizing all or some of the words in the squares. An attempt has been made in the construction of this activity and others used in the Santa Monica Project to provide for students at various levels of functioning. The teacher can change the specific directions for the assignment, making it easier, harder, longer, or shorter for individual children. This reading activity and others like it are simple enough to require only limited explanation and initially are used in place of the standard reading program of the engineered classroom until the child is well acquainted with the check-mark system and the entire class schedule. The teacher may actually modify the reading assignment wheel shown in the photograph and place the names of these reading activities over those shown. In this way each row would get each sheet during a particular hour. Teachers will recognize the endless possibilities for preparing simple work sheets and for including other types of reading activities during this introductory phase.

Once the class is functioning smoothly with the introductory materials the standard reading activities are presented one-by-one. Individual reading is usually the first introduced. This may be presented on the wheel along with two of the reading activities described earlier. Therefore, only during one 15-minute segment of the reading period would the child be doing something different.

During individual reading, each child is given a work reader—a

** The author wishes to express appreciation to Dr. Frank D. Taylor of the Santa Monica Unified School District for permission to present this and other examples of curriculum material to follow which he developed for the Santa Monica Project. Mrs. Betty Rys deserves special mention for her assistance in the rendering of these materials.

NAME _____ DATE _____

Word Block   No. 5

a^1 b^2 c^2 d^2 e^3 f^2 g^3 h^3 i^3 j^3 k^3
l^2 m^1 n^1 o^3 p^3 q^4 r^2 s^2 t^2 u^3
v^2 w^3 x^3 y^3 z^4

Use words from

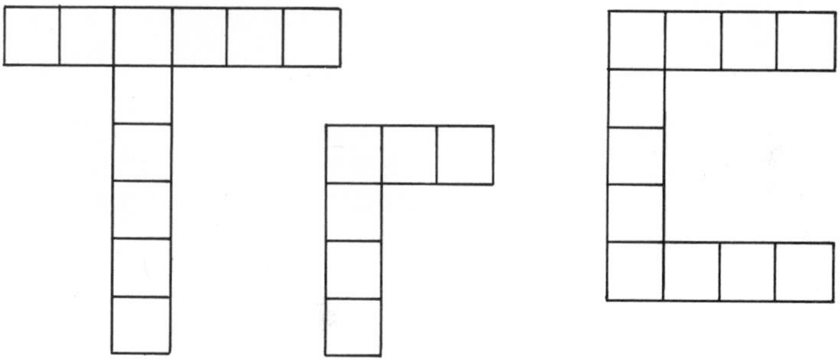

Score _____   Score _____   Score _____

DIRECTIONS

Put any_____of the above words into alphabetical order.

1 _____

2 _____

3 _____

4 _____

5 _____

FIGURE XI-1. Word block activity.

basal or remedial reading text at a vocabulary level close to his actual functioning on an achievement test. For those children who are complete nonreaders, readiness, alphabet, or other primer-level activities have to be selected. When a particular row is assigned to individual reading by means of the wheel, each child will get out his work reader and begin to study it in preparation for a three-minute oral reading

Individual reading.

session at the teacher aide's desk. The teacher remains in the student desk area circulating and assisting children assigned other reading activities.

One-by-one, children assigned to individual reading are called to the aide's desk. Once they are seated, they turn over a small three-minute hour-glass egg timer and begin to read aloud from their work reader. For each line of reading material they read correctly, the teacher will deposit one candy unit in a small paper cup. When words are miscalled, the teacher immediately corrects the child who is instructed to repeat the word aloud and go on reading. Any word the child cannot read is also provided for him. There is no sounding out of words or phonic instruction during this period. As the child is reading, the teacher keeps a record of the words he misses on the Reading Record card shown in Figure XI-2. Notation is also made of the number of lines read correctly during a three-minute period.

When a child finishes reading, the aide asks several comprehension questions to see if he has understood what he has read. Then, the child is given 3 x 5 inch cards with the words which he missed during the session printed in manuscript on them. If the child has missed more words than he can comfortably accept or study, the aide selects the most basic vocabulary words and gives these to him. An effort is made to keep each student working in a reader that is somewhat of a challenge for him. However, when he misses more than four to five words a page, the grade level of the book should be lowered.

This is the only time during the regular engineered classroom day when candy is used instead of check marks. The decision to retain this direct means of rewarding the child was based on the high degree of motivation shown by students for "practicing" their reading before coming to the aide's desk and the steady increase made in lines read correctly. When the child returns to his desk, he may eat the accumulated candy he has earned whenever he pleases. As was stated earlier, when candy is inappropriate to use because of health or other reasons, sunflower seeds, raisins, peanuts, and popcorn may be substituted.

The other two children in the row assigned to individual reading then take their turns reading at the teacher aide's desk. While waiting, the child is expected to practice reading at his desk; when he returns he may be encouraged to read ahead in anticipation of the next day's individual reading or given a reading activity sheet such as the one described previously in connection with the introductory phase of the

READING RECORD CARD

STUDENT NAME

TITLE OF BOOK	DATE	PAGES READ	LINES READ IN 3 MINUTES	WORDS MISSED

FIGURE XI-2

reading program. In selecting children to be called up for individual reading from a given row, the aide may let those who have the most difficult time waiting read first, get their candy, and return to their desks for another activity.

At the end of the first 15-minute segment of the reading period, the teacher announces from the front of the room, "Put your pencils down and your Work Record cards at the upper-left-hand corner of your desk." The assignment wheel is turned so that each row is now assigned to a different reading activity and the teacher calls attention to the new assignment. Then the direction, "Get ready for check marks," is given and both teacher and aide circulate, giving check marks and leading the children individually into the next activity.

Normally, the aide will give check marks to those children who have had individual reading and the teacher will give check marks to those with whom she has worked during the period. Throughout the day the teacher and aide try to give check marks to those children with whom they have worked during a particular period. This is especially important when problems have arisen with a given student during a work period. The person most familiar with what the student has actually done should be the one to evaluate his work and administer the check marks.

The question often arises regarding how the children perceive the teacher and aide. Will they try to pit teacher against aide or vice versa and complain, "She always gives me more check marks than you, so I want her to give me my check marks this time"? If this occurs there is no verbal defense put forth by either teacher or aide. Both are "teachers" in the room, both concerned about assigning the children tasks that they are ready for, need, and can be successful doing, and both are part of a working team devoted to giving each child exactly what he has earned for his accomplishments. If such a comment is made by the child, the teacher or aide reassures him that, "These are the check marks which you have *earned*." In general this problem arises very infrequently and is easily handled in the manner described. Of course, the importance of a close and positive working relationship between teacher and aide cannot be overemphasized. They must be mature and objective enough not to attempt to win certain children's approval and loyalty through check-mark generosity.

While the aide continues with another three children in individual reading, the teacher moves among the remaining two rows and supervises word study and skill reading.

Word study involves review of the word cards the child has been given during individual reading and is the second standard reading activity introduced. At this point, students are given individual reading and word study and only one of the introductory activities described earlier. During word study, the teacher circulates among the three assigned children and reviews their reading vocabulary cards with them. These cards are flashed before the child and he is asked to read the words on them. As each word is read correctly the teacher puts a plus on it, and after three consecutive correct recognitions, the card is filed away alphabetically in a small file box on the child's desk and no longer reviewed. Spelling words acquired during story writing, to be discussed later, are also reviewed at this time and the child asked to recall these in writing. Those words the child cannot read or recall are given him by the teacher and he is asked to repeat them aloud. No mark is made on the cards with these words on them, and the child is held to at least three later reviews of them in order to accumulate the required three consecutive pluses.

While the teacher works with one child in word study, the other two children in the row are expected to study their cards independently. Once the child finishes his review of word cards with the teacher, he may be expected to resume study of the words he has missed. As an alternative, he may be given a reading activity sheet or sent to one of the centers in the room, depending on the teacher's assessment of what would be most appropriate for him at the time.

When the second 15-minute segment of the reading period is over, the teacher calls the class's attention to the assignment wheel, turns it so that each row now is assigned to the third and final reading activity for the day, and then, both teacher and aide administer check marks for the previous segment and lead the children individually into the new activity.

Skill reading involves an independent vocabulary and comprehension reading assignment, and a wide variety of commercial materials including programed units are used. The child is given the assignment to do at his desk, and questions he has about it are answered by the teacher who circulates among the children doing both word study and skill reading. For children unable to work independently on such material, reading activity sheets similar to those used during the introductory phase may be utilized. In addition, these children may be sent to either the Order or Exploratory Center during this period since skill reading may represent a mastery activity which is too difficult for them.

The standard reading program used in the engineered class includes opportunities for oral reading, sight vocabulary building, and focus on independent reading skills. It offers considerable flexibility to the teacher and can be varied to fit the needs of the individual children. For example, skill reading can be assigned during two of the segments to those children who might profit more from this as compared with word study and individual reading. Speed reading and reference or study-skill assignments may also be given more able students during this time. Reading readiness activities can be used during the entire three segments with children unable to read at all. The reading period actually dictates only the general framework for assigning reading activities to students, and teachers must fill in the framework with assignments best suited to the functioning level of individual children.

The reading period is used at least three times weekly, usually on Monday, Wednesday, and Friday. Twice a week, on Tuesday and Thursday, story writing is focused on during this period. The use of the first major period of the day for reading and written language work has been found more successful than waiting until late morning or late afternoon when students may be tired and restless in school. Since these mastery areas are often difficult for children with learning problems, and the ones they have had most discomfort with in the past, taking advantage of the early part of the day when they are apt to be fresher and more alert is only logical.

Story writing is done by the entire class rather than by rows as was the case in reading. Usually the teacher takes 15 minutes to present a short motivation lesson in some area of interest to the class (e.g., knighthood, deep-sea life). Filmstrips, movies, and sharing of experiences by the children themselves may also be utilized. This is one period when the class is dealt with as a group and in a manner similar to a regular classroom. Check marks are given at the close of the 15-minute motivation segment and each child given a sheet of composition paper to write on. Depending on the level of the child, story writing may consist of the writing of a single sentence, a caption placed under a picture a child has drawn, or the dictation of a story to the teacher or aide. Other children may be able to write for two 15-minute work periods. Regardless of the level of the child an attempt is made to get some writing from each student. As he writes, the child is assured that any word he needs will be given to him by the teacher. This is done by writing the needed word on a 3 x 5 inch card in cursive writing, having the child study it, say it aloud, and then turn the card over and write the word on the back, saying it aloud as he writes it. The child then checks to see if he has written the word correctly and if so, places it in his story without copying it from the card. This technique is similar to that used at the second stage of the Fernald (1947) method. Kinesthetic tracing or stage one of the method involves presenting the child with words he needs written in large cursive form on 4 x 10 inch newsprint slips. For children functioning at the attention and response levels, the teacher may allow the child to copy the word directly from the word card or actually may write it in the story for him in order to encourage communication and a beginning attempt at written expression. This is an example of "reduction of the criteria of correctness" and "guaranteeing success." These are characteristics of tasks on the response level of the developmental sequence and further discussed in Chapter VI.

Children who cannot write for more than a few minutes may be given reading activity sheets or sent to one of the centers in the room. At the end of the period, the class gets ready for recess. A set routine is followed at this time. The children are dismissed by rows, put their Work Record cards back in the holder, line up by the door, and are taken to the playground by the teacher aide. Whenever possible the teacher remains in the classroom, primarily identified with learning tasks in that setting, while the aide supervises free play during recess and physical education. Since both teacher and aide may be required to supervise nine emotionally disturbed children, this plan cannot always be followed. However, arrangements do need to be made for both teacher and aide to have a short break during the program. In classes where the aide can handle this first recess period, the teacher takes her break then. During the second recess or nutrition time in the classroom, the aide may be given her break.

At this point in the discussion, some may wonder if placing the child in the more open playground situation after holding him to the planned routine of the engineered classroom will produce a "cork out of the bottle" effect. Will old maladaptive behavior patterns erupt with fury because of demands for conformity in the classroom? It can be simply stated that this has not been found to occur. Children whose previous records indicated serious problems on the playground made good improvement over the year. There actually was a decrease in "name calling" and number of fights among the children in the engineered classroom program and their classmates and children from regular classrooms. Lewin, Lippett, and White (1939) found "authoritarian" climates produced eruptions of misbehavior whenever the authoritarian adult left children unsupervised. That this did not occur in the engineered classroom is due to the inclusion of a degree of child-centered structure and "working partner" role of the teacher in the classroom itself. Structured, yes; rigidly authoritarian, no.

During the recess period, the teacher aide provides some children with game equipment for such activities as four-square, handball, basketball, and kickball. Others, who cannot function well in group activities, use playground equipment, such as swings, rings, and bars. In most cases the children were able to play either by themselves or with others for the brief recess period. More difficult problems were encountered during the longer physical education period later in the morning.

At the end of the recess, the children are again lined up, allowed to get a drink, and returned to the classroom. Bathroom needs are also taken care of at this time. Once inside the room the children pick up their Work Record cards and go to their desks. The teacher and aide immediately circulate and give check marks for behavior during the recess period. In cases where problems occurred on the playground and the teacher was not present, the aide always goes first to such children so that the number of check marks given the children truly reflects what they have earned.

ARITHMETIC PERIOD

As the check marks for recess are being administered, both teacher and aide individually introduce the first arithmetic assignment to the children. Usually the initial segment of the arithmetic period is taken up by skill arithmetic designed to strengthen the child's basic number skills in addition, subtraction, multiplication, and division. For the introduction of a particular concept such as carrying, borrowing, or long division several children may be grouped together with either the teacher or aide for a group lesson. Normally, however, all instruction during the period is individual and both teacher and aide circulate throughout the room giving help as needed.

It should be pointed out that one of the initial goals in the engineered classroom is to get the children to freely raise their hands whenever they have questions about assignments given them or when they need help. Such "hand-raising" behavior must often be encouraged and shaped by immediate recognition on the teacher or aide's part. It has been found that while many emotionally disturbed children will attempt to raise their hand to get the teacher's attention this may be quickly forgotten if any delay is encountered and old patterns of "talking out" or leaving their seats to get the teacher's help return. Therefore, it is essential that not more than five or ten seconds elapse between a given child's raising his hand and his obtaining teacher attention. If the teacher and aide are occupied with other students, a comment to the child such as, "I see your hand, Tommy. I'll be with you just as soon as I finish with Mary," is usually successful in getting the child to wait.

While circulating during any period of the day, the teacher and aide should position themselves when working with a particular child so that they can easily see all the other children in the room and immediately recognize another child's request for assistance. Sitting alongside the child for long periods and becoming engrossed in his work to the exclusion of awareness of what the other children are doing should be avoided. When a child calls across the room for help or gets up and comes to the teacher, his bid for attention has been generally ignored. Providing the reward of social attention for such inappropriate behavior will most certainly cause it to be relied on more often by the child. Most children soon "get the idea" that such a reward will only be theirs when they "follow the rules" although a comment to the effect, "You know how to ask for my help" and directing them back to their seat may have to be used initially.

Certainly the most important single factor in helping children to learn to raise their hand for help is immediate teacher recognition. For those children with severe response and order problems who are not easily involved in systematic hand-raising, awarding extra bonus check marks for "remembering to raise your hand" may provide an extra incentive. One extremely shy, withdrawn boy who never asked for help and who sat alone quietly and often unnoticed for long periods when he could not do a problem was given five extra check marks any time he raised his hand just to let the teacher know he was still there, regardless of whether he needed help or not. It was surprising to see how much more frequently he raised his hand when he really wanted the teacher's assistance as a result.

The Santa Monica staff has developed a number of flexible, multi-level arithmetic work sheets which can be quickly adapted to the individual needs of a student. Figure XI-3 illustrates one of these work sheets which is designed to assist the child in adding money and understanding the value of coins.

In Figure XI-4 we see how a teacher adapted it for a particular student, first assigning a value to the coins at the top and then by grouping the coins into sections A, B, C, and D. Not only can the number of coins included in a segment and their individual values be varied but the same sheet may also be used with a given child several times since so many variations are possible.

Figure XI-5 is another example of a multi-level arithmetic work sheet. The teacher fills in the blanks at the top of the page, directing the child to circle a specified number of digits below so that they add up to a certain sum. For example, the number of digits selected may be "2" and the sum "8." The child would survey all the numbers in the column below and combine any two numbers totaling "8" by enclosing them in a loop or circle. The task is to pair as many numbers totaling "8" as possible.

NAME _____   DATE _____

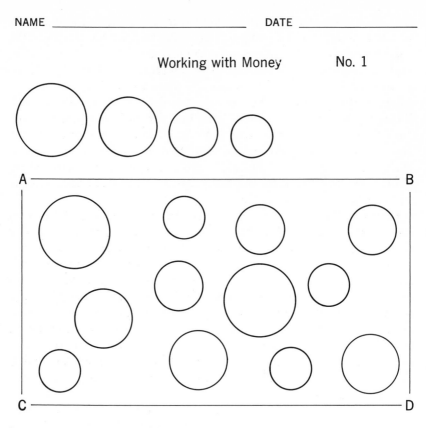

Working with Money   No. 1

1. How much do all the coins in A = ?
2. How much do all the coins in B = ?
3. How much do all the coins in C = ?
4. How much do all the coins in D = ?

Figure XI-3

Figure XI-6 is another individualized multi-level work sheet. It can be used in addition or multiplication. The teacher fills in the center segment of each circle with a number to be added or multiplied with each of the numbers which adjoin it. The answers for each addition or multiplication combination are placed in the outer ring.

In general, arithmetic is a more comfortable subject for emotionally disturbed children as compared with reading and written language, and the arithmetic period is run much as it would be in any regular classroom which carefully attended to students' remedial needs.

NAME ___Vincent___   DATE ___March 3___

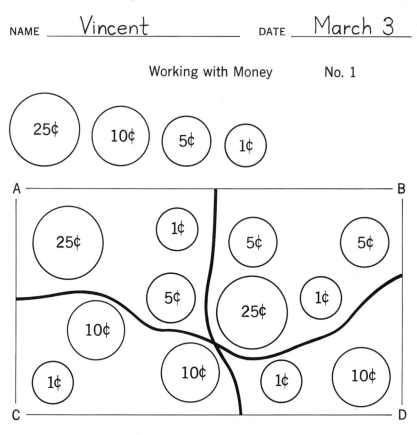

Working with Money   No. 1

1. How much do all the coins in A = ?
2. How much do all the coins in B = ?
3. How much do all the coins in C = ?
4. How much do all the coins in D = ?

FIGURE XI-4

Following the initial 15-minute work period in arithmetic, the teacher and aide circulate and check marks are given. During this time all work is corrected and the next 15-minute assignment given the student. With respect to correcting children's work, an attempt is made to have everything undertaken during a 15-minute work period completely corrected by the time the check marks are given. During the work period itself, both teacher and aide continually evaluate the student's work and correct it up to the point the student has reached in the assignment. In this way allowing the student to make errors in problem

NAME _____ DATE _____

| Arithmetic Fun | No. 2 |

DIRECTIONS

Circle ____ numbers together that add up to ____.

9	6	2	1	2	4	7	6	3	2	1	3	1	2
7	2	5	3	1	4	6	2	5	6	3	2	1	5
1	3	6	2	1	3	6	2	5	4	3	1	2	1
9	6	1	8	7	5	1	3	2	1	8	5	7	2
4	3	2	1	2	3	4	9	6	1	3	7	4	8
9	1	2	5	4	2	1	3	4	5	1	3	2	1
2	6	4	6	1	8	9	2	1	4	8	7	6	2
1	3	5	9	7	1	2	4	6	3	7	5	9	4
6	2	4	5	2	8	5	2	9	7	6	5	2	8
5	3	4	2	4	1	2	1	3	5	6	9	7	4
3	6	7	5	2	1	4	6	2	9	3	8	4	7
7	2	5	6	4	3	6	4	1	2	5	1	6	3
4	7	9	4	6	2	1	4	3	9	6	5	8	6
2	8	2	1	3	1	9	2	4	4	3	7	5	9
1	4	6	2	2	3	6	4	9	7	1	8	2	5
9	5	7	6	5	2	8	1	2	3	3	4	1	3

Figure XI-5

after problem when he does not understand a process is avoided. It also permits the teacher to reassign a child a more appropriate arithmetic assignment or other tasks in the room if it is apparent he cannot be successful with what he was originally given. Within a few weeks of the semester, however, the attention, response, order, exploratory, social, and mastery functioning levels of each student are apparent to the

NAME _____ DATE _____

Arithmetic + or ×

FIGURE XI-6

teacher so that the most appropriate intervention in school—*anticipation of the problem before it occurs and the selection of assignments accordingly*—is possible with most children.

The second and third 15-minute segments of the arithmetic period are devoted to individual arithmetic. These periods are designed to provide the child with assignments offering opportunities for application of basic number skills in problem solving. Standardized arithmetic texts and individual work sheets are used. Those children who can handle a single assignment for one-half hour may be allowed to continue on it after check marks are given at the midpoint. Those children who need a change in activity may be given simple order-type arithmetic assignments involving measurement, counting, and form discrimination during the third 15-minute segment. Of course, the Exploratory and Order Centers are always available for alternate assignments at any time.

As had been mentioned, check marks will be given following the second work segment of the arithmetic period regardless of whether or not the student continues on the same assignment through the third 15-minute segment. Questions often arise regarding the wisdom of arbitrarily interrupting a child while he is working on a task. "Won't this interfere with his train of thought?" "Shouldn't he be allowed to pursue a task as long as he wishes before stopping in order to encourage self-motivation in learning?" Despite these relevant considerations, it is the author's contention that the advantages of offering a five-minute "breathing spell" during which the child can relax, change position and activity, and receive recognition for his efforts during the previous 15-minute work period far outweigh the disadvantages. In fact, once children in an engineered classroom become accustomed to the 15-minute work period routines they are seldom distracted during this time and work efficiently, possibly motivated by the fact they are aware a "break" will occur shortly. It should be mentioned that for some children with extreme problems on the attention, response, and order levels, five-minute work periods may be more appropriate. Indeed, such an assignment schedule has been maintained when necessary in the engineered classroom, although it is generally not necessary over an extended period of time.

Following the third 15-minute arithmetic segment, the children receive check marks and are provided with a second recess or nutrition period. Snacks may be brought from home or obtained in the school cafeteria, and these are eaten in the room. Children are normally free to move about and talk informally together. However, they are not permitted to "play" with the exploratory or order materials in the two centers. Some teachers have provided a separate "free time" shelf with magazines, games, and activities not utilized at these two centers to be used by children during this second recess.

Check marks are given following the nutrition period, and the children are instructed to get ready for physical education. They are dismissed by rows and line up at the door. It has been found useful to have the children take their Work Record cards with them to the playground so that they may be given check marks in the actual setting where this period will take place. Once the children are on the playground, the Work Record cards are picked up by the aide, checks given for "leaving the room," and play initiated. Check marks also can be given for the entire period once the children are back in the room.

The children may engage in a single game such as four-square, handball, volleyball, or kickball or divide into smaller groups for more individualized recreational activities. Since some emotionally disturbed children possess limited sports skills, are poor "team" members, and are easily upset by competition, particularly the threat of losing, the teacher aide attempts to get each child involved in the game or activity which he enjoys and can successfully handle. Wargo (1960) has described the problems of disturbed children on the playground. He has also discussed the setting up of suitable recreational programs for them.

Once the physical education period is over, the children line up and are given their Work Record cards by the aide. Check marks for "being a student" during the period are administered and the group returns to the classroom after opportunities for going to the drinking fountain and bathroom are provided. Once in the room and at their desks, the children receive additional check marks for "returning and being ready to work."

EXPLORATORY PERIOD

After a 20-minute play period and almost three hours of being in school, the children may not always quickly settle down and return to work at this point. In order to gradually introduce them back into learning, a short 10- to 15-minute listening period is held before the final major activity of the day—the exploratory period. The value of listening activities in general, and reading aloud to emotionally disturbed children in particular, has been discussed in Chapter VIII. The teacher may select a children's classic with high interest value to the

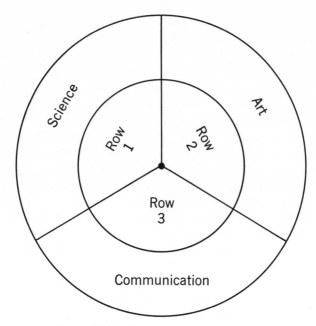

FIGURE XI-7.   Exploratory assignment wheel.

students and read a portion of a chapter each day. As the children develop a continuing interest in the events, characters, and suspense of the story, they may come to greatly anticipate this listening period.

Check marks are given for the listening period as they are for all of the periods of the day. Following this, the teacher calls the class's attention to the exploratory wheel located on the work assignment board along with the reading assignment wheel. The exploratory wheel is illustrated in Figure XI-7.

The exploratory period is the last period of the day and is designed to engage students in highly stimulating and interesting activities below the mastery level and provide a full range of rewards including social attention, task completion, multisensory experience, and social approval as well as routine check marks. In this way the probability that the day will close on a positive and successful note for each student is increased.

The exploratory hour, like the reading, written language, and arithmetic periods earlier in the day, is divided into three 15-minute segments. Two of these segments of time are devoted to science and art and are associated with the exploratory level. The third segment involves communication activities and is aimed at assisting children on the social level of the developmental sequence. As was done with reading, students are assigned by rows to one of the three activities each 15 minutes. The assignment wheel shown in Figure XI-7 is used for this purpose, and the inner wheel is rotated to indicate to the children in each row which activity they will undertake.

After the teacher calls attention to row assignments, the children are dismissed and move to one of the areas in the Exploratory Center. Work Record cards are left at the desks since the children will return after each 15-minute segment to receive check marks and be reassigned.

Once the students have found their places in the Exploratory Center, the teacher goes to the science area and prepares to introduce an experiment to the three children assigned there. The aide supervises both the art and communication areas.

The Santa Monica staff has developed some 150 basic science tasks or experiments organized into units on microscopes, magnetism, electricity, air, light, water, heat, machines, and chemistry. Each task is printed on an 8½ x 11 inch card and numbered according to its position in the unit. In developing these materials the staff was guided by the characteristics suggested for tasks at the exploratory level—multisensory experience, reality emphasis, and predictable outcomes. Three examples of science tasks are illustrated in Figures XI-8, XI-9, and XI-10.

The science experiments presented are concrete so that each child will understand them and be able to replicate them following the teacher's demonstration. They also utilize basic science equipment and supplies available in most school science departments. During the science segment of the exploratory period, the teacher presents a new task card to the three students assigned to the science area, reads the simple instructions underneath the illustration on the card, and proceeds to demonstrate the experiment for them. The illustration on the card summarizes the steps involved in the experiment in pictorial form so that students can do it on their own by referring to the picture alone. In this way, students with limited reading ability can actively participate. During the teacher demonstration, the children are asked questions about the experiment and then each given an opportunity to replicate it. The emphasis during this time is on multisensory experience rather than the teaching of science concepts, although an attempt is made to achieve balance between the two as discussed in Chapter VIII. Following the exploratory period the science task card is placed in a box in the science area for future use during classroom interventions undertaken with students on subsequent days.

TASK NO. 1 \ MAGNETS

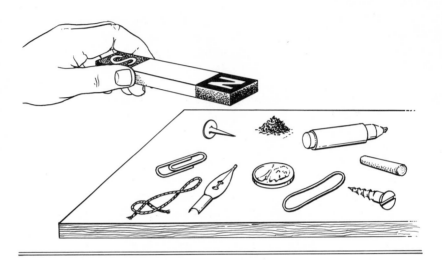

DIRECTIONS

1. Hold a magnet near each item placed on display table.
2. List the items that a magnet attracts.
3. List the items that it won't attract.

FIGURE XI-8

The art and communication areas of the Exploratory Center are supervised by the teacher aide. Art tasks are also organized on cards similar to those used in science and have been prepared by the Santa Monica staff for both teacher and student reference. Three examples of the 150 art tasks developed in the project are shown in Figures XI-11, XI-12, and XI-13. Students are given necessary materials which have been laid out in advance at the art area and then have the task explained to them by the aide. In selecting art tasks for use during this exploratory period, an attempt was made to choose activities the child could complete in 15 minutes. When this is not possible for one or more children, a particular task is carried over several days if neces-

TASK NO. 5   MACHINES

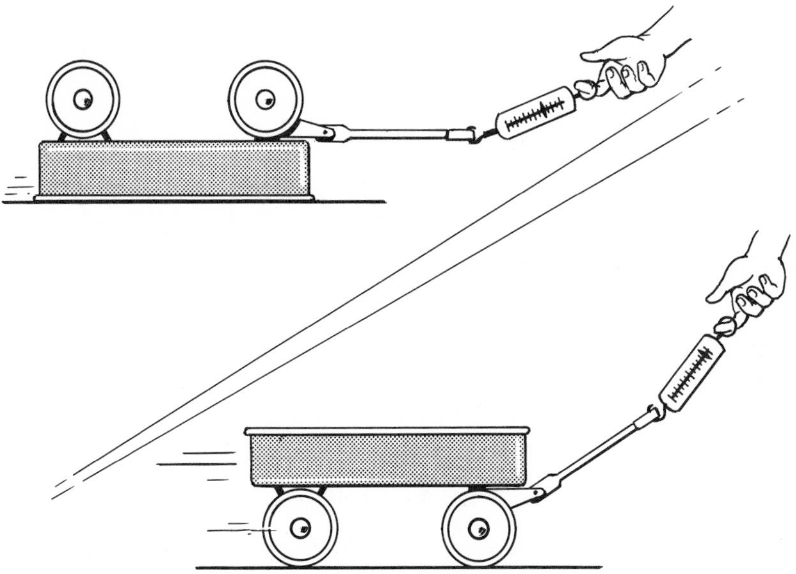

DIRECTIONS

1. Hook scale to the cart. Turn cart upside down on the floor.
2. Pay attention to the reading on the scale.
3. Place cart on wheels, noticing the scale reading.
4. Which way takes more work? Why?

FIGURE XI-9

sary. Art task cards are also filed away at the art area for future reference during interventions.

The Santa Monica staff has developed some 50 communication tasks for use during the communication segment of the exploratory period. These activities were chosen to reflect the characteristics of tasks at the social level of the developmental sequence—requiring that the child communicate with the teacher or one or more peers, that he maintain appropriate social behavior, and that he tolerate a period of delay and

TASK NO. 9 \ AIR

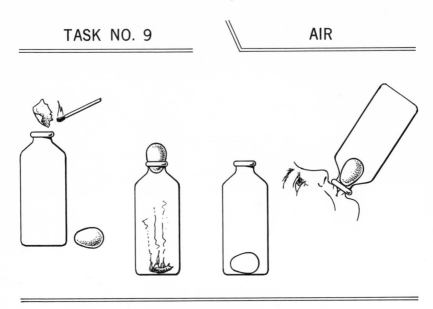

DIRECTIONS

1. Drop a burning piece of paper into a milk bottle.
2. Place a shelled hard-boiled egg on top.
   What happens? Why?
(Turn the bottle upside down and blow into the
   bottle and the egg will come out.)

FIGURE XI-10

"wait his turn." These tasks also involve the children in games or
activities where the outcome is more based on luck than skill. Three of
the communication tasks developed in the project for teacher and student reference are illustrated in Figures XI-14, XI-15, and XI-16, and
additional suggestions for communication tasks were presented in
Chapter VIII.

Because of the "game" aspect of these tasks, they may be repeated
several times during the school year. The science and art tasks also may
be repeated, although it is probably not wise to repeat them as frequently as the communication tasks.

Normally before the close of a 15-minute exploratory period segment, a one-minute warning is given so that the children may clean up
and put their work away. When the 15 minutes are up, the teacher calls

TASK NO. 123 | CRACKLE PAPER

Material: wrapping paper,
tempera paint (dark color),
newspaper, bowl, mixing stick.

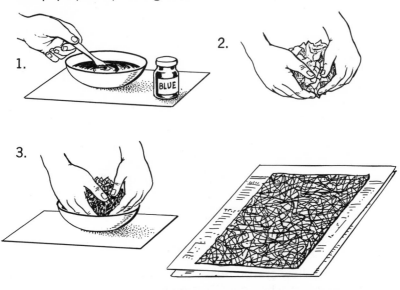

DIRECTIONS

1. Mix one teaspoonful of tempera color (a dark color) in one-half cup of water.
2. Crumple a piece of wrapping paper (14×20 inches) into a ball.
3. Dip it into the tempera mixture, squeeze. Open out and flatten on newspapers to dry.

FIGURE XI-11

all students back to their desks and both teacher and aide give out check marks. This procedure of having students return to their desks for check marks is useful in bringing closure to the activity at each area and giving the students a chance to change position and "stretch" before going on to another activity.

TASK NO. 2 \ SCRIBBLE DESIGN

Material: crayons, glue,
9×12 inch white construction paper,
dark construction paper, scissors.

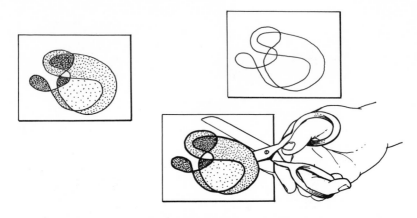

DIRECTIONS

1. Using a yellow crayon, make a scribble design on a 9×12 inch sheet of white construction paper.
2. Color each section with a different color.
3. Outline each section with a black crayon.
4. Cut out design, mount on dark background.

FIGURE XI-12

After check marks are administered, the teacher reassigns the class in groups of three to a new area by a one-third turn of the exploratory assignment wheel. After the children have moved to their new areas, the three exploratory activities are presented again by teacher and aide. The teacher repeats the science lesson and the aide directs the children at the art and communication areas. This rotation occurs one additional time so that all children have an opportunity to participate at each of the three Exploratory Center areas.

When the child returns to his desk following the third 15-minute segment, the classroom day is almost complete. All that remains to be

TASK NO. 58 \\ PAPER CONSTRUCTION

Material: yarn,
paper bag or
plate, scissors,
crayons, string,
straws.

DIRECTIONS

1. Draw a face on a paper bag or paper plate.
2. Cut eye holes and color the face.
3. Use yarn, straws, or string for hair.
4. Tie string from one hole to the other on the paper plate.
Use your own ideas.

FIGURE XI-13

done is the totaling of all check marks received for the day and the entering of these on the Work Report, the 8½ x 11 inch histogram graph affixed to the upper-right-hand corner of the child's desk which was illustrated in Figure X-3 and is shown in the photograph. As the teacher and aide administer the final check marks, they quickly add up the day's total and draw a line at the appropriate point on the graph. The child fills in the column below the line and compares his functioning that day with previous days.

The teacher then dismisses the class by rows, and as the children leave the room, they return their Work Record cards to the Work

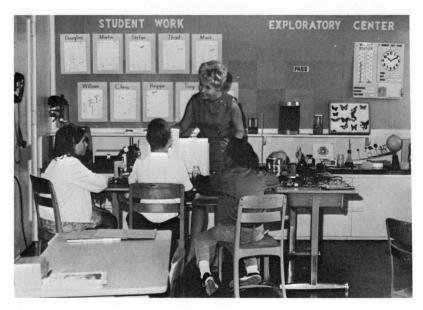

Exploratory period—science.

Exploratory period—art.

Exploratory period—communication.

Filling in the Work Report at the close of the day.

TASK NO. 5	COMMUNICATION

Puzzle Message

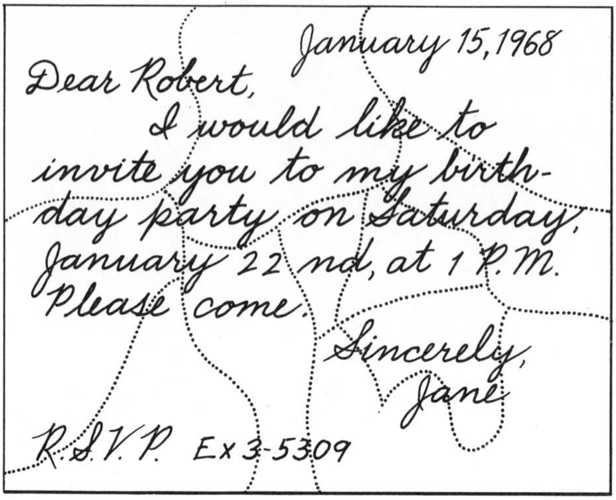

Dear Robert,   January 15, 1968
        I would like to
invite you to my birth-
day party on Saturday,
January 22nd, at 1 P.M.
Please come.
                    Sincerely,
                    Jane

R.S.V.P. Ex 3-5309

Teacher's sample

Puzzle message should not be cut into more than 12 pieces.

DIRECTIONS

Students should write message to each other and cut them up before passing them on to be decoded. Fit the pieces of the puzzle together to discover the puzzle message.

FIGURE XI-14

Record holder. In general, no homework assignments are given children in the engineered classroom. The small class size, individualization of instruction, and work orientation of the program allows for much more work accomplishment than would take place with these children in a regular classroom. Hence, there is seldom a need for outside assignments. However, as students approach the point of return to a regular classroom, homework may be introduced as a transition aid. Homework is so often a source of conflict and anxiety for emotionally disturbed children with learning problems and their parents that its removal, at least initially, in a special class program is seen as useful.

TASK NO. 11 \\ COMMUNICATION

Game of Dots

The object of this game is to form boxes. The first player draws a straight line (vertical or horizontal) connecting any two dots. No diagonal lines.

1. When a player completes a box he puts his initial in the box.
2. Player gets another turn when he completes a box.
3. Player with the most boxes wins.

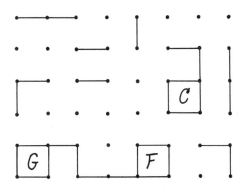

Two or more can play

FIGURE XI-15

This chapter and the last have introduced the engineered classroom design, including operations, schedule, and curriculum. The design represents an attempt to translate the goals and methodology of the developmental strategy into actual classroom practice. Despite an emphasis on structure and routine, it provides opportunities for teacher flexibility and creativity and is essentially a framework within which "good teaching" may take place on a highly individualized basis rather than a rigid and arbitrary system. As has been stated earlier, in each of the engineered classrooms in the Santa Monica Project, the personality, previous experience, and specialized teaching skills of the teachers created a unique classroom environment which made the classes different, one

TASK NO. 24	COMMUNICATION

Example: one player is **x**
           one player is **o**   Loser

x o o x x o x x x o o x o o x x x o o x

— — — — — — — — — — — — — — — — — — — —
— — — — — — — — — — — — — — — — — — — —
— — — — — — — — — — — — — — — — — — — —
— — — — — — — — — — — — — — — — — — — —
— — — — — — — — — — — — — — — — — — — —
— — — — — — — — — — — — — — — — — — — —
— — — — — — — — — — — — — — — — — — — —
— — — — — — — — — — — — — — — — — — — —
— — — — — — — — — — — — — — — — — — — —
— — — — — — — — — — — — — — — — — — — —
— — — — — — — — — — — — — — — — — — — —
— — — — — — — — — — — — — — — — — — — —
— — — — — — — — — — — — — — — — — — — —

DIRECTIONS

1. Each player takes a turn filling in one, two, or three symbols.
2. The player who ends the line of 20 blank spaces is the loser.

Figure XI-16

from the other, although all were operating within the general engineered class framework.

The next chapter reports on a research study undertaken to demonstrate and assess the engineered classroom design.

XII THE SANTA MONICA
PROJECT—EVALUATION

The purpose of the Santa Monica Project was actually twofold: first, to develop and implement the engineered classroom design in the public school as discussed in the last two chapters, and second, to evaluate its effectiveness with emotionally disturbed children as compared with a more traditional design. This chapter reports on the evaluation portion of the project (Hewett, Taylor, and Artuso, 1967).[1]

In the evaluation study, the engineered classroom design constituted the experimental condition, while the control condition or traditional classroom design consisted of any approach the teacher chose to follow which did not include the use of check marks, token, or any other tangible rewards. The independent variable, then, was rigid adherence to the engineered classroom design including the use of check marks. An attempt was made to equate all other variables in the project classrooms. The criteria utilized for assessing the effectiveness of the two classroom conditions or the dependent variables in the evaluation will be presented in a later section.

We turn now to a discussion of the setting in which the evaluation took place, selection and training of teachers, selection and grouping of students, procedures followed, results obtained, and discussion of the evaluation.

SETTING

The Santa Monica Unified School District is located west of Los Angeles in the community of Santa Monica, California, and includes the coastal area of Malibu, some 25 miles to the north. The district serves 26,000 children, adolescents, and young adults from preschool

[1]HEWETT, F., F. TAYLOR, AND A. ARTUSO, "The Santa Monica Project: Demonstration and Evaluation of an Engineered Classroom Design for Emotionally Disturbed Children in the Public School: Phase I: Elementary Level," Final Report. Project No. 62893, Demonstration Grant No. OEG—4–7–062893–0377, Office of Education, Bureau of Research, U.S. Department of Health, Education, and Welfare, 1967.

through junior college. The homes these individuals come from represent a broad range of socioeconomic levels and groups at the two extremes are well represented. In actuality, the socioeconomic distribution of the community is similar to that found in the greater Los Angeles County area and, hence, the Santa Monica Unified School District offers an ideal setting within which to conduct research.

Four elementary schools and one junior high school were selected in the district and one or two project classrooms set up in each school.* The junior high school setting was used for a pilot class and not included in the evaluation portion of the project. The project classrooms were located within the regular building areas of the schools on the basis of availability rather than consideration of special needs of educationally handicapped children. The majority of children enrolled in the project were brought to the schools by means of district buses.

TEACHER AND AIDE SELECTION AND TRAINING

Six female elementary school teachers were selected from among new teaching applicants in the Santa Monica District for the project. Two additional teachers were selected to conduct demonstration and pilot classes at the elementary and junior high level which were not evaluated but were used for visitation and continual innovation. None of the project teachers had ever taught in the Santa Monica Schools before. One had never taught and the teaching experience of the others ranged from three to eight years. Only one teacher had previously worked with children with learning problems in public schools. Selection of the project teachers was made by the Santa Monica Unified School District Personnel Office on the basis of strong qualifications and an expression of willingness to participate in a project with educationally handicapped children.**

A two-week training program was conducted in order to acquaint the teachers with the developmental strategy and the engineered classroom design. All project teachers participated in a series of daily four-hour

---

* Acknowledgment is due the following principals for their support and cooperation during the project: Mr. Ray Acevedo, Madison Elementary School; Mr. Hugh Bruce, McKinley Elementary School; Dr. Donald Cleland, Franklin Elementary School; Dr. Vincent Correll, Grant Elementary School; and Mr. Joe Day, Lincoln Junior High School.

** The author wishes to express appreciation to the project teachers: Mrs. Marcella Baughman, Miss Karen Clark, Mrs. Sandra Glina, Mr. Bill Hunt, Miss Leota Johnson, Miss Barbara Laier, Miss Rosemarie Stack, and Mrs. Roseanne Stefanopolous.

lectures and demonstrations. The training program also included having each teacher role play the part of student, teacher, and aide in a engineered classroom and then spend one day as actual teacher and later as actual aide in a room with educationally handicapped students.

At the close of the training program, each teacher's name was placed on a slip of paper, the slips shuffled, and then one at a time drawn randomly in order to determine assignment to either an experimental or control classroom. Although only teachers in the experimental classrooms were required to adhere to the engineered design, training all of the teachers in this special approach was seen as necessary in an attempt to control the amount of information, supervision, and training provided by the district prior to the beginning of teaching and to some extent, degree of teacher involvement and motivation. In addition, the random assignment of similarly trained teachers to experimental and control conditions represented a further attempt to at least partially control variability in length of previous teaching experience, individual personality factors, and teaching competence. The "teacher variable" is particularly complex to deal with in educational research. No two teachers relate to children, teach subject matter, or function in the classroom in exactly the same manner. The best-laid plans of experimenters setting up experimental teaching conditions often fail because what actually takes place in a classroom has more to do with the teacher and differences in teaching style than any other variable involved. Nevertheless, some control of the "teacher variable" can be obtained through exposing all teachers to the same prior training and then randomly assigning them to experimental or control conditions as was done in this study.

As was previously stated, experimental teachers were to adhere rigidly to the engineered design including the giving of check marks every 15 minutes, while control teachers could use any aspect of the developmental strategy or engineered classroom design they chose *except* check marks or other token or tangible rewards. Additional discussion of the two classroom conditions will follow in a later section. Throughout the study, all teachers received identical amounts of supervision from the project staff and had access to the same curriculum materials and classroom supplies.

Eight teacher aides (without prior teaching experience) were selected for the project from housewives and graduate students. They were given the same preliminary training as the teachers and then randomly paired with project teachers so that the nine students in both experimental and control classrooms were supervised by a teacher and an aide.

SELECTION AND GROUPING OF STUDENTS

Fifty-four educationally handicapped children attending school in the Santa Monica District between the ages of eight and twelve were located by school psychologists attached to the district's Department of Special Services. These children had been referred by elementary school principals throughout the district because of difficulties in adjusting to school and/or profiting from instruction. They had all been given an individual intelligence test (Wechsler Intelligence Scale for Children) and were functioning within the Full Scale IQ range of 85-113. The majority of these children were emotionally disturbed with serious problems on the first five levels of the developmental sequence and, in addition, were academically retarded.

Since the California State Department of Education does not classify children with serious attention, response, order, exploratory, social, or mastery problems in school as "emotionally disturbed" but rather uses the label "educationally handicapped" (EH) the children selected for this project met the following requirements for inclusion in a state subsidized EH classroom:

> Educationally handicapped minors are minors, other than physically handicapped minors . . . or mentally retarded minors . . . who, by reason of marked learning or behavioral problems or a combination thereof, cannot receive the reasonable benefit of ordinary education facilities.[1]

In addition to the individual intelligence tests all children were given physical examinations and were found to be free from primary physically handicapping conditions. Once the 54 project children had been selected and designated "educationally handicapped" through psychological and medical appraisal the following additional tests were given each child before the start of the project: the Reading Vocabulary, Reading Comprehension, and Arithmetic Fundamentals sections of the California Achievement Test (CAT, Elementary level), and the Reading and Spelling sections of the Wide Range Achievement Test (WRAT). The California Achievement Test was utilized to provide a measure of independent, silent reading ability and arithmetic computational skills. The Wide Range Achievement Test assessed word recognition and spelling. These tests were administered outside the classroom

---

[1] California Education Code, Chapter 7.1, Section 6750.

on a group basis by the same psychologists at the beginning, middle, and end of the project.[2]

The children were grouped into six classrooms of nine students each on the basis of IQ, age, and reading and arithmetic levels in that order of priority. Sex was a variable which was not possible to control because of the small number of girls referred to the project. Factors such as the psychologist's diagnostic impression, ethnic background, and parental socioeconomic level were also not possible to consider because of the difficulty in attempting to equate six groups with respect to IQ, age, and achievement level. Some attempt was made to place children in classes which would be housed in or near their regular elementary schools, but no child was assigned a group because it was felt he could profit more from the experimental or control condition. The class groupings were completed before any assignment of teachers or classroom condition was made. The six groups with initial individual data on project students regarding IQ, age, reading and arithmetic level, and sex are presented in Table XII-1. The mean IQ for all six groups was 94 (range 85-113), mean age 10 years, 3 months (range 8.0-11.11), mean reading achievement level was 2.8 grade equivalent (range 0-6.2), and mean arithmetic achievement level 3.3 (range 0-5.2). The original N of 54 was reduced to 45 due to incomplete data obtained on nine children during the course of the study. Therefore only the initial data on those students for whom complete records were available are reported in Table XII-1.

PROCEDURES

It was stated earlier that the central concern of this evaluation was whether adherence to the engineered classroom design and the systematic giving of check marks resulted in a more effective educational program for educationally handicapped children than a program of any type which did not offer token or tangible rewards. We come now to the design of the study itself.

With regard to the effect of a token or tangible reward system on learning and behavior several questions immediately arise:

1. What is the effect of rigid adherence to the engineered classroom design and use of a token and tangible reward system on educationally handicapped children who previously have been in a regular class?

[2] Dr. Leo Martucci and Dr. Arthur Rosenthal of the Santa Monica Unified School District were the psychologists in charge of student assessment and selection in the project.

TABLE XII-1

INDIVIDUAL DATA ON PROJECT STUDENTS

S	IQ	Age	CAT Total Reading Grade Equiv.	CAT Arith. Fund. Grade Equiv.	Sex
			Classroom 1 (N = 7)		
1	97	11–4	5.9	4.5	M
2	88	9–11	2.0	3.0	M
3	88	11–2	2.9	3.8	M
4	99	9–9	2.4	3.7	M
5	99	10–6	2.0	4.1	M
6	88	10–0	2.8	3.2	M
7	91	9–11	3.3	2.9	F
Mean = 93		10–4	3.0	3.6	
			Classroom 3 (N = 7)		
1	90	10–9	2.7	4.6	M
2	87	11–4	2.4	0	M
3	101	8–0	2.2	3.0	M
4	103	10–9	2.0	3.0	M
5	85	11–9	2.0	3.5	M
6	86	11–0	3.7	4.4	M
7	91	11–0	2.7	2.8	M
Mean = 92		10–8	2.5	3.0	
			Classroom 5 (N = 7)		
1	107	8–0	0	2.9	M
2	95	9–11	2.5	3.2	M
3	96	9–10	2.6	3.3	M
4	85	9–11	0	2.9	F
5	91	9–1	4.1	2.8	M
6	99	10–10	6.0	3.7	M
7	111	10–10	6.2	4.8	M
Mean = 98		9–9	3.0	3.4	

S	IQ	Age	CAT Total Reading Grade Equiv.	CAT Arith. Fund. Grade Equiv.	Sex
			Classroom 2 (N = 7)		
1	94	11–0	3.7	4.1	M
2	88	11–9	2.0	3.3	M
3	96	8–0	2.0	3.0	M
4	113	9–1	2.1	3.2	M
5	93	10–6	3.5	3.1	M
6	87	11–11	3.1	4.9	M
7	93	11–2	4.4	3.3	F
Mean = 95		10–6	2.9	3.5	
			Classroom 4 (N = 8)		
1	106	8–2	3.7	2.2	M
2	110	8–1	2.1	3.1	M
3	96	11–3	2.0	2.6	M
4	91	11–8	2.8	4.2	M
5	96	9–6	4.5	2.7	M
6	86	11–5	3.2	3.8	M
7	93	9–11	2.3	3.0	M
8	90	10–10	4.6	4.5	M
Mean = 96		10–1	3.2	3.3	
			Classroom 6 (N = 9)		
1	96	11–9	2.4	3.5	M
2	88	9–10	2.0	2.2	M
3	100	9–2	2.0	0	M
4	86	11–11	2.0	3.2	F
5	86	11–11	2.0	3.2	M
6	92	9–4	2.6	3.3	M
7	104	9–11	2.0	5.2	M
8	88	9–0	2.0	3.1	M
9	94	10–1	3.4	3.1	M
Mean = 93		10–4	2.3	3.0	

TABLE XII-2

ASSIGNMENT OF PROJECT CLASSES TO EXPERIMENTAL
AND CONTROL CONDITIONS

Class	Fall Semester	Spring Semester
1 (E)	Experimental	Experimental
2 (C)	Control	Control
3 and 4 (CE)	Control	Experimental
5 and 6 (EC)	Experimental	Control

2. What is the effect of rigid adherence to the engineered classroom design and use of a token and tangible reward system on educationally handicapped children who previously have been in a small individualized class which did not use such a reward system?
3. What will be the effect of abruptly withdrawing the complete engineered classroom design including the reward system from a class of educationally handicapped children which has become accustomed to it?

The design of the evaluation portion of the Santa Monica Project attempted to shed light on answers to these questions. The assignment of the classes discussed in Table XII-1 to either experimental or control conditions is shown in Table XII-2. As can be seen two of the six classes (Class E and Class C) maintained year-long programs according to either the experimental or control condition. Two classes (Classes CE) began using the control condition and rotated to the experimental condition at mid-year. For the two remaining classes (Classes EC) the reverse was true. Classes E and C were concerned with question one. Children in these rooms had been enrolled in regular public school classes prior to the fall semester when the project began. Classes E and C provided a comparison of the experimental and control conditions over a one-year period. Classes CE were focused on question two. Following a one-semester period in a small class with nine students and two teachers the experimental condition was introduced. Thus an opportunity was afforded to evaluate separately the effect of being in a small, special class as compared to being in the class with the addition of the experimental condition. Classes EC were set up to provide information on question three. Once a class has been exposed to the experimental condition, what happens when the reward system is abruptly removed?

Following the two-week teacher-training program, the selection and grouping of students, the random placement of each teacher and aide, and assignment of experimental or control condition to the classes themselves as shown in Table XII-2, the Santa Monica Project began on the first day of the fall semester. All classrooms were set up with the help of the author, the other Co-Investigators and the Project Coordinator. Classes which would utilize the engineered design were arranged specifically as described in Chapters X and XI. Classes which were to operate as controls could use any approach including the engineered classroom schedule, floorplan, Order and Exploratory Centers, and study booths but no check marks or other token or tangible rewards.

The major dependent variable utilized in Santa Monica classes to assess the effectiveness of the experimental and control conditions was *task attention*. Task attention was defined as the time spent by a student maintaining eye contact with the task or assignment given him by the teacher. In situations where eye contact was irrelevant to the task (e.g., listening to a record) or where the student's eyes could not be seen, appropriate head and body orientation toward the task was credited as "task attention."

Two observers sat in front of each of the six classrooms for two-and-one-half hours every morning during the entire year of the project. These observers were undergraduate college students recruited and trained for this assignment. Each observer held a stopwatch and was assigned either four or five children to regularly observe. The children were observed for five-minute segments throughout the two-and-one-half-hour observation periods in random order so that at least five separate samples of task attention were obtained on each student each day. The observation period in the experimental classrooms coincided with the order, reading or written language, and arithmetic periods. Teachers in the control classrooms also presented these subjects (with the possible exception of the order period which was not compulsory under the control condition) at the same times so the type of activities the students were given during the observation period was controlled.

Observers operated the stopwatches during each five-minute student task attention sample and immediately recorded the number of seconds the student's eyes (or in some cases head and body) had been appropriately oriented toward the assigned task. The criteria used for deciding when a student was "attending" appear in Appendix III.

Project observers were trained by two graduate assistants who had established a 90 percent or better agreement between themselves for task attention measurements. Each observer was then paired with one of the graduate assistants until his reliability was established at a 90 percent or better level. Every two weeks the two graduate assistants rotated through the classrooms rechecking the reliability among the observers and themselves, and at no point in the project was agreement found to be below the 85 percent level.

Daily individual task attention percentages were obtained on each child by using his total observed task attention time as the numerator in a proportion with the total observed time as a denominator. These daily percentages were totaled for all the children in a class and a weekly task attention percentage mean obtained for each project class throughout the year. Whenever a teacher was absent, task attention measures taken in her room were excluded from the data.

Once a week all six classrooms were visited by the author, the other Co-Investigators, and the Project Coordinator. An attempt was made to equate the actual time spent during such visitations in each room. In general, outside visitors were not permitted in any project classroom; a demonstration room, not included in the evaluation portion of the project, had been set up specifically for this purpose. Weekly meetings were held at which time the project teachers were either seen in two separate groups representing the experimental or control conditions or during individual conferences. At these meetings curriculum materials were made available to all teachers and specific problems of concern to the teachers discussed. Most problems regarding individual students were taken up by the Project Coordinator who was available to both experimental and control teachers alike for consultation. With experimental teachers he continually referred to the engineered classroom design and its resources for the handling of the problems. With control teachers he made similar suggestions (without reference to the giving of tangible or token rewards) but was usually less specific and offered several alternatives. Separate meetings of the project staff and the parents of the children enrolled in each class were held near the start of the project. Although each parent had given written permission for his child to be enrolled in the special program he had not been introduced to the specific nature of the project. This was done at the meeting and various questions parents raised were considered. The childrens' parents were not regularly involved in any other phase of the project.

All students were retested with the achievement tests used in the initial screening at mid-year and at the close of the project. At mid-year, Classes CE introduced the engineered design to students on the first Monday morning of the spring semester. The teachers in these rooms followed the procedures initially used by the teachers in Classes

EC in presenting the check-mark system and other aspects of the design to students as explained in Chapter X. At the same time, Classes EC abruptly withdrew the check-mark system and became control classes as shown in Table XII-2. On the first Monday morning of the spring semester the teacher simply announced, "We are not going to use check marks anymore." The room had been altered in its appearance and more traditional bulletin boards introduced. These teachers, like the control teachers initially, were free to select any other approach or to retain aspects of the engineered design as they chose except that they were required to discontinue the use of check marks or any other token or tangible reward system. Class E continued as a year-long experimental class and Class C continued as a year-long control class.

RESULTS

The results of the project evaluation will be discussed with reference to the three main questions presented earlier. In the statistical treatment of all data, a level of confidence of .05 was established. Therefore, no differences between groups are considered significant if the .05 level or better was not obtained.

What is the effect of rigid adherence to the engineered classroom and use of a token and tangible reward system on educationally handicapped children who previously have been in a regular class?

Class E and Class C were compared on the four achievement tests as shown in Table XII-3.* Group means (in raw score units) and standard deviations for these tests appear in this table. A series of analyses of covariance was done with these means comparing the classes' posttest means with the appropriate pretest as the covariate. The covariance approach was utilized to take into account differences in initial achievement level existing among students in the two classes.

Only one comparison produced significant results. This was with arithmetic fundamentals. As can be seen from Table XII-4 which presents the analysis of covariance data, Class E improved significantly more than Class C in arithmetic fundamentals over the project year. The mean arithmetic fundamentals grade equivalent for Class E was 3.9 (converted from raw score units in Table XII-3) at the start of the project and went to 5.1 at the close (total year gain 1.2 years). For Class C, the initial mean grade equivalent was 3.4 and final mean 3.8 (total year gain .4 year). Table XII-5 reports the differences between original means and the adjusted means used in the analysis of covariance.

---

* See pages 322–326 for Tables XII-3–16.

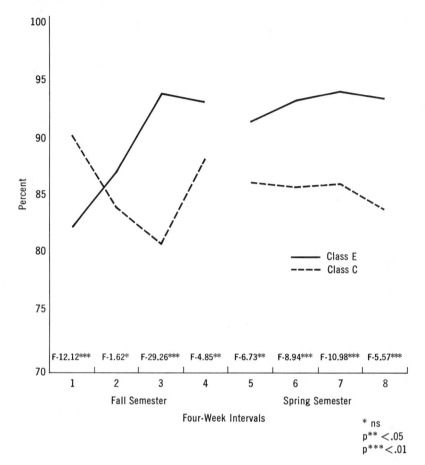

FIGURE XII-1. Graph of Class E and Class C mean task attention percentages—averaged for four-week intervals during the fall and spring semesters.

Table XII-6 presents the mean task attention percentages and standard deviations for all six classes, averaged for four-week intervals during the fall and spring semesters. Intervals 1 and 5 represent weeks 2-5 during the fall and spring semesters respectively since observations were not done the first week of either semester. The mean task attention percentages are based on five daily five-minute observations made on every child in a given class, and in most cases at least 100 such observations were made on each child during each four-week interval. These were then totaled and a resultant class mean task attention percentage obtained.

Figure XII-1 graphs the comparative four-week mean task attention percentage for Class E and Class C over the year-long project. F values obtained from analyses of variances with the means in each interval are also reported. During interval 1, Class C enjoyed a significant initial advantage over Class E but this was not maintained, and in interval 2 Class C fell slightly below Class E. Beginning with interval 3, Class E dramatically increased its task attention percentage and leveled off for the remainder of the project. From this point on, Class E's task attention percentage was always significantly higher than that attained by Class C. Class C's task attention percentage dropped rapidly during intervals 2 and 3, improved during interval 4, but fell from three to 13 percentage points below Class E from interval 2 on.

A trend analysis was performed on the four-week mean task attention percentages for Class E and Class C. The results of this analysis appear in Table XII-7. The significant F for "E-C" indicates that the overall means for the two classes were significantly different. The F for "trials" shows that the eight four-week means for both groups together are a significant trend. It is the F for the interaction between "trials" and "E-C" which is most interesting. This indicates that the trends for the two groups were significantly different. The F's for the linearity of trend indicate that though there is a significant nonlinear component, the two trends are basically linear and significantly different.

It is also evident from an examination of Figure XII-1 and Table XII-7 that the trend for Class E is increasing while that for Class C is constant or slightly decreasing.

We turn now to presentation of results bearing on the second main question of the evaluation.

What is the effect of rigid adherence to the engineered classroom design and use of a token and tangible reward system on educationally handicapped children who previously have been in a small individualized class which did not use such a reward system?

Classes CE began the project with the control condition and introduced the experimental condition at mid-year. Children in these classes were initially exposed to a highly individualized instructional program which may or may not have used aspects of the engineered classroom design but were not given systematic token or tangible rewards. During the fall semester, these classes were similar to Class C which began with the control condition and maintained it all year. Therefore Class C functioned as a control class for Classes CE during the spring semester. Differences between these two groups would offer evidence regarding the effect of adding the engineered design to a small class already under way.

Classes CE and Class C were compared on the four achievement test variables as well as task attention. The achievement test means for these classes appear in Tables XII-3 and XII-8. An analysis of variance was done with the achievement test means obtained at mid-year (when both groups were similar) and at the close of the year (after Classes CE had changed to the experimental condition). No significant F's were obtained with any of the achievement test mean comparisons except arithmetic fundamentals. Table XII-9 presents the analysis of variance table for arithmetic and indicates Classes CE made a significant gain over Class C during the spring semester. Starting with a 3.7 grade equivalent (converted from raw score units in Table XII-8) in arithmetic fundamentals at mid-year, Class CE moved to a mean of 4.5 (semester gain of .8 year). Class C made only a .1 year gain during the spring semester.

The gain made in arithmetic fundamentals by Classes CE during the spring semester (.8 year gain) was significantly greater than the gain these classes made during the fall (.2 year gain). Table XII-10 presents the t value for this comparison and reveals that there were no significant differences between fall and spring semester gains on other achievement tests by Classes CE.

In order to compare Classes CE with Class C on task attention percentages, these percentages were averaged for the last nine weeks of the fall semester when both groups were the same and again for the last nine weeks of the spring semester when they were different. An analysis of variance of these means revealed that Classes CE had made significant gains in task attention percentage over the spring semester as compared with Class C which maintained the control condition during this time. Table XII-11 presents the analysis of variance data for this comparison.

The task attention percentages of Classes CE and C were also compared during the eight four-week intervals of the entire project. Figure XII-2 graphs the mean task attention percentages attained by Classes CE and Class C for the year. Values of t obtained in the comparison of mean task attention percentages also appear in each interval. Class C achieved a significantly higher task attention level than Classes CE during interval 1. This, however, was narrowed during intervals 2 and 3 but reappeared in interval 4. The classes were not significantly different on this dependent variable during interval 5 at the beginning of the spring semester. Classes CE which introduced the experimental condition at this time, however, attained a significantly higher level during the remainder of the semester.

Comparing Classes CE with respect to task attention percentages achieved the last nine weeks of the fall semester under the control condition with those obtained the last nine weeks of the spring semester

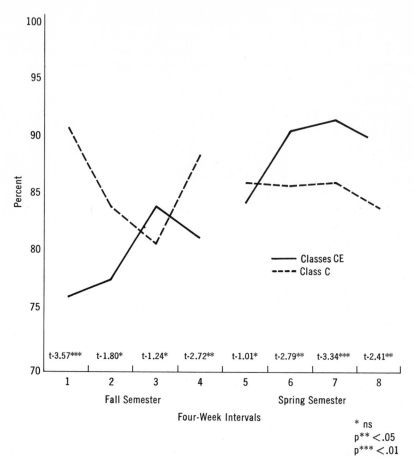

Figure XII-2. Graph of Classes CE and Class C mean task attention percentages —averaged for four-week intervals during the fall and spring semesters.

under the experimental condition produced the data presented in Table XII-12. The t value obtained is significant. Therefore, introduction of the experimental condition in Classes CE resulted in a definite improvement in task attention among students in these classes (mean gain 8.82).

The final question under consideration in the evaluation was:

What will be the effect of abruptly withdrawing the complete engineered classroom design including the reward system from a class of educationally handicapped children which has become accustomed to it?

Classes EC began the project utilizing the engineered design or experimental condition and withdrew the token and tangible reward system along with other aspects the teacher chose to change without warning at the start of the spring semester. During the fall semester these classes were similar to Class E (which maintained the year-long experimental condition), and during the spring semester this class served as a control. The achievement test means appearing in Tables XII-3 and XII-8 for Classes EC and Class E were compared between mid-year when the classes were similar and the close of the project when Classes EC had introduced the control condition. A series of analyses of variance with the data revealed that Classes EC and Class E did not differ significantly on any of the achievements tests from the mid to post points in the project.

Table XII-13 presents data comparing the achievement test mean difference scores obtained by Classes EC in the fall with those obtained in the spring. None of the t values are significant, and hence, achievement test gains made by students in these classes were not significantly affected by the change in classroom conditions.

Mean task attention percentage comparisons between Classes EC and Class E are graphed in Figure XII-3. No significant difference was found when means obtained the last nine weeks of both project semesters were subjected to an analysis of variance.

The task attention percentages for Classes EC and Class E were also compared during each of the eight four-week intervals of the project. Figure XII-3 reports the t values obtained from these comparisons. The groups were not significantly different during intervals 1 and 2 but Class E attained a significantly higher task attention percentage during intervals 3 and 4. This was maintained during the first portion of the spring semester (intervals 5 and 6), but for the final intervals, 7 and 8, no significant difference was found.

Table XII-14 reports the mean task attention percentage attained by Classes EC during the last nine weeks of the fall semester when they were maintaining the experimental condition as compared with the last nine weeks of the spring semester when they dropped it. The t value is significant, indicating that Classes EC actually improved in task attention percentage during the last part of the spring semester under the control condition.

An analysis of variance was done to evaluate the comparative mean task attention percentage gains made by Classes EC and CE during the last nine weeks of the two project semesters. Table XII-15 reports this analysis of variance and Table XII-16 the means and standard deviations upon which it is based. Class CE made a significantly higher gain in task attention than EC over the spring semester.

Classes EC and CE were also evaluated by means of t tests during

TABLE XII-3

Means and Standard Deviations for Class E and Class C
on Achievement Tests

Test	Pre				Mid				Post			
	E		C		E		C		E		C	
	M	σ	M	σ	M	σ	M	σ	M	σ	M	σ
WRAT Spelling	29.8	6.1	28.9	7.8	27.1	6.3	26.7	9.2	30.0	5.3	31.1	8.0
WRAT Reading	45.2	14.3	42.9	14.6	44.7	9.4	42.8	18.4	47.9	13.0	49.1	15.7
CAT Total Reading	31.4	34.1	23.1	19.9	33.1	38.7	34.4	24.2	38.0	30.6	34.0	28.2
CAT Arith. Fund.	15.1	12.2	10.5	6.5	20.7	13.4	13.9	7.5	24.9	11.7	14.5	8.3

TABLE XII-4

Analysis of Covariance for Class E and Class C
on Posttest Results of CAT Arithmetic Fundamentals
(covariate pretest)

Source of Variation	df	Sums of Squares	Mean Square	F
E-C	1	211.04	211.04	7.65*
Individual Differences	11	303.48	27.59	
Total	12	514.52		

*p < .05

TABLE XII-5

Means and Adjusted Means for Analysis of Covariance
for Class E and Class C on Posttest Results
on CAT Arithmetic Fundamentals (covariate pretest)

Class	Mean	Adjusted Mean
E	24.9	23.9
C	15.1	16.1

TABLE XII-6

MEAN TASK ATTENTION PERCENTAGES AND STANDARD DEVIATIONS
FOR ALL TREATMENT GROUPS, AVERAGED FOR FOUR-WEEK INTERVALS
DURING FALL AND SPRING SEMESTERS

Class		Fall Semester				Spring Semester			
		1 weeks 2–5	2 weeks 6–9	3 weeks 10–13	4 weeks 14–17	5 weeks 2–5	6 weeks 6–9	7 weeks 10–13	8 weeks 14–17
E	M	82.3	87.6	94.2	93.8	92.0	93.9	94.8	94.0
	σ	3.5	3.7	4.2	4.3	3.6	3.0	2.1	4.0
C	M	90.7	84.5	81.1	89.0	86.7	86.3	86.7	84.4
	σ	6.2	6.3	5.8	5.1	4.4	6.1	6.2	9.9
EC	M	85.5	85.8	87.7	86.6	85.6	90.0	91.8	91.3
	σ	7.7	6.6	7.3	6.9	6.5	4.7	3.8	5.3
CE	M	76.2	78.0	84.3	81.6	84.5	91.0	92.0	90.5
	σ	13.8	11.7	5.8	7.8	4.9	2.3	2.7	4.1

TABLE XII-7

ANALYSIS OF VARIANCE INDICATING TRENDS FOR CLASS E AND CLASS C
USING EIGHT FOUR-WEEK MEAN TASK ATTENTION PERCENTAGES

Source of Variation	df	Sums of Squares	Mean Square	F
Between Subjects				
E-C	1	1081.22	1081.22	9.85**
Subjects Within Groups	13	1427.35	109.80	
Within Subjects				
Trials	7	264.75	37.82	2.46*
Trials × EC	7	1162.59	166.09	10.79
Linear Trend	1	545.62	545.62	35.44**
Other	6	617.98	102.83	6.68**
Trials × Subjects				
Within Groups	91	1400.96	15.40	
	119			

* p < .05
** p < .01

TABLE XII-8

MEANS AND STANDARD DEVIATIONS FOR CLASSES EC AND CE
ON ACHIEVEMENT TESTS

Test	Pre				Mid				Post			
	EC		CE		EC		CE		EC		CE	
	M	σ	M	σ	M	σ	M	σ	M	σ	M	σ
WRAT Spelling	29.2	7.2	29.6	5.5	25.9	8.6	28.1	9.8	30.9	7.0	31.1	6.3
WRAT Reading	43.3	14.7	48.1	12.0	42.4	13.6	46.5	14.6	48.6	14.0	50.7	12.6
CAT Total Reading	28.1	28.3	24.8	16.6	32.9	23.3	33.4	17.4	35.9	29.3	37.8	19.3
CAT Arith. Fund.	10.7	6.4	11.1	7.0	15.2	8.4	13.5	10.1	19.8	9.3	19.7	9.9

TABLE XII-9

ANALYSIS OF VARIANCE FOR CLASSES CE AND CLASS C
ON CAT ARITHMETIC FUNDAMENTALS GAINS
DURING SPRING SEMESTER (MID TO POST)

Source	df	Sums of Squares	Mean Square	F
CE-C	1	135.00	135.00	4.83*
Individual Differences	18	502.80	27.93	
Total	19	637.80		

$* \, p < .05$

TABLE XII-10

TABLE OF t TESTS FOR PRE-MID VS. MID-POST
MEAN DIFFERENCE SCORES FOR CLASSES CE ON ACHIEVEMENT TESTS

Test	Fall (Pre-Mid)	Spring (Mid-Post)	Difference	t	sig.
WRAT Spelling	−2.57	2.57	5.14	1.07	ns
WRAT Reading	−1.00	3.92	4.92	.95	ns
CAT Total Reading	7.23	4.53	−2.69	.98	ns
CAT Arith. Fund.	2.00	7.61	5.61	2.89	$p < .05$

TABLE XII-11

ANALYSIS OF VARIANCE FOR CLASSES CE AND CLASS C ON MEAN TASK
ATTENTION PERCENTAGES—LAST NINE WEEKS OF FALL SEMESTER
VS. GAINS LAST NINE WEEKS OF SPRING SEMESTER

Source	df	Sums of Squares	Mean Square	F
CE-C	1	305.92	305.92	8.71*
Individual Differences	18	631.87	35.10	
Total	19	937.79		

*p < .01

TABLE XII-12

TABLE OF t VALUE FOR MEAN TASK ATTENTION PERCENTAGES—
LAST NINE WEEKS OF FALL SEMESTER VS. LAST NINE WEEKS
OF SPRING SEMESTER FOR CLASSES CE

Fall Semester (Last nine weeks)	Spring Semester (Last nine weeks)	Difference	t	sig.
82.53	91.35	8.82	5.64	p < .01

TABLE XII-13

TABLE OF t TESTS FOR PRE-MID VS. MID-POST
MEAN DIFFERENCE SCORES FOR CLASSES EC ON ACHIEVEMENT TESTS

Test	Fall (Pre-Mid)	Spring (Mid-Post)	Difference	t	sig.
WRAT Spelling	−3.93	5.68	9.62	2.06	ns
WRAT Reading	−1.00	6.37	7.37	1.41	ns
CAT Total Reading	7.33	6.66	− .67	.10	ns
CAT Arith. Fund.	4.60	4.13	− .46	.23	ns

TABLE XII-14

TABLE OF t VALUE FOR MEAN TASK ATTENTION PERCENTAGES—
LAST NINE WEEKS OF FALL SEMESTER VS. LAST NINE WEEKS
OF SPRING SEMESTER FOR CLASSES EC

Fall Semester (Last nine weeks)	Spring Semester (Last nine weeks)	Difference	t	sig.
87.56	91.40	3.84	2.91	p < .05

TABLE XII-15

ANALYSIS OF VARIANCE FOR CLASSES CE AND EC ON MEAN TASK
ATTENTION PERCENTAGES—LAST NINE WEEKS OF FALL SEMESTER
VS. LAST NINE WEEKS OF SPRING SEMESTER

Source	df	Sums of Squares	Mean Square	F
CE-EC	1	278.30	278.30	10.07*
Individual Differences	29	801.29	27.63	
Total	30	1079.59		

* p < .01

TABLE XII-16

MEANS AND STANDARD DEVIATIONS FOR CLASSES EC AND CE
ON MEAN TASK ATTENTION PERCENTAGES—LAST NINE WEEKS
OF SPRING SEMESTER

Fall Semester (Last nine weeks)				Spring Semester (Last nine weeks)			
EC		CE		EC		CE	
M	σ	M	σ	M	σ	M	σ
87.6	6.3	82.5	6.4	91.4	3.9	91.3	3.1

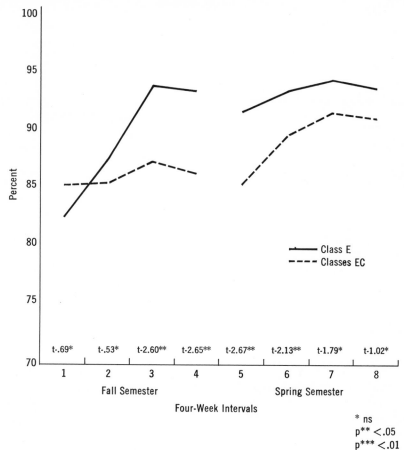

Figure XII-3. Graph of Classes EC and Class E mean task attention percentages averaged for four-week intervals during the fall and spring semesters.

each four-week interval of the project as shown in Figure XII-4. During intervals 1 and 2, Classes EC were significantly higher in task attention than Classes CE. There was no significant difference in interval 3 but one favoring Classes EC appeared again during interval 4. Over the spring semester (intervals 5, 6, 7, and 8) the classes attained quite similar task attention percentages and no significant differences were found.

DISCUSSION

In the section which follows we shall discuss the differences in gains in arithmetic fundamentals made by project classes, changes in task

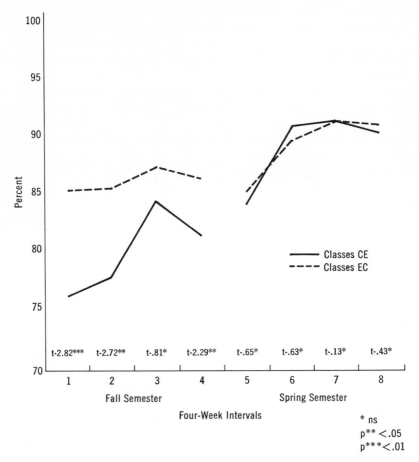

FIGURE XII-4. Graph of Classes EC and Classes CE mean task attention percentages—averaged for four-week intervals during the fall and spring semesters.

attention occurring among groups, the impact of the classroom conditions on students, and conclusions and implications which may be drawn from the evaluation.

A consistent finding in the evaluation was that the presence of the experimental condition was positively correlated with student achievement level in arithmetic fundamentals as measured by the California Achievement Test. Class E attained a significant improvement in arithmetic as compared with Class C over the year. Classes CE made significantly greater gains in arithmetic during the spring semester when they introduced the experimental condition than they had made during the fall semester when they maintained the control condition. They also made significant gains during the spring semester as compared with the year-long control Class C. Classes EC made approximately the same gains in arithmetic during the fall semester when they introduced the experimental condition as they had during the spring semester when they withdrew it.

In the Santa Monica Project, one hour daily was set aside for arithmetic (the second hour in the morning), and all experimental and control classes adhered to this schedule. Differences in the emphasis which teachers place on arithmetic and their competencies for teaching it are obvious determinants of arithmetic gains made by their students. However, the significant arithmetic improvement made by classes following the experimental condition as compared with those using the control condition suggests that the teacher variable was not alone responsible. The nature of the experimental condition with its 15-minute work periods followed by check marks may have been conducive to more consistent work efforts on the part of children in a class operating under this condition. The routine of the class which emphasized putting everything in its place, following directions, having all work corrected each 15 minutes and even counting the daily check marks may well have supported improvement in arithmetic skills. From an observational viewpoint the author was impressed with the amount of time teachers under the control condition spent in handling behavior problems during academic work periods. This took away from actual teaching time available and may have limited the amount of individual remedial help given to students. Children in classes using the experimental condition were observed to work better independently and for longer periods of time without distraction. The task attention data to be discussed later support this observation.

Classes EC did not show a significant difference in their degree of improvement in arithmetic during the fall semester as compared with the spring semester. Their gains, much like those of Class E, were similar during both the fall and spring semesters as shown in Tables XII-3 and XII-8. This may be a reflection of the advantage of starting with the experimental condition and establishing a structured working routine which then carries over one semester to the next regardless of changes made, such as removal of the check-mark system.

The experimental condition in the Santa Monica Project had a facilitating effect on student task attention as illustrated in Figures XII-1–4. In Figure XII-1 we see how Class E overcame an initial disadvantage as compared with Class C during the earlier part of the fall semester and repeatedly attained a significantly higher task attention percentage, than Class C over the remainder of the year. In this respect, the initial four-week interval of the fall semester is interesting to consider. All project teachers were trained in the use of the developmental sequence and the engineered classroom design prior to random assignment to either experimental or control classrooms. The teacher in Classroom C was particularly interested in this approach to the education of emotionally disturbed children and sought to implement as much of it as possible while adhering to the control condition which precluded the use of the check-mark system. Her efforts are reflected in the 90 percent mean task attention percentage level her class attained during the initial portion of the semester.

The author was impressed with the teacher's application of behavior modification techniques using exploratory, social, and mastery level emphasis. While no check marks or candy were present in her program, she effectively provided many high interest arts and crafts projects, games, and other exploratory activities, in addition to continual social attention and praise. The teacher in Class E and the two teachers in Classes EC during the fall semester had to get used to a unique system of 15-minute work periods, check-mark giving, and regular use of classroom interventions. During the first few weeks which it took for these routines to be established for both teachers and children in Classes E and EC their task attention percentage level was below that of Class C. By the second four-week interval, however, both classes had attained a slightly higher task attention percentage as reflected in Table XII-6. From that point on (with one exception during interval 4, when Classes EC were slightly below Class C) Class E and Classes EC maintained their task attention advantage utilizing the experimental condition. The teacher in Class C encountered more difficulty in maintaining her initially higher level due to what seemed a diminishing effectiveness of exploratory, social, and mastery rewards with her students. The more basic attention, response, and order reward system inherent in the engineered classroom design, while slower to achieve effectiveness, appears to have greater long-range benefits than use of higher level rewards initially. The initial significant difference in task attention between Class C and Classes CE during interval 1 of the fall semester would appear a reflection of the teacher variable in these classes and the greater success enjoyed by the teacher in Class C in the use of exploratory, social, and mastery rewards.

That "launching" children by use of the engineered design moves them up the developmental sequence and makes them susceptible to maintenance of a consistently high task attention level without the use of check marks and rigid adherence to the engineered design is suggested by Figure XII-3 which depicts the task attention gains made by

Classes EC as teachers gave up the check-mark system and relied on exploratory, social, and mastery rewards during the spring semester. These gains were apparently not due to time and enrollment in a small individualized class alone, for the task attention percentages attained during the control phase of Classes EC were consistently superior to those of Class C during the same period. In addition, Class E reached its peak task attention level in interval 3 and leveled off for the remainder of the year rather than demonstrating a second semester increase. The sharp increase in task attention percentage displayed by Classes CE when the experimental condition or engineered design was introduced during the second semester offers further evidence of the facilitating effect of the design on children who had been accustomed to a small class.

The dependent variable of task attention was selected primarily as a measure of student functioning on the attention, response, and order levels of the developmental sequence. One of the hypotheses advanced throughout this text has been that getting children ready for learning through emphasis on fundamental competencies in learning is extremely important. Such a readiness training goal is basic to the design of the engineered classroom and the evidence obtained from the evaluation suggests: 1) that there is a positive relationship between the design and improved task attention functioning and 2) once an investment is made in building attention, response, and order behaviors, the child naturally moves to higher levels on the developmental sequence and does not need the continuing support of the check-mark system, tangible rewards for learning, or emphasis on routine. An important additional possibility to consider is that the teachers in Classes E and EC increased their effectiveness as secondary social reinforcers due to their initial association with a success-oriented program and primary reward system. The teachers in Classes EC, therefore, were able to rely on social reinforcement during the spring semester and maintain successful control with it while the teacher in Class C diminished in her effectiveness because of lack of opportunity to initially establish herself as such a positive social reinforcer.

The validity of task attention as a measure of learning or performance may be questioned by some. Eye, head, or body orientation toward a task does not reflect whether or not the student is actually working on the assignment, whether he understands what he is doing, or whether he is making academic progress from day to day. The possibility that a given child may be daydreaming even though his eyes are on the task also cannot be ruled out. Despite these limitations, the assumption that a child is attending, responding, and following directions when his eyes are directly on a task (or in some cases, when his head or body are properly oriented toward it) is considered reasonable and warranted. "Task attention" is not a qualitative measure of learning but it has definite quantitative advantages with respect to assessing the three lowest levels of the developmental sequence. In addition, the high degree of observer reliability which is possible using this direct behavioral measurement allows discussion with some certainty if differences are found between experimental and control conditions.

The author was aware when formulating the evaluation of the Santa Monica Project that one explanation of any change which might occur among the students would relate to the "Hawthorne effect." Several decades ago, evidence was provided by Roethlisberger and Dixon (1939) that changes in working conditions initially improved worker morale and subsequent performance level. Since that time the immediate positive effect derived from introducing novelty or change into a working situation has come to be known as the "Hawthorne effect." At the beginning of the Santa Monica Project, all students were exposed to a powerful novelty effect. Coming into a small class with two teachers after having been in regular classrooms with 30 or 35 other students where instruction was group oriented and where grade level curriculum was emphasized along with competition and grades constituted a marked modification of working and learning conditions in school. While Figures XII-1–4 reflect four-week interval mean task attention percentages, and daily and weekly measures are not reported, such data did indeed offer evidence that in all classes the first few days or in some cases the first few weeks when a new condition was introduced produced a task attention advantage which diminished to varying degrees immediately following. At the start of the second semester when Classes EC withdrew the check-mark system and tangible rewards, they too, experienced such an initial spurt which quickly diminished. Here is an example of the effect of "taking away" what would seem to be a highly desirable element in the classroom but which nevertheless altered the working conditions and produced a positive result. The continued improvement of Classes EC over this semester has been discussed previously in relation to the increased effectiveness of exploratory, social, and mastery rewards rather than the removal of the check-mark system and tangible rewards alone. Such continued gains cannot be explained merely as the result of the Hawthorne effect.

The full year duration of the Santa Monica Project provided an opportunity for a thorough assessment of the Hawthorne effect. Class E maintained a high level of task attention over the major portion of the year; certainly a larger one than would be accountable for on the basis of novelty alone. Classes CE immediately improved in task attention the first few days when the engineered design was introduced during the spring semester, but this diminished soon after. Their consistent improvement from that point on is viewed as the result of the attention, response, and order emphasis introduced through the experimental condition or engineered design.

The overall results of the Santa Monica Project can be interpreted in the framework of the deconditioning model utilized with Peter and the white rabbit presented in Chapter III. The small classes with a teacher and aide constituted a unique and positive setting within which to introduce demands for learning and appropriate behavior. The individualization of work assignments and gradual increase in their complexity which was possible in all six classes can be likened to the slow but steady introduction of the white rabbit to Peter while he was engaged in highly satisfying and rewarding activities. One of the pieces of missing information in the evaluation is a base line measure of the task attention level of the project children the previous year while they were all in regular classes. While no systematic or long-range observations were made, three of the children were timed for a brief period at the close of the semester prior to the project and task attention percentages of from 27 to 33 percent obtained. This suggests that all six project classes were successful to a considerable degree in improving the task attention functioning level of their students.

The engineered design, however, may well have included additional positive and rewarding elements through its check-mark system, emphasis on the most fundamental levels of the developmental sequence, and systematic use of interventions which aimed at continually guaranteeing the child success. Children in the engineered classes may then have experienced even more success and satisfaction while the "white rabbit" of school and learning was introduced. Certainly the results of the evaluation answer some critics' claim that use of tangible rewards in the classroom dooms the child to dependence on them. The evidence obtained indicates that emotionally disturbed children can and do move on to responding positively to more traditional rewards such as multisensory experiences, social praise, and knowledge of results. Again it should be emphasized that the use of tangible rewards alone is not enough. It is their inclusion in a well-organized, consistent process such as the check-mark system that makes them of real value.

The engineered classroom design appears basically a launching technique for initiating learning with children who often fail to "get off the ground" in school. It does not appear to be essential in its present form for more than one semester with many children, and indeed as additional work is done it may be found that children profit from it primarily the first few weeks of the program after which they are ready to move on to a more traditional learning environment. In fact, the elaborate intervention procedures were not extensively used with most students in the Santa Monica Project after a period of seven to ten weeks. Efforts need to be made to assess transition usage of the reward system, such as having the child start the semester receiving check marks and tangible exchange items (Phase I), then moving on in six to eight weeks to exchanging the check marks for privilege time (Phase II) in line with the Premack principle cited earlier, and finally, moving to merely graphing the check marks on a Work Report as a form of "grade" (Phase III). This means of modifying rewards parallels the developmental sequence and moves from the attention to the exploratory and finally the mastery level.

Teachers of children with emotional, behavioral, and learning problems in one way or other have been doing many of the things discussed in the last three chapters of this book for years. That they have not always experienced success with such difficult children may be largely due to a need to refocus on readiness training and the value of a systematic approach for launching children into learning. Such a reorientation of teachers and emphasis on systematically helping children get ready for school while they are actually there has been the major purpose of this text.

Appendix I

STUDENT ASSESSMENT ACCORDING TO

A DEVELOPMENTAL SEQUENCE

OF EDUCATIONAL GOALS

Inventory

Frank M. Hewett, Ph.D.
University of California, Los Angeles

TASK

Attention

1. Child does not pay attention to learning tasks.

☐	☐	☐
(ALWAYS)	(SOMETIMES)	(RARELY)
Child never pays attention to learning tasks	Child often does not pay attention to learning tasks	Child occasionally does not pay attention to learning tasks

2. Child prefers fantasy to reality.

☐	☐	☐
(SEVERE)	(MODERATE)	(MILD)
Child out of contact with reality	Child often daydreams	Child occasionally daydreams

3. Child engages in repetitive behavior which interferes with learning.

☐	☐	☐
(SEVERE)	(MODERATE)	(MILD)
Child preoccupied with constant self-stimulation	Child preoccupied with rituals or other compulsive behavior	Child preoccupied with neatness, cleanliness, or correctness

4. Child's beliefs and interests are inappropriate.

☐	☐	☐
(SEVERE)	(MODERATE)	(MILD)
Child has extremely bizarre beliefs and interests	Child has distorted beliefs about his environment	Child's beliefs and interests immature for sex and age

5. Child does not pay attention to teacher.

☐	☐	☐
(ALWAYS)	(SOMETIMES)	(RARELY)
Child never pays attention to teacher	Child often does not pay attention to teacher	Child occasionally does not pay attention to teacher

6. Child does not profit from instruction.

☐	☐	☐
(ALWAYS)	(SOMETIMES)	(RARELY)
Child never retains and uses instruction he has been given	Child often does not retain and use instruction he has been given	Child occasionally does not retain and use instruction he has been given

Response

7. Child does not respond to learning tasks.

☐	☐	☐
(ALWAYS)	(SOMETIMES)	(RARELY)
Child will never undertake a learning task	Child often will not undertake a learning task	Child will occasionally not undertake a learning task

8. Child maintains a constricted level of performance.

□	□	□
(ALWAYS)	(SOMETIMES)	(RARELY)
Child always controlled and rigid with learning tasks	Child often controlled and rigid with learning tasks	Child occasionally controlled and rigid with learning tasks

9. Child exhibits a narrow range of learning interests.

□	□	□
(ALWAYS)	(SOMETIMES)	(RARELY)
Child will never try a new or different learning task	Child often will not try a new or different learning task	Child occasionally will not try a new or different learning task

10. Child withdraws from teacher and peers.

□	□	□
(ALWAYS)	(SOMETIMES)	(RARELY)
Child always avoids contact with teacher and peers	Child often avoids contact with teacher and peers	Child occasionally avoids contact with teacher and peers

11. Child cannot function in a regular classroom.

□	□	□
(SEVERE)	(MODERATE)	(MILD)
Child does not respond to tasks in individual tutoring	Child does not respond to tasks in a special class or program	Child does not respond to tasks in a regular classroom except for brief periods of time

Order

12. Child does not follow directions.

□	□	□
(ALWAYS)	(SOMETIMES)	(RARELY)
Child never follows directions when doing learning tasks	Child often does not follow directions when doing learning tasks	Child occasionally does not follow directions when doing learning tasks

13. Child is uncontrolled in learning.

☐	☐	☐
(ALWAYS)	(SOMETIMES)	(RARELY)
Child always approaches learning tasks in an impulsive, uncritical manner	Child often approaches learning tasks in an impulsive, uncritical manner	Child occasionally approaches learning tasks in an impulsive, uncritical manner

14. Child is disruptive in group.

☐	☐	☐
(ALWAYS)	(SOMETIMES)	(RARELY)
Child always is disruptive in group	Child often is disruptive in group	Child occasionally is disruptive in group

15. Child does not finish learning tasks.

☐	☐	☐
(ALWAYS)	(SOMETIMES)	(RARELY)
Child never finishes learning tasks	Child often does not finish learning tasks	Child occasionally does not finish learning tasks

Exploratory

16. Child does not adequately explore his environment.

☐	☐	☐
(ALWAYS)	(SOMETIMES)	(RARELY)
Child's exploration of his environment extremely limited	Child's exploration of his environment moderately limited	Child's exploration of his environment limited to a few specific areas

17. Child overly dependent on others for choice of interests and activities.

☐	☐	☐
(ALWAYS)	(SOMETIMES)	(RARELY)
Child completely dependent on others for choice of interests and activities	Child excessively dependent on others for choice of interests and activities	Child usually dependent on others for choice of interests and activities

18. Child cannot do learning tasks because of motor, physical, sensory, perceptual, or intellectual deficits.

☐ | ☐ | ☐
(SEVERE) | (MODERATE) | (MILD)
Child severely impaired by motor, physical, sensory, perceptual, or intellectual deficits | Child moderately impaired by motor, physical, sensory, perceptual, or intellectual deficits | Child mildly impaired by motor, physical, sensory, perceptual, or intellectual deficits

Social

19. Child does not gain approval from others.

☐ | ☐ | ☐
(SEVERE) | (MODERATE) | (MILD)
Child never gains approval from others | Child often does not gain approval from others | Child occasionally does not gain approval from others

20. Child overly dependent on attention or praise from others.

☐ | ☐ | ☐
(SEVERE) | (MODERATE) | (MILD)
Child will only work with constant supervision and attention from teacher | Child will only work for brief periods of time without attention and praise from others | Child often seeks attention and praise from others while doing learning tasks

Mastery

21. Child's functioning level in self-care and intellectual skills below capacity.

(self-care)

▽ | ▽ | ▽
(SEVERE) | (MODERATE) | (MILD)
Extreme discrepancy between child's capacity and functioning level in self-care | Considerable discrepancy between child's capacity and functioning level in self-care | Slight discrepancy between child's capacity and functioning level in self-care

(intellectual skill)

◿   ◿   ◿
(SEVERE)   (MODERATE)   (MILD)
Extreme dis-   Considerable dis-   Slight discrepancy
crepancy between   crepancy between   between child's
child's capacity   child's capacity and   capacity and
and functioning   functioning level   functioning level
level in intellec-   in intellectual and   in intellectual and
tual and academic   academic skills   academic skills
skills

REWARD

a. Child not rewarded by tangible rewards (e.g., food, money)
   in learning.
   ☐   ☐   ☐
   (ALWAYS)   (SOMETIMES)   (RARELY)
   Child's responses   Child's responses   Child's responses
   never controlled   often not con-   occasionally not
   by tangible   trolled by tangible   controlled by
   rewards   rewards   tangible rewards

b. Child not rewarded by social attention in learning tasks.
   ☐   ☐   ☐
   (ALWAYS)   (SOMETIMES)   (RARELY)
   Child's responses   Child's responses   Child's responses
   never controlled   often not con-   occasionally not
   by social attention   trolled by social   controlled by social
                               attention   attention

c. Child is not rewarded by finishing learning tasks.
   ☐   ☐   ☐
   (ALWAYS)   (SOMETIMES)   (RARELY)
   Child's per-   Child's perform-   Child's perform-
   formance never   ance often not   ance occasionally
   controlled by task   controlled by task   not controlled by
   completion   completion   task completion

d. Child not rewarded by multisensory experiences in learning.

☐	☐	☐
(ALWAYS)	(SOMETIMES)	(RARELY)
Child's responses never controlled by multisensory rewards	Child's responses often not controlled by multi-sensory rewards	Child's responses occasionally not controlled by multisensory rewards

e. Child not rewarded by gaining approval and avoiding disapproval for learning tasks.

☐	☐	☐
(ALWAYS)	(SOMETIMES)	(RARELY)
Child's responses never controlled by social approval and disapproval	Child's responses often not controlled by social approval and disapproval	Child's responses occasionally not controlled by social approval and disapproval

f. Child not rewarded by doing learning tasks correctly.

☐	☐	☐
(ALWAYS)	(SOMETIMES)	(RARELY)
Child's responses never controlled by knowledge of results	Child's responses often not controlled by knowledge of results	Child's responses occasionally not controlled by knowledge of results

g. Child not rewarded by acquiring knowledge and skill.

☐	☐	☐
(ALWAYS)	(SOMETIMES)	(RARELY)
Child's performance never controlled by acquisition of knowledge and skill	Child's performance often not controlled by acquisition of knowledge and skill	Child's performance occasionally not controlled by acquisition of knowledge and skill

Appendix II

PARENT AND TEACHER RATING SCALES

Parent Rating Scale

Name of student_____ Date_____

Person filling out Rating Scale_____

Relationship of this person to student_____

Below are 18 statements describing a student and his work at school. Please read each statement and decide how it applied to your child over the past school semester. A simple rating scale to the right can be checked. 1. NEVER—if the statement never applied, 2. RARELY—if the statement rarely applied, 3. SOMETIMES—if the statement sometimes applied, 4. OFTEN—if the statement often applied, and 5. ALWAYS—if the statement always applied. Base your ratings on your child's behavior during the semester he has just completed and make a check mark on the scale to show your rating.

1. He was happy in school.

NEVER	RARELY	SOMETIMES	OFTEN	ALWAYS
1	2	3	4	5

2. He wanted to stay home from school.

NEVER	RARELY	SOMETIMES	OFTEN	ALWAYS
1	2	3	4	5

3. He discussed school at home.

NEVER	RARELY	SOMETIMES	OFTEN	ALWAYS
1	2	3	4	5

4. He said he liked
   school.

NEVER	RARELY	SOMETIMES	OFTEN	ALWAYS
1	2	3	4	5

5. He said he disliked
   school.

NEVER	RARELY	SOMETIMES	OFTEN	ALWAYS
1	2	3	4	5

6. He said he liked his
   teacher.

NEVER	RARELY	SOMETIMES	OFTEN	ALWAYS
1	2	3	4	5

7. He said he disliked
   his teacher.

NEVER	RARELY	SOMETIMES	OFTEN	ALWAYS
1	2	3	4	5

8. He said he liked his
   classmates.

NEVER	RARELY	SOMETIMES	OFTEN	ALWAYS
1	2	3	4	5

9. He said he disliked
   his classmates.

NEVER	RARELY	SOMETIMES	OFTEN	ALWAYS
1	2	3	4	5

10. He made friends in
    school.

NEVER	RARELY	SOMETIMES	OFTEN	ALWAYS
1	2	3	4	5

11. He was interested in
    reading.

NEVER	RARELY	SOMETIMES	OFTEN	ALWAYS
1	2	3	4	5

12. He was interested in
    arithmetic.

NEVER	RARELY	SOMETIMES	OFTEN	ALWAYS
1	2	3	4	5

13. He improved in his
    reading.

NEVER	RARELY	SOMETIMES	OFTEN	ALWAYS
1	2	3	4	5

14. He improved in his
    arithmetic.

NEVER	RARELY	SOMETIMES	OFTEN	ALWAYS
1	2	3	4	5

15. He concentrated well.

NEVER	RARELY	SOMETIMES	OFTEN	ALWAYS
1	2	3	4	5

16. He got into trouble
    in school.

NEVER	RARELY	SOMETIMES	OFTEN	ALWAYS
1	2	3	4	5

17. The school under-
    stood what he
    needed.

NEVER	RARELY	SOMETIMES	OFTEN	ALWAYS
1	2	3	4	5

18. The school provided
    a good program
    for him.

NEVER	RARELY	SOMETIMES	OFTEN	ALWAYS
1	2	3	4	5

Teacher Rating Scale

Name of student_____ Date_____

Name of teacher reporting _____

Ratings based on period of observation from_____ to _____

Below are a series of statements about this student's functioning and behavior. Read each statement and rate it according to the 5-point scale to the right based on your impressions of the student during the past semester. Place an X at the appropriate point on the scale.

1. Student showed
   enthusiasm for
   school in general.

NEVER	RARELY	SOMETIMES	OFTEN	ALWAYS
1	2	3	4	5

2. Student showed
   enthusiasm for
   learning to read.

NEVER	RARELY	SOMETIMES	OFTEN	ALWAYS
1	2	3	4	5

3. Student showed
   enthusiasm for
   learning arithmetic

NEVER	RARELY	SOMETIMES	OFTEN	ALWAYS
1	2	3	4	5

4. Student showed enthu-
siasm for participat-
ing in class activities.

/	/	/	/	
NEVER	RARELY	SOMETIMES	OFTEN	ALWAYS
1	2	3	4	5

5. Student showed
concern with progress
in reading.

/	/	/	/	
NEVER	RARELY	SOMETIMES	OFTEN	ALWAYS
1	2	3	4	5

6. Student showed
concern with progress
in arithmetic.

/	/	/	/	
NEVER	RARELY	SOMETIMES	OFTEN	ALWAYS
1	2	3	4	5

7. Student completed
assignments in
reading.

/	/	/	/	
NEVER	RARELY	SOMETIMES	OFTEN	ALWAYS
1	2	3	4	5

8. Student completed
assignments in
arithmetic.

/	/	/	/	
NEVER	RARELY	SOMETIMES	OFTEN	ALWAYS
1	2	3	4	5

9. Student worked well
independently.

/	/	/	/	
NEVER	RARELY	SOMETIMES	OFTEN	ALWAYS
1	2	3	4	5

10. Quality (handwriting,
organization, neat-
ness) of student's
work acceptable.

/	/	/	/	
NEVER	RARELY	SOMETIMES	OFTEN	ALWAYS
1	2	3	4	5

11. Student made
progress in reading.

/	/	/	/	
NEVER	RARELY	SOMETIMES	OFTEN	ALWAYS
1	2	3	4	5

12. Student made prog-
ress in arithmetic.

/	/	/	/	
NEVER	RARELY	SOMETIMES	OFTEN	ALWAYS
1	2	3	4	5

13. Student made
progress in degree of
participation in class
activities.

/	/	/	/	
NEVER	RARELY	SOMETIMES	OFTEN	ALWAYS
1	2	3	4	5

14. Student became
    frustrated.

    ___/___/_____/___/___
    NEVER RARELY SOMETIMES OFTEN ALWAYS
      1   2   3   4   5

15. Student became
    tearful.

    ___/___/_____/___/___
    NEVER RARELY SOMETIMES OFTEN ALWAYS
      1   2   3   4   5

16. Student became
    angry.

    ___/___/_____/___/___
    NEVER RARELY SOMETIMES OFTEN ALWAYS
      1   2   3   4   5

17. Student had an ade-
    quate attention span.

    ___/___/_____/___/___
    NEVER RARELY SOMETIMES OFTEN ALWAYS
      1   2   3   4   5

18. Student daydreamed.

    ___/___/_____/___/___
    NEVER RARELY SOMETIMES OFTEN ALWAYS
      1   2   3   4   5

19. Student respected
    class rules and
    routine.

    ___/___/_____/___/___
    NEVER RARELY SOMETIMES OFTEN ALWAYS
      1   2   3   4   5

20. Student had to be
    sent out of the room.

    ___/___/_____/___/___
    NEVER RARELY SOMETIMES OFTEN ALWAYS
      1   2   3   4   5

21. Student took
    direction well.

    ___/___/_____/___/___
    NEVER RARELY SOMETIMES OFTEN ALWAYS
      1   2   3   4   5

22. Student appeared to
    want to please
    teacher.

    ___/___/_____/___/___
    NEVER RARELY SOMETIMES OFTEN ALWAYS
      1   2   3   4   5

23. Student worked well
    independently.

    ___/___/_____/___/___
    NEVER RARELY SOMETIMES OFTEN ALWAYS
      1   2   3   4   5

24. Student occupied a position of leadership with his peers.

	NEVER	RARELY	SOMETIMES	OFTEN	ALWAYS
	1	2	3	4	5

25. Student withdrew from peers.

	NEVER	RARELY	SOMETIMES	OFTEN	ALWAYS
	1	2	3	4	5

26. Student was subjected to teasing by peers.

	NEVER	RARELY	SOMETIMES	OFTEN	ALWAYS
	1	2	3	4	5

27. Student was involved in physical fights with peers.

	NEVER	RARELY	SOMETIMES	OFTEN	ALWAYS
	1	2	3	4	5

Please use remaining space for any additional comments you wish to make.

Appendix III

TASK ATTENTION CRITERIA

Eye attention is the primary criterion, but head and body attention are acceptable subject to specifications listed below.

I. EYE ATTENTION

    a. Child's eyes must be on task or teacher when:
1) Teacher talking to class.
2) Teacher giving him checks.
3) Teacher talking to him individually or helping him.
4) Child doing an assignment at his desk.

Note: Eyes not to shift to folders, box, etc. during a task unless these are being employed during task.

During task at desk, no loud noises or talking to others, but whispering to self permitted.

II. HEAD ATTENTION

    a. Child's head must be facing task when:
1) Back turned to observer in study booth or at Exploratory or Order Centers.

III. BODY ATTENTION

    a. Child must be sitting in chair quietly when:
1) Hand up waiting for teacher.
2) Waiting for checks, following receipt of checks, or while waiting for others to receive their checks.
3) All other waiting periods (e.g., when finished task, before recess and dismissal).

IV. GENERAL

a. Child not credited when he calls out to teacher, talks to classmate during work periods, or sits and plays with objects at desk.

b. If leaves seat or room without permission, do not time until he returns.

c. If sent on errand in room (e.g., to get pass, go to center, sharpen pencil, etc.) credit for body attention (e.g., does not disturb others, touch irrelevant objects, and goes directly to assigned area). Do not time child when sent out of room by teacher on errand or when goes to bathroom or for drink outside.

d. If taken from room for misbehavior (e.g., time-out room or to be sent home) do not time. An exception here is the response intervention when observer credits child for body attention as child is being taken to door by teacher.

e. Child who holds pencil during waiting period is not docked unless he plays with it.

f. When teacher says "stop" child has 30 seconds to put pencil down and work away before being docked.

g. Any time an observer sees or hears an assignment being disobeyed by child, the child must be docked (e.g., if it can be seen that child has not finished all math problems and he has put himself into a waiting period instead of completing task). If, however, an observer cannot see whether task is completed or not, or if he has not heard the teacher assign child to a specific task, the child is not docked for a self-imposed waiting period: the criterion being that he engaged in task for at least 30 seconds before stopping.

h. Child is not docked for looking at date on blackboard or any other words, etc. which teacher wrote there that are a part of the assigned task.

Bibliography

ABRAHAMSON, D., "Status of Mental Hygiene and Child Guidance Facilities in the Public School in the United States," *Journal of Pediatrics*, 1955, 46, pp. 107–118.

ACKER, L., "Errorless Discrimination Training in Autistic and Normal Children" (doctoral dissertation, University of California, Los Angeles, Department of Psychology, 1966).

ADAMS, A., "Identifying Socially Maladjusted School Children," *Genetic Psychology Monographs*, 1960, 61, pp. 3–36.

AICHHORN, A., *Wayward Youth*, New York: The Viking Press, 1965.

ALLEN, K., B. HART, J. BUELL, F. HARRIS, AND M. WOLF, "Effects of Social Reinforcement on Isolate Behavior of a Nursery School Child," *Child Development*, 1964, 35, pp. 511–518.

ANTONITIS, J. AND G. BARNES, "Group Operant Behavior: An Extension of Individual Methodology to a Real Life Situation," *Journal of Genetic Psychology*, 1961, 98, pp. 95–111.

ARPS, G., "A Preliminary Report on 'Work with Knowledge versus Work without Knowledge of Results,'" *Psychology Review*, 1917, 24, pp. 449–458.

————, "Work without Knowledge of Results versus Work with Knowledge of Results," *Psychological Monographs*, #125, 1920.

AYLLON, T. AND E. HAUGHTON, "Control of the Behavior of Schizophrenic Patients by Food," *Journal of Experimental Analysis of Behavior*, 1962, 5, pp. 343–354.

AYLLON, T. AND J. MICHAELS, "The Psychiatric Nurse as a Behavioral Engineer," *Journal of Experimental Analysis of Behavior*, 1959, 2, pp. 323–334.

BATEMAN, B., "Three Approaches to Diagnosis and Educational Planning for Children with Learning Disabilities," *Proceedings: 1967 International Convocation on Children and Young Adults with Learning Disabilities,* Pittsburgh: Home for Crippled Children, 1967, pp. 120–130.

————, "Young MR Curriculum," speech presented to the Special Study Institute for Administrators of Special Education, sponsored by the California State Department of Education and the University of Southern California, Sacramento, October, 1967.

BEILIN, H., "Teachers' and Clinicians' Attitudes towards the Behavior Problems of Children: A Reappraisal," *Child Development,* 1959, 30, pp. 9–12.

BENDER, L., "Childhood Schizophrenia," *Psychiatric Quarterly,* 1953, 27, pp. 663–681.

————, "Schizophrenia in Childhood: Its Recognition, Description, and Treatment," *American Journal of Orthopsychiatry,* 1956, 26, pp. 499–506.

BEREITER, C. AND S. ENGELMANN, *Teaching Disadvantaged Children in the Pre-School,* Englewood Cliffs: Prentice-Hall, 1966.

BERKOWITZ, P. AND E. ROTHMAN, *The Disturbed Child,* New York: New York University Press, 1960.

BERRES, F., J. COLEMAN, W. BRISCOE, AND F. HEWETT, *The Deep Sea Adventure Series,* San Francisco: Harr Wagner and Company, 1958.

BETTELHEIM, B., *Love Is Not Enough,* Glencoe: The Free Press, 1950.

————, "A Noncontribution to Educational Research," *Harvard Educational Review,* 1963, 33, p. 329.

————, *The Empty Fortress: Infantile Autism and the Birth of the Self,* New York: The Free Press, 1967.

BIJOU, S. AND D. BAER, *Child Development: A Systematic and Empirical Theory,* New York: Appleton-Century-Crofts, 1961.

BIRCH, H., ed., *Brain Damage in Children: The Biological and Social Aspects,* Baltimore: Williams and Wilkins, 1904.

BIRNBRAUER, J., S. BIJOU, M. WOLF, AND J. KIDDER, "Programmed Instruction in the Classroom," in L. Ullman and L. Krasner, eds., *Case Studies in Behavior Modification,* New York: Holt, Rinehart and Winston, 1965.

BIRNBRAUER, J. AND J. LAWLER, "Token Reinforcement for Learning," *Mental Retardation,* 1964, 2, pp. 275–279.

BOUSFIELD, W., J. ESTERSON, AND G. WHITMARSH, "The Effects of Concomitant Colored and Uncolored Pictorial Representations on the Learning of Stimulus Words," *Journal of Applied Psychology,* 1957, 41, pp. 165–167.

BOWER, E., "A Process for Identifying Disturbed Children," *Child,* 1957, 4, pp. 143–147.

————, *The Education of Emotionally Handicapped Children*, Sacramento, California: California State Department of Education, 1961.

BROWN, J., "Prognosis from Presenting Symptoms of Preschool Children with Atypical Development," *American Journal of Orthopsychiatry*, 1960, 30, pp. 382–390.

CALL, J., "A Psychodynamic View of the Learning Process," in M. Gottsegen and G. Gottsegen, eds., *Professional School Psychology*, Vol. II, New York: Grune & Stratton, 1963, pp. 1–17.

————, Personal Communication, 1968.

CARTWRIGHT, D., "The Effect of Interruption, Completion and Failure upon the Attractiveness of Activities," *Journal of Experimental Psychology*, 1942, 31, pp. 1–16.

CHARTERS, W., "Is There a Field of Educational Engineering?" *The Educational Research Bulletin*, 1945, 24, pp. 29–37.

————, "Idea Men and Engineers in Education," *Educational Forum*, 1948, 12, pp. 399–406.

CLEMENTS, S., "Minimal Brain Dysfunction in Children," *NINDB Monographs*, No. 3, United States Public Health Service, Washington, 1966.

CLEMENTS, S. AND J. PETERS, "Minimal Brain Dysfunctions in the School Age Child," *Archives of General Psychiatry*, 1962, 6, pp. 185–197.

COALADARCI, A., Presentation at School Psychology Conference, University of California, Berkeley, 1967.

COOLIDGE, J., P. HAHN, AND A. PECK, "School Phobia: Neurotic Crisis or Way of Life?" *American Journal of Orthopsychiatry*, 1957, 27, pp. 296–306.

CRITCHLEY, M., *Developmental Dyslexia*, London: Heinemann, 1964.

CRUICKSHANK, W., F. BENTZEN, F. RATZEBURG, AND M. TANNHAUSER, A *Teaching Methodology for Brain-Injured and Hyperactive Children*, New York: Syracuse University Press, 1961, pp. 14, 424.

CRUSE, D., "The Effect of Distraction Upon the Performance of Brain-Injured and Familial Retarded Children," in E. Trapp and P. Himmelstein, eds., *Readings on the Exceptional Child*, New York: Appleton-Century-Crofts, 1962.

CUNNINGHAM, R., *Understanding Group Behavior of Boys and Girls*, New York: Teachers College, Columbia University, 1951.

DAVIDSON, S., "School Phobia as a Manifestation of Family Disturbance: Its Structure and Treatment," *Journal Child Psychology and Psychiatry*, 1961, 1, pp. 270–287.

DEVEREUX, G., *Therapeutic Education: Its Theoretical Bases and Practice*, New York: Harper & Row, 1956.

DOLL, E., *The Vineland Social Maturity Scale*, Minneapolis: Educational Testing Bureau, 1946.

DOUGLAS, K., "The Teacher's Role in a Children's Psychiatric Hospital Unit," *Exceptional Children*, 1961, 27, pp. 246–251.

DUNN-RANKIN, P., Personal Communication, 1967.

DURRELL, D., *Improvement of Basic Reading Abilities*, New York: World Book Company, 1940.

EISENBERG, L., "The Autistic Child in Adolescence," *American Journal of Orthopsychiatry*, 1956, 112, pp. 607–612.

————, "School Phobia: A Study of the Communication of Anxiety," *American Journal of Orthopsychiatry*, 1958, 114, pp. 712–718.

EKSTEIN, R., K. BRYANT, AND S. FREEDMAN, "Childhood Schizophrenia and Allied Conditions," in L. Bellak, ed., *Schizophrenia: A Review of the Syndrome*, New York: Logos Press, 1958.

ELLWELL, J. AND G. GRINDLEY, "The Effect of Knowledge of Results on Learning and Performance," *British Journal of Psychology*, 1938, 29, pp. 39–53.

ERIKSON, E., *Childhood and Society*, New York: W.W. Norton, 1950.

EYSENCK, H., ed., *Behavior Therapy and the Neuroses*, New York: The Macmillan Company, 1960.

FERNALD, G., *Remedial Techniques in Basic School Subjects*, New York: McGraw-Hill Book Company, 1943.

FERSTER, C. AND M. DE MYER, "A Method for the Experimental Analysis of the Behavior of Autistic Children," *American Journal of Orthopsychiatry*, 1962, 32, pp. 89–98.

FREUD, A., "The Relation between Psychoanalysis and Pedagogy," in *Psychoanalysis for Teachers and Parents* (trans. by B. Low), New York: Emerson Books, 1954.

————, *Normality and Pathology in Childhood*, New York: International Universities Press, Inc., 1965.

FREUD, S., *An Outline of Psychoanalysis*, New York: W.W. Norton, 1949.

————, "Analysis Terminable and Interminable" (original publication 1937), in *Collected Papers of Sigmund Freud*, London: Hogarth Press, 1950.

————, "Inhibitions, Symptoms and Anxiety" (original publication 1926), in *Standard Edition of the Complete Psychological Works of Sigmund Freud*, Vol. 20, London: Hogarth Press, 1959.

FREY, R., "The Effects of Verbal Reinforcers on Group Operant Behavior" (master's thesis, University of Maine, 1960).

FROSTIG, M., A *Developmental Test of Visual Perception*, Palo Alto: Consulting Psychologists Press, 1964.

————, *The New Frostig Program for the Development of Visual Perception*, Chicago: Follett Publishing Company, n.d.

FROSTIG, M., D. LEFEVER, AND D. AND J. WHITTLESEY, "A Developmental Test of Visual Perception for Evaluating Normal and Neurologically Handicapped Children," *Perceptual Motor Skills*, 1961, 12, pp. 383–394.

GAGNÉ, R., *The Conditions of Learning*, New York: Holt, Rinehart and Winston, 1965.

GALLAGHER, J., "Children with Developmental Imbalance: A Psychoeducational Definition," in W. Cruickshank, ed., *The Teacher of Brain-Injured Children*, Syracuse: Syracuse University Press, 1966, p. 27.

GLANZER, M., "Curiosity, Exploratory Drive, and Stimulus Satiation," *Psychological Bulletin*, 1958, 55, pp. 302–315.

GOLDFARB, W., P. BRAENSTEIN, AND I. LORGE, "A Study of Speech Patterns in a Group of Schizophrenic Children," *American Journal of Orthopsychiatry*, 1956, 26, pp. 544–555.

HAEUSSERMANN, E., *Developmental Potential of Preschool Children*, New York: Grune & Stratton, 1958.

HARING, N. AND T. LOVITT, "Operant Methodology and Educational Technology in Special Education," in N. Haring and R. Schiefellbusch, eds., *Methods in Special Education*, New York: McGraw-Hill Book Company, 1967.

HARING, N. AND E. PHILLIPS, *Educating Emotionally Disturbed Children*, New York: McGraw-Hill Book Company, 1962, pp. 9–10, 240.

HARRIS, A., *How to Increase Reading Ability*, New York: Longmans, Green & Company, 1950.

HAVIGHURST, R., *Developmental Tasks and Education*, New York: Longmans, Green & Company, 1952.

HAY, L., "A New School Channel for Helping the Troubled Child," *American Journal of Orthopsychiatry*, 1953, 23, pp. 676–683.

HAYES, J., "The Maintenance of Play in Young Children," *Journal of Comparative and Physiological Psychology*, 1958, 51, pp. 788–794.

HEWETT, F., "An Investigation of the Effect of Pleasant and Unpleasant Affective Tone on Learning and Recall of Words Among Delinquent and Nondelinquent Adolescents with Reading Problems" (unpublished manuscript, 1961).

————, "Teaching Reading to an Autistic Boy through Operant Conditioning," *The Reading Teacher*, 1964, 17, pp. 613–618.

————, "A Hierarchy of Educational Tasks for Children with Learning Disorders," *Exceptional Children*, 1964, 31, pp. 207–214.

————, "Teaching Speech to an Autistic Child through Operant Conditioning," *American Journal of Orthopsychiatry*, 1965, 35, pp. 927–936.

————, "The Tulare Experimental Class for Educationally Handicapped Children," *California Education*, 1966, 3, pp. 6–8.

————, "Reinforcement Preferences of an Austistic Boy" (unpublished manuscript, 1966).

————, "A Hierarchy of Competencies for Teachers of Emotionally Handicapped Children," *Exceptional Children*, 1966, 33, pp. 7–11.

————, "Educational Engineering with Emotionally Disturbed Children," *Exceptional Children*, 1967, 33, pp. 459–467.

HEWETT, F., D. MAYHEW, AND E. RABB, "An Experimental Reading Program for Neurologically Impaired, Mentally Retarded, and Severely Emotionally Disturbed Children," *American Journal of Orthopsychiatry*, 1967, 37, pp. 35–48.

HOBBS, N., "Helping Disturbed Children: Psychological and Ecological Strategies," *American Psychologist*, 1966, 21, pp. 1105–1115.

HOLLAND, J., "Teaching Machines: An Application of Principles from the Laboratory," *Journal of the Experimental Analysis of Behavior*, 1960, 3, pp. 275–287.

HULL, C., *Principles of Behavior*, New York: Appleton-Century-Crofts, 1943.

ISOM, J., paper presented at *The Troubled Child Workshop: The Neurologically Handicapped*, University of Oregon, Eugene, Oregon, 1967.

ITARD, J.M.G., *The Wild Boy of Aveyron*, New York: Appleton-Century-Crofts, 1962.

JACOBSON, S. AND C. FAEGRE, "Neutralization: A Tool for Teachers of Disturbed Children," *Exceptional Children*, 1959, 25, pp. 243–246.

JENSEN, C., Personal Communication, 1966.

JENSEN, G. AND M. WOMACK, "Operant Conditioning Techniques Applied in the Treatment of an Autistic Child," *American Journal of Orthopsychiatry*, 1967, 37, pp. 30–34.

JOHNSON, A., E. FALSTEIN, S. SZVERK, AND M. SVENDSON, "School Phobia," *American Journal of Orthopsychiatry*, 1941, 11, pp. 702–712.

JONES, M., "A Laboratory Study of Fear: The Case of Peter," *Pedagogical Seminary*, 1924, 31, pp. 310–311.

KANNER, L., "A Discussion of Early Infantile Autism," *Digest of Neurological Psychiatry*, 1951, 19, pp. 158–159.

KANNER, L. AND L. EISENBERG, "Notes on the Follow-up Studies of Autistic Children," in P. Hoch and J. Zubin, eds., *Psychopathology of Childhood*, New York: Grune & Stratton, 1955.

KELLER, F., *Learning: Reinforcement Theory*, New York: Random House, 1954, pp. 3–4.

KEPHART, N., *The Slow Learner in the Classroom*, Columbus, Ohio: Charles E. Merrill Books, Inc., 1960, p. viii.

————, "Perceptual-Motor Aspects of Learning Disabilities," *Exceptional Children*, 1964, 31, pp. 201–206.

KIRK, S. AND J. MCCARTHY, "The Illinois Test of Psycholinguistic Abilities— An Approach to Differential Diagnosis," *American Journal of Mental Deficiency*, 1961, 66, pp. 399–412.

KISH, G., "Studies of Sensory Reinforcement," in W. Honig, ed., *Operant Behavior: Areas of Research and Application*, New York: Appleton-Century-Crofts, 1966, pp. 109–159.

KOUGH, J. AND R. DE HAAN, *Identifying Children with Special Needs*, Vol. I, Chicago: Science Research Associate, 1955.

KRATHWOHL, D., B. BLOOM, AND B. MASIA, *Taxonomy of Educational Objectives, Classification of Educational Goals, Handbook II: Affective Domain*, New York: Longmans, Green & Company, 1956.

LECKY, P., *Self-Consistency—A Theory of Personality*, New York: Island Press, 1945.

LEVIN, G. AND J. SIMMONS, "Response to Praise by Emotionally Disturbed Boys," *Psychological Reports*, 1962, 11, p. 10.

LEWIN, K., R. LIPPITT, AND R. WHITE, "Patterns of Aggressive Behavior in Experimentally Created 'Social Climates,'" *Journal of Social Psychology*, 1939, 10, pp. 271–299.

LEWIS, W., "Project Re-ED: Educational Intervention in Children's Behavior Disorder," *Proceedings: 1967 International Convocation on Children and Young Adults with Learning Disabilities*, Pittsburgh: Home for Crippled Children, 1967, pp. 263–274.

LONG, E., J. HAMMOCK, F. MAY, AND B. CAMPBELL, "Intermittent Reinforcement of Operant Behavior in Children," *Journal of Experimental Analysis of Behavior*, 1958, 1, pp. 315–339.

LONG, N., W. MORSE, AND R. NEWMAN, *Conflict in the Classroom: The Education of Emotionally Disturbed Children*, Belmont, Calif.: Wadsworth, 1965.

LORBER, J., "Hydrancephaly with Normal Development," *Developmental Medicine and Child Neurology*, 1965, 7, pp. 628–633.

LOVAAS, O., J. BERBERICH, B. PERLAFF, AND B. SCHAEFFER, "Acquisition of Imitative Speech by Schizophrenic Children," *Science*, 1966, 151, pp. 705–707.

LOVAAS, O., G. FREITAG, M. KINDER, B. RUBENSTEIN, B. SCHAEFFER, AND J. SIMMONS, "Experimental Studies in Childhood Schizophrenia: II.

Establishment of Social Reinforcers," paper presented to Western Psychological Association, 1964.

MABRY, C., "Prolonged Neonatal Anoxia without Apparent Adverse Sequelae," *The Journal of Pediatrics*, 1959, 55, pp. 211–215.

MACKIE, R., W. KVARACEUS, AND H. WILLIAMS, *Teachers of Children Who Are Socially and Emotionally Maladjusted*, Washington, D.C.: U.S. Department of Health, Education and Welfare, 1957.

✓ MACPHERSON, S., V. DEES, AND G. GRINDLEY, "The Effect of Knowledge of Results on Learning and Performance. II. Some Characteristics of Very Simple Skills," *Quarterly Journal of Experimental Psychology*, 1948, 1, pp. 68–78.

————, ————, AND ————, "The Effect of Knowledge of Results on Learning and Performance. III. The Influence of the Time Interval between Trials," *Quarterly Journal of Experimental Psychology*, 1949, pp. 167–174.

MAHLER, M., "Remarks on Psychoanalysis with Psychotic Children," *Quarterly Journal of Child Behavior*, 1949, 1, pp. 18–21.

————, "On Child Psychosis and Schizophrenia. Autistic and Symbrotic Infantile Psychoses," in *The Psychoanalytic Study of the Child*, Vol. 7, New York: International Universities Press, 1952.

MANEY, E., *Visual Readiness Skills (2 levels), Seeing, Listening, and Differentiating (3 levels)*, Elizabethtown: The Continental Press, Inc., n.d.

MARTIN, J. AND J. DAVIDSON, "Recall of Completed and Interrupted Tasks by Achievers and Underachievers," *Journal of Educational Psychology*, 1964, 55, pp. 314–316.

MARTIN, W. AND C. STENDLER, *Child Behavior and Development*, New York: Harcourt, Brace & World, 1959, pp. 349–350, 355–356.

MASLOW, A., *Motivation and Personality*, New York: Harper & Row, 1954.

MAYHEW, D. AND J. FERJO, "The Use of In-Patient Adolescents as Teacher Assistants in an Elementary Classroom in a Psychiatric Setting," paper presented at the Forty-Fifth Annual Meeting of the American Orthopsychiatric Association, Chicago, 1968.

MAZURKIEWITZ, A., "Socio-Cultural Influence and Reading," *Journal of Developmental Reading*, summer, 1960.

MONEY, J., ed., *Reading Disability: Progress and Research Needs in Dyslexia*, Baltimore: The Johns Hopkins Press, 1962.

————, ed., *The Disabled Reader, Education of the Dyslexic Child*, Baltimore: The Johns Hopkins Press, 1966.

MONTESSORI, MARIA, *The Montessori Method*, Philadelphia: F. A. Stoker, 1912.

MOORE, R. AND I. GOLDIAMOND, "Errorless Establishment of Visual Discrimination Using Fading Procedures," *Journal of Experimental Analysis of Behavior*, 1964, 7, pp. 269–272.

MORSE, W., "Working Paper; Training Teachers in Life Space Interviewing," *American Journal of Orthopsychiatry*, 1963, 33, pp. 727–730.

————, "The Crisis Teacher," in N. Long, W. Morse, and R. Newman, eds., *Conflict in the Classroom: The Education of Emotionally Disturbed Children*, Belmont: Wadsworth, 1965.

————, "Public Schools and the Disturbed Child," in P. Knoblock, ed., *Intervention Approaches in Educating Emotionally Disturbed Children*, Syracuse: Syracuse University Press, 1966, pp. 113–128.

————, "The Education of Socially Maladjusted and Emotionally Disturbed Children," in W. Cruickshank and G. Johnson, eds., *Education of Exceptional Children and Youth*, 2nd ed., Englewood Cliffs: Prentice-Hall, 1967.

MORSE, W. AND E. SMALL, "Group Life Space Interviewing in a Therapeutic Camp," *American Journal of Orthopsychiatry*, 1959, 29, pp. 27–44.

MYKELBUST, H., "Aphasia in Children—Language Development and Language Pathology," in V. Travis, ed., *Handbook of Speech Pathology*, New York: Appleton-Century-Crofts, 1957.

NEWMAN, R., "The Acting Out Boy," *Exceptional Children*, 1956, 22, pp. 186–190.

————, "The Assessment of Progress in the Treatment of Hyperaggressive Children with Learning Disturbances within a School Setting," *American Journal of Orthopsychiatry*, 1959, 29, pp. 641–642.

NEWMAN, R., C. BLOOMBERG, R. EMERSON, M. KEITH, H. KITCHNER, AND F. REDL, *Technical Assistance*, Report to the Washington School of Psychiatry, Washington, D.C., 1964.

ORTON, S. T., *Reading, Writing, and Speech Problems in Children*, New York: W. W. Norton, 1937.

OSGOOD, C., *Method and Theory in Experimental Psychology*, New York: Oxford Press, 1953.

OTT, J., "Teaching the Emotionally Disturbed Teenage Student," *Bulletin of the National Association of Secondary School Principals*, 1958, 42, pp. 180–181.

PAGE, E., "Teacher Comments and Student Performances: A Seventy-Four Classroom Experiment in School Motivation," *Journal of Educational Psychology*, 1958, 49, pp. 173–181.

PATE, J., "Emotionally Disturbed and Socially Maladjusted Children," L. Dunn, ed., *Exceptional Children in the Schools*, New York: Holt, Rinehart and Winston, 1963.

PATTERSON G. AND M. EBNER, "Applications of Learning Principles to the Treatment of Deviant Children," paper read at American Psychological Association, Chicago, September, 1965.

PAVLOV, I., *Conditioned Reflexes* (trans. by G.V. Ansep), London: Oxford University Press, 1927.

PEARSON, G., *Emotional Disorders of Children*, New York: Norton, 1949.

————, *Psychoanalysis and the Education of the Child*, New York: Norton, 1954.

PETER, L., *Prescriptive Teaching*, New York: McGraw-Hill Book Company, 1965.

PFAFFMAN, C., "The Pleasures of Sensation," *Psychological Review*, 1966, 67, pp. 253–268.

PIAGET, J., *The Psychology of Intelligence*, London: Routledge and Kegan Paul, 1950.

PORTER, D., "What Does Learning Theory Contribute to the Classroom?" *Audiovisual Instruction*, 1962, 7, pp. 14–15.

PREMACK, D., "Toward Empirical Behavior Laws: I. Positive Reinforcement," *Psychological Review*, 1959, 66, pp. 219–233.

QUAY, H., "Remediation of the Conduct Problem Child in the Special Class Setting," *Exceptional Children*, 1966, 32, pp. 509–515.

QUAY, H., W. MORSE, AND R. CUTLER, "Personality Patterns of Pupils in Special Classes for the Emotionally Disturbed," *Exceptional Children*, 1966, 32, pp. 297–301.

RABB, E. AND J. BUSCH, "Developing Speech with Non-verbal Autistic Children through Reading," paper presented at the Forty-Fifth Annual Meeting of the American Orthopsychiatric Association, Chicago, 1968.

RABINOW, B., "The Role of the School in Residential Treatment," *American Journal of Orthopsychiatry*, 1955, 25, p. 691.

————, "A Proposal for a Training Program for Teachers of the Emotionally Disturbed and the Socially Maladjusted," *Exceptional Children*, 1960, 26, pp. 287–293.

REDL, F., "The Phenomenon of Contagion and Shock Effect in Group Therapy," in K. Eissler, ed., *Searchlights in Delinquency*, New York: International Universities Press, 1949, pp. 315–328.

————, "Strategy and Techniques of the Life Space Interview," *American Journal of Orthopsychiatry*, 1959, 29, pp. 1–18.

————, *When We Deal with Children*, New York: The Free Press, 1966, p. 125.

REDL, F. AND D. WINEMAN, *Children Who Hate*, Glencoe: The Free Press, 1951.

————— AND —————, *Controls from Within*, Glencoe: The Free Press, 1952.

REGER, R., *School Psychology*, Springfield: Charles C. Thomas, 1965, pp. 190–191.

RHEINGOLD, H., W. STANLEY, AND G. DOYLE, "Verbal and Auditory Reinforcement of a Manipulatory Response in Young Children," *Journal of Experimental Child Psychology*, 1959, 61, pp. 317–322.

RIGGS, M., "Recall and Organization of Aggressive Words under Varied Conditions of Emphasis," *Perceptual Motor Skills*, 1956, 6, pp. 273–284.

RIMLAND, B., *Infantile Autism*, New York: Appleton-Century-Crofts, 1964.

ROETHLISBERGER, F. AND W. DICKSON, *Management and the Worker*, Cambridge: Harvard University Press, 1939.

ROZENWEIG, S., "Preference in the Repetition of Successful and Unsuccessful Activities as a Function of Age and Personality," *Journal of Genetic Psychology*, 1933, 42, pp. 423–441.

————— , "The Preferential Repetition of Successful and Unsuccessful Activities," *Psychological Bulletin*, 1936, 33, p. 797.

ROWLEY, V. AND E. KELLER, "Changes in Children's Verbal Behavior as a Function of Social Approval and Manifest Anxiety," *Journal of Abnormal Social Psychology*, 1962, 65, pp. 53–57.

ROWLEY, V. AND F. STONE, "Changes in Children's Verbal Behavior as a Function of Social Approval, Experimenter Differences and Child Personality," *Child Development*, 1964, 35, pp. 669–676.

RUSSELL, D., The Ginn Basic Readers: *My Little Red Story Book, My Little Green Story Book, My Little Blue Story Book, The Little White House*, Boston: Ginn and Company, 1957.

SCHWITZGEBEL, R., *The Science of Learning and the Art of Teaching*, paper presented at the First Annual Educational Engineering Conference, University of California, Los Angeles, 1965.

SEARS, R., "Social Behavior and Personality Development," in T. Parson and E. Shills, *Toward a General Theory of Action*, Cambridge: Harvard University Press, 1951.

SHIRLEY, M., *The First Two Years, II. Intellectual Development*, Minnesota: University of Minnesota Press, 1933.

SKEELS, H., "Effect of Adoption on Children from Institutions," in J. Frost and G. Hawkes, eds., *The Disadvantaged Child: Issues and Innovations*, Boston: Houghton Mifflin Company, 1966, pp. 116–119.

SKINNER, B., *Science and Human Behavior*, New York: The Macmillan Company, 1953.

————— , "Operant Behavior," *American Psychologist*, 1963, 18, pp. 503–515.

————, "Why Teachers Fail," *Saturday Review*, 1965, 48, pp. 80–102.

STAATS, A., K. MINKE, J. FINLEY, M. WOLF, AND L. BROOKS, "A Reinforcer System and Experimental Procedures for the Laboratory Study of Reading Acquisition," *Child Development*, 1964, 35, pp. 209–231.

STAATS, A., C. STAATS, R. SCHUTZ, AND M. WOLF, "The Conditioning of Textual Responses Using 'Extrinsic' Reinforcers," *Journal of Experimental Analysis of Behavior*, 1962, 5, pp. 33–40.

STANCHFIELD, J., "A Study of Boys' Reading Interests in Relationship to Reading Achievement" (doctoral dissertation, University of California, Los Angeles, Department of Education, 1961).

STARK, W. AND F. BENTZEN, "Integrating the Emotionally Disturbed Child in the School," in M. Krugman, ed., *Orthopsychiatry and the School*, New York: American Orthopsychiatric Association, 1958, pp. 82–95.

STEVENSON, H. AND R. ODOM, "Effects of Pretraining on the Reinforcing Value of Visual Stimuli," *Child Development*, 1961, 32, pp. 739–744.

STRAUSS, A.A. AND L.E. LEHTINEN, *Psychopathology and Education of the Brain-Injured Child*, New York: Grune & Stratton, 1947.

Sullivan Programmed Reading Series, New York: McGraw-Hill Book Company (Webster Division), 1966.

TALBOT, M.E., *Edouard Seguin: A Study of an Educational Approach to the Treatment of Mentally Defective Children*, New York: Bureau of Publications, Teachers College, Columbia University, 1964.

TERRACE, H., "Discrimination Learning with and without 'Error,'" *Journal of the Experimental Analysis of Behavior*, 1963, pp. 1–27.

THORNDIKE, E., *Educational Psychology*, New York: Columbia University Press, 1913.

THURSTONE, T., *Reading for Understanding*, Chicago: Science Research Associates, Inc., 1958.

ULLMAN, L. AND L. KRASNER, *Case Studies in Behavior Modification*, New York: Holt, Rinehart and Winston, 1965.

VALETT, R., "A Developmental Task Approach to Early Childhood Education," *Journal of School Psychology*, 1967, 2, pp. 136–147.

WALLIN, N. AND R. TRAVERS, "Analysis and Investigation of Teaching Methods," in N. Gage, ed., *Handbook of Research on Teaching*, Chicago: Rand, McNally and Company, 1963, pp. 448–505.

WARGO, G. "Recreation for Emotionally Disturbed Children," *The Physical Educator*, 1962, 19, pp. 99–100.

WATSON, J., *Behaviorism*, New York: The People's Institute, 1925.

WEISS, H. AND B. BORN, "Speech Training or Language Acquisition? A Distinction When Speech Training Is Taught by Operant Conditioning Procedures," *American Journal of Orthopsychiatry,* 1967, 37, pp. 49–55.

WERNER, H. AND A. STRAUSS, "Pathology of Figure-Background Relationship in the Child," *Journal of Abnormal and Social Psychology,* 1941, 36, pp. 236–248.

WERRY, J., "The Diagnosis, Etiology, and Treatment of Hyperactivity in Children," in J. Hellmuth, ed., *Learning Disorders,* Seattle: Special Child Publications, in press.

WHELAN, R., "The Relevance of Behavior Modification Procedures for Teachers of Emotionally Disturbed Children," in P. Knoblock, ed., *Intervention Approaches in Educating Emotionally Disturbed Children,* Syracuse: Syracuse University Press, 1966.

WHELAN, R. AND N. HARING, "Modification and Maintenance of Behavior through Systematic Application of Consequences," *Exceptional Children,* 1966, 32, pp. 281–289.

WHITE, M. AND M. HARRIS, *The School Psychologist,* New York: Harper & Row, 1961.

WICKMAN, E., *Children's Behavior and Teachers' Attitudes,* New York: Commonwealth Fund, 1928.

WITTY, P. AND S. GOLDBERG, "The Army's Training Program for Illiterates," *Elementary English Review,* 1943, 20, pp. 306–311.

WOLPE, J., A. SALTER, AND L. RENYA, eds., *The Conditioning Therapies,* New York: Holt, Rinehart and Winston, 1965.

WOODWORTH, R. AND H. SCHLOSBERG, *Experimental Psychology,* New York: Holt, Rinehart and Winston, 1954, p. 687.

ZEIGARNIK, B., "On Finished and Unfinished Tasks," in W.D. Ellis, ed., *A Source Book of Gestalt Psychology,* New York: Harcourt, Brace & World, 1938.

ZIMMERMAN, E. AND J. ZIMMERMAN, "The Alteration of Behavior in a Special Classroom Situation," *Journal of Experimental Analysis of Behavior,* 1962, 5, pp. 59–60.

Index

DATE DUE

DEC 1 5 '71	JAN 3 '72		
MAR 2 9 '72	MAY 12 '72		
MAR 1 9 '74	FEB 9 '76		
JUN 26 '74	JUN 2 6 '74		
MAR 6 '81	MAR 5 '81		
AP 27 '82	APR 26 '82		
OC 13 '82	SEP 26 '82		
APR 2 5 1991	APR 29 '91		
NOV. 3 0 1993	DEC 8 '93		
DEC 6 '94	DEC 0 6 1994		
GAYLORD			PRINTED IN U.S.A.